To Verona Stellet, Aileen and Michael (Wallace); Theresa, Eoin, Sean and Tadhg (Gunnigle); Monica, Laura, Alison and Kevin (McMahon); and Michael, Kitty and Aonghus (O'Sullivan) with thanks for all your support.

GILL & MACMILLAN

Gill & Macmillan
Hume Avenue
Park West
Dublin 12
with associated companies throughout the world
www.gillmacmillan.ie

© Joseph Wallace, Patrick Gunnigle, Gerard McMahon,
Michelle O'Sullivan 2013

978 07171 4381 8

Print origination by Carrigboy Typesetting Services
Printed by GraphyCems, Spain
Indexed by Cliff Murphy

*The paper used in this book comes from the wood pulp of managed forests. For every tree
felled, at least one tree is planted, thereby renewing natural resources.*

A CIP catalogue record is available for this book from the British Library

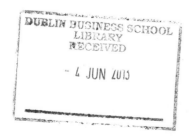

Contents

CHAPTER 1 INDUSTRIAL RELATIONS: A CONTEXTUAL AND THEORETICAL OVERVIEW

CHAPTER 2 COLLECTIVE LABOUR LAW IN A HISTORICAL, SOCIAL AND POLITICAL CONTEXT

CHAPTER 3 TRADE UNIONS

CHAPTER 4 EMPLOYER ORGANISATIONS

CHAPTER 5 DISPUTE RESOLUTION AND WAGE-SETTING INSTITUTIONS

CHAPTER 6 INDIVIDUAL EMPLOYMENT LAW

Chapter 7 Collective and Individual Workplace Procedures

Chapter 8 The Management of Industrial Relations

Chapter 11 Negotiations

CHAPTER 12 EMPLOYEE INVOLVEMENT, EMPLOYEE PARTICIPATION AND WORKPLACE PARTNERSHIP

CHAPTER 13 NATIONAL COLLECTIVE BARGAINING

Acknowledgements

Ms Linda Edgeworth, Cook Ireland

Ms Aileen Wallace

Ms Grainne O'Donovan

Dr Jimmy Donaghey, Warwick University

Ms Mairead Regan, Central Statistics Office

Mr P.J. Stone, Garda Representative Association

Mr John Clinton, Prison Officers' Association

Mr Anthony Kerr, University College Dublin

Ms Marian Geoghegan, Irish Bank Officials Association

Ms Carol Nolan, Boots Retail Ireland

Supt Margaret Nugent, An Garda Síochána

Mr Adrian Cummins, Local Jobs Alliance

Mr Paul Joyce, Free Legal Advice Centres

Mr Michael McDonnell, Chartered Institute of Personnel & Development

Ms Wendy Sullivan, Chartered Institute of Personnel & Development

Mr Karl O'Connor, Culture and Employee Engagement, Ulster Bank

Mr Paddy Keating, IMPACT Trade Union

Mr Eamonn Collins & Ms Celine Kelly, National Qualifications Authority of Ireland

Ms Maeve Lewis, One in Four

Mr Joseph Greenan, Jesuit Community of Ireland

Ms Suzanne Mullins, City of Cork VEC

Mr Brian McGann, Irish Postmasters Union

Ms Lorraine Crawford, The Teaching Council

Mr Darragh Horan, ESB International

Mr Maurice Dowling, Irish Rugby Football Union

Mr Graham Harding, Noyeks Newmans

Mr Edward Conlon, Dublin Institute of Technology

Dr Mary Prendergast, Dublin Institute of Technology

Ms Maeve Kelly, Dublin Institute of Technology

Ms Marian Jennings, Dublin Institute of Technology

Mr Pat Cuffe, Dublin Institute of Technology

Mr Kevin O'Leary, Dublin Institute of Technology

Mr Paul Sweeney, Irish Congress of Trade Unions

Dr John McCartney, Central Statistics Office

Dr Caroline Murphy, University of Limerick

Dr Tony Dobbins, Bangor University

Dr Tony Dundon, NUI Galway

Prof. Bill Roche & Teresa Brannick, University College Dublin

Mr Michael Kinsella, Analog Devices BV

Mr Tom O'Leary, Millpore

Mr Adrian Beatty, Dairygold

Mr Conor McDonnell, Fidelity Investments

Mr Alan O'Leary, SIPTU

Mr Brian Sheehan & Mr Colman Higgins, *Industrial Relations News*

Labour Market and National Accounts Section, Central Statistics Office

Ms Gillian Chamberlain & Ms Barbara Nestor, Irish Business & Employers Confederation

Mr Robert Ahern, Department of Jobs, Enterprise and Innovation

Ms Deirdre Keogh, Irish Congress of Trade Unions

Dr Brian Harney & Prof. David Collings, Dublin City University

Dr Jonathan Lavelle, Dr Juliet MacMahon, Dr Sarah MacCurtain, Dr Jean McCarthy, Dr Tom Turner, Prof. Mike Morley & Ms Aisling Danagher, University of Limerick

Peter Reilly, UL Business Studies Librarian

List of Figures and Tables

Figures

Tables

CHAPTER 1

Industrial Relations:
A Contextual and Theoretical Overview

INTRODUCTION: WHAT DO WE MEAN BY INDUSTRIAL RELATIONS?

The subject area of industrial relations is one of the most-discussed specialist areas of organisational and national economic management. The public prominence of the topic is primarily attributable to its headline-making capacity when in the throes of industrial action, mass redundancy or wage bargaining activities. These events materialise at plant, industry and national level, commanding extensive media coverage and widespread public interest and concern. However, the subject is frequently shrouded in confusion and anxiety at the expense of insightful analysis – a factor contributing to periodic public pronouncements urging dramatic and often ill-conceived policy changes, e.g. to outlaw strikes.

The primary focus of industrial relations or employee relations is on the employment relationship of around 2 million employees in the Republic of Ireland, working across all employment sectors and entity types. The term 'industrial relations' (or 'labour relations') has connotations of the traditional unionised blue-collar working environment in the manufacturing sector, while the term 'employee relations' conjures up images of the non-union or less unionised white-collar services sector. In recent years, the term 'employment relations' – which merges the more individualist 'employee relations' with the more collectivist 'industrial relations' – has gained currency. This text retains the term 'industrial relations', not least because it is the one most commonly used by practitioners, but also because it is used in legislation in Ireland. However, the text covers both the collective and individual aspects of the employment relationship.

The subject itself can be best understood and interpreted in the wider context of the historical, political, social and economic processes that have shaped the regulation of working lives in this jurisdiction. That is, the subject draws upon a range of disciplines to facilitate an understanding of both individual and collective relationships in white- and blue-collar work environments and at plant, national and international levels. The complexity of the subject necessitates consideration of an array of other specialisms in order to accommodate a comprehensive analysis of all issues affecting people at work, e.g. labour law, sociology, political science and labour economics.

Traditionally, the topic has been preoccupied with considerations about trade unions. This emphasis, while understandable, fails to appreciate the importance of contextual matters and contrasting (non-union) perspectives on the same phenomena. Both issues, of the context and perspectives on industrial relations, are addressed in this opening chapter. In so far as is possible, the text also attempts to adopt a factual and unbiased approach to the study of the subject matter. However, the subject's very nature inevitably means that many aspects of the topic are contentious. Accordingly, an effort is made in this text to take an independent line, while outlining the central strands of the differing viewpoints that have been expressed on various dimensions of the subject.

A most attractive aspect of the subject is that it allows students to develop their own opinions and to make up their own minds as to the merits of the contrasting perspectives outlined. Of course, opinions need to be informed and this text adopts a *research-based* approach. This is facilitated via a general overview of the more significant contextual, theoretical, institutional, substantive and procedural aspects while reviewing what are generally adjudged in the literature to be the more salient features and trends in industrial relations. This text also addresses 'debatable' dimensions of the subject, including the range of political arguments and the plethora of factual data, which lend themselves on occasion to a number of possible interpretations. The intention is to encourage students to engage in debate and to form their own views on the matters in question. However, it is important that the development of particular viewpoints and perspectives be embedded in an appreciation of the many central features and facts around which the industrial relations system operates. Accordingly, this text endeavours to provide a balanced and comprehensive treatment of the topic without an undue emphasis on any specific area. It is designed to address the key practical and theoretical aspects of the subject. Should students wish to explore particular topics in more detail, an extensive bibliography is provided.

In this chapter, readers are introduced to the topic via a contextual and theoretical overview of the subject. This enables Chapters 2, 3, 4 and 5 to delve further into key features associated with collective labour law (Chapter 2), trade unions (Chapter 3), employer organisations (Chapter 4) and the associated institutional framework (Chapter 5). Chapter 6 outlines the extensive provisions and precedents established under individual employment law. Chapter 7 explores theoretical and practical aspects of workplace procedures. Chapter 8 provides in-depth examination of the management of industrial relations. Chapter 9 provides insight into what is perhaps the most high-profile feature of the system: conflict and industrial action. This enables Chapter 10 to explore the specific area of strikes and the theory and practice of conflict resolution through negotiation is explored in Chapter 11. Employee participation and consultation (including workplace partnership) is covered in Chapter 12, while Chapter 13 examines the evolution and development of collective bargaining in Ireland (including national social partnership and its aftermath).

Figure 1.1 presents a working model or overview of the Irish system of industrial relations. Each component of this model is outlined and critically evaluated at an appropriate point in the text. In this opening chapter the main contrasting theoretical perspectives and contextual factors that determine the shape of the industrial relations system are reviewed. The system itself can be viewed from many perspectives. No single perspective yields a full understanding, but each can add to our insights. The location of five theoretical perspectives on the outer perimeter of Figure 1.1 is designed to convey the potential of each of these theories to provide their own insights. That is, these theoretical perspectives or frames of reference offer contrasting explanations of the same phenomena or features of the industrial relations system. They are also reflected in consequential decisions taken by the key actors therein, e.g. legal changes, union recognition practices, etc.

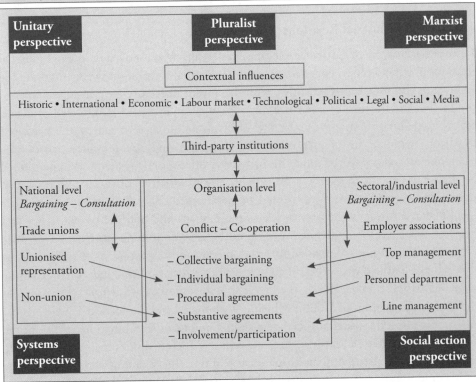

Figure 1.1
Model of the Irish System of Industrial Relations

The prevalence of dual direction arrows depicts the relationship between the various components of the system. This may be reflected in a vast array of exchanges, such as:

- trade union opposition to legal intervention on grounds of history or tradition;
- the reform of third-party dispute-settling agencies due to the nature and volume of (conflict) cases coming before them; or
- the impact of the terms of a collective agreement reached at national, industrial or organisational level by employees and employer(s) (or their representative organisations) on the state of the economy.

THE CONTEXTUAL SETTING OF INDUSTRIAL RELATIONS

Any initiative designed to analyse and prescribe in the area of Irish industrial relations requires some familiarity with those prominent influences that have helped or forced the system to adopt its present shape and character. Hence, Salamon (2000: 3) defines industrial relations as encompassing 'a set of phenomena, both inside and outside the workplace, concerned with determining and regulating the employment relationship'. The key features of this system can be more gainfully assessed from a knowledge base spanning three centuries that has thrown up a vast range of economic, political and social changes. While there has been a wide array of such interrelated influences, in this section an attempt is made to accommodate the more salient influences under the interrelated themes of history, economics, the labour market and politics.

History and Industrial Relations

Historical factors are of particular relevance in developing an understanding of industrial relations in Ireland today. For example, as the Industrial Revolution swept Britain in the eighteenth and nineteenth centuries, with the advent of factory-cum-machine types of production and the further concentration of population in the large industrial cities and towns, trade unions emerged and grew. This was an attempt to redress the perceived imbalance wrought by private enterprise capitalism and the prevalent laissez-faire economic orthodoxy. At the time, this orthodoxy or economic system was underpinned by the belief that the market was the only means by which all prices, including wages, profits and economic priorities, should be determined. Therefore, trade unions were identified as a threat to the prevalent economic, social and political order. Sidney and Beatrice Webb (1897: 1) defined a trade union as a 'continuous association of wage earners for the purpose of maintaining and improving the conditions of their working lives'. They identified the earliest such union as an association of London hatters in the reign of Charles II (Boyd 1984). The first Irish trade union to be identified by name was the Regular Carpenters of Dublin, which it is estimated was founded in 1764.

There is also evidence that there were several unions or 'combinations' active in the Cork area in the middle of the eighteenth century. Their activities included organising strikes, picketing, destroying tools, materials and machinery, and ostracising employers who would not give in to their demands. Eventually Parliament declared that anyone in Cork city found guilty of being a member of an unlawful trade union should be 'imprisoned not above six months, whipped in public and released only on giving recognisance of good behaviour for seven years' (Boyd 1972: 14). From 1770 there is an account of two weavers who were found guilty of 'combination' and were whipped through the streets of Dublin from Newgate Prison to College Green. In 1780 the Irish Parliament passed further legislation for the suppression of all trade unions, while members of the Irish clergy had condemned unions as 'iniquitous extortions' (Boyd 1972: 10). Despite the legal and social pressures, unions maintained their influence, as individual employers disregarded the legal scenario and negotiated with them. The state's role at this time was one of facilitating the unfettered operation of the free market and to confront and control any challenge which was considered to be in 'restraint of trade' (e.g. trade unions). Consequently, by the beginning of the nineteenth century a series of statutory and judicial decisions (dating back to 1729) had served to make them illegal under a variety of headings.

The official hostility towards trade unions may be primarily attributed to the aforementioned laissez-faire economic 'religion' of the time. This debarred any interference with the laws of supply and demand in the marketplace. However, the minority ruling class also feared the onset of civil disturbance. This had already been witnessed in the Irish rural context, with such secret societies as the Whiteboys and the Ribbonmen, and had been central to the outbreak of the French Revolution of 1789.

The ruling class were also disturbed by the ideas of democracy and republicanism, which subsequently spread throughout Europe, and trade unions were wrongly indentified as a factor in the French Revolution.

Irish craft workers' unions continued to surface, to a large extent as a branch of their unions in the United Kingdom, of which Ireland was a part at that time. According to Ó Gráda (1994), in the earlier part of the nineteenth century most crafts in Irish towns and cities appear to have been highly unionised. In a society plagued by unemployment, destitution and illness, the skilled tradesmen enjoyed a relatively privileged place in society by virtue of their relatively high wages and permanent employment. For the purpose of maintaining that position, they sought to increase the value of their trade by restricting access to it via an apprenticeship system. Such apprenticeships were generally confined to relatives. In addition, the craft unions endeavoured to increase the security of their members by providing mutual unemployment and sick benefits.

Inter-union co-operation in Ireland formally emerged for the first time in the shape of trades councils (i.e. organisations representing trade unionists in individual towns and cities). Such councils were founded in Belfast in 1881 and in Dublin in 1884, and though primarily concerned with the interests of craft workers, their formation was a significant step in the overall development of the Irish trade union movement. With the growing disenchantment of Irish representatives at the lack of priority accorded their business by the British Trade Union Congress, in 1894 the Irish Trade Union Congress (ITUC) was established. By 1900 a total of 60,000 workers were members of the ITUC. However, Boyle (1988: 105) notes that unionisation amongst unskilled workers was extremely limited, estimating that the total membership of Irish labourers' unions did not exceed 4,000 at any one time over the period 1889 to 1906.

Around this time, the first real efforts in Ireland to organise unskilled workers began. Together with the lessons learned from the experiences of their British general worker counterparts from the late 1880s and from their rural countrymen (via the Land League movement), mass organisation, solidarity and organised struggle arrived on the trade union agenda at the behest of unskilled general workers. Unlike the craft unions, the general workers' unions were open to all, charged low subscription rates, provided no mutual benefits, had no control over access to work, were more inclined towards frequent and aggressive industrial action and retained quite explicit and radical political links.

The struggle to extend union membership and recognition beyond the relatively privileged craft workers was a bitter and sometimes bloody affair, on occasion involving the police and army in a series of repressive measures. Major confrontations occurred in Belfast in 1907, Dublin in 1908, Cork in 1909 and Wexford in 1911 (McNamara *et al.* 1994). Directly related to these events was the establishment of the Irish Transport and General Workers' Union (ITGWU) in 1909 by James Larkin. The most renowned confrontation that this union became involved in was the 1913 Dublin Lockout (Nevin 1994; Yeates 2000). This was sparked by the dismissal (lockout) of 200 tramway workers who had refused to leave the union. A bitter five-month conflict ensued between the ITGWU, led by Larkin, and the Dublin Employers' Federation, established by the prominent businessman William Martin Murphy. Within one month of the start of the lockout, over 400 employers and 25,000 workers were in the throes of a violent confrontation. In the face of police assaults, the workers established a self-defence group called the Irish Citizens' Army. A key tactic of the employer grouping was to effectively starve the strikers and their families into submission – a tactic that was eventually to prove successful. However, it was arguably a Pyrrhic victory. In the strike's immediate aftermath, the union reorganised and eventually grew to become the largest trade union in the country (Larkin 1965). In 1920 the ITGWU recorded a membership of 120,000 (Roche and Larragy 1986), of whom nearly 50,000 were newly recruited farm labourers. Furthermore, affiliation levels to the ITUC jumped from 110,000 in 1914 to 300,000 by 1921.

The Dublin Employers' Federation involved in this dispute had been established in 1911, two years after its Cork counterpart, on which it was modelled. It subsequently played a major role in the founding in 1942 of the Federated Union of Employers (FUE), which later changed its name to the Federation of Irish Employers (FIE). In 1992, it merged with the Confederation of Irish Industry (CII) to become the foremost Irish employers' representative organisation, the Irish Business and Employers Confederation (IBEC).

By the early twentieth century the central objectives of trade unionism had been clearly established. Trade unions aimed to secure recognition, procure collective agreements covering the terms and conditions of employment of their members and influence the state's legislative and policy-making process in such areas as employment conditions, housing, healthcare, social welfare and education. Effectively, the labour movement was accepting the emerging industrial society while exerting effort to mould it to its advantage. This purpose was accompanied by significant changes in the state's attitude towards trade unionism – from one of hostility, intransigence and legal suppression to one of recognition and accommodation, subject to trade unions' acceptance of the main economic, political and social structures of society. Therefore, between 1871 and 1906 the British Parliament passed a series of key enactments, serving to grant legality to trade unions, protect union funds from court action, recognise collective bargaining and legalise peaceful picketing.

Economics and Industrial Relations

The policies and practices adopted by Irish trade unions over the years have been characterised by constant adaptations to the realities of political and economic life. Changes in these spheres have primarily prompted a reactive and pragmatic response, as the trade union movement adjusts its priorities, postures and principles in what is perceived to be in the best interests of its membership and potential membership (the unemployed) at the time. These are primarily pursued through ICTU's influence on government policies, such as job creation, pay determination and labour law. While individual trade unions may participate in this process (either through ICTU or in an independent capacity), their primary preoccupation is to protect and improve the pay and conditions of their membership at plant, industry and national levels. Because of this, some authorities have ascribed the rampant inflation of the 1960s and 1970s, together with subsequent unemployment levels and the demise of the Celtic Tiger economy, to the unreasonable pay demands and labour market rigidities respectively sought, secured and imposed by trade unions.

The relatively slow growth of Irish trade unionism in the nineteenth and earlier part of the twentieth centuries may be attributed to the relatively belated arrival of the Industrial Revolution to Ireland. The absence of high-grade coal and iron ore, at least in comparison with Britain, was a contributory factor in this tardy development. However, one cannot disregard the historical determinants, such as the colonisation of Ireland by England, which proceeded from the middle of the sixteenth century onwards and undoubtedly prevented the growth of industry well before the Industrial Revolution. Such restrictions, which included a spell of tariff impositions and export constraints, prevailed up until 1922, since Ireland was perceived as not just a political but also an economic threat to Britain. Consequently, throughout the nineteenth and early twentieth centuries Ireland remained primarily an agricultural economy. In fact, the Cumann na nGaedheal government of 1922 had no industrial policy, believing agriculture to be the mainstay of the economy. Half the workforce was in agriculture, food and drink made up most exports and there was a huge market 'next door' in Britain. The belated transition to a modern industrial economy was a hesitant and slow process.

Between 1914 and 1920 trade union membership increased from 110,000 to 250,000 (Roche and Larragy 1989), but it declined again with the depression in agriculture and trade during the 1920s. Enjoying the aforementioned legal tolerance secured by their British counterparts (which had been incorporated into the new state's legislature), trade unions surfaced hesitantly, addressing themselves to issues of growth, consolidation and adaptation to the prevalent and primarily hostile economic order. Indeed, such was the stagnant nature of society and the related lack of vision amongst the nation's leadership that considerable trade union energy was devoted to the establishment and maintenance of wage differentials, rather than the attainment of any wider economic and social goals. It could be said that a status, rather than a class, consciousness prevailed.

Throughout the 1930s significant moves towards economic development were made inside protectionist economic policies. These were designed to promote greater national economic self-sufficiency and proved effective in securing the development of new industries and the expansion of older ones. However, the onset of World War II and the consequent material supplies shortage contributed to a decline of over a quarter of industrial output during this period. In fact, as late as 1946 agriculture accounted for 47 per cent of total employment, services for 36 per cent and industry for just 17 per cent. Even that 17 per cent was predominantly characterised by small establishments, so that by 1958 only forty concerns outside the public service employed more than 500 workers (Lee 1980). Over the period 1945 to 1950 a short post-war recovery was experienced, which was accompanied by an increase of about 70 per cent in both strike frequency and union membership levels.

The recovery of the late 1940s concealed the limitations of the protectionist strategy. In contrast with the rest of Europe, the 1950s proved to be a miserable decade for Irish society. Economic performance was disappointing – marked by emigration, unemployment, balance of payments difficulties and virtual stagnation – with an actual decline in national output in the last half of the decade. In O'Hagan's assessment

(1987), there was a lack of quality economic policy-making and effective leadership in both government and civil service at this time. While the level of trade union membership increased by over 7 per cent during the 1950s (as it benefited from state intervention in the economy), the level of strike frequency dropped significantly from its post-war heights, as trade unions resigned themselves to the economy's stagnation or lack of growth. The fact that by 1960 there were 123 operating trade unions – of which 84 had an enrolled membership of less than 1,000 – offers some insight into the priority accorded status or relativity factors by the Irish worker, in preference to class consciousness or solidarity considerations (Lee 1980).

In the late 1950s Ireland entered a period of sustained economic growth arising from the adoption of a new development strategy. Economic isolationism and aspirations for self-sufficiency were abandoned in favour of free trade as 'Ireland opened a wider window on the world' (MacSharry and White 2000: 357). This was despite the continued prevalence of obsolete management techniques and primitive employer–worker relationships. The 1960s and early 1970s were periods of sustained and unprecedented improvements in living standards and considerable economic growth. There was an emphasis on attracting direct foreign investment through generous incentives. Commenting on the changing social climate of the 1960s, McCarthy (1973) suggested that it was 'a decade of upheaval' or period of national adolescence, with the old authoritarian societal structures facing unprecedented challenges. The demise of 'the deferential worker' transpired, as previously accepted values, attitudes and institutions came under challenge. The expansion of educational opportunities and media influences increased awareness of the outside world and facilitated a greater preparedness to question previously sacrosanct practices and institutions. Allied to this awakening was an opening up of educational and social possibilities that were previously denied or non-existent.

Consequent to this economic development – with 1,000 foreign operations comprising a labour force of 87,600 established in Ireland – trade union membership levels rose by nearly 50 per cent between the mid-1960s and the late 1970s, while strike frequency levels escalated significantly between 1960 and the mid-1970s. The barriers of pay relativity which had been established were now being reinforced, as both white- and blue-collar workers engaged in some of the most notorious industrial actions in Irish industrial relations history as they clamoured to preserve their differentials and position on the social ladder (McCarthy 1973; McCarthy *et al.* 1975).

Over the 1960s and 1970s, following in the path of its main trading partners, the Irish government opted to relegate the laissez-faire approach to economic affairs and adopt a Keynesian approach to economic growth management and planning. This involved successive governments stimulating demand through budgetary deficits and increased expenditure. These yielded higher levels of economic activity and reduced levels of unemployment. However, this route to the idyllic economy brought with it a new set of ills. Chief amongst these was the spiralling level of inflation, which the social partners (government, employers and trade unions) attempted to halt via a series of national-level pay agreements commencing in 1970. In addition, the surge in economic confidence brought with it a drift of power to the workplace, with shop stewards (workplace representatives) dominating the collective bargaining scene at plant level. An upsurge in unofficial strike action (action without official trade union authorisation) also materialised, as workers seized upon the boom climate created by economic expansion.

By the 1980s two problems of significance had materialised. First, the accumulated foreign debt had grown (from £126 million in 1972 to £7,900 million by 1985), bringing with it an increase of over £730 million in annual debt interest payments. Second, unemployment levels had escalated from about 6 per cent to 17 per cent over the period 1971 to 1986 – with worse to follow. In brief, the Irish economy was under severe pressure from an explosive national debt, oppressive taxation, high emigration and rising unemployment. There was a concern amongst Ireland's political and banking community at this time that the International Monetary Fund (IMF) would step in to impose the economic stringency that the politicians had failed to apply (MacSharry and White 2000). Once again, following on international trends, the government opted for 'fiscal rectitude' through monetarist policies, primarily designed to tackle the balance of payments deficit and the attainment of international competitiveness. The policies of particular relevance in the industrial relations context included moderate pay rises and reduced government spending – with consequences for welfare benefit levels, government subsidisation of Irish industry and public sector employment. In effect, this constituted a neo-laissez-faire economic route, involving reduced state intervention with the economy left largely to the devices of the marketplace.

The advent of this 'new realism' in the 1980s and early 1990s was accompanied by reduced trade union bargaining power. This was expressed in falling unionisation levels, spiralling unemployment, a greater prevalence of non-union employments and an upsurge in managerial confidence, together with instances of 'macho management' practices. As the international recession heightened in the early 1990s, a persistent balance of payments problem, increased unemployment and rising interest rates all combined to create real constraints and tensions. A consequence of this downturn was the intensification of divisions within society, as unemployment spiralled and welfare benefits and services declined. Nevertheless, the various indices used to measure industrial action or strike levels reveal a general downward trend, accompanied by a decline in trade union density (the percentage of employees who are union members). Reflecting on the social and political impact of the crisis of liberal capitalism, Bew *et al.* (1989) noted the relative lack of class conflict, radical politics, industrial militancy or any fundamental change in the nature of Irish society. Ireland remained a conservative society, imbued with the values of Catholicism, nationalism and ruralism, although apparently less stridently so than in earlier periods.

By the mid-1990s the 'Celtic Tiger' had arrived, bringing with it a new economic confidence and aura. This was reflected in such factors as the fastest growth rates in the European Union (EU), the healthiest exchequer returns ever, a large balance of payments and current budget surplus, low mortgage interest rates, declining unemployment, booming profits and incomes and the lowest crime rate for nearly twenty years. Inflation was below the EU average from 1987 to 1997, although thereafter it drifted above that level. No economic model had predicted such a reversal of fortune. According to O'Donnell and O'Reardon (1996), the much needed recovery from the disastrous early and mid-1980s was largely attributable to the social partnership deals. A relevant feature of the first social partnership agreement was the wage restraint (and industrial peace) which unions traded in return for an input to the wider economic and social agenda. According to Roche (2007a), the main thrusts of successive social partnership agreements since 1987 have been the promotion of economic recovery, the maintenance of national competitiveness, adjusting to European economic integration and monetary union and the promotion of improvements in wages, living standards and social services at levels consistent with economic and political imperatives.

The period of the Celtic Tiger was not a homogenous one. Commentators have generally distinguished between the period up to 2000 and the period thereafter. Up to 2000 the economic growth was based on a sound economy characterised by increased competitiveness; thereafter it was based on a property bubble and ever-increasing public spending. By 2007 the housing market had entered into decline, leaving the banking system in a perilous state. By September 2008 the government felt forced to intervene in order to save the banks, and the controversial bank guarantee was introduced.

There was a dramatic turnaround in 2008 and the economy officially entered into recession in the first half of the year. By the third quarter of 2010 the economy was contracting. Associated with this contraction, consumption and investment levels declined, reflecting continued weakness in the demand for housing and domestic services. Banking bailouts and budgetary cutbacks adversely affected consumer confidence and unemployment rose to 14.7 per cent by the end of 2010. In response to these deleterious indicators, the government initiated public sector pay and pension reforms over the period 2009 to 2010, entering into the Croke Park Agreement 2010–2014 with public sector unions. This agreement served to secure co-operation for these (and related work practice) reforms in exchange for a commitment to no redundancies or further pay cuts. Consequent to the recession, employers' industrial relations focus turned to finding ways of controlling and reducing pay and headcounts (McMahon 2011). A feature of this trend is the sense among trade union officials that their role is to 'rubber stamp' decisions already made by employers, while employees remain largely compliant and fearful for their livelihoods:

> The current recession has led to the collapse of the formal national social partnership arrangements ushered in during the previous recession … The 'Croke Park' agreement … and the joint accord between IBEC on public policy priorities and private sector pay reflect the legacy of social partnership and its continuing informal or depleted influence on employment relations in Ireland. (Roche *et al.* 2011: 245)

In the context of the economic framework, developments in the labour market exert a significant influence on industrial relations and human resource management policies and practices. Many of the key influences on such policies and practices are summarised in Table 1.1.

Table 1.1

Key Changes in the Irish Labour Market 1922–2011

- After a lethargic forty-year period subsequent to the foundation of the state (characterised by a predominantly agricultural economy with high emigration rates) pursuant to modest industrial development in the 1960s, in the following decade a boom in the economy transpired, facilitating high levels of employment. In the 1980s a contraction in the domestic economy led to an employment crisis. In the 1990s employment improved in the export and international services sector but unemployment rates remained persistently high. In the 2000s a construction boom occurred in the domestic economy, facilitating full employment. In the period 2008 to 2011 a contraction of the domestic economy led to an employment crisis, although the export economy remained relatively stable throughout the boom–bust period.

- Up to 2008 the size of the (better educated, more skilled) labour force had been constantly increasing over a period of forty years. Reflecting the change in Ireland's economic fortunes over the period 1971 to 2008, there was an increase of nearly 90 per cent in the size of the labour force. By 2011, out of a population of almost 4.5 million, 1.8 million were in the labour force, of whom 86 per cent were employed. This is attributable to a combination of the underlying growth in the population aged fifteen years and over, increased female participation rates and immigration. The level of female participation in the labour force escalated from 28 per cent in 1971 to approximately 52 per cent by 2011. This increased participation level is particularly evident in retail distribution, insurance, financial/business, professional and personal services. Reflecting the sizeable immigration trend is the fact that it more than doubled from 21,000 in 2004 (when EU enlargement took place) to 48,000 in 2007 (CSO 2011). However, consequent to the aforementioned recession, emigration increased sharply over the period 2010 to 2011, and was estimated to have reached 76,400 in the year to April 2011.

- A salient feature of the changing composition of the labour force has been the substantial shift in employment levels from the agricultural to the services sector. The period since 1926 has witnessed major changes in the relative employment shares of the three broad sectors of economic activity: agriculture, industry and services. The diminishing importance of agriculture is clearly evident, as is the growth of the services sector since 1971. The composition of industrial types of employment has altered significantly, with contractions in many of the older, labour-intensive, indigenous sub-sectors (e.g. textiles, clothing and footwear) and expansions in technology-related, export-oriented and foreign-owned employments. A notable characteristic of the changing sectoral composition of the labour force is the decline in male manual jobs in the manufacturing sector, alongside a sizeable increase in the number of (predominantly female) part-time jobs, posing practical problems for trade union organisers. Alongside increased immigration levels, these changes also have implications for a host of areas related to industrial relations and human resource management (HRM). These include labour market segmentation, 'atypical' work patterns, trade union recognition, working methods, job content, wage differentials, skill protection practices, the incidence and extent of low pay, job security, downsizing, subcontracting, outsourcing, job displacement, 'race to the bottom', the management of diversity, equal opportunities, decreased union density and collective bargaining strength, and the protection of collectively agreed pay and employment standards (above legally fixed minima) and initiatives in respect of (and arising from) protective labour laws.

> • Technological advances generally accompany (if not prompt) major waves of economic and
> social change, e.g. the Industrial Revolution. New technologies energising post-industrial
> societies are rooted in information technology (IT). The IT revolution is not confined to
> the economic sphere of production: it is changing the social, cultural and political arenas
> of society at an accelerating rate. The technological impact on matters such as the size,
> spread, location and duration of employment is sizeable (e.g. the electronics/information
> technology revolution). The quickening pace of technological change has a dramatic impact
> on the structure and nature of the labour market and numerous job types therein. A notable
> impact of this trend is the aforementioned move away from manual work together with
> the ease of workplace relocation. Technology also affects cost structure and consequently
> impacts on key aspects of industrial relations, e.g. job security, deskilling, demarcation lines,
> reward systems and relative bargaining power positions.
>
> *Source:* Ahearne (2010) and www.cso.ie

Politics in Industrial Relations

The role of the state in the industrial relations arena has been most significant over the
past century. This has seen it adjust from the casting of trade unions as illegal entities to
an accommodation in a social partnership or neo-corporatist model (see Chapter 13)
with union involvement in the national-level decision-making processes covering the
whole gamut of economic and social affairs. Although the state aspires to the role of
independent referee and regulator of labour relations matters, as it addresses the worst
excesses of liberal capitalism, it would be inappropriate to evaluate its role as only that
of an impartial facilitator. In any democratic society, the state reflects the differences
in power between capital and labour and endeavours to side with whomever yields the
greatest political influence. In effect then, through their various powers and agencies,
successive Irish governments have upheld the established norms, values and culture
of liberal capitalism. Over time, the state has tended to refine the extremes of laissez-
faire ideology and concede some trade union demands, so long as they are peacefully
presented and pursued, constitutional and maintain due deference to property rights
and industrial capitalism.

The Irish Free State inherited the legislative framework laid down in UK statutes
from 1871 to 1906 and these continued to apply so long as they were in accordance with
the 1922 (and later the 1937) Constitution. However, the first Free State government
displayed some disdain for entitlements granted by their British predecessors, as it
proceeded to alienate many working-class voters and rejected the application of Whitley
procedures to Ireland (the provision of arbitration machinery for the civil service).

In line with the eventual adherence to an 'auxiliary' or accommodative strategy, the state
largely supported the voluntarist principle in labour relations by mainly confining legal
interference to the provision of mediation services. Such a strategy, while successfully
isolating trade union militancy and dampening popular support for the route to
revolutionary socialism, forced the trade union movement to (generally) separate and
seek its ideologically driven aspirations through a political wing, e.g. via the Labour
Party or tripartite/corporatist structures such as the 'social partnership' agreements.

The Irish Labour Party was established in 1912 at the initiative of James Connolly and James Larkin at the Trade Union Congress. However, between preoccupations with the burning 'national' question (which has consumed the overwhelming majority of political thought and action over many centuries) and a negligible industrial base (at least until the 1960s), the scope for the development of strong working-class communities and culture was severely restricted. Of some further relevance to the relatively modest influence of the Labour Party is the fact that, together with the ITUC, it decided not to contest the 1918 General Election. According to Kavanagh (1987), this policy of abstention (since the party sidestepped the independence question) removed Labour from centre stage in Irish politics for many years.

In any case, a working class consumed by sacrosanct relativities and occupational status was unlikely to fill the ranks of a vibrant left-wing movement along western European lines. A striking consequence of this void is that there has been little substantial difference in policy stances between successive Irish governments on economic and social issues. Given the ideological similarities across the main political parties and governments, there has been relatively mild opposition to the directions, policies and actions of the governmental process.

The absorption of working-class demands into the existing industrial and political structures has also facilitated the maintenance of widespread support for those parties representing the values and beliefs of liberal capitalism. Indeed, up to the 1970s the state adopted such an 'auxiliary' role as it avoided direct coercive interference in the industrial relations process, leaving the parties to resolve their own differences via free collective bargaining.

The progressive creation of a welfare state in the decades succeeding World War II reflected a belief within society that the state should accept responsibility for the provision of education, health and related social services. This perspective also dominated in the economic arena, as the government maintained and persisted with semi-state industries such as the ESB, Aer Lingus and Bord na Móna. Of course, the gradual creation of a welfare state facilitated the maintenance of political consensus, stability and legitimacy. The emergence of a corporatist or interventionist ideology was accompanied by an integration of political, economic and social decision making. From the 1960s onwards, the state's policy of corporate control came into evidence as trade union representatives were invited onto consultative bodies with a role in economic planning, notably the National Industrial and Economic Council (NIEC). The advent of tripartite consultations was adjudged important, given the need for economic adaptation, restructuring and the establishment of appropriate and realistic planning targets. The government therefore had to fall back on those interests involved on the ground in order to acquire the necessary information and understanding as well as to secure their co-operation in the implementation of policy. The downgrading of enterprise and sector-wide free collective bargaining and the emergence of national-level tripartite bargaining (involving government, employers and trade unions) marked a new phase in the relationship between the state and the trade union movement.

The decision to enter the European Economic Community (EEC) with effect from 1973 was another important development in the political environment of industrial relations.

An immediate impact was felt in areas of industrial development and individual labour law. Indeed, this latter feature has made persistent inroads into almost every facet of day-to-day interactions at the workplace. Furthermore, the influx of multinational enterprises is commonly accredited with a greater level of professionalism in the area of personnel or HRM, together with an increase in trade union membership-cum-preproduction employment agreements and non-union establishments (McMahon 1990).

The advent of contemporary national-level partnership arrangements, covering a host of economic (including pay) and social issues, can be traced back to the maintenance men's dispute of 1969–70. This was, according to the Dublin Chamber of Commerce, 'the greatest crisis in industrial relations ever experienced in the history of the state', producing a 20 per cent wage rise over eighteen months (Ó Gráda 1997: 103). The expectations sparked by this settlement promptly raised industrial relations on the government's agenda. Such a large settlement threatened the government's economic management aspirations in the desire to control incomes and inflationary pressures, thus eventually giving rise to the national tripartite arrangements.

Over the 1970s these arrangements had expanded in scope to accommodate a plethora of economic and social affairs under the title of 'national understandings'. The temporary demise of the consensus approach at national level during the 1980s can be primarily attributed to a hardened negotiating stance on the part of both employers and state. Related to this was a change in government, with the more populist or pragmatic Fianna Fáil party being replaced by a Fine Gael–Labour coalition. A subsequent change of government facilitated the resurgence of the social partnership-type approach from 1987 onwards, as national-level agreements emerged again to embrace a range of economic and social issues. However, in this regard it is also pertinent that the monetarism or neo-laissez-faire economic policies espoused particularly by Thatcher's Conservative government in Britain and Reagan's Republican government in the US prevailed. The choice for the Irish unions, in an era of declining membership and rising unemployment, spanned probably futile industrial action or participation in the nation's key decision-making forums. The participative model (initiated by Seán Lemass in the late 1950s) was accepted by the majority of trade unions and employer organisations.

By the early 1990s a persistent international recession and constraints on remedial initiatives imposed by membership of, and adherence to, the EU and Single European Market, respectively, combined to signal a new era in the management of industrial relations. Political developments in many industrialised economies (including the resurgence of laissez-faire individualism, with its emphasis on monetarism, free enterprise, open markets, deregulation and privatisation) and the demise of socialist economies in eastern Europe forced the recall and revision of many left-wing and trade union ideological aspirations. This helped reinforce for the trade union movement the merits of operating inside the neo-corporatist model and the furtherance of its more immediate demands under the auspices of the prevalent liberal capitalist political system.

In return for involvement, trade unions were expected to deliver industrial peace. This quid pro quo exchange was particularly evident in the Celtic Tiger phase. Given the contention that in the absence of such (social) partnership agreements, income determination would have been more fractious, with more strikes and higher pay settlements (Sweeney 1998: 93) and that relative industrial peace prevailed in this period, various sources accorded social partnership a fundamental role in the economic miracle (Auer 2000; MacSharry and White 2000; NESC various years; O'Donnell and O'Reardon 1996, 2000). This role is not unchallenged, however. Baccaro and Simoni (2004) point out that although the economic transformation began in 1987 and overlapped in time with the institutionalisation of social partnership, much of the economic literature discounts this overlap as sheer coincidence. It is salutary to note that the view of social partnership has changed, with critics claiming it contributed to excess state spending, especially through the benchmarking process within the public sector.

In any case, it is apparent that the social partnership model effectively constituted a 'new form of governance' or a parallel political system within the state in this era (Roche 2007a). Subsequent to the demise of the Celtic Tiger and the onset of the economic crisis, the consensus approach to social and economic policy-making faded, while the formal institutional process governing collective bargaining was dropped. Related to this, the Taoiseach of the new government (elected in 2011) labelled the shift as one from 'social partnership' to 'social dialogue' (Sheehan 2011c).

THE ROLE OF THEORY IN INDUSTRIAL RELATIONS

The role of theory is to facilitate the analysis and appraisal of the processes, structures and institutions of industrial relations in as objective a manner as is possible with any of the social sciences. This section of the text attempts to outline and evaluate the main academic theories that have been developed in an effort to provide a logical and consistent means of understanding and interpreting industrial relations realities.

Over time there have been a series of prescriptions for change designed to improve the conduct of industrial relations in Ireland, e.g. laws on strikes, worker participation/involvement schemes and trade union recognition. Such proposals can often be highly contentious, and the theoretical principles and value judgments upon which they are founded are rarely made explicit. Accordingly, this section introduces and assesses the main theoretical perspectives and related value judgments on the nature of the world of work. Familiarity with the underlying values of the various theoretical perspectives facilitates insightful analysis. As each theory originates from a different base or set of assumptions, it would be inappropriate to insist upon a single 'best' theory of industrial relations. However, it would be remiss not to acknowledge the traditional primacy of the pluralist analysis in Irish industrial relations practices and debates.

Pluralist Analysis

The pluralist model is based on the existence of a 'post-capitalist' society, where industrial and political conflict have become institutionally separated, ownership is distinguished from management, and authority and power in society are more widely distributed. In effect, this analysis acknowledges that society is comprised of a range of individuals, interest and social groups, each in pursuit of their own objectives. As in society, the employing entity is comprised of an accommodation or alliance of different values and competing sectional interests. So it is only through such an accommodation or alliance that work organisations can attempt to operate with any degree of continuity and success. Just as the political system is institutionalised and regulated through a party political and parliamentary process, so too is the industrial system institutionalised and regulated through representative organisations and appropriately structured processes. According to Fox (1973), these competing organisational values and interests have to be 'managed' for the purpose of maintaining a viable collaborative structure.

This perspective acknowledges the legitimacy of trade union organisation, interests and the right to contest managerial prerogative. This is done through collective bargaining, which engenders greater industrial relations stability and adaptability than the outlawing of trade unions (Clegg 1975). Accordingly, conflict is viewed as a logical and inevitable feature of the world of work and consequently it requires management by a variety of role players, representatives, procedures, processes and specialist institutions.

A central feature of this post-capitalist perspective is that the class conflict by-product of the Industrial Revolution has now abated. The Marxist analysis of the powerful capitalists and weak wage earners – of the socially elite and the socially weak – is (allegedly) no longer an appropriate model. Contemporary society, it is argued, is more open and mobile, with the franchise (vote) extended for the further democratisation of politics, greater accessibility of educational opportunity opening hitherto closed occupational routes and the advent of the welfare state serving to alleviate the worst extremes of deprivation and inequality. Furthermore, the spread and diffusion of property ownership, status and authority in the post-capitalist society has irretrievably removed the sharp divisions between those who were once industrially and politically powerful and their counterparts, who were weak and powerless in both these crucial spheres.

With the separation of industrial and political conflict, collective bargaining has become the focus of attention at the workplace for the regulation of relations. With the emergence, structuring and regulation of representative organisations on both sides of industry, appropriate forums have been established to address the tensions and conflicts arising at all levels between these sectional interest groups. For example, in the event of failure to resolve differences at plant level, an array of third-party institutions provides a generally acceptable route for the resolution of contrasting objectives and conflict. According to Dahrendorf (1959), these developments are well reflected in:

- the organisation of conflicting interest groups, e.g. trade unions and employer associations;
- the establishment of 'parliamentary' negotiating bodies in which these groups meet, e.g. social partnership forums;
- the institutions of mediation and arbitration, e.g. the Labour Relations Commission and Court;
- formal representations within the individual enterprise, e.g. via shop stewards/employee representatives; and
- tendencies towards an institutionalisation of workers' participation in industrial management, e.g. consultation initiatives.

Therefore, pluralists acknowledge the inevitability of conflict but point to the relative stability of a society that institutionalises, manages and contains any differences via collaboration, negotiated compromises and mediation.

Unitary Analysis

The basic premise of the unitary analysis is that all employment units are, or should be, cohesive and harmonious establishments with a total commitment to the attainment of a common goal. Being unitary in structure and purpose – with shared goals, values and interests and one source of (managerial) authority – staff relations are set upon a plinth of mutuality and harmony. There is no conflict between those contributing the capital (the owners) and the contributors of labour (the employees). Consequently, all staff members agree unreservedly with the aspirations of the organisation and the means deployed to give effect to them. Through this team or complementary partnership approach, it is assumed that both sides can satisfy their common goals of high profitability and pay levels, job security and efficiency. Furthermore, it is implicitly acknowledged that competent and strong leadership or management are a prerequisite to the pursuit of organisational effectiveness. In practice this may give rise to elements of paternalism and/or authoritarianism on the part of management in their approach to employee relations matters.

Paternalism may be reflected in a managerial concern for staff needs, together with a rejection of union recognition and collective bargaining practices. Authoritarianism may also materialise in a dominant managerial value system, characterised by a minimal concern for employee welfare and outright opposition to union recognition and collective bargaining initiatives. For example, during the nineteenth century many employers adopted an aggressive unitary stance, actively excluding unions while employing women and children on low pay for long hours in unsanitary working conditions. In either scenario – paternalism or authoritarianism – trade unionism is opposed as a threat to the organisation's unity of purpose and managerial prerogative, as it competes for employee loyalty and commitment. The consequent rejection of collective bargaining is therefore based on management's perceived legitimate prerogative to proceed without the incumbency of negotiation to attain consent to their decision-making initiatives and responsibility. In such settings it is assumed that management will insert an appropriate communications structure to alert staff to organisational priorities and to manage the expectations of staff in respect of same. In response, members of staff are expected to give effect to these instructions and to show loyalty to the entity for the realisation of common goals.

In essence, the unitary theory rejects the concept of enduring conflict or organisational factionalism, as such collision or competition distracts from what are assumed to be non-competing, co-operative initiatives. The existence of conflict is not perceived to be a structural feature of organisational life.

The unitary philosophy is therefore predominantly managerialist. It legitimises management authority under the heading of commonality, largely attributes the source of conflict to subordinates and serves as a means of justifying managerial decisions to any interested parties, while explaining opposition to same as either ill-informed or perverse. Increased levels of opposition to trade union recognition and the associated rise in the number of non-union establishments have significantly strengthened the prevalence and validity of this particular model in Ireland. Accordingly, it provides 'the subconscious foundation' (Salamon 2000) for managers in their choice of issues upon which they are prepared to negotiate and those upon which they are only prepared to consult. Furthermore, it provides a raison d'être for many of the now prevalent HRM practices in Irish employments.

Radical or Class Conflict Analysis

The radical or class conflict perspectives endorse the Marxist view of capitalist societies being divided into antagonistic class forces. Although Marxist analyses of industrial relations are more a by-product of a theory of capitalist society and social change rather than of labour relations, they provide a useful framework for the interpretation of the relationship between capital and labour. Marxism is more concerned with the structure and nature of society than with the actual workplaces that society accommodates. When the original Marxist analysis of the nature and structure of society was conceived, the phenomena of trade unionism and collective bargaining were barely established. Consequently, the application of the original Marxist analysis to contemporary labour relations institutions and phenomena is problematic. Classical Marxism saw capitalism as an advanced stage in societal development, with class conflict over the distribution of the 'surplus value' of workers' efforts giving rise to irreconcilable antagonism between capital and labour. It predicted the impoverishment of an ever-growing working class, eventually leading to revolutionary change.

This body of theory is essentially an analysis of the evolution of society, of which the capitalist (or bourgeois) state is only one phase. Therefore, Marxism depicts a series of developments or phases of social change: from the initial state of primitive communism, through an era of feudalism, to capitalism (which it is predicted would give rise to a class war between the 'bourgeoisie' and the 'proletariat'), culminating in a dictatorship of the proletariat before progressing to socialism and eventually a utopian, classless society.

In essence, Marxism is based upon the premise that class (i.e. capital and labour) conflict is at the root of societal change. This conflict is not a simple consequence of contrasting demands and tensions at the workplace; it is the product of an inequitable distribution of power and wealth in wider society. Such inequity is also reflected in society's social and political institutions, serving to maintain the position of the dominant establishment group (i.e. the owners of the means of production). Therefore, social and political conflict (and social change) is the consequence of economic inequity within society, between the owners/capitalists and the labouring classes. Accordingly, conflict reflects the difference between these groups, with their diametrically opposed economic and political interests. This class and political conflict is linked to industrial conflict, which Marxists adjudge to be a permanent feature of capitalism, as the competing interests seek to consolidate and advance their relative positions in the economic power structure, contesting the distribution of the entity or society's power, wealth and 'surplus value'. Hence, the industrial relations system is viewed as a marginal forum for the conduct of this class war, although some Marxists suggest that it will ultimately spill over into a more fundamental political revolution.

Neo-Marxist and radical sources attribute the industrial relations system with a limited role, via the resolution of pay and condition issues and the delineation of the boundaries of managerial prerogative, although conflict is seen as a reflection of the opposing economic interests engendered by capitalism. The starting point for those holding the radical reference frame is the largely unequal distribution of power between the employer and the employee, while radicals do not see the collective organisation of employees (e.g. in unions) as restoring the power balance between the 'propertied' and the 'unpropertied'.

Radical writers (e.g. Fox 1977) suggest that conflict is contained and stability maintained by the social and political system and associated trade-offs. In other words, the institutions of industrial relations serve to institutionalise conflict. In this context, unions are viewed as a collective response to the exploitation of capitalism, with a role in the wider political process for the attainment of significant alterations to the economic and social system. However, Marxists adjudge the operation of (national, industrial and enterprise-based) bodies of joint regulation as accommodating, consolidating, legitimising and effectively enhancing management's prerogative and power position, while projecting an image or veneer of power sharing. The collective bargaining process is perceived to (at least temporarily) accept, facilitate and ultimately support the inherent contradictions of capitalism. Furthermore, Marxists view the state's legislative framework as a related piece of armoury designed to support managements' interests (Hyman 1975).

In summary, Marxists argue that economic and political issues cannot be separated and they place great emphasis on the antagonistic interests of capital and labour. In sharp contrast with alternative analytical frameworks, this theoretical perspective focuses on the importance of assessing the power held by opposing interests and so offers a valuable insight into the mechanics of the industrial relations system.

Social Action Analysis

The social action perspective on industrial relations 'stresses that the individual retains at least some freedom of action and ability to influence events' in the manner they adjudge to be most appropriate or preferable (Jackson 1982). This theory emphasises the role players' or actors' definitions, perceptions and influences on reality. It is these definitions and perceptions that determine, in part, their relationships, behaviours and actions. Therefore, with this frame of reference, social and industrial relations actions are best understood in terms of their subjectively intended meanings. Concentration on observed behaviour at the workplace restricts the value of any interpretation, since it would overlook the deeper intent of the actors. The actors' decisions are determined not just by the specific work situations they find themselves in, but by a plethora of wider and underlying influences such as the attitudes, values, experiences and expectations developed over a lifetime, both inside and outside of the workplace. The central relevance of this particular perspective is that it attributes to the individual actors some prerogative or discretion to shape the actual workplace and society in which they exist along (their) desired lines. However, in this context, they are restricted by their own perception of reality. Thus, the social action analysis accords some control or priority to the individual over the structure or system in which they find themselves. It offers a frame of reference that concentrates on the range of industrial relations system outputs as being as much the end result of the actions of its constituent parts as of the structure of the system itself. This theory is rooted in a well-developed sociological school of thought which argues that just as 'society makes man … man makes society' (Silverman 1970). The impact on Irish industrial relations of people like James Larkin and William Martin Murphy arguably provides support for the social action view that individuals have a capacity to influence and shape events.

Systems Analysis

The systems theory of industrial relations originated in the late 1950s in the US when John Dunlop proposed that industrial relations is a system made up of actors, contexts and an ideology serving to bind the system together, producing a body of rules that govern the actors at the workplace (Dunlop 1958). Dunlop's construction of an integrated model is based on a view of the system as one which, though overlapping and interacting with the economic and political decision-making systems, is nevertheless a societal subsystem in its own right. This subsystem's output or product is comprised of a set of rules pertaining to the employment relationship, which spans their design, application and interpretation. Accordingly, the industrial relations system is primarily concerned with an output of rules covering all matters of pay and conditions, together with the installation of procedures for their administration and application. It is based on the standard *input–process–output* model, which Dunlop argues may be applied regardless of the prevailing economic or political system.

Under *input*, three sets of influences apply: *actors, environmental contexts* and *ideology*. These combine in the bargaining, conciliation and legislative processes, yielding a body, network or web of *rules*. The *actors* include the different worker categories (whether organised or unorganised), various layers of management (together with their respective representatives) and the range of third-party agencies. The *environmental context* impinging on the system is comprised of technological, market/budgetary and societal power location and distribution variables. The technological impact is reflected in such factors as the size, skill and sexual breakdown of the workforce, its concentration or distribution and the location and duration of the employment. The market or budgetary constraints, whether applied locally, nationally or internationally, affect all enterprise types – not just the entity's management but also, ultimately, all of the system's role players. The *power* input relates to the degree of autonomy afforded to the industrial relations system by wider society, as significantly influenced by the distribution of power in that society. The *ideological* input recognises that while each group of actors in the system may have their own set of ideas, these are sufficiently congruent for a level of mutual tolerance, common belief or unifying ideological compatibility to prevail.

Conclusion and Critique of Models

Given their contrasting premises and prognoses, the various models of industrial relations are the subject of critical evaluation. For example, despite its prevalence, the pluralist analysis has been criticised for its undue emphasis on consensus and integration, alongside a ready acceptance of the social and political status quo and a fundamental conservatism which assumes an illusory balance of power between the various interest groups (Fox 1973; Goldthorpe 1974). Furthermore, it tends to ignore the decision-making powers resident beyond the collective bargaining process. In this regard, radical theorists point out that power is also about the ability to prevent matters becoming the subject of negotiation. Yet unlike both the unitary and Marxist theories, pluralism appears less value driven, though it does veer towards prescriptions favouring the constant negotiation of conflicts based on compromise (Clegg 1975).

The unitary perspective is cautioned for its unrealistically utopian outlook, limited applicability (e.g. to non-union entities) and a paternalistic, management orientation that assumes a generally accepted value system. Indeed D'Art and Turner's overview of Irish industrial relations serves as a sturdy challenge to this perspective. Their findings support the case 'for the utility and continuing relevance of trade unions and collective bargaining' (2002: 303).

The classic Marxist analysis is adjudged to be anachronistic given that, among other things, the nature of class conflict has substantially changed and contemporary society (with its mixed economy and welfare state) is now more open and socially mobile. The distribution of power, property and social status in society is also more widely diffused today (at least in the developed world) than it was in the nineteenth century. Furthermore, capitalism has been successful in developing wealth in certain parts of the globe, though the distribution of that wealth remains an issue with which many neo-Marxists and radical writers take issue. It is also pertinent that 'revolution' came to pass not in the developed West but in the less developed East. In addition, a number of predictions of classical Marxism have failed to materialise, although the growth of large-scale business or monopoly capital is one area of Marxist analysis with contemporary resonance, as is the current international economic and financial crisis (Resnick and Wolff 2010). In drawing attention to the nature of power and control in the workplace and society, the neo-Marxist and radical analysis presents a valuable intellectual challenge to unitarist and pluralist thinking.

With regard to social action theory, critics point to its neglect of those structural features that influence the action of its actors. This oversight reflects the theory's inability to explain the very nature of the wider system inside which these actions occur.

Systems theory has also been subjected to considerable critical evaluation, refinement and modification (Gennard and Judge 2010). For example, it is contended that the model's narrow focus omits the reality of and mechanisms for the distribution of wealth and power in society. In effect, its convenient unifying ideology-cum-status quo inclination (which takes society as given) merely accords the industrial relations system some functional role in the maintenance of stability and overlooks a range of issues, including industrial relations change, the source of conflict and the system's interrelationship with the 'outside' political, economic and social scene. It is also argued that its structural emphasis leads to an output, or rules focus, at the expense of the actual decision, or rule-making processes. It also fails to explain important behavioural variables (i.e. why actors act as they do) and it is suggested that this model ought to accommodate the significant role of the owners of business, who warrant inclusion as actors and in their contextual capacity. Wood (1978) also recommends that a distinction be made between the (industrial relations) system which 'produces' the rules and the (production) system which is governed by these rules.

CONCLUDING COMMENTS

Far from being a subject based on a single analytical framework or a set of incontrovertible facts and statistics, political and theoretical controversy is inherent to the subject of industrial relations. There are many ways of interpreting what is going on and a multitude of opinions about what ought to be happening. The fact that there is no universally accepted global theory is unavoidable and ought to be accepted by the student as an attractive dimension to a topic that easily lends itself to contrasting perspectives, opinions and debate. It is for the student to make up their own mind on these matters, since this book endeavours to take a neutral line, presenting the different sides of the various issues under examination.

CHAPTER 2

Collective Labour Law in a Historical, Social and Political Context

INTRODUCTION

This chapter examines the role of common law, legislation, the 1937 Irish Constitution (Bunreacht na hÉireann) and recent European Union (EU) developments in the area of collective industrial relations law. The historical origins and the main collective legal provisions are examined. There are a number of reasons why a historical appreciation of collective labour law (and its political and social context) is essential. First, the laws enacted prior to the foundation of the state in 1922 remain in place except where they have been repealed or found to be repugnant to the Constitution (Kerr 1989). Second, much of the recent legislation is based on legislative principles developed prior to 1922 and an understanding of the conceptual basis of these legal principles is essential. Third, the law cannot be understood in the absence of its social and institutional context. In this regard, the impact of social activism through trade unions on the development of industrial relations legislation has been especially important. Fourth, historical experience can mark the boundaries of what is practicable and possible in legislating for industrial relations and for those considering resort to legal remedies. Finally, an understanding of the evolution of collective legislation is essential to critically evaluate contemporary debates on the role of the law in industrial relations.

OVERVIEW

Prior to 1824 the approach of both politics and the law to trade unions – or 'combinations' as they were then known – was one of trenchant opposition. The restrictive approach adopted by the law has been ascribed to two factors. One is that the attitude of the judiciary, which was drawn from the ruling class, lacked any understanding or empathy with working men and was biased against working-class organisations. The second and probably more important factor is that the legal judgments arose out of the logic of the individually based 'common law' system, which was at odds with the collective values embodied in trade unionism. Common law is judge-made law. It is based on the notion that rights are vested in individuals. A key principle of common law is that 'restraint of trade' is illegal. This means that interference with the right of individuals or businesses to pursue their own ends, including commercial ones, is contrary to the underlying principles of common law.

As trade unions sought to *collectively* regulate the terms and conditions of employment (to restrain trade), they were inevitably brought into conflict with common law. However, common law arose from liberal ideas that embodied competing principles. The first liberal idea is that individuals should be free to maximise their own welfare and that collective interference with this right is in restraint of trade. The other is that individuals should be free to combine together to promote their own interests. This latter principle implies a right of association that would, if adopted, vindicate workers' entitlement to collectively organise in trade unions.

The evolution of state policy towards trade unions in the UK during the eighteenth and early nineteenth centuries can be seen as a recurring conflict between these two competing liberal principles – restraint of trade and freedom of association. In this conflict, the political system tended to deliver greater liberties to trade unions, while the common law legal system restricted and rowed back on these liberties. This meant that trade unions developed in conjunction with liberal democracy and were arguably a key component of that democracy.

The tension between the individually based common law system and collective industrial relations continues to be a feature of industrial relations to this day. Where legislation or the Constitution does not cover an aspect of collective industrial relations, common law principles apply. In addition, legislation and the Constitution have tended to be interpreted in terms of common law individual liberal principles rather than the collectivist principles applying in a number of EU countries. This has not, however, stopped the issue of commercial rights and collective rights colliding at EU level in recent cases and these are reviewed below.

EARLY LEGAL RESTRICTIONS

The early legal and political hostility to the emergent trade unions (or combinations) dates back to the sixteenth century when 'combinations of workmen were made illegal' (Boyle 1988: 7). Prior to the rise of capitalism, the skilled trades were regulated by the medieval guilds. Although the guilds were organisations of masters (employers), they fulfilled an indirect function of protecting labour. As the power of the medieval guilds progressively weakened in the eighteenth century, the skilled trades were exposed to competition. Shorn of the indirect protection provided by the guilds, workers in the skilled trades formed trade clubs for protection. In time, these trade clubs became known as 'combinations' and later trade unions. Thus, the origin of trade unions in Britain and Ireland was in the skilled trades and among relatively privileged workers – not the deprived and exploited semi-skilled and unskilled workers of the Industrial Revolution.

Combinations were banned under a range of legislation in the eighteenth century, culminating in the Anti-Combinations Acts of 1799–1800. In 1803, the 1800 Act was extended to Ireland but with provision for the maximum jail sentence of six months, compared to three months on the British mainland (D'Arcy 1994: 9). Despite their coercive intent, the various legal attempts to suppress combinations failed, as evidenced by their growth in the skilled trades (Boyd 1972; Boyle 1988).

There are a number of reasons for the failure of legal suppression. The laws were difficult to enforce because of the secrecy of the combinations. Social pressure was sometimes brought to bear on owners and intimidation (even violence) against masters. Intimidation and violence were, however, more evident among non-union workers. This is demonstrated by the non-unionised Luddites who opposed the introduction of new technology in textiles in the period 1811 to 1813. By far the most important reason for the failure of the Anti-Combination Acts was the scarcity of the skills possessed by craftsmen, which made employers reluctant to use the law. There was no such reluctance among employers in opposing unionisation among unskilled or semi-skilled workers. It is important to note that resort to the law was not the main weapon of employers. Simply replacing workers who joined unions or went on strike was the most common and effective tactic. Over time, employers required workers to sign an undertaking not to join unions – this was the so-called 'document' that was at the root of the 1913 Dublin Lockout.

In 1824, the Anti-Combination Acts 1799–1800 and other provisions banning unions were repealed following the campaigning work of Francis Place (a master tailor and an employer) and David Hume, MP. Among the key arguments used to support the case for repeal was the ineffectiveness of the Acts and evidence that they actually worsened relations between master and workmen. Boyle (1988: xi) notes that while the repeal of the combination laws gave trade unions a legal existence, this had only limited effect for two reasons. First, an 1825 Act created crimes of intimidation, obstruction and molestation, which resulted in 'criminal prosecution of workers engaged in industrial action' (Kerr and Whyte 1985: 214). Second, trade unions were vulnerable to arcane laws on the taking of oaths.

In 1834, the significance of the illegality of taking oaths became apparent in the celebrated Tolpuddle Martyrs case, which was the subject of the 1986 film *Comrades*. The martyrs were six Dorset farm labourers who had formed the Friendly Society of Agricultural Labourers to resist wage cuts: they refused to work for less than 10 shillings per week. The oath of secrecy they had taken to protect their identity was found to be illegal and seditious. The six were sentenced to seven years' transportation to Australia. There was outrage at the sentence. Although the men were transported, they were eventually pardoned and repatriated following a campaign led (surprisingly) by the establishment newspaper *The Times* of London.

More long-lasting than repressive legislation was the doctrine of common law conspiracy. This doctrine meant that an action that was otherwise legal was made illegal if two or more workers combined in that action. This obviously placed the primary purpose of unions – the improvement of terms and conditions of employment through *collective* action – outside the law. In 1859, the British Parliament moved to allow a limited use of industrial action in the Molestation of Workmen Act of that year. However, the intentions of Parliament were frustrated by judicial interpretations which found that the Act provided no protection for a breach of contract (a common law offence), which a strike was said to involve.

Not all employers used the law and by the 1850s a growing number had begun to deal with the first nationally organised craft-based 'model unions' in the UK. These had grown out of the new trades formed by the Industrial Revolution. The model unions were viewed as being responsible because of their careful use of the strike weapon. Their acceptance was promoted by the buoyancy of the British economy based on industrial innovation and an expanding empire. In such a buoyant market, it made little sense for employers to engage in industrial conflict with skilled workers when they were needed by the expanding industry. The model unions quickly extended their influence to Ireland. By and large, they formed the basis of the Irish trade union organisation until the foundation of the Irish Transport and General Workers' Union (ITGWU) in 1908. This gave the union movement a distinctly conservative character and set up early clashes with the ITGWU, which operated on the principles of syndicalism. Such syndicalism was associated with militant political activism, free use of the strike weapon and an aspiration to overthrow capitalism.

THE CRIMINAL LAW AND COLLECTIVE INDUSTRIAL RELATIONS

By 1870 a growing acceptance of trade unions in the skilled trades had set the groundwork for change to the doctrine of *criminal* conspiracy. This was aided by the extension of the franchise (vote) to smallholders (those who owned small houses), many of whom were skilled workers and members of the model unions. In the 1870 elections, the unions delivered support to the Liberal Party under Gladstone. That party in turn introduced reforming legislation – the Trade Union Act of 1871. This Act, as subsequently amended, still governs the legal status of trade unions in Ireland today. It legalised the existence of trade unions but carefully sought to refrain from giving them corporate status, i.e. entities capable of suing and being sued in their own name.

While legitimising the existence of unions, the 1871 Act did not provide protection against the underlying common law concept of a criminal conspiracy. In *Regina* v. *Bunn (1872)*, the judiciary found that the existence of a combination (two or more people acting together) converted an otherwise non-criminal act into a crime. The employer had a right to employ whomever he wished and any union interference with this was a criminal offence (O'Hara 1981: 16). It was 'unjustifiable annoyance and interference with the masters in the course of their business' (Kerr and Whyte 1985: 215). Furthermore, picketing was also held to be a criminal offence and even minor expressions of opinion were sufficient to lead to a jail sentence. Picketing is the congregation of workers (usually outside a place of work) for the purpose of communicating a grievance and persuading other workers not to work. It is viewed as central to an entitlement to strike, since it limits the possibility of striking workers being replaced by substitute labour.

The effect of *Regina* v. *Bunn* and other judicial decisions was to frustrate the operation of trade unions and they again looked to politics for relief. In the election of 1874, the model unions switched their allegiance to the Conservative Party, led by Disraeli, in return for a promise of favourable legislation. The Conservatives won the election and there followed a period of legislative activity. The main Act was the Conspiracy and Protection of Property Act 1875, which restricted the remit of the criminal law. It decriminalised peaceful picketing and specified that no one is liable for any act committed *'in contemplation or furtherance of a trade dispute'* unless the act would also be a crime if committed by one person. In effect, it removed the notion of a criminal conspiracy from a peaceful trade dispute. Although the Act was repealed in the UK in 2008, it is still on the statute books in Ireland and continues to serve to limit the role of the criminal law in industrial disputes. The Employers and Workmen Act 1875 followed. It removed criminal liability from employees for breach of their employment contract and limited the penalty to civil damages. Since there was little point in employers suing individual workers, the Act limited the impact of the doctrine that a strike was a breach of contract.

The broad effect of legislative changes in the 1870s was to establish a *voluntarist* system of industrial relations (or 'legal abstentionism') in which the law was designed to play a minor role. In effect, this voluntarism represented a resolution of the conflict between a social movement seeking *collective* regulation of industrial relations and the *individually based* common law system. Trade unions were granted *immunities* from acts that would otherwise have been criminal offences, but they were not given rights. The net effect of the legislative provisions of this time is that the criminal law today applies to industrial relations only in so far as actions are in themselves criminal acts.

The Civil Law and Industrial Relations

The legislation introduced by Parliament did not go unchallenged. Denied the use of criminal liabilities, employers challenged the legality of picketing and had resort to the notion of civil conspiracy under the law of tort (Kerr and Whyte 1985). A tort is a civil wrong arising from a breach of a duty of care and it gives rise to an entitlement to damages. A series of cases in the 1890s made unclear the common law position on picketing. However, the most important developments during this period were in relation to the role of the law of tort – namely, civil liability.

Two cases were important in this regard. In the Belfast case of *Quinn* v. *Leathem (1901)*, an inducement to breach a third-party contract was found to be a civil offence not protected by the 1875 Act. The second case is the celebrated *Taff Vale* case, the full name of which is the *Taff Vale Railway Company* v. *Amalgamated Society of Railway Servants (1901)*. In this case, a union official, Bell, had persuaded substitute workers hired by the employer (Taff Vale) to undermine a strike not to pass pickets. This persuasion, although peaceful, was deemed to have induced a breach of a third-party contract. More significantly it was found that, contrary to the prevailing belief, a trade union could be sued in its *own* name despite the 1871 Act provisions which had been carefully drafted to avoid that possibility. The union was found liable for some £35,000 in damages and costs – a very substantial sum at the time. The impact of this case threatened the very existence of trade unions, since they could quickly become insolvent if they pursued industrial action.

Yet again, the trade union movement turned to the political process in order to overturn the precedents established by *Taff Vale* and similar cases (Boyle 1988; Saville 1967). Following the 1906 elections, a Liberal government was able to assume office because of the support of fifty-four Lib-Lab deputies. These were MPs who supported the trade unions: the Lib MPs were members of the Liberal Party and the Lab MPs were members of the Labour Representation Committee. (Neither the Irish nor UK Labour Party existed at this stage.) Indeed, the campaign over *Taff Vale* is credited with leading to the establishment of the British Labour Party. Following the election, and in return for the support of the fifty-four Lib-Lab MPs, the Liberal government enacted the Trade Disputes Act 1906.

The 1906 Act granted unions and their members immunity from the tort of civil conspiracy, reinforced the protection for peaceful picketing and granted immunities from defined common law liabilities. The immunities in the Act were available to union members and union officials only where they were *acting in contemplation or furtherance of a trade dispute* – the so-called 'golden formula', a phrase coined by noted labour lawyer Lord Wedderburn (1965: 222). Trade unions enjoyed stronger immunities, since they were granted a *total* immunity from being sued under the law of tort. This reversed in its entirety the *Taff Vale* decision that unions could be sued in their own name. Von Prondzynski (1989: 214) notes that the Trade Disputes Act 1906 adopted a very simple technique: it identified the main judicial decisions that had disabled trade unions and gave unions immunities from these judicial precedents.

Known as a 'Bill of Rights for Workers', the 1906 Act actually provided no legal rights and specifically did not confer a right to strike. It met a demand of unions that is encapsulated in Wedderburn's (1965: 9) celebrated phrase: 'they wanted nothing more from the law than it should leave them alone'. Kerr and Whyte (1985) report that the trade unions opposed the enactment of a comprehensive labour law code with positive rights and obligations. They opted instead for the pragmatic immunities approach that had been employed in the 1870s. This 'legal abstentionism' contrasts with the approaches adopted in a number of European countries where, although initially subject to severe legal restrictions, positive rights to union organisation and industrial action were introduced during the twentieth century.

In northern Europe, positive rights systems today normally distinguish between *disputes of rights* and *disputes of interest*. Disputes of rights involve situations where a pre-existing rule can be used to decide on the rights and wrongs of a dispute. In legally based systems, employment legislation or a collective agreement constitutes such a rule. Such disputes are said to be justiciable (capable of being decided by a legal authority) and strikes are not legally protected in such cases (Commission of Inquiry on Industrial Relations 1981). In contrast, strikes involving disputes of interests *are* protected. An example of such a dispute is where on the termination of a collective agreement, a trade union makes a claim for increased pay of 5 per cent and an employer responds with a demand for a pay freeze. There is no pre-existing rule that can be used to decide between these two positions and strikes in pursuit of such issues are legal.

While it arose from the demands of trade unions, it is important to stress that voluntarism also had advantages for employers. In the collective arena, no requirements were placed on employers to recognise or negotiate with trade unions. It left management free to decide on a pragmatic basis if they would or would not deal with them. Legal abstentionism also extended to the area of individual employment law, leaving employers with few obligations. Notably, there was no prohibition on discrimination, no general right to minimum pay or maximum working time (Hepple 2002) and no protection against unfair dismissal; an employer could dismiss for 'any reason or none'. (These issues are developed further in Chapter 6.)

The final piece of collective legislation enacted prior to 1922 (which remains on the statute books) was the Trade Union Act 1913. This Act allows trade union funds to be applied for political purposes provided that political purposes are included in the union's objectives and a separate political fund is set up. As a result, unions in Ireland may operate a political fund but they must offer members an easy way of opting out of paying the political contribution. The issue of whether or not trade unions should be allowed to contribute to political parties has arisen again in recent years, with the debate being framed in the context of limiting or abolishing corporate donations. It has been argued by some that any restrictions on donations should equally apply to trade unions.

COLLECTIVE LEGISLATION, 1922–1990

The trade union movement in the newly independent Irish state was concerned with preserving the legacy embodied in the acts of the UK Parliament and it did not seek positive rights (McGinley 1990). Table 2.1 summarises the main legislative developments in Irish collective labour law since 1922.

Table 2.1
Collective Labour Legislation Enacted by the Oireachtas, 1922–2012

Statute	Provisions
Trade Union Act 1935	Trade unions allowed to own unlimited amount of land
Trade Union Act 1941	Negotiation licences, sole representation rights
Trade Union Act 1942	Exemptions from negotiation licences, appeals in sole rights situations
Industrial Relations Act 1946	Establishment of the Labour Court
Trade Union Acts 1947–1952	Six Acts extending power to reduce deposits to be maintained in the High Court by Irish unions by 75 per cent
Industrial Relations Act 1969	Enlargement of the Labour Court, establishment of Office of Rights Commissioners
Trade Union Act 1971	New negotiation licence rules: £5000 deposit, 500 members, eighteen-month wait
Trade Union Act 1975	Encouraged the amalgamation of trade unions by providing funding for expenses for successful mergers
Industrial Relations Act 1976	Established a Joint Labour Committee (JLC) for agricultural workers and allowed them access to the Labour Court
Worker Participation (State Enterprises) Act 1977–1988	Elected worker directors
Trade Disputes (Amendment) Act 1982	Extended immunities of the 1906 Act to all except the Defence Forces and Gardaí

Table 2.1 (continued)	
Collective Labour Legislation Enacted by the Oireachtas, 1922–2012	
Statute	**Provisions**
Industrial Relations Act 1990	Established the Labour Relations Commission, repealed 1906 and 1982 Trade Disputes Acts, pre-strike secret ballots, immunities restricted, injunctions curbed, funding for trade union rationalisation even if unsuccessful
Industrial Relations (Amendment) Act 2001	Deals with disputes arising out of union recognition – allows for legal determination of terms and conditions of employment but not statutory recognition
Industrial Relations (Miscellaneous Provisions) Act 2004	Reduces the period for Labour Court determinations (from the 2001 Act)
Industrial Relations (Amendment) Act 2012	Amendments to JIC and JLC institutions
Source: Adapted and extended from McGinley (1990)	

The first major piece of legislation post-1922 was the Trade Union Act of 1941. That Act sought to regulate collective bargaining. It established a requirement that in order to engage in collective bargaining, organisations had to possess a negotiation licence or be deemed an excepted body. Any organisation granted such a licence, including an employer organisation, would then be an 'authorised trade union'. The immunities in the Trade Disputes Act 1906 were then confined to authorised trade unions. The Trade Union Act 1941 led to conflict within the trade union movement over limitations placed on UK unions. Following a constitutional challenge, Part III of the Act was struck down in 1947 (McCarthy 1977). This is examined further in the section on the Constitution (see pp. 36–9).

Controversy also dogged the proposed Trade Union Bill 1966, which sought to legislate for secret ballots prior to industrial action and to remove the 1906 Act immunities from those engaged in unofficial industrial action. Although initially supported by the Irish Congress of Trade Unions (ICTU), the Bill was strongly opposed by individual trade unions and union activists and was allowed to lapse in 1969. The jailing of strikers in the Electricity Supply Board (ESB) in 1968 backfired, since taxis had to be sent by the authorities late at night to Mountjoy Prison in order to facilitate the strikers' release (the strikers had refused to leave until this was done). For the government of the day, the embarrassment seemed to reinforce the limitations of the law and the incident was instrumental in the dropping of the 1966 Bill. These experiences emphasised the need for consensus as a requirement for successful legislation. The institutional provisions in the Industrial Relations Acts of 1946 and 1969 (including the establishment of the Labour Court) enjoyed such a consensus, as did the Trade Union Act 1971, which limited the formation of new unions, and the Trade Union Act 1975, which encouraged union mergers. However, amending trade disputes law was a highly charged issue.

The Operation of Voluntarism in Ireland

In the 1950s, trade dispute law was not subject to major controversy. This was a manifestation of the low strike levels in that decade. With the growth in strikes in the 1960s, it became common to find commentators decrying the imperfections of the Irish system, especially the Trade Disputes Act 1906. Among some of the readily identifiable defects of the 1906 Act from an employer perspective was the availability of protection for unofficial strikes, strikes by a minority of workers and strikes in breach of collective agreements. The most famous denunciation of the Act was made by Justice Parke in *Goulding Chemicals Ltd* v. *Bolger (1977)*:

> The Trade Disputes Act 1906 was a child of political expediency hastily conceived and prematurely delivered. It has now survived more than the allotted span of life with all its inbred imperfections still uncorrected. (Quoted in Commission of Inquiry on Industrial Relations 1981: 222)

Parker's views were seen by critics as evidence of continuing judicial bias against workers, and they have not gone unchallenged. Far from being a rushed response to a political situation, Kidner (1982) notes that the 1906 Act was the subject of great care and consideration. It has also been pointed out that the imperfections had largely been used to restrict the intended effect of the Act (Kerr and Whyte 1985; von Prondzynski and McCarthy 1984). The most serious of these restrictions related to the granting of injunctions. Injunctions are restraining orders preventing named individuals from engaging in certain actions. An injunction may be granted on an interim, interlocutory or permanent basis. An interim injunction is one granted pending a hearing on the application for an injunction. Employers could seek interim injunctions on an *ex-parte* basis, i.e. without the union being present. An interlocutory injunction is one granted pending a full hearing of the case. A permanent injunction is one granted following a full hearing of a case.

Prior to 1990 an interim or interlocutory injunction was available to an employer if they met the following two criteria:

- there was a fair case that there was a legal problem with the union action; and
- the balance of convenience was in favour of granting the injunction.

The requirement that there was a fair case that there was a legal problem is a very low threshold and, once established, the court would proceed to consider where the 'balance of convenience' lay. This was almost invariably decided in favour of an employer. An employer could easily demonstrate that they would incur financial loss that could not be recovered from the union, since they possessed immunity under the law of tort. This might suggest that employers had frequent resort to injunctions. However, this was not the case, since an injunction was not without its problems. Employers were reluctant to enforce injunctions if employees disregarded them, since this could lead to the jailing of strikers and the generation of public sympathy. This possibility arose because in order to enforce the injunction an employer would have to have employees cited for contempt of court.

THE DEBATE ON LEGAL REFORM

By the mid-1970s, calls for reform had intensified. In response, the Fianna Fáil government in 1978 established a Commission of Inquiry on Industrial Relations (Duffy 1993). The Commission, from which ICTU withdrew shortly after it was established, recommended the repeal of the legislation on trade disputes and its replacement by new consolidated legislation (Commission of Inquiry on Industrial Relations 1981). In essence, this legislation would place procedural requirements on trade unions and would make them again liable to be sued in tort if the procedures were not observed. On the other hand, the Commission favoured the retention of the immunities-based approach to the criminal law in the Conspiracy and Protection of Property Act 1875.

The Commission's report, while generally welcomed by employers, drew negative reaction from trade unionists and academics. For trade unions, the recommendations were totally unacceptable, since they would have reversed the gains of the 1906 Act. Academics pointed to both methodological and practical flaws in the report. Von Prondzynski and McCarthy (1982) highlighted the absence of any original research and the selective and misleading use of secondary research. Kelly and Roche (1983) noted that the recommendations were not congruent with the voluntarist tradition of Irish industrial relations. Subsequently, a study by Wallace and O'Shea (1987) covering the years 1978 to 1986 undermined a claim by the Commission that unofficial strikes – a major concern of the Commission – were associated with small unions. The study found that unofficial action was actually overwhelmingly associated with members of larger unions – the direct opposite of the Commission's assertion.

In 1986 the Department of Labour, with Ruairi Quinn as Minister, published proposals for a 'positive right to strike' – an apparent total rejection of the Commission's recommendations (Department of Labour 1986a). The unions soon became concerned at restrictions to be placed on the positive rights and the proposals were dropped primarily because of the unenthusiastic response of ICTU (Bonner 1989). In 1988, revised departmental proposals were presented, which were described as an attempt to achieve a balance between the competing interests of employers and trade unions. It quickly became clear that even if the proposals did not enjoy total consensus, there was general acceptance of them – notably by trade unions and ICTU.

A number of factors have been suggested for this acceptance (Wallace and O'Sullivan 2002). Unions had a major concern over the threat of a constitutional challenge to the 1906 Act. First, it was feared that the total immunity unions enjoyed under the Act would not survive a legal challenge based on Article 34 of the Constitution, which guarantees access to the courts. Second, the unions may have feared more severe legal restrictions based on Thatcherism in the UK. Third, ICTU may have been attracted to the intention to strengthen the position of union leadership at the expense of 'unruly activists'. In addition to this, because of the 1980s recession, union activists were in a weaker position to organise opposition than in the 1960s (at the time of the 1966 Bill).

THE INDUSTRIAL RELATIONS ACT 1990

The Industrial Relations Act 1990 is the most significant piece of collective industrial relations legislation in Ireland. Its stated purpose is 'to put in place an improved framework for the conduct of industrial relations and for the resolution of trade disputes [with] the overall aim ... to maintain a stable and orderly industrial relations climate' (Department of Labour 1991: 1). When the Bill was presented to the Dáil, there were some sharp criticisms led by Pat Rabbitte TD and Eamon Gilmore TD of the Workers' Party. They criticised the provisions on the grounds that the Section 9 requirements (see below) would make the position of shop stewards vulnerable and that they would lead to more, not less, intervention into industrial relations by the courts – in effect a dilution of voluntarism (Rabbitte and Gilmore 1990). Apart from these points, there was general support for the Bill and it was passed into law. The most significant amendment during the Dáil debate was one that provided protection for the all-out picketing provision of ICTU. An all-out picket is an ICTU-sanctioned picket that requires members of all unions in an employment to observe it during a strike. It was introduced by ICTU in 1970 to regulate picketing in companies with multi-union representation and it requires consultation with all unions prior to sanction being granted.

TRADE DISPUTES AND TRADE UNION PROVISIONS OF THE 1990 ACT

The following is a summary of the main trade disputes provisions.

1. Section 8 contains definitions of an employer, a trade dispute, a trade union, a worker, industrial action and a strike. Some key points from the definitions are as follows:
   - A worker does not include a member of the Defence Forces or of An Garda Síochána.
   - A trade dispute only covers disputes between employers and workers or former workers. This has the effect of withdrawing protection from worker versus worker (inter-union) disputes.
   - The purpose of a strike must be to compel an employer to accept or not accept certain terms or conditions affecting employment. This requirement excludes political strikes over such matters as taxation or a general strike (Meenan 1999) or a protest at the imprisonment of an individual (Kerr 1991).

2. Section 9 withdraws immunities from any form of industrial action in individual disputes that are in breach of agreed procedures contained either *in writing, in custom or in practice*. Should an employer not observe procedures or should there be no procedures in place, workers are not required to follow procedures.

3. Section 11 is designed to both clarify and restrict the provisions for picketing as follows:
   - Picketing is lawful at a place where an employee works or where an employer carries on business or, where this is not practical, at the approaches to the place of work.

- Workers may only picket *their* employer or, in the case of secondary action, picket another employer if that (secondary) employer is seeking to frustrate the industrial action by directly assisting the primary employer.
- Normal commercial activity does not meet the criterion for frustration of industrial action, nor does any sympathy action in support of workers by workers in other companies.
- All-out strikes and pickets and secondary action involving more than one union are required to be sanctioned by ICTU.

4. Section 12 provides exactly the same immunities against civil conspiracy and combination as did the 1906 Act.

5. Under Section 13, the previous total immunity that trade unions enjoyed from being sued under the law of tort is withdrawn and is now only available where they can show they are 'acting in contemplation or furtherance of a trade dispute'.

6. Section 14 requires that a secret ballot be conducted in the event of *any form of industrial action* and that specific rules on this be incorporated in union rule books. Immunities are withdrawn from any industrial action where a majority of workers vote against such action in a secret ballot. Should unions persistently disregard the balloting provisions, they may have their negotiation licence withdrawn.

7. Section 19 places limitations on the granting of *ex-parte* injunctions. An injunction will not be granted where all of the following conditions have been met:
   - a secret ballot has been held;
   - a majority has voted in favour of industrial action; and
   - seven days' notice of such action has been given to an employer.

Interlocutory injunctions (injunctions pending a full trial) are not available to an employer where, in addition to the previous requirements, the union establishes a fair case that it is acting in contemplation or furtherance of a trade dispute.

Continuity and Change

There is considerable continuity between the 1906 and 1990 Acts, most notably regarding the approach to the retention of the immunities and the absence of any right to strike. The provisions in Section 11 largely confirm previous case law on secondary and sympathy picketing, which do not enjoy protection under the 1990 Act. The section clarifies the law on picketing. For example, it allows for picketing on the premises of a shopping centre with multiple owners where employees are only in dispute with one company. Section 12 is unchanged from the 1906 Act. Kerr (1991) makes it clear that unofficial action does not necessarily lose immunity, as is sometimes suggested. Unofficial action that complies with the balloting provisions and where employees served the required seven days' notice (perhaps an unlikely situation) would continue to enjoy immunities.

Major changes include withdrawal of immunity from individual disputes where procedures have not been exhausted. This departure can be seen as representing a step on the road to a distinction between dispute of rights and dispute of interest. It is noteworthy that strikes over individual issues are nowadays a rarity, although this development predated the 1990 Act. The requirement that a union should be able to prove it was acting in contemplation or furtherance of a trade dispute places a new onus on trade unions if they are to enjoy the immunities. The requirement to incorporate balloting provisions in union rules represented a substantial change not just because of the requirement to ballot, but because of the specification of the exact rules unions should incorporate. Unions had previously resisted any intrusion into their internal affairs since the 1870s.

THE OPERATION OF THE INDUSTRIAL RELATIONS ACT 1990

The 1990 Act can be seen as a modest adaptation of trade disputes law in order to allow trade disputes to be brought back within the area of the legal system without compromising the principles of voluntarism. However, bringing the law back into the area of trade disputes opened up a host of potential issues. Within a short time, trade unions found themselves involved in a number of cases that clashed with the stated intention to remove the law from industrial relations and reinforce voluntarism (Kerr 1991; Wallace 1991). These cases indicated that judicial interpretation was going to be a key factor in the operation of the 1990 Act (Kerr 2010). The *G&T Crampton* and *Nolan Transport* cases are particularly important in establishing how the Act was going to be applied.

In *G&T Crampton* v. *BATU (1997)*, the Supreme Court found that the onus lay on the party resisting an application for an interlocutory injunction (the union) to prove a number of requirements had been met. The requirements were that:

- a secret ballot had been held;
- it had been properly conducted;
- the outcome was in favour of the action taken; and
- the required notice (a minimum of one week) had been given.

If these conditions were met, then the union needed 'to establish a fair case that it was acting in contemplation or furtherance of a trade dispute' for an employer's application for an injunction to be refused.

The Nolan Transport Cases, 1993–1998

The series of cases running from 1993 to 1998 between Nolan Transport and SIPTU have been the most important under the 1990 Act. The dispute revolved around the issue of union recognition and the claimed dismissal of two employees (members of SIPTU) for union activism. The key legal issues revolved around the conduct of the ballot for strike action and the existence of a trade dispute. In the High Court case in 1994, Justice Barron found that the ballot for strike action was fraudulent and did not constitute a valid trade dispute because the dispute was really an attempt by the union to gain recognition and this did not constitute a trade dispute. Given these findings,

Justice Barron concluded that the immunities were not available to either SIPTU or union members. The union was ordered to pay damages of £600,000 and costs. With accusations of judicial bias being made at union conferences, the Nolan Transport judgment drew parallels with Taff Vale. A survey found that 73 per cent of union officials thought that 'the 1990 Act was a mistake which should not have been accepted in its current form' (Wallace and Delany 1997: 114).

The High Court decision was appealed to the Supreme Court, and this led to the judgment being overturned in 1998. The Supreme Court found that the employees 'at the very least, had good grounds for thinking themselves dismissed' and that, as a result, a trade dispute did exist. In addition, the Supreme Court determined that a recognition dispute did qualify as a trade dispute and that union liability in tort did not follow from an improperly conducted ballot. The prescribed penalty was the loss of a union's negotiating licence but this applied only if there was persistent disregard of the balloting provisions.

Not surprisingly, the outcome of the Supreme Court appeal was greeted with a sigh of relief from trade unions (O'Keeffe 1998). While the decision has seen controversy over the Act largely disappear, this does not mean that the Act is without potential difficulties for trade unions. Despite the restrictions in Section 19, injunctions that impede industrial action continue to be granted. Kerr (2010) notes three leading cases that were successful at full trial but where the industrial action had been injuncted. There are also a considerable number of issues that still await clarification some twenty years after the Act was introduced, e.g. whether or not secret ballots comply with Section 14 of the Act (Kerr 2010). Given their importance, the balloting requirements in Section 14 are reproduced in Table 2.2. Even observing the requirements in Table 2.2 is not sufficient to ensure compliance. The key issue is not whether a secret ballot has been held or not, but whether or not a union can prove this to be the case. However, Kerr (2010) notes that issues arising under case law indicate that the standard of proof that is to be applied is unclear and that this leaves unions somewhat in limbo.

THE CONSTITUTION AND INDUSTRIAL RELATIONS

As noted earlier, nineteenth-century liberal ideas supported the right of individuals to combine to promote their own interests. Such a right is known as a 'right of association' and is incorporated in the 1937 Irish Constitution in the following Articles:

- Article 40.6.1 (iii) guarantees 'the right of citizens to form associations and unions. Laws, however, may be enacted for the regulation and control in the public interest of the foregoing right'.
- Article 40.6.2 specifies that the laws regulating this right 'shall contain no political, religious or class discrimination'.

Part III of the Trade Union Act 1941 provided for the establishment of a tribunal that could grant 'a determination that a specified union (or unions) alone should have the sole right to organise workers of a particular class'. In effect, this was an exclusive right to organise, which encouraged 'sole negotiating rights' (Forde 1991: 29). It was aimed

Table 2.2

Balloting Requirements Applying to Any Industrial Action

1. the union shall not organise, participate in, sanction or support a strike or other industrial action without a secret ballot, entitlement to vote on which shall be accorded equally to all members whom it is reasonable to believe will be called upon to engage in the strike or other industrial action;

2. the union shall take reasonable steps to ensure that every member entitled to vote in the ballot votes without interference from, or constraint imposed by, the union or any of its members, officials or employees and, so far as is reasonably possible, that such members shall be given a fair opportunity of voting;

3. the committee or management or other controlling authority of a trade union shall have full discretion in relation to organising, participating in, sanctioning or supporting a strike or other industrial action notwithstanding that the majority of those voting in the ballot, including an aggregate ballot, favour such strike or industrial action;

4. the committee or management or other controlling authority of a trade union shall have full discretion in relation to organising, participating in, sanctioning or supporting a strike or other industrial action against the wishes of a majority of those voting in a secret ballot, except where, in the case of ballots by more than one trade union, an aggregate majority of all votes cast favours such strike or other industrial action;

5. where the outcome of a secret ballot conducted by a trade union which is affiliated to the Irish Congress of Trade Unions or, in the case of ballots by more than one such trade union, an aggregate majority of all the votes cast is in favour of supporting a strike organised by another trade union, a decision to take such supportive action shall not be implemented unless the action has been sanctioned by the Irish Congress of Trade Unions; and

6. as soon as practicable after the conduct of a secret ballot the trade union shall take reasonable steps to make known to its members entitled to vote in the ballot (i) the number of ballot papers issued, (ii) the number of votes cast, (iii) the number of votes in favour of the proposal, (iv) the number of votes cast against the proposal and (v) the number of spoilt votes.

Source: Adapted from Industrial Relations Act 1990

at curbing the operation of British-based unions in Ireland, since they could not be granted the sole right to organise (O'Hara 1981). Part III was highly controversial and within a short time the provision was tested as a result of an inter-union dispute. In 1945 the ITGWU applied to the tribunal for the sole right to organise workers in the road passenger service of Córas Iompair Éireann (CIÉ). A British-based union, the National Union of Railwaymen (NUR), and a number of its members initiated a constitutional challenge against Sullivan (the chairman of the tribunal). Regarding it as merely a regulation of the right to form a union, the High Court found the provision to be constitutional. This judgment was overturned in the Supreme Court, which found 'the denial of a person's choice of which union he can join is not a control of the exercise of the right of freedom of association but a denial of it altogether' (Forde 1991: 18).

The right to join unions does not automatically create a right to be accepted into membership by a trade union, as indicated in the case of *Tierney* v. *Amalgamated Society of Woodworkers (ASW) (1995)*. In this case Tierney had sought to join the ASW in pursuit of a right to work. His application was refused because he had not served an apprenticeship and the union did not accept he was a genuine carpenter. Tierney failed in both the High Court and the Supreme Court on a number of grounds, including that the Constitution provided no support for the case as the union had acted fairly within their rules (Forde 1991).

The most significant interpretation of the right of association in the 1937 Constitution is that it has been found to imply an equal and opposite right of disassociation. The *Educational Company of Ireland* v. *Fitzpatrick (1961)* case involved thirty-six Irish Union of Distributive Workers and Clerks (IUDWC) workers who went on strike and picketed in pursuit of enforcing a closed shop. A closed shop involves a situation in which all employees in a particular class of employee are required to be union members. In this case an injunction was granted against the picket but not against the strike. It was suggested that there was a pre-existing higher-order right to strike that was not contradicted by anything in the Constitution. This claimed 'higher-order' right to strike has not subsequently been developed or legislated for. The picketing was found not to be protected by the immunities in the 1906 Act as these were subordinate to the right of disassociation of the non-union members. Of course, the strike collapsed without the protection for picketing being available.

The existence of a right of disassociation was confirmed in the case of *Meskell* v. *CIÉ (1973)*. John Meskell, a bus conductor with 15 years' service, was dismissed for failure to give an undertaking to 'at all times' remain a member of one of four named unions. He lost his appeal against dismissal in the High Court but was successful in the Supreme Court. The company argued that it was entitled in common law to dismiss. However, the entitlement to dismiss in common law was found to provide no justification for the dismissal because of the superior position of the employee's constitutional right of disassociation as established in the *Educational Company* case.

The above two cases do not limit the right of employers to require workers to join specified unions prior to them commencing employment (Kerr and Whyte 1985). Thus, while the post-entry closed shop is unconstitutional, the pre-entry (prior to employment) closed shop may well be constitutional. This is because, while it guarantees the right to work, the Constitution does not guarantee a right to employment and generally employers can employ whomever they wish – see *Becton Dickinson* v. *Lee (1973)*.

The right of association has been found not to place any requirement on an employer to recognise or negotiate with any particular trade union. The leading case in this regard is that of *Abbott and Whelan* v. *the Southern Health Board and ITGWU (1982)*. About half of a particular category of workers in the Southern Health Board (SHB) left the ITGWU and joined the Amalgamated Transport and General Workers' Union (ATGWU). The SHB refused to recognise their new union and continued to negotiate with the ITGWU. Two employees, Abbott and Whelan, initiated a High Court case requiring the SHB to recognise and negotiate with the ATGWU and to prevent the ITGWU from purporting to negotiate with the SHB on their behalf. They lost on both grounds. The High Court found that as the SHB was not required to recognise any union, the SHB did not have to recognise the ATGWU. Neither was there any constitutional right to have negotiations conducted by a union of one's choice. The SHB could not be prevented from negotiating with the ITGWU. The Abbott and

Whelan case only concerned an application for an injunction, but this interpretation was affirmed in the case of the *Association of General Practitioners v. Minister for Health* (1995), which went to full trial. Justice O'Hanlon's judgment in that case clearly laid out the current law on union recognition and negotiation rights in Ireland:

> I do not consider that there is any obligation imposed by ordinary law or by the constitution on an employer to consult with or negotiate with any organisation representing his employees or some of them, when the conditions of employment are to be settled or reviewed. The employer is left with freedom of choice as to whether he will negotiate with any organisation or consult with them on such matters, and is also free to give a right of audience to one representative body, and refuse it to another if he chooses to do so. (Daly and Docherty 2011: 328)

These principles have been subsequently confirmed in the complex series of cases taken by the Irish Locomotive Drivers' Association (Higgins 2000b). Taken together, the judgments make it clear that although the Constitution provides for a right to form unions, this right does not have as a corollary the rights to recognition, negotiation or representation. In effect, under the 1937 Constitution these are voluntary options for an employer.

The Constitution in Context

A number of the above decisions have given rise to controversy. On the one hand, the *NUR* v. *Sullivan* decision has been criticised for restricting government's capacity to regulate trade unions. It is, of course, an open question as to the extent to which such government regulation is desirable in a free society. On the other hand, the decisions establishing an implied right of disassociation have been criticised for converting a collective right into an individual one. Kerr and Whyte (1985: 12) write that 'the right to *form* unions is of its very nature a collective right, so it is difficult to see how its corollary can be a right not to join unions, which is an individual right'.

The controversy over the Educational Company case largely petered out in the twenty-five years following the decision. Although procedure agreements that require employees to be union members still exist, newer agreements tend to deal with the issue of union recognition in a different fashion. These make it a matter for the union involved to recruit employees if the employees wish to join and they require the union to take into membership all such eligible employees. The growth in union density to over 60 per cent by the early 1980s demonstrated the capacity of trade unions to grow their membership irrespective of the Supreme Court's individualist interpretation of the right of association. This demonstrates that the restrictive constitutional interpretations had little practical effect on the fortunes of unions. It also hints that favourable constitutional provisions may only have a limited impact if other factors work against unionisation.

THE INDUSTRIAL RELATIONS ACTS 2001–2004

With the reversal of the historical growth in union density in the 1990s, recognition and negotiation rights appeared back on the union movements' agenda. For unions, there was a manifest contradiction between their involvement in social partnership at national level and the growing inability to gain recognition from employers at company level. However, trade unions had some reservations about reversing the voluntary approach and lobbying for a legal right to union recognition, as occurred in the UK in 1999. There was a fear that a law prescribing union recognition could lead to union derecognition, as the right of association had led to a right of disassociation. A high-level group set up under Partnership 2000 considered the issue and this led to the Industrial Relations (Amendment) Act 2001.

The 2001 Act represented an attempt by government to resolve trade union complaints about anti-union employers without interfering in the principle of voluntary union recognition. The Act allowed unions to refer cases to the Labour Court over disputes where an employer did not engage in negotiations with groups of employees or unions and dispute resolution procedures had failed to resolve the dispute. While unions would not be entitled to mandatory recognition or negotiation rights, the Act had potentially significant consequences for employers, since the Labour Court had the power to set legally binding wages and conditions of employment in an organisation. The Industrial Relations (Miscellaneous Provisions) Act 2004 introduced time limits for Labour Court determinations as well as anti-victimisation provisions. The legislation was initially very attractive for unions but many of the cases they took were largely used in small to medium enterprises.

However, in 2004 IMPACT (and its branch, the Airline Pilots Association (IALPA)) requested a Labour Court investigation under the Acts on behalf of a number of pilots in Ryanair, which did not negotiate with unions. The union sought an investigation about a number of issues relating to the conditions attached to an offer by Ryanair to retrain pilots on a new aircraft. One particular issue was that the pilots would have to repay training costs if the company was forced to recognise the union (O'Sullivan and Gunnigle 2009). The Labour Court first had to consider whether it could investigate these issues because Ryanair argued that the conditions required for hearing a case under the Acts were not met. The conditions were that there had to be trade dispute, that the company did not engage in collective bargaining and that dispute resolution procedures had failed to resolve the issues. Ryanair argued that the Labour Court could not hear the case, one of the reasons being that collective bargaining did take place through the company's Employee Representative Committees (ERCs). The Labour Court found that the conditions had been met. Ryanair challenged the Labour Court's decision in the High Court and it subsequently upheld the Labour Court's decision. However, Ryanair appealed this in the Supreme Court and it overturned the High Court's decision in 2007. It found that the Labour Court erred in:

- finding that a trade dispute within the terms of the 2001 Act existed; and
- dismissing Ryanair's claim that collective bargaining existed without hearing direct oral evidence from at least one of Ryanair's pilots.

The Supreme Court also found that internal machinery of ERCs, which could have conducted collective bargaining, had not been exhausted. The Court concluded that these were excepted bodies within the meaning of the Trade Union Act 1941 and these could have conducted collective bargaining, but the Labour Court had not investigated properly whether this was the case or not. Notably, the Court said that 'Ryanair is perfectly entitled not to deal with trade unions nor can a law be passed compelling it to do so'. While it is accepted that employers have never been compelled to recognise unions, there is debate as to whether or not a statutory union recognition law *could* be introduced. D'Art and Turner expressed astonishment at what they term the pre-emptive assertion by the Supreme Court that a law could not be passed to compel union recognition. They note this would place Ireland in 'a relatively unique position among the western democracies', as laws providing for union recognition are found in a range of countries, including the UK, Scandinavia, Canada and the US (D'Art and Turner 2007a: 21). The outcome of the case was that it undermined the usefulness of the 2001–2004 Acts from a trade union's perspective and it has led to significant debate over the meaning of collective bargaining.

Contemporary International Legal Developments

The ILO Dimension

Ireland has international obligations under a number of international treaties and conventions. These can come in the form of soft law, such as obligations arising from our membership of the United Nations International Labour Organisation (ILO), the EU and the Council of Europe. In recent years our membership of all three bodies has come to have potential implications for Irish collective industrial relations law.

Shortly after the Supreme Court judgment in the Ryanair case, D'Art and Turner (2007a: 19) claimed that an 'unintended consequence' of the Ryanair decision 'is to leave the Irish state in breach of ILO Convention 98'. This convention prohibits 'company' or 'house' unions that are not independent of the employer. D'Art and Turner argued that the ERCs in Ryanair are such bodies. They also took issue with the Court's use of a dictionary definition of collective bargaining and its failure to refer to the relevant definition in ILO Recommendation 91. D'Art and Turner noted that it was open to the unions to initiate a complaint against Ireland to the ILO and this was done by ICTU in 2010. In its response, the state relied strongly on arguments based on voluntarism and noted that Articles 1–4 of ILO Convention 98 'do not require the imposition of any obligation on employers to recognise trade unions or to negotiate with trade unions' (ILO 2012: 213). The state went on to claim that ICTU was seeking 'compulsory collective bargaining' and that this was contrary to ILO provisions (ILO 2012: 230). It was also pointed out that IMPACT had failed to prove the three conditions required under the 2001 Act actually existed in Ryanair and that this could not form a basis for a complaint against the state for breach of Convention 98.

The ILO reported on the complaint in 2012. It reaffirmed the voluntary nature of the ILO provisions on union recognition and noted the state's argument that it was the failure of IMPACT to prove the issues in dispute that led to the case being lost, not any defect in Irish law. However, the ILO was highly critical of the possibility that inducements might have been offered to Ryanair pilots not to unionise. It considered:

> that the alleged offer of conditional benefits by the company provided that it would not be required to enter into a collective bargaining relationship with the union, if true, would be tantamount to employer interference in the right of workers to form and join the organisation of their own choosing. (ILO 2012: 228)

The report also drew attention to the fact that ILO Recommendation 91 provides that representatives of unorganised workers are only to be granted a 'role in collective bargaining solely when no workers' organisation exists', i.e. in the absence of a trade union (ILO 2012: 230). In conclusion, the report requested the Irish government to carry out an independent inquiry into the alleged acts of employer interference in Ryanair. It also asked that a review of the existing framework and consideration of appropriate measures (including legislative ones) be conducted 'to ensure respect for the freedom of association and collective bargaining principles' (ILO 2012: 231).

International Developments

A number of recent cases have dealt with industrial action and the regulation of employment in organisations operating on a transnational basis within the EU. The first was *International Transport Workers' Federation* v. *Viking Line ABP (2008)*. This case concerned a Finnish shipping company that was reflagged to Estonia and employed Estonians at lower wages. The Finnish Seamen's Union (FSU) threatened industrial action and sought the International Transport Workers' Federation (ITF) support by requiring affiliate unions not to negotiate with Viking. The case was referred to the Court of Justice of the European Union (CJEU), which recognised that the right to strike was a fundamental right but considered it was to be strictly circumscribed. The Court identified the following four conditions that strike action would have to meet. It must:

- be justified and have a legitimate aim;
- be for overriding reasons of public interest;
- be suitable for securing the attainment of the objective pursued; and
- not go beyond what is necessary in order to attain it.

In effect, the decision of the Court established a strong proportionality test that any strike involving the provision of cross-national services would have to meet. The Court determined that these conditions had not been met by the union in this case.

Judgment in a second important case was issued a week after the Viking case: *Laval Un Partneri Ltd* v. *Svenska Byggnadsarbetareförbundet*. This case involved 'posted workers' (workers sent to another country) sent from Latvia to Sweden. The Swedish unions sought to conclude a collective agreement on wages and working conditions covering them. To avoid this, Laval signed a collective agreement in Latvia for lower wages and conditions. In return, Swedish electrical unions blockaded the work site and engaged in 'solidarity or secondary action', which is legal in Sweden. The CJEU found that the strike, although legal under Swedish law, was illegal under EU law and was secondary to the right of businesses to supply cross-border services.

Hug and Tudor (2012: 16) claim that the CJEU 'identified the right to strike as a fundamental right' and then 'appeared to strangle that right at birth'. Responding to these judgments, Barnard (2012: 264) pointed out that the CJEU adopted an asymmetrical approach in which once it considered that an 'economic right has been infringed by the exercise of the social right ... the onus is on the trade union to justify this breach and show that it is proportionate'. She argued that this 'asymmetrical approach' meant that 'economic rights were likely to prevail' and warned of the dangers this has for a social Europe (Barnard 2012: 124). Finally, she notes that the proportionality test creates many practical difficulties for trade unions that place their funds at risk in the event of strike action, since they cannot know whether they have met a proportionality test in advance of a court case.

In contrast to the Viking and Laval cases, two leading cases under the European Convention on Human Rights (ECHR) have suggested that priority must be given to the right to bargain and to engage in strike action. Like the Irish Constitution, the ECHR incorporates a right to freedom of association. This is contained in Article 11, which states that 'everyone has the right to freedom of peaceful assembly and association, including the right to form and join trade unions for the protection of his interests'. Because the member states have an obligation to accede to the ECHR as a result of the Lisbon Treaty, its provisions are especially important for all member states, including Ireland.

Article 11 had long been interpreted as not implying a right to union recognition or negotiation rights – still less a right to strike (Ewing 2012). Only a very limited individual right to representation had been recognised in the *National Belgian Police Union* v. *Belgium (1975)*. The unanimous reversal of this approach by the seventeen-member European Court of Human Rights (ECtHR) in the case of *Demir and Baykara* v. *Turkey (2008)* was a major surprise. In that case, the Court found that Article 11 of the ECHR had to be seen as involving a right to bargain collectively. It considered that restrictions on this right could only apply in so far as they met the requirements of ILO conventions. In effect, soft law was influencing hard law. In 2009, this decision was further expanded in *Enerji Yapi-Yol Sen* v. *Turkey*, in which it was found that a right to strike was required as part of a trade union's right to defend their members' interests.

Commentary on Recent Developments

The significance of the European cases and the ILO report on Ryanair has yet to be worked out. At a practical level, the Ryanair decision means that the 2001–2004 Acts have lost much of their force. Unions are generally not prepared to expose their members to giving direct legal evidence against their employers. However, union recognition and negotiation rights and protection for strike action continue to be live issues because of the ILO dimension. Minister for Enterprise, Jobs and Innovation, Richard Bruton

TD, has said that there will not be an independent inquiry into Ryanair, since the case had already been through the courts. Minister Bruton also argued that the government could not conduct an inquiry under industrial relations legislation because a trade dispute would have to exist and the Supreme Court had decided that it had not been established that it was a trade dispute in Ryanair (Sheehan 2012e). Minister Bruton said the government will act on the other ILO recommendations and will reform the Industrial Relations (Amendment) Act 2001 but this will not mean the introduction of compulsory union recognition (Sheehan 2012e). The exact nature of this reform is uncertain but it seems to be in the direction of restoring, at least in part, the original intention of the 2001–2004 Acts (Sheehan 2012a).

Because the Viking and Laval cases relate only to the provision of transnational services, they have had limited impact on domestic strike laws to date. Irish employers and trade unions have been divided along predictable lines on the cases. The Director of Industrial Relations for IBEC, Brendan McGinty, has favoured the EU developments and even (surprisingly) suggested that a positive right to strike with restrictions would be preferable to the immunities approach in the 1990 Act (McGinty 2010). On the other hand, both the European Trade Union Confederation (ETUC) and ICTU have (unsurprisingly) called for EU law to be brought into line with the requirements of the ECHR.

Ewing (2012) considers that the ECtHR decisions will provide a basis for rolling back the restrictive interpretations of the rights to strike under EU and UK law. Others are sceptical of human rights legislation when applied to the industrial relations arena. For example, Hepple has 'doubts about the willingness of courts in the common law countries to embrace ILO jurisprudence'. He also argues that judicial involvement in deciding on abstract principles 'hardly seems a suitable way to settle labour disputes in the modern globalised economy' (Hepple 2010: 15). Recent EU proposals to deal with the decisions of the CJEU and the ECtHR do not give primacy to either economic freedoms or fundamental social rights. Ewing is highly critical of this approach, claiming it to be 'either naïve or disingenuous'. He points out that it is fundamental in 'disputes between economic freedoms and social rights that both cannot prevail simultaneously' (Ewing 2012: 14).

In an Irish context, given the significance of direct foreign investment and the influence of bodies such as the American Chamber of Commerce, there must be some scepticism about any major changes over and above those originally intended in the 2001–2004 Acts. In this regard, Sheehan (2012c: 5) suggests that the ILO report may provide a way for the government 'to steer a diplomatic course between seemingly polarised positions, and perhaps lead to a final resolution of what has, for decades, been something of a conundrum for industrial relations watchers and employment law experts'. This echoes an earlier suggestion by Docherty (2009: 401) that Irish legislation 'pre its emasculation in the Ryanair case' might be worthy of exploration as 'an alternative model' to resolve the restrictions on collective bargaining placed by the CJEU decisions. This would involve reinstating the ILO definition of collective bargaining and would have the benefit of allowing for unions to take cases to protect wage norms and not just minimum rates. However, he sees little joy for the unions in terms of union growth because taking cases is time consuming and costly, and even pre-Ryanair the legislation did not lead to any significant growth in union recognition. This in and of itself is not likely to make legislation based on the 2001–2004 Acts attractive to EU countries with strong union traditions, such as those in Scandinavia.

Concluding Comments

Over 200 years after the Combination Acts, tensions continue to characterise the role of the law in industrial relations. Irish law is based on a system of immunities that has been in existence for over 145 years in the criminal area and over 100 years in the civil area. While the revisions in the 1990 Act have clarified some areas of law, others are still unclear. The experience with the 2001–2004 Acts has raised questions over Ireland's compliance with ILO requirements. There is also a conflict between the recent decisions of the EU and the requirements of the ECHR that remains to be resolved. These international developments demonstrate that tensions over the role of the law in industrial relations are not confined to common law systems and are not just of historical interest, but are evidence of continuing underlying problems that apply to legal systems and industrial relations, whether these be characterised by systems of immunities or rights.

CHAPTER 3

Trade Unions

INTRODUCTION

The study of work, management, law, politics and economics is not complete without an examination of trade unions, which are the most common form of employee representation across the world. In much the same way that students' unions were created by students for students, trade unions were created by employees to give a collective voice to employee needs. Employees believed that they would have more bargaining power to improve their conditions by acting together than by acting individually. When trade unions emerged they were strongly resisted by employers but, particularly after World War II, employers grew to accept and negotiate with them and union membership grew strongly. Some employers viewed negotiating with a trade union as more advantageous than negotiating with employees individually and, particularly in western European countries, trade unions were seen as a legitimate and essential part of a democratic society.

Trade unions have had important effects on individuals and societies. Research shows that unions can increase the life satisfaction of citizens and stimulate people's participation in politics and elections (D'Art and Turner 2007b; Flavin *et al.* 2010). However, since the 1980s, trade unions across the world have been finding it more difficult to retain members. It could be argued that employees do not want trade unions in a modern economy. Yet surveys across Europe indicate that the vast majority of people, including employers and managers, consider that workers need trade unions in order to protect their pay and working conditions. In this chapter, we examine the factors that influence union joining and these help to explain why the percentage of employees who join unions is dropping. We examine how unions are responding to this challenge and we consider whether other organisations can be viable alternatives to unions. First, we will explain what trade unions do, examine how and why they emerged and discuss trade union organisation in Ireland.

WHAT ARE TRADE UNIONS?

Trade unions have traditionally been seen as the most effective means of countering employer power and achieving satisfactory pay and working conditions for employees. The basic strength of a union lies in its ability to organise and unite employees. Sidney and Beatrice Webb (1920: 1) wrote the first comprehensive history of trade unions and defined them as 'a continuous association of wage earners with the objective of improving or maintaining conditions of employment'. Unions generally try to achieve this objective through collective bargaining, i.e. negotiation with a single or multiple employers on the pay and conditions to apply to a group of employees. While the Webbs' definition aptly describes the workplace collective bargaining role of trade unions, it fails to explicitly address the broader societal role of trade unions in advancing employee interests in the political arena. In essence, trade unions are organisations that aim to unite workers with common interests while seeking to define those interests, express them, safeguard and advance them through their interactions (particularly collective bargaining) with individual employers, employer associations, government, government agencies and other parties.

In the workplace, unions engage in a range of activities. They:

- give information and advice to employees on working rights and employment law;
- represent employees when they have grievances at work, e.g. pay, working hours, work duties, bullying, etc;
- sanction industrial action by employees in a dispute with their employer;
- represent employees when management initiate disciplinary procedures/actions against them;
- represent employees in cases/disputes in state dispute resolution body hearings, e.g. the Labour Court;
- contribute to the development of management policies and procedures, e.g. on equality;
- challenge management decisions that they believe are not in employee interests;
- engage in collective bargaining by negotiating with employers on employees' pay, conditions, the introduction of change in the workplace, redundancies, etc;
- offer services to members, e.g. discounted travel and car insurance;
- offer education and training to members on issues such as employment law and the representation of members; and
- organise campaigns to recruit new members into the union.

At a national level, unions:

- lobby and make submissions to the government and its agencies on a range of issues, e.g. the introduction of employment law, the government's budget, the economy and social welfare;
- present trade union views in the media; and
- engage in collective bargaining with multiple employers and governments in order to set pay and conditions for employees across an industry or nationally (the extent to which this happens varies across countries).

THE ORIGINS AND GROWTH OF TRADE UNIONS UP TO THE 1970S

The early 'combinations' of workers were almost exclusively composed of skilled craftsmen or 'journeymen', as they were known. They were purely local bodies and their existence was often tenuous. The historical development of trade unions is inextricably linked to the development of industrial relations. The current nature of the trade union movement in Ireland has its origins in the dramatic changes brought about by the Industrial Revolution, beginning in Britain in the eighteenth century and later spreading

Table 3.1

Case Study

What Unions Do – the Student Nurses' Dispute

In December 2010, the Department of Health announced plans to phase out payments to student nurses on rostered clinical placements. Fourth year student nurses, during the thirty-six-week period when they are rostered for full duties, received a payment of 80 per cent of the minimum of the staff nurse scale. Under the proposed changes, this would be reduced to 76 per cent of the minimum point on the new lower scale in 2011. In 2012 the rate would be reduced to 60 per cent; in 2013 to 50 per cent; in 2014 to 40 per cent; and the payment would be abolished in 2015. According to the Department, the plans would result in anticipated savings of €32.5 million.

The Irish Nurses and Midwives Organisation (INMO) general secretary Liam Doran said the cuts were 'cruel and unnecessary' and called it the introduction of 'slave labour' in the health service. Nursing unions – INMO, supported by SIPTU, and the Psychiatric Nurses Association (PNA) – launched a campaign with a lunchtime protest on 9 February 2011 involving about 6,000 nurses and midwives. A protest march and rally was held in Dublin on 16 February. The nursing unions also planned a ballot for industrial action for existing fourth year students who were on placement, up to and including strike action. In addition, the INMO took a case to the Labour Court, claiming that the Department of Health/HSE breached their obligations under the EU Information and Consultation Directive in the manner in which they introduced the pay reduction for student nurses.

In October 2011, the Minister for Health announced that the pay rates for student nurses and midwives would be reduced in stages over the coming years, but that the cuts would not be as deep as those set out by the former minister. Pay rates for student nurses in their fourth year on placement would be set at 76 per cent of the staff nurse salary in 2011. In 2012, the pay rate was set at 60 per cent and from 2013 onwards the pay rate is reduced again to 50 per cent of the first point of the relevant staff nurse/midwife salary scale. The original proposal to eliminate from 2015 the payment for student nurses for their work placement period has been dropped. The INMO said that in view of the minister's decision, a planned national protest against the cuts (which was scheduled for 9 November 2011) would be postponed. It said that this would allow time for nationwide consultation and balloting on the revised arrangements. The INMO balloted its student nurse members on the issue and they voted to accept the amended government proposals.

Discussion Points

1 Why do you think the unions engaged in a protest and rally first, rather than go on strike?
2 Would you consider the unions' campaign to be a successful one or not?
3 If you were one of the students involved, how would you have voted in the ballot?

Source: Farrelly (2011a); Wall (2011b)

to Europe and North America. There was a gradual change from a largely peasant society based on agriculture and craft production to an industry-based society with new social divisions where greater numbers of people worked in the 'factory system' and relied on wages for their existence. In this new order, people now worked together in much larger numbers and on much more tightly defined tasks. This scenario led to the emergence of modern management as a result of the need to plan, control, direct and organise the use of equipment, capital, materials and people in the factory system. By and large, early factory owners adopted authoritarian approaches to workers. Working conditions were poor, working hours were long and 'sweated labour' was common. Workers themselves could do little about this situation, since they had little or no economic or political power. It was only the skilled workers who were successful in establishing any significant permanent unionisation in Ireland up to the early twentieth century. Until 1850 even the trade unions of skilled workers were modest and local in terms of their organisation. A new type of trade union was prompted by the foundation of the Amalgamated Society of Engineers (ASE) in the UK in the period 1850 to 1851.

In Ireland in the early 1900s the growth in influence and power of the 'new unionism', which primarily sought to organise unskilled workers, was most obviously manifested in the leadership skills of Jim Larkin who founded the Irish Transport and General Workers' Union (ITGWU) in 1909. Many employers refused to engage with this trade union, and since the workers were unskilled, they had little power as individuals and they could easily be replaced. Therefore, unions such as the ITGWU frequently engaged in industrial action in the form of strikes in order to force employers to recognise and negotiate with them and to improve the pay and conditions of members. The festering conflict between employer and worker interests came to a head in the Dublin Lockout of 1913 (Yeates 2000). The fallout from this bitter dispute initially dealt a severe blow to the ITGWU: their membership declined from 45,000 in 1913 (prior to the lockout) to 5,000 afterwards. However, by 1919 membership had recovered to 100,000 (Boyd 1972; McNamara *et al.* 1988). An important effect of this turbulent period was that it served to accelerate the organisation of employees into trade unions and employers into employer associations, thus placing an ever-increasing emphasis on industrial relations. After the difficulties and confrontation of 1913, labour relations slowly moved towards a more constructive approach based on negotiations and bargained agreement. The union movement had arrived and employers had to take steps to accommodate it. This was done through multi-employer bargaining via employer associations and through the employment of labour relations officers to deal with personnel and industrial relations matters at organisation level. The period 1914 to 1920 has been described as the 'first phase of rapid mass union membership growth in Ireland', when union membership rose from 110,000 in 1914 to 250,000 in 1920 (Roche 1997: 54; Roche and Larragy 1986).

The decade of the 1920s saw a reversal in unions' fortunes. Membership fell in the face of economic recession and external competition, as the government pursued an open economy policy. However, union membership rose steadily from the early 1930s. Between 1930 and 1940, trade union membership increased from 99,500 to 151,600; the percentage of employees who were union members rose from 20 to 26 per cent (Roche 1997). This trend reflected the acceleration in the level of industrialisation and economic activity. This was aided by the closed economy policy and promotion of infant industries, pursued by the Fianna Fáil government from 1932 onwards.

The rate of growth in union membership slowed during World War II, a development that Roche (1997) attributes to a cyclical downturn in economic activity

Table 3.2
Dublin Lockout 1913

Jim Larkin moved to Belfast as a union organiser in 1907. He subsequently extended his organising activities to Dublin and other Irish cities and he established the ITGWU in 1909. James Connolly subsequently became active in the labour movement and joined the ITGWU, becoming an organiser in Belfast. In August 1913, Larkin's union organised to have 200 union members in the Dublin Tramway Company abandon their tramways on O'Connell Street after the chairman, William Martin Murphy, refused to allow workers to join the unions. (Murphy also had business interests in Clerys Department Store and the Irish Independent and Evening Herald newspapers.) However, Murphy had replacement workers operating the tramways within one hour. Murphy then persuaded other employers to lock most of Dublin's unionised workers out of their jobs until they signed a document renouncing the ITGWU. The lockout lasted six months and saw violent riots, thousands of people evicted from their homes, an unknown number killed, thousands living in poverty and severe increases in infant mortality. By December 1913 and January 1914, workers eventually succumbed, renounced the ITGWU and returned to work.

Source: Doherty and O'Riordan; Yeates (2003)

(and employment) as a result of the war, combined with the effects of wage tribunals that controlled the level of wage rises and thus restricted union influence on wage movements over the period. The period of fastest growth in union membership was during the immediate post-war years from 1945 until the early 1950s. Aggregate union membership increased from 172,000 in 1945 to 306,000 in 1955, representing a growth in membership of 80 per cent and an increase in employment density of 64 per cent (from 28 per cent in 1945 to 46 per cent in 1955). One reason for this growth was the greater cohesion of the union movement in negotiating increases in pay and improvements in employment conditions through the 'wage round' system (see Chapter 13). The establishment of the Labour Court in 1946 symbolised the advent of a more tolerant or supportive approach to trade unions on the part of the Irish state. A similar change in state strategy was responsible for the granting of recognition to public service unions and the establishment of the civil service conciliation and arbitration schemes, the first of which was introduced in 1953 (see Chapter 5).

Table 3.3
Measures of Union Membership: Density

* **Workforce density:** The percentage of the total civilian workforce, i.e. including those employed and those seeking employment, who are trade union members.

* **Employment density:** The percentage of civilian employees who are trade union members.

For the remainder of this chapter, 'union density' refers to employment density.

The 1950s witnessed a continued but much less rapid increase in trade union density, although the economic recession of the 1950s slowed union growth. The economic climate of the 1960s was quite different and was marked by significant economic expansion and employment growth. The decade saw continued steady growth in union membership and density, along with other developments including the growth in the number and importance of shop stewards and the growth in white-collar trade unionisation. The early 1970s saw a slowing of the pace of unionisation, with only modest growth in levels of union membership. Roche (1997) attributes this to a saturation effect, where there was almost full unionisation in those sectors of the economy where unionisation was easiest to achieve (e.g. in manufacturing industries, rather than in small firms). After 1976 there was a further increase in unionisation due to the expansion of the public sector by the Fianna Fáil government elected in 1977. (Developments in unionisation after 1980 are discussed later in the chapter.)

How to Establish a Trade Union

Trade unions are defined under the 1941 Trade Union Act as bodies carrying on negotiations for fixing wages or other conditions of employment. This legal definition of trade unions is very broad and embraces employer organisations. Apart from certain 'excepted bodies' (e.g. the Irish Hospital Consultants Association and the Irish Dental Association), only 'authorised' trade unions holding a negotiating licence are permitted to engage in collective bargaining on pay and working conditions. Trade unions must first register with the Registrar of Friendly Societies and then apply for a negotiation licence from the Department of Jobs, Enterprise and Innovation. To get a licence, a union must meet criteria in three areas:

- **Notification:** Trade unions must notify the Minister for Jobs, Enterprise and Innovation and the Irish Congress of Trade Unions (ICTU) at least eighteen months before applying for a licence.
- **Membership:** Trade unions must have a minimum of 1,000 members in order to gain a licence.
- **Finance:** Trade unions must have deposits ranging from €25,395 for up to 2,000 members to €55,869 for more than 20,000 members. They must also have €1,016 for each additional 1,000 members (or part of 1,000 members) in excess of 20,000 members to a maximum of €76,184.

Types of Trade Unions

Not all employees have the same interests and it is for this reason that multiple trade unions have been established to cater for differing needs. For example, the union representing nurses is likely to have different concerns from those of clerical staff or doctors in a hospital. Trade unions in Ireland have traditionally been grouped into three broad categories: craft unions, general unions and white-collar unions. It should be noted that it is extremely difficult to categorise unions as 'pure' craft, general or white collar, so the categorisation should be interpreted as broadly indicative of union types.

Craft unions represent the first form of union organisation. They have their origins in the early unions that emerged in Britain at the start of the nineteenth century. Craft unions catered for workers who possessed a particular skill in a trade where entry was

Table 3.4
Largest Trade Unions in the Republic of Ireland, 2010

Trade Union	Membership (% of ICTU membership)	
Craft		
Technical, Electrical and Engineering Union (TEEU)	39,000	(6.7%)
Union of Construction and Allied Trades and Technicians (UCATT)	8,750	(1.5%)
Building and Allied Trades Unions (BATU)	4,000	(0.7%)
General		
Services, Industrial, Professional and Technical Union (SIPTU)	199,881	(34.4%)
Mandate (The Union of Retail, Bar and Administrative Workers)	40,286	(6.9%)
Unite	31,594	(5.4%)
White Collar		
Irish Municipal Public and Civil Trade Union (IMPACT)	63,566	(10.9%)
Irish Nurses and Midwives Organisation (INMO)	40,100	(6.9%)
Irish National Teachers' Organisation (INTO)	31,363	(5.4%)
Communications Workers' Union (CWU)	19,550	(3.4%)
Association of Secondary Teachers Ireland (ASTI)	18,025	(3.1%)
Irish Bank Officials' Association (IBOA)	16,002	(2.8%)
Teachers' Union of Ireland (TUI)	15,800	(2.7%)
Civil and Public Services Union (CPSU)	13,775	(2.4%)
Public Services Executive Union (PSEU)	12,000	(2.1%)

Source: Data provided by ICTU

restricted to workers who had completed a prescribed apprenticeship programme or equivalent. Craft unions no longer control entry to the trade and their relative influence has decreased over time in accordance with increased mechanisation and consequent de-skilling. However, craft unions remain an important part of Ireland's industrial relations system (see Table 3.4).

General unions adopt an open approach, taking into membership all categories of workers regardless of skill or industry. The origins of general trade unions lie in the organisation of semi-skilled and unskilled workers employed in the large factories in the late nineteenth and early twentieth centuries in Britain and Ireland. They initially organised general labourers and dock-workers and were noted for both their aggressive bargaining style in attempting to improve pay and working conditions of their members and for their greater political consciousness in attempting to advance working-class interests. Their development in Ireland is especially associated with the arrival of Jim Larkin in 1907. He was gneral secretary of the ITGWU and later became general secretary of the Workers' Union of Ireland, which was a breakaway union from the ITGWU, formed in 1924. The largest union in the country is the Services, Industrial, Professional and Technical Union (SIPTU), which was formed in 1990 following the merger of the ITGWU and the Federated Workers' Union of Ireland (FWUI). The FWUI was a descendent of the Workers' Union of Ireland. SIPTU has many other organisations affiliated to it or in receipt of support from it, e.g. the Professional Footballers' Association of Ireland (PFAI) and the National Union of Journalists (NUJ).

White-collar unions normally cater for professional, supervisory, technical, clerical and managerial grades. Such workers have long-established unions: the Irish National Teachers' Union (INFO) formed in 1868, the Teachers' Union of Ireland (TUI) formed in 1899 and the Irish Banks Officials' Association (IBOA) formed in 1918 (Logan 1999). There was significant growth in white-collar union membership in the period from the late 1960s until the early 1980s. The dramatic growth in the services sector, particularly in the public sector, was a significant factor facilitating the growth of white-collar unionisation. While some white-collar workers were reluctant to join trade unions, Kelly (1975) notes that poor job design and general quality of working life were important factors encouraging white-collar unionisation. Another significant aspect in white-collar unionisation was the large advances in pay and conditions secured by blue-collar unions representing manufacturing and craft workers, which encouraged hitherto more conservative white-collar workers to unionise. Today, most of the largest white-collar unions are in the public sector.

How Trade Unions Are Governed

At workplace level, the shop steward or employee representative is the key union representative. Their role is to represent employee interests on workplace issues, liaise with union officials and keep members *au fait* with union affairs. In practice, shop stewards may become involved in much workplace bargaining involving local grievances or disputes. On more serious issues, their role is to support the trade union official and give feedback to the membership. Shop stewards are elected or appointed by fellow trade union members at elections, which normally take place once a year. Shop stewards are also employees of the organisation and, as such, must perform their normal job. The Code of Practice on Duties and Responsibilities of Employee Representatives from the Labour Relations Commission states that such representatives should be afforded 'necessary' time off to perform their representative duties and should not be dismissed because of their union activities. Equally, trade union representatives are charged with representing their members in a fair and equitable manner and co-operating with management in implementing agreements. A section committee is normally comprised of an elected group of shop stewards. It allows stewards representing various sections/ groupings in the organisation to meet regularly in order to discuss common problems and decide on policy.

Many unions have a branch system in which the branch acts as a channel of communication; disseminates policy and instructions downward and the views of the membership upward; manages the internal affairs of the union; and strives for improvements of the terms and conditions of employment for members (McPartlin 1997: 82). The branch comprises a group of trade union members, normally from different organisations but working in a particular geographical area, although the branch can sometimes be based in a single workplace. The branch decides policy at ordinary general or general meetings and at the branch annual general meeting. The election of union officers takes place at the annual (ADC) or biannual delegate conference. The general officers are usually full-time employees of the union and usually consist of a general president, a general secretary, a general vice-president and a general treasurer. Motions concerning the union and its policies are also discussed and voted on. The ADC is comprised of branch delegates, the union's National Executive Council (NEC) and the union's General Council. As well as forming resolutions, a second function of the ADC is to act as a controlling body to which the NEC and the general officers of the union are

Figure 3.1
Indicative Trade Union Structure

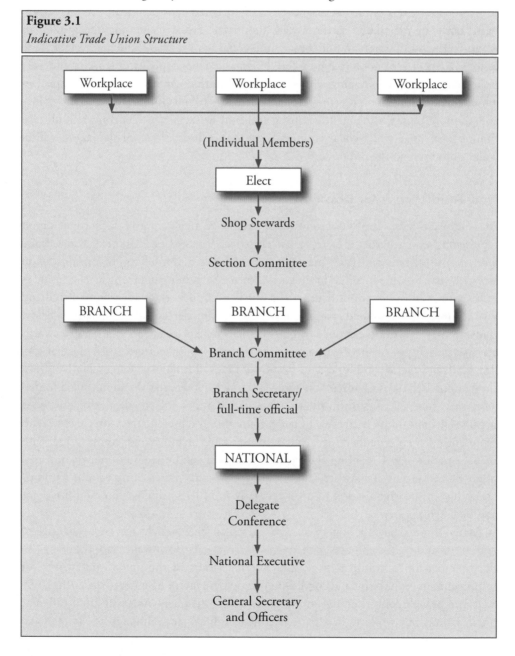

accountable. In particular, it appoints a union's full-time branch officials and appoints staff employed by the union. Most of a union's revenue comes from membership fees and many employers facilitate unions by deducting fees from employees' pay ('deduction at source'). Membership fees vary across unions. In the case of SIPTU, fees in 2012 were on a progressive scale from €1 a week for someone earning €127 or less to €4.70 a week for someone earning over €500. Unemployed members pay €0.30 a week (2012, www.siptu.ie).

IRISH CONGRESS OF TRADE UNIONS

The Irish Congress of Trade Unions (ICTU) is the central co-ordinating body for the Irish trade union movement (union confederation). Most trade unions are affiliated to ICTU and they retain a large degree of autonomy over their activities. Unlike the unions affiliated to it, ICTU does not represent individual members or negotiate for them in the workplace. Instead, its function is to voice the common interests of unions to government, state bodies, employer organisations and the media. It also nominates people to participate on various national institutions or agencies (e.g. the Labour Court) and it represents Irish unions internationally through membership of the European Trade Union Confederation (ETUC). Another key function of ICTU between the years 1987 and 2009 was to represent member unions in the negotiation of national wage agreements, along with the government, employer associations, farming and voluntary sector representatives (see Chapter 13).

ICTU was established in 1959 as a result of a merger between the Irish Trade Union Congress (ITUC) and the Congress of Irish Unions (CIU). This merger served to heal a longstanding rift in the Irish union movement, which was partially related to personality differences but also as a result of ideological differences and differences between Irish and British unions (IDS/IPD 1996). The CIU was founded in 1945 and had primarily represented some ten Irish-based unions (most notably the ITGWU), while the ITUC, which was founded in 1894, was composed of the remaining Irish- and British-based unions. In 1958, the year prior to the merger, the CIU had unions with 188,969 affiliated members, while the figure for the ITUC was 226,333 (McCarthy 1977). At the end of 2010, ICTU had forty-nine unions affiliated to it in the Republic of Ireland and Northern Ireland – with 581,376 members in the Republic and 217,711 members in Northern Ireland (data provided by ICTU).

Ultimate decision-making power within ICTU is vested in the delegate conference. Here, delegates from affiliated unions consider various resolutions presented by union delegates and those adopted become ICTU policy. Both trade unions and trades councils (voluntary groupings of unions on a regional or local basis) are allowed to send delegates to these conferences and to vote on motions; voting rights are based on membership size. The ICTU Executive Council is elected at the delegate conference and is responsible for policy execution as well as general administration and management. Various committees operate under the auspices of ICTU. One is the Disputes Committee, which deals with disputes between member unions around jurisdiction over membership. The Demarcation Committee deals with inter-union disputes concerning which union should organise particular workers (see Table 3.5) and the Industrial Relations Committee deals with applications for an 'all-out' picket in disputes. An all-out picket obliges all union members employed in the organisation in dispute not to pass the picket, i.e. a protest in which striking workers encourage other workers not to work and try to persuade management to concede to their demands. An all-out picket differs from a normal picket in that only members of one union participate in the latter (see Table 3.6).

Table 3.5

What Is Demarcation? Central Bank Dispute

In 2006, a dispute arose between the Central Bank and SIPTU in relation to work being carried out by counting staff at the counting section of the Central Bank Currency Centre. The union claimed that the counting staff should not be carrying out vault work, since it did not form part of their duties and there were supervisory staff trained and available to do the job. Management argued that it could delegate work as it deemed appropriate in order to meet its operational needs. The dispute could not be resolved at local level and was referred to the Labour Court (see Chapter 5). The Court recommended that the supervisors should, whenever possible, be assigned to the vault work. Only in cases of their unavailability should the counting staff be called upon. The Court said that counting staff should continue to co-operate where requested and should avail themselves of opportunities to work in the high-security area.

Source: Central Bank and SIPTU (Labour Court Recommendation No. LCR18568)

Table 3.6

An All-Out Picket: Blarney Woollen Mills

In January 2010, ICTU sanctioned an all-out picket of the Blarney Woollen Mills in Bunratty, Co. Clare as a result of two chefs being made compulsorily redundant at the Bunratty restaurant. A union official said 'essentially the ICTU has requested that all trade union members not pass the picket at the Blarney Woollen Mills. We expect that it will affect drivers and delivery persons as well as union members who would ordinarily use the premises'.

Source: Farrelly (2010a)

WHY DO PEOPLE JOIN OR NOT JOIN TRADE UNIONS?

The process of union joining is not as straightforward as someone deciding whether to join or not. There are a significant number of factors that can affect the process of union joining and we examine some of these in this section. There are two steps to union joining: (1) the availability of a union and (2) the decision to join a union (Green 1990). Regarding availability, key determinants of membership are that a union has access to a workplace and that people are asked to join a union (Kerr 1992). If someone works in an organisation that does not have union members (or does not recognise or negotiate with unions), then there is much less chance that they will be asked to join a union. There are a range of *structural* factors that influence union supply, i.e. a change in the social structure and social values (Ebbinghaus and Visser 1999). These can include type of job or sector, change in the type of job, firm size, proportion of part-time workers and extent of a collectivist or individualist orientation (Beaumont and Harris 1991; Blanchflower 2006; Green 1991; Roche 1997). In certain types of jobs, industries and occupations, trade unions have a strong presence, while in others they have a weak presence. There can be a self-fulfilling cycle where strong union presence leads to more new members, which in turn allows unions to maintain a strong union presence.

One of unions' greatest difficulties is recruiting members in organisations and industries where they have a weak presence. In Ireland and many other countries, trade unions tend to have a stronger presence in the public sector than the private sector. Table 3.7 shows that union density is highest in public administration and defence, education and health. Within the private sector, unions have generally been strong in traditional manufacturing jobs (e.g. food and drink) and weak in services sector employments and hi-tech manufacturing jobs. Unionisation is lowest in food and accommodation services and agriculture. The low density in agriculture is unsurprising given that the sector is characterised by self-employed people and small holdings. The food and accommodation sector has low unionisation rates internationally and this is related to the nature of employment – part time, seasonal and small-sized businesses. Smaller organisations are less likely to have a union and unionisation is highest in organisations with over a hundred employees. Over time, the structure of the labour market has changed, with a decline or stagnation of employment in traditionally highly unionised sectors and growth in sectors which have traditionally posed difficulties for union penetration, e.g. electronics/computing and private services (Roche 1997; Roche and Ashmore 2001).

Table 3.7
Union Density in Ireland by Economic Sector, 2009

Sector	Union Density (%)
Agriculture, forestry and fishing	7
Industry	29
Construction	25
Wholesale and retail trade; repair of motor vehicles and motorcycles	16
Transportation and storage	53
Accommodation and food service activities	6
Information and communication	23
Financial, insurance and real estate activities	35
Professional, scientific and technical activities	13
Administrative and support service activities	17
Public administration and defence; compulsory social security	81
Education	61
Human health and social work activities	50
Other NACE activities	15

Source: CSO (2010)

Individual characteristics can affect union joining, e.g. age, gender, education levels and political orientation. In many countries, unionisation is higher among older workers and full-time employees; this is also the case in Ireland. Traditionally, men had higher unionisation rates than women, since women tended to work in jobs that were short term and 'marginal to the main (male) labour force' (Turner *et al.* 2008: 481). Some argued that women were less interested than men in trade unions; however, a number of studies show that women have positive attitudes towards unions and are active in them (Wajcman 2000: 187; Walters 2002; Turner and D'Art 2012). While men still have higher union density rates in many countries, in Ireland 35 per cent of women are union members, compared to 32 per cent of men (Blanchflower 2006; CSO 2010).

Table 3.8

Who Are More Likely to Be Union Members in Ireland?

- Employees aged 45–59
- Employees in the Midlands area
- Irish nationals
- Married people
- Employees in professional and associate professional jobs
- Those with third-level education

Source: CSO (2010)

Another set of factors that is important in determining union membership is that of *cyclical factors*, i.e. the impact of unemployment and inflation on unionisation (Ebbinghaus and Visser 1999). It might be expected that people will be less inclined to join trade unions when the economy is in recession and unemployment is high and vice versa (Roche 1997). It has been argued that people will be more likely to join unions when wage levels rise, since unions receive credit for the increase (credit effect), and when inflation rises, since people seek to protect the value of their wages (threat effect) (Roche and Larragy 1989). If we examine union membership and density trends in Ireland, we can see that the business cycle was particularly influential in the 1980s. Union membership and employment density peaked in 1980 but then fell throughout the 1980s. This decline is principally attributed to the economic recession and increased unemployment. The harsh economic climate of the early to mid-1980s dramatically changed the industrial relations environment. This period, which was characterised by widespread company rationalisations and redundancies, significantly altered the power balance in negotiations, with adverse consequences for unions. Employers increasingly sought to address issues such as payment structures and levels of wage increases, the extent of demarcation and the erosion of managerial prerogative by trade unions.

The business cycle was again influential when the economy began to recover in the 1990s and boomed until the late 2000s. As employment increased, so did the number of people joining unions. Between 1990 and 2007, the number of union members had increased by 15 per cent, from 491,000 to 565,000. However, union density continued to fall throughout the economic boom. Why did this happen? As a hypothesis, let us say that the number of people in employment in a country is 100,000 and 50,000 of these are union members, i.e. the union density rate is 50 per cent. Let us imagine one year later: the number of people in employment increases to 150,000 and the number of union members grows to 55,000. The union density rate would *fall* to 36.6 per cent.

A similar scenario happened with Ireland's unionisation. Even though more people were joining unions, the increase in union membership could not keep pace with the increase in employment, so union density actually fell. Union density continued to decline until a slight increase occurred in 2009. It is likely that this is due to the fact that union membership did not fall at the same pace as employment when the economy went into recession. In addition, employment and union density remained strong in the public sector, though recent large-scale redundancies in the public sector may contribute to a decline when new figures for density become available.

The economic recession of the late 2000s has had a similar impact on human resources as the 1980s, with companies introducing pay freezes, wage cuts, redundancies, re-deployment and reduced working hours (Roche *et al.* 2011). Research suggests that HR managers believe they have engaged with unions on how to respond to the recession, but union officials believe that management have sought to introduce change unilaterally and ignore collective agreements (Roche *et al.* 2011). Roche *et al.* (2011: 239) have concluded that 'the recession has debilitated trade unions' and they have been unable to respond to the recession more assertively because of the scale of the recession, the collapse of national wage agreements and because employees are subdued and fearful for their jobs.

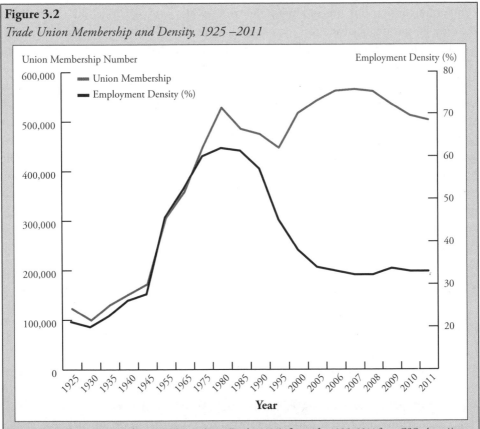

Figure 3.2
Trade Union Membership and Density, 1925–2011

Source: Figures for 1925–1990 from DUES Data Series (Roche 2008); figures for 1995–2011 from CSO <http://www.cso.ie/en/media/csoie/releasespublications/documents/labourmarket/2011/TableS11a.xls.>
For a discussion on the differences in data sources, see Roche (2008b) and CSO (2010).

Institutional factors focus on the effects of a 'country's particular historical development and the specific national institutions governing industrial relations' (D'Art and Turner 2006b: 168; Roche 1997). Key issues here include the nature of collective bargaining, employer ideology (including their attitudes to trade unions) and the role of government in regulating the operation of labour markets and industrial relations interactions. In relation to employer attitudes to unions, we noted earlier that Irish employers grew to accommodate and negotiate with unions, particularly after World War II. Unions that are recognised by employers are more likely to grow (Bain and Price 1983). However, trade unions have been finding it more difficult to gain recognition from employers and union officials have reported an increase in the use of coercive tactics by employers who did not want to recognise unions (D'Art and Turner 2005, 2006b).

An important issue in the Irish context is the managerial values of MNCs because Ireland is so heavily reliant on foreign direct investment. In 2010, foreign-owned companies supported by the Industrial Development Authority (IDA) employed almost 140,000 people and almost 72 per cent of these were in US-owned companies (Forfás 2011). The country of ownership of MNCs is important because it can influence the managerial values of the MNC in the host country, i.e. Ireland. Evidence suggests that there is a 'country of origin' effect, with a trend of union avoidance among US-owned companies coming into Ireland since the mid-1980s, particularly in the information technology and financial services sectors (Geary and Roche 2001; Gunnigle *et al.* 1997; Lavelle 2008). A large-scale study of MNCs has found that 42 per cent of US-owned companies recognise unions compared with 81 per cent of Irish companies (Lavelle 2008). It has been argued that this is due to the 'anti-union sentiment characteristic of the US national business system' compared with the more pluralist tradition of the Irish system (Lavelle 2008: 58). Even when MNCs are long established in one part of the country and recognise trade unions, many of these same companies later set up newer, non-unionised plants in another part of country. This practice is known as 'double breasting' (Gunnigle *et al.* 2009; Lavelle 2008). The increased resistance of employers to unions is not unique to Ireland. It has been suggested that there has been 'renewed unilateralism in personnel issues pursued by company management' internationally and that, with globalisation, trade unions have become more exposed to threats by companies to move locations (Pedersini 2010: 5).

A Comparative Perspective

Compared to other countries, Ireland's union density is in the middle: higher than the US and UK but much lower than Scandinavian countries (see Table 3.9). The overall trend is one of falling union density across OECD countries between 1980 and 2009. The international decline in unionisation has been explained by rising unemployment, the changing composition of the labour force, more union-resistant employers, politics and internal union inadequacies (Pedersini 2010; Waddington 2005).

As an institutional factor, national politics are a key determinant of unionisation trends (Schmitt and Mitukiewicz 2011). It has been argued that countries with close links to social democratic parties (Sweden, Denmark, Norway and Finland) had small

Table 3.9
Union Density in Selected OECD Countries, 1980 and 2009

	1980 (%)	2009 (%)
Australia	48.5	19.0
Austria	56.7	28.6
Belgium	54.1	52.0
Canada	34.0	27.3
Denmark	78.6	68.8
Finland	69.4	69.2
France	18.3	7.6*
Germany	34.9	18.8
Iceland	66.2	79.4*
Ireland	54.3	33.7.
Italy	49.6	34.7
Japan	31.1	18.5
Luxembourg	50.8	37.3*
Netherlands	34.8	19.4
Norway	58.3	54.4
Portugal	54.8	20.1
Sweden	78.0	68.4
Switzerland	27.7	17.8
United Kingdom	49.7	27.2
United States	22.1	11.8

*2008 figures
Source: For comparability purposes, the following dataset is used: http://stats.oecd.org/Index.aspx?DataSetCode=UN_DEN# .
For an explanation of sources, see http://www.oecd.org/els/employmentpoliciesanddata/Trade%20union%20density_Sources%20and%20methodology.pdf.

decreases in union density since 1980; 'liberal market economies' (Ireland, US, UK, Australia, New Zealand, Canada and Japan) had sharp drops in density; and countries with Christian democratic traditions (Germany, Austria, Italy, the Netherlands, Belgium, France and Switzerland) had moderate declines in union density (Schmitt and Mitukiewicz 2011: 3). In addition to having social democratic parties in government, some Scandinavian countries operate a 'Ghent' system, under which unemployment benefits are administered by trade unions, giving employees a strong incentive to join; this has contributed to higher union density. A liberal market economy (e.g. Ireland) is one in which employers have a lot of freedom to pursue their own employment practices (Roche *et al.* 2011). While Irish trade unions have links to the Labour Party, the party has historically been relatively small and not as influential in politics as Fianna Fáil or Fine Gael. These parties appeared to be supportive of trade unions, setting up bodies like the Labour Court and negotiating with them on national wage agreements (or social partnership). In the 1960s and 1970s, state agencies recommended to MNCs that they recognise trade unions; however, this practice had been abandoned by the 1990s (Gunnigle *et al.* 2009). In addition, it has been argued that the national wage agreements and government policy allowed MNCs to avoid unions and governments have refused to introduce statutory union recognition legislation, i.e. a law that would compel employers to recognise and negotiate with a union (McDonough and Dundon 2010).

Caution is needed when interpreting union density rates in different countries, since the figures do not always give a full picture of union strength. Another measure of union strength or influence is collective bargaining coverage, i.e. the percentage of employees whose pay and conditions are governed by a collective bargaining agreement, whether or not they are members of a union (see Table 3.10). The coverage of collective bargaining is a major issue. If a country has an industrial relations system in which collective bargaining agreements can cover a large percentage of employees, then trade unions may not be too concerned about a lower union density. In many European countries there is provision for extending union–employer agreements reached at sectoral, industry or national level to non-union workers in an industry or to a wider section of employees in an economy. This is referred to as the 'extension of collective bargaining' and is frequently done in legal systems where the agreements are legally binding. This extension of collective bargaining means that the coverage of collective bargaining is routinely greater than union density. For example, in France only 8 per cent of employees are in a union but 90 per cent of employees are covered by a collective bargaining agreement.

If countries have an industrial relations system in which collective bargaining agreements generally cover union members only, then a fall in union density presents a major problem for unions and for employees. This is the case in Ireland, where there is no general provision for extension of collective bargaining and, as a result, a steep decline in union density generally means a decline in collective bargaining coverage as well. This represents something of a crisis for unions, particularly in the private sector (which has much lower unionisation than the public sector). Of course, even in countries with declining density and bargaining coverage, there are examples of individual unions that have shown considerable strength through bargaining power, political engagement, high levels of member activism and improved pay and conditions, e.g. the National Union of Rail, Maritime and Transport Workers (RMT) in Britain (Behrens *et al.* 2004; Connolly and Darlington 2012). However, the overriding picture for the union movement in many countries is bleak.

The responses of political and financial institutions (institutional factor) to the global financial crisis (cyclical factor) has influenced collective bargaining structures in some countries. When Greece received loans from the IMF/EU/ECB, these bodies in turn demanded radical changes to labour market regulation and wage determination, including a shift from national and sectoral collective bargaining to firm-level bargaining. Koukiadaki and Kretsos (2012: 292) argue that:

> … the priority that is given to firm-level agreements over those concluded at sectoral level, in conjunction with the prohibition on extending agreements,

points to significant deregulatory trends in the collective bargaining system, with negative implications not only for workers but also for employers who are members of the signatory organisations of the sectoral collective agreements, who now face being undercut.

In Ireland, trade unions, employer organisations and the government could not agree new pay rates in negotiations on a new social partnership agreement in 2009 in the context of the recession and the negotiations collapsed. This means that collective bargaining shifted from the national level to the firm level for those private sector firms that were part of social partnership previously.

Table 3.10
Collective Bargaining Coverage in Selected OECD Countries, 2008

High CB Coverage (%)		Low–Medium CB Coverage (%)	
Austria	99***	Switzerland	48
Belgium	96	Portugal	45**
Sweden	91	Ireland	44
Finland	90*	Australia	40
France	90	United Kingdom	32.7**
Iceland	88	Canada	31.6**
Netherlands	82.3	Japan	16
Italy	80**	United States	13.1***
Denmark	80*		
Norway	74		
Germany	62**		
Luxembourg	58		

*2007 **2009 ***2010
Source: ICTWSS (Database on Institutional Characteristics of Trade Unions, Wage Setting, State Intervention and Social Pacts)

WHY DO INDIVIDUALS DECIDE TO JOIN UNIONS?

Traditionally, in some heavily unionised industries and companies, employees had no choice but to join a union. Unions operated a 'closed shop', whereby every employee was required to be a member, often with the approval of employers. When everyone was a union member, there was no 'free rider' problem. A free rider is someone who is not a union member but who still receives the pay and conditions negotiated by a union. However, the closed shop practice has dwindled and most new members voluntarily choose to join. Generally there are four categories of reasons for people joining unions. One is a collectively based reason, where people join because they want the benefits of collective strength and they want to address a perceived injustice, have support if they encounter a future problem and improve pay and conditions (Wheeler and McClendon 1991). A number of international studies show that the collective category is the strongest motivation for people to join unions (Peetz 1997; Tolich and Harcourt 1999; Waddington and Whitson 1997). A second category is individual based, where people want the services offered by a union, e.g. legal advice and financial services. While legal advice can be a strong reason to join a union, studies indicate that the financial services offered by unions (e.g. cheaper car insurance) are rarely an attraction for potential members (Kerr 1992; Tolich and Harcourt 1999; Waddington and Whitson 1997). A third category is ideological: people join because they believe in trade unions. A fourth reason for people joining is peer related: people feel they should join because their relatives and colleagues are already members.

Why Does a Decline in Unionisation Matter?

There are a whole range of consequences that result from a decline in unionisation – for the individual, the organisation and society. For a non-unionised individual, it means that they may have to rely on their own individual bargaining power to seek to defend or improve pay and conditions. However, if they do not have unique skills (e.g. those of a star football player), they may have very limited bargaining power. There may be an internal employee association in the company (see later discussion) but these would not have the collective power a union can bring. Part of a union's role within an organisation is a democratic one in which they challenge management decisions, try to ensure decision making is fair through the introduction of rules and procedures, and act as a voice mechanism for employees. If employees do not have access to a union, these benefits may be lost. In addition, disputes within an organisation may be less likely to be resolved collectively in the absence of a union and disputes can become individualised. This phenomenon is already evident in the types of disputes that are referred to state dispute resolution bodies. The number of cases referred by individuals to the Rights Commissioners (who deal with individual disputes) increased dramatically between 2000 and 2010 (see Chapter 5). The high number of individual cases has led to significant delays in disputes being resolved. This contrasts with the Swedish industrial relations system, which has strong trade unions, a collective orientation to dispute resolution and lower levels of individual disputes (Teague 2009). At a societal level, research shows that countries with high union density are associated with lower levels of income inequality (Blanchflower 2006). Unions do this directly through collective bargaining, which reduces wage dispersion (the spread of wages between higher and lower paid) within a firm. Similarly, when collective bargaining is at sectoral or national level, wage dispersion across firms is reduced (Freeman 2007). Indirectly, trade unions lobby governments to make economic and political choices that reduce inequality. Strong trade unions tend to be associated with social democratic governments and larger welfare states, and these reduce inequalities (Bradley *et al.* 2003; Baccaro 2008).

It could be argued that a decline in union density is not problematic if there is a fall in the demand for unions, i.e. if people no longer need unions in a modern economy. However, the evidence suggests otherwise. In a 2002 survey of fifteen EU countries, 72 per cent of respondents agreed that workers need trade unions in order to protect their pay and working conditions (Turner and D'Art 2012). In the survey, 72 per cent of Irish non-union employees believed that workers needed strong trade unions. Even among young employees, who have generally lower unionisation rates than older employees, research suggests that the former can have even more positive attitudes to unions than the latter (Haynes *et al.* 2005). The difference between actual unionisation rates and attitudes to unions suggests there is a *representation gap* – the proportion of employees who would join a union but are unable to (Freeman and Rogers 1999). There are two key issues that arise as a result of this phenomenon. The first is that because the fall in unionisation has meant less collective strength and revenue for unions, they have had to enact various strategies to manage and reverse the decline. The second is the question as to whether or not there are alternatives to unions that can satisfy the representation demands of employees. We will now examine each of these issues.

TRADE UNION RESPONSES TO DECLINE

Rationalisation

Trade unions have responded to the decline in unionisation in a number of ways. Some unions have rationalised by ceasing to operate, transferring membership and finances to another union or merging together to form a new union. Between 1977 and 1998, there were eighteen transfers of engagements and eight amalgamations (Wallace *et al.* 2000). Two significant mergers were that between the Federated Workers' Union of Ireland and the ITGWU to form SIPTU in 1990; and between the two British-based unions, Amicus and the Amalgamated Transport and General Workers' Union (ATGWU), to form Unite in 2007. Irish governments have supported the rationalisation of unions and the Industrial Relations Act 1990 makes available financial assistance to unions who attempt (successfully or not) to merge. Unions in other countries have also merged in order to try to improve their position. Merging is a complicated process involving tensions amongst officials and large transaction costs. Research suggests there are mixed results from union mergers and they do not always lead to greater efficiency or improved services for members (Undy 2008; Waddington 2005).

Recruitment and Organising

A second strategy aimed at responding to the decline in unionisation has been an increased emphasis on recruitment of new members in workplaces where unions already exist and in non-unionised workplaces. Traditionally, unions did not invest heavily in recruiting new members because of strong unionisation and closed shop arrangements. Particularly since the mid-1990s, Irish trade unions invested more in recruiting by employing specialist recruitment officers who would target certain types of employees and industries. For example, SIPTU has targeted young people, women, atypical workers, workers in MNCs and migrant workers. They have also focused on industries that were considered 'ripe' for union drives, e.g. security, construction, hotels, catering, cleaning and nursing homes (Dobbins 2003, 2004). Other unions, such as IBOA, Mandate, Unite and CWU, invested in recruitment initiatives (Dobbins 2008).

Unions in other countries have also made extensive efforts to recruit more people such as students, migrant workers and women (Pedersini 2010).

More recently, unions have sought to organise workers as well as recruit them. Organising is the idea that workers are 'empowered' to define and pursue their own interests through the medium of collective organisation (Heery *et al.* 2000: 38). Instead of members being reliant on the full-time union official to serve their needs, they would become more active and try to address their needs collectively themselves within an organisation. This emphasis on organising arose because union officials were spending too much time representing the problems of individual employees; they had very little time to recruit new members and members had an expectation of being 'serviced' by the union rather than being active in it. This problem was also experienced by unions in the US, UK and Australia and unions there sought to move away from 'servicing' much sooner than Irish unions.

SIPTU has undergone significant internal restructuring in order to allow union officials to concentrate on organising and representing members on collective issues rather than representing individual members with employment rights issues. Union officials now represent members in one sector rather than companies in different sectors, allowing them to build up knowledge of a sector and generate organising activity. Members refer their individual rights problems to the union's Membership Information and Support Centre, which assigns an Advocate to the case. SIPTU aims to spend 25 per cent of membership fees on organising by 2013, up from 6 per cent in 2007 (Higgins 2009a). Research to date indicates that union efforts at organising have yielded mixed results (Murphy and Turner 2011, 2012). Challenges for unions include difficulties in gaining access to workplaces and union organisers relying on employees with previous union membership experience to become activists (Murphy and Turner 2011, 2012). Union attempts to reverse the decline in density will be a difficult task in the current economic and industrial relations climate, with increased unemployment, globalisation and the ability of MNCs to change locations in order to avoid unionisation.

Union Recognition

Since union access to a workplace is critical in the process of union joining, Irish unions have lobbied for legislation to deal with employers who are opposed to them. There is no constitutional or legal right to union recognition. Union recognition is the process whereby 'trade union(s) are formally accepted by management as the representative of all, or a group, of employees for the purpose of jointly determining terms and conditions of employment' (Salamon 2000: 189). Historically, this lack of statutory provision in relation to trade union recognition was not a major problem in Irish industrial relations. Most medium and large employers traditionally recognised and concluded collective agreements with trade unions. However, unions have been finding it increasingly difficult to gain recognition from employers. While trade union action or a recommendation of the Labour Court may convince employers to accede to union recognition, it is largely an issue of management discretion. Employers can choose to recognise and negotiate with one union, multiple unions or none. It was in this context that unions lobbied for legislation, the result of which was the Industrial Relations Acts 2001–2004 (see Chapter 2). Given that unionisation is falling and unions are finding it more difficult to get access to workplaces, and that these trends are unlikely to be reversed at least in the medium term, the next section examines whether there are viable alternatives to unions for employees.

ALTERNATIVES TO TRADE UNIONS? INTERNAL COMPANY ASSOCIATIONS AND CIVIL SOCIETY ORGANISATIONS

In the absence of a trade union, employees in some companies may have no alternative mechanism for collective representation. In other organisations, there are internal structures that have a representative function; these include employee forums, works councils and employee associations. They are introduced by management either voluntarily or because of legal requirements, e.g. the EU Works Council Directive and the EU Directive on Information and Consultation. Such structures can be used for information sharing or to allow employees to participate in decision making, though the extent of this varies widely. The issue of employee participation is discussed in more detail in Chapter 12. Unlike trade unions, an employee association consists only of employees who work in the same organisation. Joining an employee association gives some of the benefits of collective organisation: by joining together, workers can present a united front to employers and redress some of the bargaining imbalance. Employee associations provide a collective voice for employees without the introduction of an 'outside' third party, and management may view these associations as easier to deal with and less likely to engage in confrontation. However, work-based associations have been criticised because of their lack of independence, i.e. they are often established and resourced by management. The issue of independence has gained particular prominence following the finding in the Ryanair case that the company's employee representative committees could have engaged in collective bargaining. As noted in Chapter 2, there is now a live debate as to whether Ireland meets the requirement for worker organisation independence as required by the ILO. Employee associations may also be at a serious disadvantage due to the absence of an external organisation structure and lack of access to bargaining expertise or legal advice. These factors may combine to limit the bargaining power of employee associations in their interactions with management. Traditionally, trade unionists have taken a cynical view of employee associations, seeing them as a poor apology for a real trade union and responsible for inhibiting collective solidarity.

Other possible alternatives to trade unions are bodies that have been variously termed 'non-worker organisations', 'community unions', 'quasi-unions', 'non-bargaining actors', 'non-member organisations' and 'civil society organisations' (Williams et al. 2011: 70). These include charities, voluntary associations, advocacy bodies, social movement organisations and non-governmental organisations such as citizens' advice bodies and migrant worker centres (Abbott et al. 2011). It has been suggested that the activities of these bodies partly fill the vacuum left by the decline in unionisation and that they challenge unions' 'alleged neglect of interests grounded in gender and minority status or in vulnerable labour market positions' (Heery et al. 2012: 156–77). Unlike employee associations, but like trade unions, these civil society bodies are independent of management and are external to the organisation. They are not established like trade unions with the objective of advancing employees' pay and conditions, but some of their activities are similar to those of trade unions. They advise employees on their rights, engage in political lobbying and campaigns and try to influence legislation (Abbott 2006; Fine 2007; Meager *et al.* 2002; Pollert 2008; O'Sullivan and Hartigan 2011). Others have, on occasion, undertaken activities previously the preserve of unions, e.g. acting on behalf of individual employees or groups who have problems in the workplace and representing them in hearings of state dispute resolution bodies (O'Sullivan and Hartigan 2011). It has been argued that the legitimacy and non-adversarial approach of voluntary organisations allow them to influence employers (Heery 2010; Williams *et al.* 2011). However, there is still a view that there is no viable alternative model of employee representation to trade unions and that only workers' collective power can counter the power of employers (D'Art and Turner 2006b; Smith and Morton 2006). In this sense, civil society organisations are an inferior form of employee representation because they do not have a constant presence in the workplace and cannot exert employees' collective power.

Concluding Comments

This chapter has reviewed the growth, operation and evolution of trade unions in Ireland. Unions have had a tumultuous history that has somewhat come full circle. They are lobbying the government for measures to help them get recognition by employers and increase membership – key issues for unions a hundred years ago. The review of union joining indicated that union membership is not a simple process of a person deciding whether or not to join one. There are many factors that affect whether or not individuals have access to a union and this is critical to the union joining process. A key influence on union stability across countries is the institutional environment – in particular, how supportive employers and political parties are of unions. The approach of employers to unions varies considerably from one of support, to acceptance to outright opposition. In Chapter 4 we will examine employer representative bodies, which have traditionally accepted and negotiated with unions.

CHAPTER 4

Employer Organisations

INTRODUCTION

As with employee organisations, employers also combine for purposes associated with employment and labour matters. The major impetus for the growth of employer organisations was undoubtedly the perceived need to counter growing union power. Employer organisations have had a much less complex and tumultuous history than trade unions. They represent a smaller number of members than trade unions and most represent employers from the same industry. While employer organisations in Ireland do not affiliate to a particular political party (as trade unions often do), their role is not just confined to micro-level issues but also to larger societal-level matters such as political control and economic and social policies. Employer organisations offer a variety of services to members. They have negotiated with trade unions on behalf of an individual employer in an organisation or on behalf of all members at a national level. It has been noted that the collective organisation of employers is potentially more difficult than for employees because of the diversity of business interests based on their organisational size, market position, geographical location and competitive relationships (Thornthwaite and Sheldon 1997: 342; Tolliday and Zeitlin 1991). Indeed, the diversity of employer interests in Ireland has become apparent in recent years. Employer organisations have offered more services in order to attract employers (particularly non-unionised employers) and there have been varying perspectives amongst employer organisations on the need for collective bargaining. This chapter considers the role of employer organisations by examining their operation, structure, membership and the services they provide. We begin by considering employers' objectives in industrial relations, which crystallises the reasons why employers join associations.

EMPLOYER OBJECTIVES IN INDUSTRIAL RELATIONS

The primary concern for organisations operating in a competitive environment is to maximise organisational effectiveness and generate satisfactory returns for the owners/ stakeholders. Such returns are often expressed in terms of cost effectiveness and, for commercial organisations, profitability. Management's primary role is to organise the factors of production, including labour, in order to achieve these objectives. It is difficult to assess the degree to which employers have specific industrial relations objectives because employing organisations vary so greatly. Indeed, it is clear that a particular organisation's industrial relations priorities and approach are heavily influenced by a combination of internal and external variables, such as product market conditions and business goals, and these differ considerably between organisations. Nevertheless, it is worth considering some general beliefs common among employers. Thomason (1984) identifies a number of generic employer objectives in industrial relations as follows.

1. **Preservation and consolidation of the private enterprise system:** This has larger political overtones and relates to employer desires to develop and preserve a 'business-friendly' political and economic environment conducive to achieving business objectives at enterprise level. They will be particularly concerned that principles such as private ownership, the profit motive and preservation of authority and control in decision making are maintained and fostered.

2. **Achievement of satisfactory returns for the owners:** In order for commercial organisations to survive in the long term, satisfactory profit levels must be achieved. Managerial approaches and strategies will always be influenced by this primary concern. Non-profit-making organisations will also be concerned with cost effectiveness and the quality of their product or service.

3. **Effective utilisation of human resources:** One of the challenges of the employment relationship is the indeterminate nature of employees' effort. When an employee is offered a job, they are told how much they will be paid, the benefits they will get and how many hours they will work. It is much more difficult for employers to predetermine the level of effort they will get from employees. Therefore, an objective of employers is to ensure that employees achieve the maximum level of effort and productivity. This can be done through a range of practices: positive ones, such as training and promotion, or negative ones, such as reduced bonuses or disciplinary procedures.

4. **Maintenance of control and authority in decision making:** Employers/senior management are the prime decision makes in the organisation. Even when organisations negotiate with trade unions or devolve some decision-making power to employees, senior management will often ensure that they retain authority on major issues, such as the company strategy and employee numbers. Employers may decide to share information but not necessarily share decision-making power with employees.

5. **Good employer–employee relations:** Employers will also strive to maintain good working relations with employees but this must be achieved within the operational constraints of the organisation. The scope to agree attractive remuneration levels and conditions of employment, for example, will vary according to the organisation's market position and profitability, as well as its human resource philosophy. Effective industrial relations will be a priority, since it constitutes an important ingredient in ensuring the organisation achieves its primary business goals (as well as being laudable in itself). To help achieve such objectives, particular employers have found it beneficial to combine with other employers into permanent organisations.

WHAT ARE EMPLOYER ORGANISATIONS?

Oechslin (1985) defines employer organisations as 'formal groups of employers set up to defend, represent or advise affiliated employers and to strengthen their position in society at large with respect to labour matters as distinct from commercial matters'. Employer organisations defend the interests of capital as a whole and the specific interests of their members (Gardner and Palmer 1992). Employer organisations include those that specialise in labour market interests and those that are concerned about labour market and other business interests – 'dual associations' (Traxler 2004). For example, the Irish Hotels Federation (IHF) represents employers in negotiating minimum wages for the industry and it also promotes hotels to tourists. Employer organisations should not be confused with trade associations, which only represent the commercial and market interests of an industry and generally are not involved in industrial relations, e.g. the Retail Jewellers of Ireland and the Associated Craft Butchers of Ireland.

There are a number of reasons why employer organisations developed. The first was because employers wanted to counteract the growing power of trade unions. Employer organisations undoubtedly existed before the emergence of modern trade unionism and some possibly had connections with the guilds of the Middle Ages. Adam Smith observed as far back as 1776 that employers were likely to combine into associations for purposes related to employment and labour matters generally. However, employers began to co-ordinate with each other in a number of countries as a response to 'new unionism' in the late nineteenth and early twentieth centuries (Barry and Wilkinson 2011). Some employer organisations, such as those in Germany, distributed lists of pro-union workers and co-ordinated lockouts in response to strikes (Silvia and Schroeder 2007). A second reason why employers formed associations was to prevent harmful economic competition with each other. In some countries, it was employers who sought the regulation of wages in order to prevent their competitor employers from undercutting them on the basis of low wages (Barry and Wilkinson 2011). A third reason for the formation of employer organisations was a response to growing state regulation of employment, since governments began to introduce laws on health and safety, minimum wages and working hours (Barry and Wilkinson 2011; Howell 2005).

The functions of employer organisations include the following.

1. **Exchange of views:** Employers came together not only to exchange information, but to agree common policies and strategies. This led to a greater formality in the organisational structure of employer organisations. This role is still important today. However, it is practically difficult to get a wide input into any general discussions on policy issues of national significance, although such opportunities can possibly be afforded at regional level. For larger associations, the policies and positions are generally decided by a limited representative body of employer opinion.

2. **Lobbying:** It has been argued that the measure of employer organisation influence includes their capacity as pressure groups to shape public policy to suit their preferred regulatory settings (Schmitter and Streeck 1999). As governments became more active in economic and social affairs in the twentieth century, employers saw a need for their views to be effectively represented to government. This political representation role is now well established in many countries. Employer organisations will generally support conservative economic policies, which protect the interests of capital, and

they will attempt to prevent, or at least lessen, the effects of protective labour or social legislation. In Ireland, when government seeks employers' views, it will generally approach the appropriate employer organisations and they often make written and oral submissions to the government on proposed legislation, e.g. information and consultation and minimum wages. The overall objective of employer organisations in responding to state intervention is to seek to defend managerial prerogative (Howell 2005).

3. **Media relations:** Allied to the political representation role of employer organisations is their role in representing employer views to the public at large on relevant issues. This will commonly be achieved through the general media or the associations' research and publications section.

4. **Provision of specialised services to members:** Employer organisations will provide a range of specialised industrial relations and related services for their affiliated membership. These include information, research and advice, education and training and consultancy on human resource management practices (Thornthwaite and Sheldon 1997). The growth of collective industrial relations legislation and individual employment legislation since the early 1970s has led to a significant increase in employer demand for specialist legal advice on these matters. Employer organisations are expected to provide specialist legal advice and assistance to members in areas such as dismissal, redundancy, employment conditions, employment equality and industrial disputes. It is now usual for larger employer organisations to have a specialist legal section that provides such advice and assistance in addition to information guidelines on legislation for the general membership.

A more traditional service concerns the provision of information and advice on both basic wage rates and levels of pay increases to member firms. Most employer organisations carry out surveys and analyses of wage rates and fringe benefits for differing occupations, regions and sizes of organisation. Consequently, they are able to provide member firms with up-to-date information on local, regional and national pay trends and advise such firms on reward issues. It is common for larger employer organisations to provide training and development programmes for their membership in a variety of areas, such as in employment law, health and safety, management and industrial relations. Providing training has become a more important part of employer organisations' activity and it acts as a source of revenue for them, outside of membership fees.

5. **Collective bargaining and representation:** By far the most obvious service provided by employer organisations for their affiliated membership is in the conduct of collective bargaining. The role of employer associations in representing members in collective bargaining is important at two levels: multi-employer bargaining at industrial, regional or national level and enterprise-level bargaining. Enterprise-level bargaining involves negotiations between a single employer and their employer organisation representative and employees and their trade union. In periods of

decentralised bargaining or so-called 'free collective bargaining' (1982–1987 and 2009–present in Ireland), much of the decision making on employees' pay occurs at enterprise level. The role of employer organisations ranges from being the key employer actor in pay negotiations to a more supportive role in providing advice and assistance to individual enterprises and co-ordinating approaches to pay negotiations.

Multi-employer bargaining involves one or more employer organisations negotiating with one or more trade unions on the pay and conditions of employees in a number of companies, including in a whole industry, region or country. As mentioned, employers, particularly larger ones, fought to have multi-employer bargaining as this resulted in standardised pay, so that lower pay could not be used as a source of advantage amongst competitors, providing a 'cartelising function' (Barry and Wilkinson 2011: 152). In such negotiations, individual companies delegate bargaining responsibilities to their employer organisations, thus making them and not the individual employer the main actor on the employer side in negotiations on pay and associated issues. In many EU countries the negotiation of pay for employees for a whole industry or sector is common. National-level bargaining was a key feature of Irish industrial relations during the late twentieth century. During these periods of centralised pay agreements (1970–1982, 1987–2009), employer organisations (particularly IBEC) played a pivotal role in representing employer opinion to the other social partners (government, trade unions, farming and voluntary community). The agreements provided for pay increases to be paid over a period of time, usually three years, to unionised employees. Employers who were not members of IBEC were not obliged to pay the increases but could do so if they wished.

In addition to negotiating pay and conditions of behalf of members, employer organisation staff provide advice to members on all aspects of employment, such as pay, contracts, conditions of employment, recruitment, discipline and dismissal. They also represent members in cases or disputes referred to the Labour Relations Commission (LRC), Labour Court, Employment Appeals Tribunal (EAT)and other third-party hearings (see Chapter 5). Affiliated firms will normally call on the services of their employer organisation if involved in third-party proceedings, although the extent of such utilisation may only involve obtaining advice and direction. At Labour Court hearings in particular it is common for the employer case to be presented by an employer organisation official. This may also occur at EAT hearings, although employers are more likely to be represented by private legal representation in that forum.

EMPLOYER ORGANISATIONS IN IRELAND

Employer organisations and trade associations must register with the Registrar of Friendly Societies. Employer organisations that are involved in industrial relations must hold a negotiating licence under the terms of the Trade Union Act 1941. This distinguishes them from trade associations, which are not required to hold such a licence. Employer organisations are, in effect, trade unions of employers and fall within the same legal definition as a trade union. While this may not initially seem significant, it can have important implications for the role and membership of employer organisations. In particular, it suggests an approach to industrial relations which emphasises the role of collectives or combinations as opposed to individuals. In 2010 there were eleven employer organisations registered with the Registrar of Friendly Societies (see Table 4.1). While the number of employer organisations with negotiation licences is considerably less than their trade union counterparts, there is great diversity in membership composition. Within this listing are examples of traditional masters' associations, industry-based associations and a general association that is national in scope – IBEC, which has been the major employer force in both labour and trade matters.

Table 4.1

Employer Organisations Holding Negotiation Licences, 2010

- Construction Industry Federation
- Cork Master Butchers Association
- Dublin Master Victuallers Association
- Irish Business and Employers Confederation
- Irish Commercial Horticultural Association
- Irish Hotels Federation
- Irish Pharmacy Union
- Irish Printing Federation
- Licensed Vintners Association
- Regional Newspapers and Printers Association of Ireland
- Society of the Irish Motor Industry

Source: Registry of Friendly Societies (2011)

Irish Business and Employers Confederation (IBEC)

By far the largest employer organisation in Ireland is IBEC, which was formed in 1993 as a result of the merger of the Federation of Irish Employers (FIE, formerly the Federated Union of Employers) and the then dominant trade/commercial association, the Confederation of Irish Industry (CII). IBEC represents business and employers in all matters relating to industrial relations, labour and social affairs. In 2012 IBEC stated that it had over 7,500 member organisations, which employ over 70 per cent of the private sector workforce (2012, www.ibec.ie). As the country's major representative of business and employers, IBEC seeks to shape national policies and influence decision making in a manner that protects and promotes member employers' interests. IBEC's mission is to 'promote the interests of business and employers in Ireland by working to foster the continuing development of a competitive environment that encourages sustainable growth, and within which both enterprise and people can flourish' (2012, www.ibec.ie). Table 4.2 indicates IBEC's services to members. It represents industry in matters of trade, economics, finance, taxation, planning and development; it develops policies on this wide range of topics through consultation with members and research; and it represents employer interests to government and to the public.

Table 4.2

IBEC Services

- Industrial relations: advice and representation
- Employment law: information, advice and representation
- HR best practice: information and case studies on employee engagement, HR strategy, leadership and diversity
- Health and safety: information and support
- Training and development: programmes on management training, health and safety, equality and environment
- Management consulting: assistance to organisations to develop leadership effectiveness, enhance employee performance and motivation, carry out investigations into bullying and harassment allegations and audit HR and people-related systems
- HR networking
- Online compliance tools: online audits to ensure an organisation's policies meet legislative requirements
- Sample policies and procedures, e.g. on parental leave, annual leave, bullying and harassment, and internet usage
- *HR News*: monthly magazine that includes research on pay trends, past cases at EAT and the Labour Court

Source: IBEC (2012, www.ibec.ie)

IBEC plays a particularly prominent role in representing business and employer views on bodies such as the National Economic and Social Council (NESC), which was established by the government as a forum for the discussion of the principles relating to the efficient development of the national economy; the National Authority for Occupational Safety and Health, known as the Health and Safety Authority (HSA), which controls the operation and enforcement of occupational health and safety legislation in Ireland; and the Equality Authority (to become the new Irish Human Rights and Equality Commission), which is the statutory authority with responsibility for the elimination of discrimination and the promotion of equality of opportunity in employment. IBEC is also a member of the European employers' body, BusinessEurope, which represents employers' interests at an EU institutional level.

Table 4.3

BusinessEurope

BusinessEurope is a Brussels-based organisation that represents 20 million companies from thirty-five countries. Its aim is to preserve and strengthen corporate competitiveness. It does this by influencing policy and legislation developed by EU institutions (BusinessEurope website 2012). In addition to having forty-one employer organisations in its membership, individual companies can join it and contribute to its working groups. In 2012, high-profile members included Accenture, Microsoft, Pfizer and NBC Universal.

Source: BusinessEurope (2012, www.businesseurope.eu)

One of IBEC's most important functions was its participation in the negotiation of social partnership (or national wage) agreements between 1987 and 2009 with the government, trade unions, farming and voluntary organisations. While a few other employer organisations were also involved in negotiations, IBEC was the significant employer player (see Chapter 12). It is noteworthy that after the breakdown of social partnership, IBEC and ICTU (the primary union representative) negotiated with each other to produce a 'protocol' or set of commitments about the conduct of industrial relations in the private sector. This was done because unions and employers who followed the national wage agreements would have little experience of negotiating pay rates with each other at the company level, since they were previously determined at the national level. While employer organisations and trade unions often have conflicting interests and can be presented as 'them and us', the protocol shows that they have common interests (see Table 4.4). Two other notable features of the protocol are: (1) the commitment of the parties not to engage in strikes or other industrial action and (2) the acceptance that pay may have to be adjusted because of a firm's specific competitiveness issues. These are significant commitments from ICTU's perspective, since industrial action is a union's main bargaining leverage and it implies an acceptance that pay may have to be cut because of the prevailing economic circumstances.

Table 4.4

IBEC/ICTU National Protocol for the Orderly Conduct of Industrial Relations and Local Bargaining in the Private Sector, 2010

1 Both IBEC and ICTU are agreed that the maximisation of sustainable employment is the most important objective to be secured during the economic downturn.

2 The parties will work together to facilitate economic recovery through agreed strategies within their sphere of influence.

3 The parties are committed to preserving stability by ensuring that industrial relations are conducted in an orderly manner and to serve the primary purpose of protecting jobs. Specifically, the parties will:
   (a) promote meaningful and timely engagement at local level in relation to issues in dispute;
   (b) encourage their members to abide by established collective agreements; and
   (c) utilise the machinery of the state – the Labour Court and LRC (or other agreed machinery) – to resolve disputes.

4 The parties recognise that they are operating in a new context without a formal agreement on pay determination. However, bearing in mind the shared commitment to maximising the sustainability of employment, it is accepted that the economic, commercial, employment and competitiveness circumstances of the firm are legitimate considerations in any discussion of claims for adjustments to pay or terms and conditions of employment. It is not the intention of the parties to alter their historical approach to dealing with normal ongoing change.

5 The parties will try to achieve common ground for the purposes of persuading government to take action on priority issues, including job retention and creation, pensions and home repossessions.

6 The parties are committed to ensuring that their respective members do not engage in strikes, lockouts or other forms of industrial action in respect of any matters covered by this protocol where the employer or trade union concerned is acting in accordance with its terms.

Source: Adapted from IBEC (2010, www.ibec.ie)

Construction Industry Federation (CIF)

Unlike IBEC, which represents employers from a range of industrial sectors, the CIF is essentially an industry-based association dealing with both trade/commercial and industrial relations matters affecting the construction industry. Some of the CIF's services include advice on construction, tendering and financial planning. The CIF nominates a representative to NESC and to the Construction Industry Disputes Tribunal, a tribunal set up by the CIF and construction unions to assist in dispute resolution in the construction industry. In the area of industrial relations, the CIF is one of the few employer organisations involved in industry collective bargaining. It negotiates with trade unions to set legally binding pay and conditions for construction workers across the country through a Registered Employment Agreement (REA). The CIF also represents members in negotiations with unions and dispute resolution hearings (e.g. the Labour Court) and advises members on employment law and other employment matters.

Table 4.5

Case Study

The CIF – For or Against Lower Wages?

In 2010, the CIF wrote to the Minister of State at the Department of Enterprise, Trade and Employment with special responsibility for Labour Affairs, Dara Calleary TD, about proposed changes to the Industrial Relations (Amendment) Bill 2009, which would regulate the system of REAs, of which there is one for the construction sector. One of the Bill's provisions was that firms who experience financial difficulties in paying the wage rates set by the REA could claim 'inability to pay' and apply to the Labour Court to pay reduced wage rates for a particular period of time. While other employer organisations like IBEC and ISME welcomed the 'inability to pay' provision, the CIF objected to it. Instead the CIF preferred to seek reduced pay rates in the REA, which would then apply to all employers.

Discussion Points

1 Why do you think the CIF was not in favour of an 'inability to pay' provision for individual firms?
2 The ISME favoured the Bill's provision. What features of the construction industry might help explain the differing perspectives of the CIF and other employer organisations?

Source: Higgins (2010c)

Irish Small and Medium Enterprises Association (ISME)

Thomason (1984) differentiates between entrepreneurs, who essentially own (at least partly) and run their businesses, and abstract corporate entities that are run by professional management. The corporate business firm has replaced the older entrepreneurial firm as the prevalent type of organisation in membership of employer organisations. Thomason suggests that this mix partly explains the diverse philosophies and roles of different employer organisations. ISME claims to be the only Irish employer organisation that represents entrepreneurs. It points out that 'independence enables it to speak out fearlessly' on behalf of competitive and entrepreneur-driven business and that 'by joining forces with other business owners across the country, members can share in protecting the health of their firms and resisting the dominance of government, trade unions and big business' (2012, www.isme.ie). ISME was established in 1993 by a group of small and medium-sized enterprises (SMEs) that broke away when the FIE and CII amalgamated to form IBEC. While ISME does not hold a negotiating licence and thus does not meet the established definition of an employer organisation, it has been prominent in commenting on economic and social affairs, including industrial relations. ISME's primary function is to represent the interests of its members to government, government bodies and other organisations impacting on business. It has lobbied for labour market deregulation and has been critical of the system of social partnership (O'Donnell and Thomas 2002). It has also been critical of IBEC and its role in social partnership (see Table 4.6). O'Donnell and Thomas (2002: 180) argue that this criticism stems from ISME's resentment at not being offered a role in social partnership. Other services offered by ISME include advice on employment law and other employment issues, discounts on financial products and management education programmes.

Table 4.6
Snapshots of ISME Views on IBEC and Social Partnership

1997
ISME claimed that IBEC was the body appointed by government to represent industry and argued that IBEC represented an 'elite grouping' of 'employee-managed big business'. ISME says it was seeking 'parity of esteem' with big business. It claimed that it had been 'locked out' of the social partnership process, which was 'the exclusive preserve of big business, the public sector unions and the government'. ISME argued that the political parties (Fianna Fáil and the Progressive Democrats) had promised that ISME would participate in social partnership should they be elected to government.

2009
ISME chairperson Eilis Quinlan outlined that:

> ISME, over twelve months ago, were the only organisation to identify that wage rates were not sustainable in the economic climate and that cuts were necessary. This was at the same time when the social partners, including the big business lobby IBEC, were actually agreeing a deal that would increase wages by 6.5 per cent. This is the same grouping that has allowed the public sector pay bill to increase by 36 per cent in the last five years alone. If the SME sector had been allowed proper representation at partnership level, there is not a hope in hell that this scenario would have been allowed to develop.

Source: ISME (2009); Sheehan (1997)

Other Employer Organisations in Ireland

Most of the other employer organisations are primarily concerned with trade and commercial issues, although they have some role in industrial relations. The Society of the Irish Motor Industry (SIMI) is mostly concerned with trade and commercial issues but it does provide human resources and industrial relations advice and assistance, including negotiating with trade unions and representing members in disputes. The most significant industrial relations function of a number of other employer organisations is the representation of members' interests on Joint Labour Committees (JLCs), which are state bodies that set minimum pay and conditions of employment for workers in certain sectors, e.g. hotel and catering (see Chapter 5).

The main industrial relations activity of the IHF and the Licensed Vintners Federation (LVF) has been to represent their members' interests on JLCs. While these employer organisations negotiate with trade unions on the JLCs, they do not get involved in negotiations with trade unions at enterprise level. One of the newest employer organisations created is the Quick Service Food Alliance (QSFA). It was established in 2008 to represent the interests of 200 fast-food employers, including Supermac's, McDonald's and Subway (2011, www.qsfa.ie). It does not provide industrial relations services but has had an impact on Ireland's industrial relations institutions. In 2008 it took a legal challenge against the Catering JLC and the Labour Court, claiming that the power of the JLC to set minimum pay was unconstitutional. It won the case in 2011 (further discussion in Chapter 5).

Chambers Ireland is not an employer organisation in the traditional sense but is a business network that aims to promote the economic and social development of chamber communities and represent business interests on various forums and committees, e.g. on the NESC (alongside IBEC and the CIF). Traditionally Chambers Ireland was not involved in employment relations, but in 2004 it launched ChamberHR, a human resources and industrial relations arm run by a HR consultancy company. ChamberHR provides HR advice and information and offers indemnification to employers against the financial costs involved in defending an employment law claim as well as against any compensation awarded against an employer in an employment law claim at a state third party, e.g. EAT (2010, www.chamberhr.ie).

An employer representative body that has had a growing voice on public policy matters is the American Chamber of Commerce Ireland (Amcham). Amcham is the representative voice of American MNCs located in Ireland and its mission is 'to promote a business environment that is attractive' to these companies (2012, www.amcham.ie). Policy is developed by Amcham through its working groups on taxation, employment law, HR leadership, and research, development and innovation and this policy is presented to media and the government. Indeed, a study of MNCs in Ireland found that Amcham had a high level of access to senior government officials and that this had influenced the content of Irish laws that transposed EU Directives (Collings et al. 2008). Collings et al. (2008: 258) argue that 'most of these directives have been enacted along lines which are broadly pro-business and tend to impose the minimal possible restrictions on business and management'. Amcham have proposed that the the low level of corporation tax in Ireland should be maintained. They have also stated that Irish salary structures need to be aligned with EU norms because 'wage costs for manufacturing workers in Ireland exceed that of the OECD average and the US by approximately 20 per cent and this is not sustainable' and that 'public sector reform must increase productivity and reduce inefficiencies' (Sheehan 2010a). In the area of union recognition and collective bargaining, Amcham has consistently lobbied the government against introducing compulsory union recognition or collective bargaining involving unions. In 2011 the president of Amcham, Gerard Kilcommins, said that 'any dilution of the current voluntary model would create a barrier to job creation and could damage our capacity to attract and retain inward investment' (Higgins 2011c). It could be argued that Amcham's lobbying has been influential, since the Minister for Jobs, Enterprise and Innovation in 2012, Richard Bruton TD, said that any new legislation the government introduces will not provide for mandatory union recognition (Sheehan 2012a).

MEMBERSHIP OF EMPLOYER ORGANISATIONS

The issue of public sector organisations becoming members of an employer organisation is a relatively recent phenomenon. While initially it might seem incompatible for public sector organisations to join an employer organisation (traditionally a bastion of free enterprise), some have taken up membership as a result of high levels of unionisation and the consequent need for expertise and advice on industrial relations issues. The amount spent by public sector organisations and semi-state bodies on employer organisation fees has led to some controversy in recent years in the context of the financial crisis. It was reported that Coilte paid €95,000, ESB paid over €150,000 and the Dublin Airport Authority paid €135,000 in fees to IBEC in 2007, while the Irish Film Board paid €5,000 and the Citizens Information Board paid €19,000 in 2010 (Sheehan 2011b). Local authorities can avail of the services of the Local Government Management Services Board, a government body which provides human resources and industrial relations research and advice and negotiates with trade unions on behalf of the local authority sector.

There is some debate as to the impact of firm size on employer organisations. For example, it has been suggested that small firms have more to gain by joining employer organisations (ILO 1975). Such firms are not generally in a position to employ HR specialists and owner/managers may not have either the necessary time or expertise to effectively handle such matters. However, subsequent research showed that employer organisations were not more frequently used by smaller organisations (Brown 1981; Daniel and Millward 1983). It has been suggested that small companies can be problematic for employer organisations because they are less committed to a collective identity and 'provide fewer membership resources relative to the demands they make on those resources' (Sheldon and Thornthwaite 2005: 20). Certainly larger companies are important to associations' membership strength because of the number of employees they have and the fees they pay. Research on employer organisations suggests there are often tensions between satisfying the interests of larger and smaller employers (Grote *et al.* 2007) and Traxler (2004) argues that associations internationally 'may have been less able to maintain their capacity to integrate smaller companies'. In Germany it has been argued that larger, export-oriented companies are having an increasing influence within employer organisations and have encouraged them to concede to trade union demands in order to avoid industrial action, while smaller companies are leaving the organisations

(Thelen and van Wijnbergen 2003). Similarly, we noted earlier the tensions between ISME and IBEC over which body can best represent smaller employers.

Membership of employer organisations is seen as a useful indicator of preferred management approaches to industrial relations (see also Chapter 9). Membership has traditionally been associated with the pluralist industrial relations model. Past research indicated that trade union recognition and formalised collective bargaining arrangements appeared to be key factors in determining membership of an employer organisation (Brown 1981). Therefore, it might be expected that companies that unilaterally determine pay and conditions and do not negotiate with trade unions are less likely to be members of an employer organisation. This would be expected to be the case with non-union MNCs (such as Intel, Dell, Google and Microsoft), which are now an integral part of the industrial scene. Some of these firms have brought with them a particular corporate approach to industrial relations that emphasises dealing with employees on an individual basis rather than through trade unions. Some international research indicates that MNCs generally avoid being members of employer organisations in the country they invest in (Marginson *et al.* 2004). However, a recent large-scale survey of 260 MNCs in Ireland found that 92 per cent were members of an employer organisation and most of these were members of IBEC (86 per cent). Interestingly, there was not a significant difference in membership rates between unionised MNCs (92 per cent) and non-unionised MNCs (85 per cent) (Lavelle *et al.* 2009). This suggests that non-union companies here do not view membership of an employer organisation as a *de facto* acceptance of collectivism and that they see other benefits of membership.

It is estimated that 60 per cent of employees in Ireland work in companies that are members of an employer organisation (Table 4.7). This is much higher than the employer density rate (the proportion of employees in employment whose employer is a member of an employer organisation) in the UK but similar to many other EU countries. As Table 4.7 shows, some European countries have very high employer density rates and this can be related to institutional factors. The institutional context can include legal requirements, trade union density and collective bargaining practices. In Austria, employers are legally required to be members of the principal employer peak organisation (the 'umbrella' organisation; there is no higher body), the WKÖ. In Belgium, the Netherlands and Spain, employers are not legally required to be members of employer organisations but they have to pay fees to a central fund for their sector, some of which goes towards funding employer organisations (Traxler 2004).

Employers may be more likely to be members of an employer organisation where there are strong trade unions (Sheldon and Thornthwaite 2005: 20). This can be viewed as the continuing relevance of the key rationale for the creation of employer organisations, i.e. to deal with unions. Traxler (2004: 56) argues that that 'the fate of employer organisations is closely linked to the fate of multi-employer bargaining to which extension practices are referring'. In Chapter 3, we noted the practice in some EU countries of extending collective agreements to a larger group. Employers engage in extending agreements or in industry-level bargaining to prevent each other from competing through lower wages. However, if companies are under significant cost pressures, they may deem it disadvantageous to have their pay rates set at the industry or national level and they may leave the employer organisation. Silvia and Schroeder (2007) argue that for many firms in Germany, increased costs and quality pressures as a result of globalisation are the main explanations for a decline of membership in employer organisations.

Alternatively, when collective bargaining is decentralised so that there is less inter-industry or national-level bargaining, terms and conditions are more likely to be determined within a company. Employer organisations then run the risk of being less relevant, since companies are less incentivised to join for solidarity reasons and the needs of companies in industrial relations become more diverse (Sheldon and Thornthwaite 2005). The evidence suggests that when multi-employer bargaining is replaced by single-employer bargaining, the result is a drop in employer density (Traxler 2004). As noted earlier, industry-level bargaining in Ireland is mostly confined to Joint Labour Committees and Joint Industrial Councils, although these have been challenged by new and old employer organisations in recent years (see Chapter 5).

Table 4.7
Employer Organisation Density

Country	Employer Organisation Density (%)
Austria	100*
Belgium	76**
Denmark	65
Finland	72.7***
France	75
Germany	60
Ireland	60
Italy	58
Luxembourg	80
Netherlands	85
Norway	65
Portugal	65
Sweden	83**
United Kingdom	35

*2010 **2009 ***2006
Source: ICTWSS (Database on Institutional Characteristics of Trade Unions, Wage Setting, State Intervention and Social Pacts)

Employer organisations have responded to changes in the economy and changes in collective bargaining levels with strategies to maintain and attract members. Strategies have included reducing membership fees; improving the range of services or conversely, cutting the range of services; charging on a fee-per-service basis; focusing more on the product market or commercial interests of employers; and merging with other associations (Traxler 2004). As noted earlier, IBEC was formed as a result of a merger and some of its services are on a fee basis, e.g. management consulting and training. Increased political lobbying and opinion formation have become another strategy used by employer organisations in order to increase their influence and membership (Barry and Wilkinson 2011; Traxler 2004). For example, in Australia employer organisations lobbied extensively in 2011 for changes to labour legislation, some of which they claim has had a negative impact on productivity and flexibility (Todd 2012). It has been argued that the reason why a large proportion of non-union MNCs are members of employer organisations in Ireland is because of their political influence in economic and social policy, particularly during the period of national wage agreements (Lavelle *et al.* 2009b). It remains to be seen if they can maintain political influence in the absence of the national agreements and what effect this will have on its membership.

Advantages and Disadvantages of Employer Organisation Membership

The potential advantages and disadvantages of employer organisation membership for individual organisations are summarised in Table 4.8. One of the disadvantages of employer organisation membership is a possible reduction of *autonomy* in decision making for the individual organisation. Employer organisations will be keen that members maintain a standard line in negotiations on pay and conditions of employment through the development of agreed policy guidelines. The individual organisation must decide if such norms are appropriate to its particular needs. This is less of an issue in Ireland since the breakdown of the national wage agreements in 2009: companies now have greater autonomy to decide on pay and conditions. *Comparability* is also an important factor. By virtue of association membership, a particular organisation's pay and conditions will generally be compared to that pertaining in other member firms. A traditional negotiating tactic of trade unions is to use the terms of collective agreements (particularly wage increases) struck with some member firms as leverage to secure similar terms with other organisations.

The issues of autonomy and comparability reflect the difficulties employer organisations face in developing common policies for a diverse membership. They also highlight the difficulties employer organisations face in enforcing policy guidelines, and they raise the issue of control over affiliates. Breaches of agreed policy guidelines by individual member organisations can detrimentally affect the credibility of such guidelines and may incur the wrath of sections of the affiliated membership. This has occasionally resulted in firms withdrawing from membership or being disaffiliated by the association. Such breaches of discipline are almost inescapable in associations where membership is voluntary and general policies are laid down for a diverse membership. Employer organisations will often exercise only informal authority over members, relying on persuasion and peer pressure to secure adherence to common policies. They are generally reluctant to punish non-conforming members, particularly where expulsion is considered. Should a large number of enterprises (or even a few significant employers) decide not to join an employer organisation, its representativeness is clearly called into question. This became an issue in 2008 in relation to the REA for the electrical contracting industry: a number of employers argued that the employer organisations which negotiated the REA were not representative of the industry (Higgins 2010b). See Chapter 5 for further discussion.

Table 4.8	
Advantages and Disadvantages of Employer Association Membership	
Advantages	**Disadvantages**
Collective approaches and uniform policy	Cost of membership
Advice on trade union matters	Loss of autonomy
Technical advice and information	Loss of flexibility
Skilled negotiators	Comparisons with other firms
Expert advisory and consultancy services	Greater acceptance of role for trade unions
Standardised pay and employment conditions	Greater formalisation in industrial relations
On par with regional/industry norms	
Assistance in industrial relations difficulties	
Influence on government/national affairs	

An issue of concern for employers with regards to membership can be how association membership fits in with the *corporate personnel/HR philosophy*. As noted, employer organisations have traditionally sought to deal with their employee counterparts through collective bargaining. However, some firms have a clear preference for a non-union status and may view membership of an employer organisation as incompatible with their HR philosophy. Conversely, we noted earlier that many non-union MNCs have joined an employer organisation. A more pragmatic reason for non-membership is related to *cost*. An important issue here can be that firms pay the full cost of membership regardless of services used. By contrast, an organisation that uses management consultants normally pays on the basis of services rendered. Most employer organisation subscriptions are related to the size of the firm (number of employees) or to the companies' total salaries and wages or turnover in a financial year. Subscription costs can be substantial for larger organisations (Ridgely 1988). Related to the issue of costs may be the perception among firms with a highly developed and well-resourced HR function that they do not need the services provided by an employer organisation. This is based on the premise that such services can be adequately provided by the company's own HR function (Reynaud 1978). We have seen (above) that the research evidence does not support this view and it seems that large firms use employer organisations more than small ones (Brown 1981; Daniel and Millward 1983).

THE GOVERNING STRUCTURE OF EMPLOYER ORGANISATIONS

In general, employer organisations are organised so that ultimate decision-making power resides with the affiliated membership. With various models of internal government in evidence, we can merely generalise on common themes with respect to governing structures. Windmuller (1984) suggests that the governing structures of the major employer associations will be composed of three or four levels:

1. Assembly or general meetings
2. General or executive council
3. Executive board or management committee
4. Presiding officer (president/general secretary/chairperson).

This structure attempts to cater for membership participation while allowing day-to-day management to be carried out by full-time staff (Windmuller 1984). Windmuller (1984) notes that general assemblies or meetings rarely occur more than once year and are largely a vehicle through which the membership influence and communicate with the central administration of the association. They help decide on general policy issues and elect the various committees. In commenting on their role, Windmuller (1984) suggests that general meetings have little power beyond the election of executive bodies. In contrast, the executive or general council tends to be much smaller. It is normally comprised of elected representatives and some officeholders will often be representative of various industrial, regional or sectional interests and will meet with greater frequency. The executive or general council is usually responsible for the appointment of the various committees and monitors their work and the general running of the association. Perhaps the most important layer in the governing structure of employer organisations is the management or executive board. This is normally much smaller and meets regularly. Its membership consists of representatives usually elected on a regional basis from the various branch/industrial divisions from the major enterprises and some officeholders of the association. Such bodies may also elect the various standing committees (finance, industrial relations, law, etc.) depending on whether there is a general council or not. Such committees often have the power to co-opt members and this influence is often used to bring in prestigious and powerful people from the business community who can make a valuable contribution to committee work. The executive board or general council exerts considerable influence on association policies and approaches and, together with the association president and the senior staff, is primarily responsible for policy formulation and execution.

For many associations, the position of chairperson or general secretary is a part-time position held by a senior manager from an affiliated enterprise. However, with the increasing demands of association work, this often creates a dilemma for the incumbent as this job requires considerable time away from their employer. The director general is normally expected to administer all the association's affairs according to the policy guidelines laid down by the general assembly, the general council and/or the executive board. A primary role for the director general will be to manage the professional staff of the association. The numbers of staff working in employer organisations has generally increased over time.

It appears that while employer organisation structure presents an image of active participatory democracy, this may be somewhat misleading. For pragmatic purposes, control and direction of association affairs is generally vested in the hands of a small number of affiliated members who together with the president and full-time staff oversee the general running of the association. There are parallels in this regard with the suggestion that there is a tendency towards oligarchy in trade unions (Michels 1962).

That is not to say that employer organisation affairs take little account of the wishes of the membership. On the contrary, since affiliation to employer organisation is voluntary and because they strive to be the authentic representative voice of their constituency, such organisations must be very circumspect to take on board the needs and wishes of their membership.

IBEC's Organisational Structure

IBEC's central decision-making authority is the National Council (see Figure 4.1). This consists of seventy members: a cross-section of the highest officers within IBEC and representatives from IBEC's members from business sector associations and policy committees. There are over sixty business sector associations, i.e. forums in which employers can discuss issues relevant to their industry. Examples of these associations are Retail Excellence Ireland, PharmaChemical Ireland and Financial Services Ireland. One of the most prominent associations is the Small Firms Association (SFA), which represents over 3,000 small firms of fewer than fifty employees (2012, www.sfa.ie). It provides networking opportunities and information, advice and representation on matters of human resources and industrial relations. It also lobbies the government and undertakes research.

IBEC's fifteen Policy Committees consist of member companies who assist in devising IBEC's position on a range of policy issues such as transport, education, economics, taxation and EU policy. This process helps IBEC to try to influence public policy by lobbying politicians and presenting its views to the media (2012, www.ibec.ie). IBEC's board is 'responsible for its corporate governance and strategic direction' (2012, www. ibec.ie). The board consists of fourteen members and it meets eight or nine times a

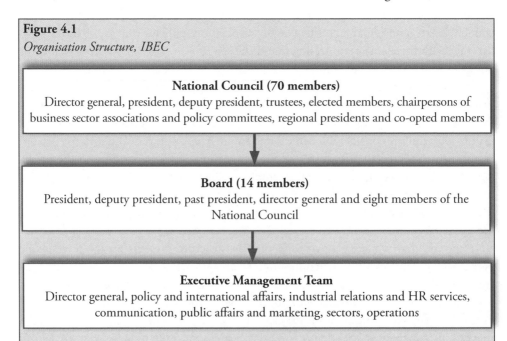

Figure 4.1
Organisation Structure, IBEC

National Council (70 members)
Director general, president, deputy president, trustees, elected members, chairpersons of business sector associations and policy committees, regional presidents and co-opted members

Board (14 members)
President, deputy president, past president, director general and eight members of the National Council

Executive Management Team
Director general, policy and international affairs, industrial relations and HR services, communication, public affairs and marketing, sectors, operations

year. The Executive Team consists of IBEC's full-time staff, who are responsible for carrying out the primary activities and services of the association. The team includes the director general position (currently held by Danny McCoy) and directors of five divisions. Brendan McGinty is director of the Industrial Relations division. IBEC has six offices: in Dublin, Waterford, Cork, Limerick, Galway and Donegal.

CONCLUDING COMMENTS

This chapter has reviewed the structure and functions of employer organisations. Employer organisations were generally created to deal with trade unions and their functions have broadened over time. Many are now heavily engaged in lobbying and presenting their positions on a variety of public policy issues. In the EU, there is a strong tradition of employer organisations negotiating with unions at an industry level and the function of employer organisations in this case is to co-ordinate the employers' negotiating position. In Ireland, there is only limited industry bargaining and employer organisations, including IBEC, have to adjust to a changed industrial relations landscape in which pay bargaining has shifted from national to firm level. Chapter 5 considers the differing perspectives of employer organisations on collective bargaining and there is discussion on recent developments in minimum wage setting.

CHAPTER 5

Dispute Resolution and Wage-setting Institutions

INTRODUCTION

While employers and employees have a common interest in keeping companies open and creating employment, they can also have conflicting interests over a range of issues such as pay, workload and working hours. For this reason, many organisations have procedures and mechanisms for addressing conflict in order to avoid lengthy disputes or poor working relationships. As well as organisations having their own internal mechanisms, governments recognise that some disputes can be difficult to resolve and employers and employees may need third-party assistance. The need for dispute resolution institutions is driven by a need to promote social justice and also by political and economic imperatives. Political pressure can arise from a need for the state to act in the role of industrial peacemaker, especially in the case of disputes in essential services like electricity, water and police (Farnham and Pimlott 1990). The study of industrial relations has long been concerned with the role of institutions. Early industrial relations scholars such as Flanders (1965) and Dunlop (1958) gave institutions a central role in the study of industrial relations, while others from radical or Marxist perspectives criticised this institutional focus. Radical thinkers drew attention to the need to study industrial relations as a struggle for power and control (Edwards 2003; Fox 1973; Hyman 1975). Despite such differences of emphases, there is general agreement amongst scholars, practitioners and policymakers that institutions are an important part of industrial relations.

In Ireland there are numerous bodies responsible for assisting employers and employees to resolve disputes and for adjudicating on employment rights. The LRC and the Labour Court deal mainly with collective disputes that involve unionised employees, e.g. the Aer Lingus cabin crew dispute in 2011 and the Vita Cortex redundancy dispute in 2012. The Employment Appeals Tribunal (EAT), the Equality Tribunal and Rights Commissioners generally deal with disputes involving individual employees who claim that their rights under a particular employment law have been breached, e.g. unfair dismissals or maternity legislation. Another area in which the state is often involved in industrial relations is in minimum wage setting. Ireland has a somewhat unusual minimum wage structure in that there is a National Minimum Wage but there are certain sectors where pay setting is undertaken by Joint Industrial Councils (JICs) or Joint Labour Committees (JLCs). The issue of whether a country should have a minimum wage was an issue of contentious debate for over a hundred years and this debate has re-emerged in Ireland since the economic crisis. The current operation of JICs and JLCs is regulated by the Industrial Relations Act 1946. Later we will discuss their functions and the challenges to their survival which have emerged in recent years. First, we will examine the dispute resolution bodies currently in operation in Ireland.

LABOUR COURT

The Labour Court was established at a time when there was very little by way of employment legislation. The original function of the Court was not to determine legal rights but to promote harmonious relations between workers and their employers and 'for this purpose to establish machinery … for the prevention of trade disputes' (Industrial Relations Act 1946). The creation and operation of the Labour Court reflected the voluntarist nature of Irish industrial relations. This voluntarism means that parties are generally free to attempt to resolve disputes through the process of collective bargaining. Irish law places no compulsion on employers or employees to engage in collective bargaining or to reach agreement. It also places no onus on employers to negotiate with trade unions. However, many employers and employees tend to seek agreement rather than risk the costs associated with either side taking industrial action in order to achieve their demands. The Labour Court fits into this voluntarist system because in the collective industrial relations areas it deals with, the parties are generally free to choose whether to use the Court or not and parties are free to accept or reject the recommendations of the Court. In this respect, the Labour Court is very unlike a 'court of law'. Other differences between the Labour Court and a court of law are that the Labour Court aims to find agreement between parties in a fast, fair, informal and inexpensive way. It rarely uses its powers to summon witnesses and hear evidence on oath and its composition differs from that of a court of law (Labour Court Annual Report 2010). Indeed, the Labour Court has been aptly described by the High Court as 'a mix of arbitrator, facilitator and inquisitor. It is a tribunal with specialist expertise in a wide area including labour law, labour relations, social and political policy' (Duffy 2010: 69). In addition to adjudicating on cases, prior to 1990 the Court also engaged in conciliation and investigated equality complaints. However, under the Industrial Relations Act 1990, the conciliation function and Equality Officers were transferred to the Labour Relations Commission (LRC).

The Labour Court currently consists of a chairman, two deputy chairmen and six 'ordinary members' (three employer members and three worker members). The Minister for Jobs, Enterprise and Innovation appoints the ordinary members after receiving nominations from IBEC and ICTU. However, the ordinary members do not act as representatives of these bodies – while sitting on the Labour Court they act independently. The members of the Court are former industrial relations practitioners with no requirement for legal qualifications, although some members do have legal qualifications. Up to 2003 the chairman was Finbar Flood, who was previously chief executive of Guinness Breweries. The current chairman, Kevin Duffy, was previously assistant general secretary of ICTU. The Court normally sits in a division comprising three people: the chairman (or a deputy chairman), an employer member and a worker member. In special circumstances, all of the members of the Court may sit on a case.

The number of cases dealt with by the Labour Court rose dramatically throughout the 1970s, reaching 1,045 recommendations in 1983 (see Figure 5.1). The number of cases completed fell in the 1990s when compared to the 1980s. Recent years have seen a return to high usage levels, with the number of cases completed peaking in

2010. This contrasts with the situation in the 1960s, when the Court heard on average 100 cases per year. The high usage of the Labour Court emphasises the high degree of reliance on institutional usage in Ireland and this has been attributed to the growth in proceduralisation and the requirement in procedure agreements that parties in dispute refer an issue to the Labour Court prior to any strike, lockout or other form of industrial action (Wallace and McDonnell 2000; Wallace and O'Sullivan 2002). While it may be understandable that third parties will voice concerns about the level of usage, it is arguable that this is an integral part of the industrial relations system. It is also a system that the actors (as measured by their revealed preferences at least) appear content to utilise on a regular basis.

Figure 5.1
Labour Court Cases Completed, 1973–2010

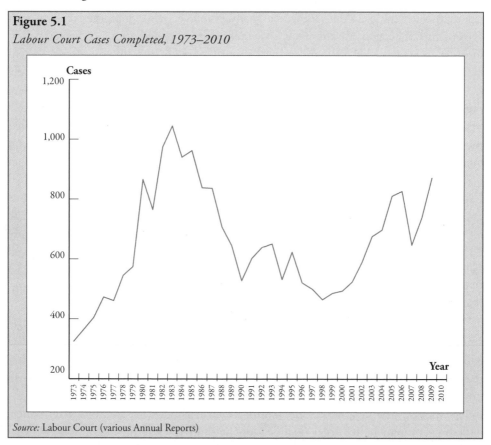

Source: Labour Court (various Annual Reports)

Industrial Relations Functions

The Labour Court has the following functions in relation to industrial relations. It must:

- investigate trade disputes under the Industrial Relations Acts 1946–2004;
- investigate (at the request of the Minister for Jobs, Enterprise and Innovation) trade disputes affecting the public interest, or conduct an inquiry into a trade dispute of special importance and report on its findings;
- hear appeals of the recommendations of Rights Commissioners under the Industrial Relations Acts;

- establish JLCs and decide on questions concerning their operation;
- register, vary and interpret employment agreements;
- register JICs;
- investigate complaints of breaches of registered employment agreements;
- investigate complaints of breaches of codes of practice made under the Industrial Relations Act 1990; and
- give its opinion as to the interpretation of a code of practice made under the Industrial Relations Act 1990. (2012, www.labourcourt.ie)

Under the Industrial Relations Acts 1946–2004 there are prescribed circumstances in which the Labour Court may investigate disputes. The Court may investigate when:

- it receives a report from the LRC that no further efforts on its part will help to resolve the dispute;
- it is notified by the chairperson of the LRC that it has waived its function of conciliation in the dispute;
- it is hearing an appeal in relation to a recommendation of a Rights Commissioner;
- it decides after consultation with the LRC that exceptional circumstances of the case warrant a Labour Court investigation; and
- there is a direct referral to the Labour Court and an advance acceptance of the Court's recommendation under Sections 20(1) and 20(2) of the Industrial Relations Act 1969.

Most cases are referred to the Labour Court by one or both of the parties to a dispute, but occasionally the Court will intervene in a dispute and invite the parties to a hearing. This tends to occur in high-profile cases of national importance, e.g. the air traffic controllers' dispute that disrupted flights in 2008. Most of the cases referred to the Court are those that have already used the conciliation service of the LRC but have failed to reach agreement, or those that are appeals of decisions of Rights Commissioners. Table 5.1

Table 5.1
Industrial Relations Referrals to the Labour Court, 2000 and 2010

Activity	2000	2010
Breach of registered employment agreement	64	328
Appeal against RC recommendation	147	184
Cases referred directly by the workers or both parties under the Industrial Relations Act 1969	130	130
Cases referred by the LRC	315	229
Cases referred directly under the Industrial Relations Act 1990 (exceptional circumstances)	0	1
Industrial Relations (Amendment) Act 2001	0	7
Interpretation of REA/JLC/Code of Practice/ERO/Agreement	5	114
Total	**661**	**993**

Source: Labour Court Annual Reports (2000–2010)

indicates a change in the type of industrial relations issues considered by the Court in 2010 compared to 2000. In particular, there were significant increases in the numbers of cases related to the legally binding regulations of JLCs (Employment Regulation Orders) and JICs (Registered Employment Agreements). A significant proportion of these were cases concerning the scope of the Construction REA (i.e. who it covered) or cases taken by trade unions and the employer body, the Construction Industry Federation (CIF), against employers for alleged breaches of the Construction REA. This reflects the increased challenges facing pay-setting institutions during the economic crisis.

Employment Law Functions

Although it was initially solely an industrial relations body, the Labour Court now has an additional range of functions in the area of employment law. Under these provisions, employees can make a claim alleging that one of their individual employment rights has been breached by an employer. This can happen in relation to legislation dealing with equality, minimum wage, organisation of working time, fixed-term work, part-time work, and safety, health and welfare at work. Some employment law issues go directly to the Labour Court but many reach the Court when an employer or employee is dissatisfied with the previous decision made by the Rights Commissioner or Equality Tribunal and they appeal it to the Court. Most of the Labour Court's caseload relates to the Organisation of Working Time Act 1997 and appeals of decisions of the Equality Tribunal under equality legislation. Table 5.2 shows the increase in employment laws for which the Court has been allocated responsibility in the last decade. Its increased work in this area has had a number of implications. First, the Labour Court (2011: 4) notes that although employment law cases constitute about a third of its *caseload*, they account for a greater percentage of the *workload* of Court members because of 'the complex issues of fact and law' that they raise. The Court (2011: 4) itself has been critical of the waste of resources arising from hearing appeals of employment law cases

Table 5.2 *Employment Rights Referrals to the Labour Court, 2000 and 2010*		
Category	**2000**	**2010**
Equality	52	88
Working time	66	279
National minimum wage	n/a	21
Fixed-term work	n/a	45
Safety and health	n/a	16
Part-time work	n/a	10
Information and consultation	n/a	0
Exceptional collective redundancies	n/a	0
Total	**118**	**459**
Source: Labour Court Annual Reports (2000–2010)		

that it believes are 'clearly unmeritorious'. While the Equality Tribunal can throw out cases it believes to be frivolous, the Labour Court must hear all cases that come before it. Second, the Court has expressed some discomfort at the adjudicative functions it has been given for employment law. It has stated that employment law cases 'necessitate different skills and different procedures than were traditionally required' and court procedures have to 'reflect the legal principles inherent in the determination of legal rights and responsibilities' (Duffy 2010: 68; Labour Court 2008: 4). In industrial relations disputes the remit of the Court is to 'resolve disputes', but in employment law cases the Court has less discretion in regard to how it reaches its decisions and it must follow the legislation's provisions with regard to redress (actions it can take to award the successful claimant). For example, equality legislation stipulates the maximum amount of compensation the Court can award in equal pay and equal treatment cases.

Investigations and Outcomes

The Labour Court investigates disputes by requiring the parties to attend a hearing, although there is no compulsion on them to attend. The hearings are usually held in private, unless one of the parties concerned requests a public hearing. The majority of hearings take place in Dublin, but hearings take place in other cities as necessary. The Court requires that each side make a written submission to it outlining the background to the dispute and their arguments. In industrial relations cases, written submissions should reach the Court no later than five days in advance of a hearing and in many of the employment law cases, written submissions must be made no later than seven days before a hearing. At the hearing, a spokesperson from each side will read out the written submission to the Court and the parties are free to make additional arguments and raise queries on each other's case. The members of the Court may also seek clarification or elaboration on the arguments of the employer or the employee. The outcome of a Labour Court investigation is a recommendation. In standard industrial relations cases, the Court aims to issue these recommendations within three weeks (Labour Court 2001). Where the ordinary members of the Court agree on the recommendation, then the chairman has no role in decision making. The chairman's role arises when the ordinary members do not agree on the recommendation; then, the chairman makes the final decision on the matter. A recommendation normally takes the form of a summary of the case submitted by each party to the dispute followed by a rationale for the Court's recommended solution. Occasionally the Court may issue an oral recommendation. If any member of the Court dissents from the recommendation (i.e. disagrees with it), this is not issued. The Labour Court publishes its recommendations on its website.

The Industrial Relations Act 1969 outlines that 'the Court having investigated a trade dispute may make a recommendation setting forth its opinions on the merits of the dispute and the terms on which it should be settled'. This marked a change from the Industrial Relations Act 1946, which required the Court to have regard to a number of issues when making recommendations. This included the public interest, the promotion of industrial peace, the fairness of the terms to the parties concerned and the prospect of the terms being acceptable to them. This section was repealed in 1969, since it was clear to the Court that it was almost impossible to reconcile all of the criteria (Kerr and Whyte 1985). R.J. Mortished, the first chairman of the Court, highlighted this when he wrote that 'a settlement acceptable to the parties might be against the public interest and one which was not acceptable to the parties would not promote industrial peace' (Labour Court 1948). The role of the Court has been described as one of persuasion, cajoling and the promotion of accommodation amongst the parties before it. Its recommendations have been described as soft regulation instruments (Duffy cited in Forde 1991; McCarthy 1984; Teague and Thomas 2008; von Prondzynski 1998). At times, the Court has been accused of being anti-employer, anti-union or anti-government, but such criticisms generally relate to the perceived effectiveness of the Court or the acceptability of its recommendations, not its role within the industrial relations institutional framework (see Forde 1991).

There is no regularly collected information on the extent to which Labour Court recommendations are accepted by the parties who use it. Kevin Duffy, chairman of the Court, said he believed that around three-quarters of recommendations are accepted (*Industrial Relations News* 2004). However, there is evidence of much lower acceptance rates in union recognition cases, in which a union takes a case against a non-unionised employer and seeks the Labour Court to recommend that the employer recognise and negotiate with the union. Between 1990 and 1999 only 30 per cent of employers actually recognised a union following a Court recommendation (Gunnigle *et al.* 2002). Even though the parties to a dispute are generally free to reject Labour Court recommendations, there can be significant constraints to doing this, e.g. negative publicity and the prospect of a protracted dispute. Even where rejected, a Labour Court recommendation may continue to have relevance, being used as the basis for further negotiations between parties.

In addition to recommendations, the Court may issue determinations, decisions or orders, depending on the relevant legislation under which an issue has been heard, and these can have binding effect. When issuing a decision on an appeal from a Rights Commissioner's recommendation in an industrial relations case, the decision is binding on the parties. A similar stipulation applies where workers or their trade unions refer a dispute on their own to the Court for investigation under Section 20(1) of the Industrial Relations Act 1969. In such cases, the union side has to agree in advance to accept the Court's recommendation. Such referrals have frequently been used in trade union recognition cases when a union tries to persuade an employer to recognise and negotiate with it but employers are not bound by the Court's recommendation. While the Court's recommendations may be stated as binding in these instances, there is no mechanism by which the recommendation can be enforced. The Labour Court carefully notes that 'where the recommendation of a Rights Commissioner in an industrial relations case is appealed to the Labour Court, it is *expected* that the parties will abide by the Court's decision on the appeal' (2012, www.labourcourt.ie). This seems to accept that it is not *legally* binding. By contrast, the Court indicates that there are certain types of cases in which the decision of the Court is enforceable through the civil courts, i.e. they are legally binding. Such cases include:

- appeals of decisions of Rights Commissioners under the working time, national minimum wage, part-time, fixed-term and safety and health legislation;
- appeals of decisions of Equality Officers under equality legislation;
- determinations under the Industrial Relations Acts 2001–2004;
- complaints of breaches of registered agreements; and
- Employment Regulation Orders made by the Court (2012, www.labourcourt.ie).

Despite the objective of the Industrial Relations Act 1946 to keep legal intervention out of industrial relations, the Labour Court has itself been the subject of legal challenges in recent years. A number of legally binding Labour Court decisions have been challenged by employers in the High Court and the Supreme Court. These include judicial reviews taken by Ashford Castle and Ryanair under the Industrial Relations Acts 2001–2004 and by employers in connection with Employment Regulation Orders and Registered Employment Agreements. Such challenges dilute the principle of the Labour Court being a court of last resort and they have resulted in a greater level of formality in Court procedures (Duffy 2010).

Table 5.3

The Labour Court in Action: Minimum Wage Dispute

In February 2011, the government cut the National Minimum Wage by €1 per hour to €7.65. In January 2011, all minimum wage workers in four hotels in the O'Callaghan Hotel group were called to a meeting at which they were asked individually to sign a form giving their employer consent to implement a 10 per cent pay cut with effect from 1 February 2011. Five members of the housekeeping staff were removed from the hotel roster after they declined to sign new contracts that would have reduced their pay from €8.65 an hour to €7.79. SIPTU, the trade union that represented the workers, gave notice of a strike to the hotel and held a picket from 17 February. Pickets were lifted on 1 March to allow for referral of the dispute to the Labour Court. The dispute was referred to the Court under section 20(2) of the Industrial Relations Act 1969, under which both parties agreed in advance to accept the Court's recommendation. At the hearing, the union told the Labour Court that there was no agreement with the workers, collectively or otherwise, for a reduction in their hourly rate of pay. SIPTU contended that the employer had sought the workers' consent to the pay reduction, but with the clear implication that if it was not given they would be removed from the payroll. The company maintained that due to a difficult trading period it had no choice but to take out significant costs. The Labour Court concluded that since it was not given any trading or financial information by the company, its submission could not support the contention that the reduction in pay was necessary to sustain jobs. The Court said that each affected employee should be provided with all the relevant information necessary to enable them to make an informed decision on the matter. They should also be given a reasonable period to reflect on the information and to take advice on the matter. The Court concluded that 'the employer's actions were not fair and reasonable'. It recommended that the five workers be reinstated in their jobs on their contract rates of pay of €8.65 and that they be repaid any unearned wages.

Source: Farrelly (2011c)

INDUSTRIAL RELATIONS ACT 1990

The Industrial Relations Act 1990 marked the most significant change to the collective institutional arrangements in Ireland since the Industrial Relations Act of 1946. The main change was the establishment of a new body, the LRC, and the continuation of the Labour Court with a revised and more limited role. A number of rationales underlined the institutional changes. There was a desire to encourage local settlement of disputes, to promote 'best practice' industrial relations and to restore the Labour Court to a 'court of last resort'. The then Minister for Labour, Bertie Ahern TD, noted that 'one the main reasons for establishing the Commission is to have a body with primary responsibility for the promotion of better industrial relations', which would 'be able to highlight examples of good practice and encourage others to adopt similar practices' (Dáil Debates 1990: 747–8). It was envisaged that the Court would again become 'the final authoritative tribunal in industrial relations matters' whose recommendations would once again be documents 'with great moral authority with the main responsibility for dispute resolution being shifted back to the parties themselves' (Kerr 1991). The main opposition to the changes came from the Labour Court, which expressed difficulty in understanding 'how the effectiveness of the conciliation service or the quality of its work could be better achieved under the proposed LRC than was possible under the Court' (Labour Court 1989: 108). Despite the Labour Court's opposition, the establishment of the new institutional arrangements proceeded smoothly and the LRC commenced operation in January 1991.

LABOUR RELATIONS COMMISSION

The Labour Relations Commission (LRC) is a tripartite body with trade union, employer and independent representation on its board, but its day-to-day services are carried out by Industrial Relations Officers (IROs) and Advisory Officers. The LRC's functions are listed in Table 5.4, with *conciliation* being its primary and most important function. This is evident from the extent of the demand for the service but also because cases will typically be concerned with efforts to resolve disputes involving many workers (Table 5.4). Conciliation is 'an advisory, consensual and confidential process, in which

---

Table 5.4

Summary of Functions of the Labour Relations Commission

- Provide an industrial relations conciliation service
- Provide a mediation service
- Provide a Rights Commissioners service
- Provide an industrial relations advisory service
- Assist JLCs and JICs in the exercise of their functions
- Review and monitor developments in the area of industrial relations
- Undertake industrial relations research
- Organise seminars and conferences on industrial relations and human resource management issues

Source: LRC Annual Report (2010)

parties to the dispute select a neutral and independent third party to assist them in reaching a mutually acceptable negotiated agreement' (Law Reform Commission 2010: 17). Conciliation can involve meetings or 'conferences' between the disputing parties either jointly or separately with an IRO, who steers the discussions and explores possible avenues of settlement in a non-prejudicial fashion (2012, www.lrc.ie). IROs have no power to compel the parties to reach agreement. While there are advantages and disadvantages to conciliation, it is this element of 'disputant control' that is the essential ingredient of conciliation that makes the process attractive to the parties. As noted, conciliation was originally a function of the Labour Court but this was transferred to the LRC on its establishment. Research indicates that settlement rates at conciliation have been higher since the LRC has taken responsibility for this (Table 5.4; Wallace and O'Sullivan 2002).

Table 5.5
Conciliation Service Case Load and Settlement Levels, 1946–2002 (Selected Years)

Year	Number of Disputes in which Conciliation Conferences Were Held	Number and Percentage of Disputes Settled at Conciliation	
1946–1947	166	105	63%
1947–1948	228	153	67%
1949	135	81	60%
1950	102	66	65%
1955	188	135	72%
1960	197	122	62%
1965	450	289	64%
1970	564	451	80%
1975	1,108	576	52%
1980	1,379	693	50%
1985	2,021	1,355	67%
1990	1,552	1,143	74%
1995	1,692	1,184	70%
2000	1,899	1,614*	85%
2005	1,692	1,371*	81%
2010	1,193	978*	82%

* These figures have been calculated from the rounded percentage figure and as such are approximations.
Source: Labour Court and LRC various Annual Reports

Table 5.6

LRC Conciliation in Action: Bin Collection

Two separate disputes over the outsourcing of waste by county councils were resolved in October 2010, following talks which were held at the LRC. SIPTU was involved in both disputes.

Refuse workers at Dún Laoghaire–Rathdown council had balloted for strike action over the planned outsourcing of the council's bin collection service to Panda, a private waste collection company. However, the strike – as well as the council's awarding of the contract to Panda – was deferred pending the outcome of LRC conciliation talks. The union had also balloted members at the other three Dublin councils for supporting action. An agreement reached at the LRC to end the dispute was accepted by the workers involved. The agreement includes a redundancy and compensation package, as well as the maintenance of direct labour in one of five waste collection services in the Dún Laoghaire–Rathdown council area. According to SIPTU, the union has also received a commitment by the management of the four Dublin local authorities (including Dún Laoghaire–Rathdown) to comply with the terms of the Croke Park Agreement in respect of the outsourcing of waste collection services. Furthermore, the four Dublin councils have accepted that direct labour will continue in the provision of waste collection services across the city and county. It was also agreed that any financial savings from the LRC agreement will form part of the surplus for distribution among union members. The council previously stated that it expected to 'make a substantial financial saving' from the outsourcing of the waste collection service.

In another proposed outsourcing of refuse collection, at Cork County Council, SIPTU members voted to accept outsourcing to a private contractor. The LRC settlement in this case means that staff affected by the outsourcing will have the option of redeployment within the council, a transfer of undertakings to the new contractor or a redundancy package.

Source: Farrelly (2010b)

Workplace Mediation Service

The mediation service is the newest service of the Labour Relations Commission, introduced in 2005. Mediation is 'a facilitative, consensual and confidential process, in which parties to the dispute select a neutral and independent third party to assist them in reaching a mutually acceptable negotiated agreement' (Law Reform Commission 2010: 17). In practice, there is often very little difference between conciliation and mediation, but the distinction within the Labour Relations Commission relates to the types of disputes for which mediation and conciliation are used. The LRC's mediation service is aimed at workplace disputes that have not already been referred to the conciliation service, the Rights Commissioner service, the Labour Court or other dispute resolution body. These disputes are relatively small scale, involving individuals and small groups. Typical issues referred to mediation may be interpersonal differences, a breakdown in a working relationship, bullying, issues arising from a grievance and disciplinary procedure and group dynamics (LRC Annual Report 2006). The mediation service received thirty-eight referrals in 2010 (LRC Annual Report 2010).

Advisory Service

The introduction of the advisory service of the LRC was a particularly innovative feature of the Industrial Relations Act 1990. The Act provides that 'the Commission may if it thinks fit, on request or on its own initiative, provide for employers, employers' associations, workers and trade unions such advice it thinks appropriate on any matter concerned with industrial relations'. Duffy (2010: 66–7) notes that the creation of the LRC 'emphasised the importance of promoting good industrial relations practice so as to avoid industrial conflict, rather than merely seeking to resolve disputes when they arise'. This conflict prevention element is most relevant to the Advisory Service, which can assist employers and employees in non-dispute situations to help build and maintain positive working relationships and effective dispute resolution mechanisms in the workplace (LRC Annual Report 2010). According to the Minister for Labour in 1990, Bertie Ahern TD, the reasoning behind the establishment of the Advisory Service was that there were some organisations using the Labour Court's conciliation service regularly and it was clear that there were underlying problems that needed to be addressed in a more fundamental manner (Dáil Debates 1990). Disputes may be merely a symptom of greater underlying problems in the workplace and such problems often remain after a dispute has been settled. To this end the Advisory Service carries out industrial relations reviews. These involve an examination of an organisation's industrial relations procedures and practices by an Advisory Officer, followed by the issuing of a report containing recommendations for the parties involved and, if needed, by follow-

---

Table 5.7

LRC Advisory Services

- Reviews of industrial relations practices and procedures
- Joint Working Parties
- Preventative mediation/facilitation/training
- Advice
- Facilitation
- Frequent Users' Initiative
- Preparation of codes of practice

Source: LRC Annual Report (2010); www.lrc.ie

Table 5.8

Number of Advisory Service Projects, 2010

Facilitation	33
Training	16
SI 76	7
IR Reviews	6
Working Parties	4
Total	66

Source: LRC Annual Report (2010)

up assistance through joint working parties (LRC Annual Report 2000). In 2010, significant areas of activity within the Advisory Service were facilitation and training (Tables 5.7 and 5.8). Facilitation occurs when the LRC offers assistance to companies that want to improve work organisation and procedures, e.g. introducing new work practices and structural change (LRC Annual Report 2010). The LRC offers training to organisations on areas such as grievance and disciplinary procedures, negotiations and consultations (LRC Annual Report 2010).

Another Advisory Service function is to draft *codes of practice* in consultation with employer and trade union organisations and other interested parties (Table 5.9). When approved by the LRC, the draft is then submitted to the Minister for Jobs, Enterprise and Innovation, who can make a statutory instrument. The codes are intended to give guidance to employers and trade unions on particular issues and are intended to have strong moral authority. Codes of practice are not directly enforceable as a breach of the code and will not attract any civil or criminal sanction. They are, however, 'admissible in evidence' in cases before the state third parties. For example, in unfair dismissals cases a Rights Commissioner or the Employment Appeals Tribunal may inquire if an employer has followed the dismissals steps recommended by the Code of Practice on Grievance and Disciplinary Procedures.

One of the more controversial codes of practice in recent years has been Statutory Instrument (SI) Number 76, the Code of Practice on Voluntary Dispute Resolution. Under the code, the LRC provides assistance in cases taken by workers/unions about pay and conditions of employment where there is no collective bargaining in a company, i.e. in generally non-unionised companies. The code of practice and the accompanying legislation (the Industrial Relations (Amendment) Acts 2001–2004) have been the subject of much debate, and since a Supreme Court case involving Ryanair in 2007, the use of the Act and the code has diminished. Only seven cases were referred to the LRC under the Code of Practice on Voluntary Dispute Resolution in 2010 compared with 82 in 2006 (LRC Annual Reports 2006 and 2010). (See Chapter 2 for more about the Ryanair case.)

Table 5.9

LRC Codes of Good Practice

- Dispute procedures, including procedures in essential services
- Duties and responsibilities of employee representatives
- Grievance and disciplinary procedures
- Compensatory rest periods
- Sunday working in the retail trade
- Voluntary dispute resolution
- Procedures for addressing bullying in the workplace
- Victimisation
- Access to part-time work
- Protecting persons employed in other people's homes
- Guide to work-related stress

Source: LRC Annual Report (2010)

RIGHTS COMMISSIONERS

The office of Rights Commissioner was created under the Industrial Relations Act 1969 with a view to preventing minor issues becoming major disputes (Cashell 2010). The cases that can be heard by Rights Commissioners cannot involve rates of pay, hours or times of work, or annual holidays of a body of workers, since it was envisaged that these issues would be dealt with by the Labour Court (Cashell 2010). Therefore, most Rights Commissioner cases relate to individual employees, though there have been instances of groups of employees involved in the same dispute submitting individual cases. For example, in 2009 twenty-eight Dell employees in Limerick who had been made redundant submitted twenty-eight individual claims to the Rights Commissioners, claiming breaches of their rights during the redundancy process. In that instance, the employer and employees agreed that the Rights Commissioner's decision in the first case heard would be applied to the other twenty-seven cases (Higgins 2009b). The Rights Commissioner can only hear cases involving employees who have access to the Labour Court. This requirement means that certain categories of state employees (e.g. civil servants and Gardaí) cannot refer cases to Rights Commissioners, since they are not permitted to use the Labour Court. Instead, these state employees have their own separate systems of dispute resolution. Any case heard by Rights Commissioners cannot have already had a Labour Court recommendation about the dispute; this is to prevent cases being appealed from the Labour Court, which would undermine the Court's recommendations. Finally, a party to the dispute must not have objected in writing to a Rights Commissioner investigation under the Unfair Dismissals Acts 1977–2007 and Industrial Relations Acts 1969–1990.

Initially, the Rights Commissioner service operated from the Department of Labour; since 1991 it has been attached to the LRC and there were fifteen Commissioners in 2010 (LRC Annual Report 2010). The Minister for Jobs, Enterprise and Innovation appoints Rights Commissioners from a panel submitted by the LRC, which in practice builds the panel following nominations from ICTU or IBEC (Cashell 2010). Investigations are held in private, with Rights Commissioners obliged to issue a written recommendation or decision. These can be appealed to either the Labour Court or Employment Appeals Tribunal depending on the legislation involved. Under the Industrial Relations Acts 1969–1990, a recommendation by a Rights Commissioner is not legally binding and there is provision for an appeal to the Labour Court, which must be applied for within six weeks from the date of the recommendation. Frequent issues that arise in cases under the Industrial Relations Acts are pay, unfair dismissals, disciplinary matters and unfair treatment/harassment (Cashell 2010; Hann and Teague 2008). The focus on individual disputes delineates the service from conciliation in the LRC, although individual disputes may also be dealt with at conciliation. However, there is one vitally important distinction between the two services. When a Rights Commissioner's recommendation is appealed to the Labour Court, the decision is binding. This does not apply when the case is referred to the Labour Court following LRC conciliation; the difference can be hugely important for either an employer or employee considering referring a case to a Rights Commissioner. Appeals against a Rights Commissioner's recommendation under individual employment legislation are made to the EAT and all appeals here must also be made within six weeks.

The Rights Commissioner service was intended to resolve disputes on day-to-day industrial relations issues but the work has shifted to dealing with complaints under an extensive number of employment laws (Cashell 2010). In recent years, there has been major growth both in the number of pieces of legislation for which Rights Commissioners have responsibility and in the usage of the Rights Commissioners' service. The Rights Commissioners cover thirty-three different laws and regulations (full list available on www.lrc.ie). Figure 5.2 shows the number of referrals to the Rights Commissioners has increased dramatically, particularly since 2004. Between 2000 and 2010, the number of referrals increased by over 388 per cent. The pieces of legislation that have accounted for most referrals to the Rights Commissioners between 2000 and 2010 were the Payment of Wages Act 1991, the Unfair Dismissals Acts 1977–2001, the Organisation of Working Time Act 1997 and the Industrial Relations Acts 1969–1990.

The increase in the number of referrals is likely due to the increased amount of employment law, the reduction in union density (so that fewer disputes are likely to be resolved collectively) and the economic recession (with more disputes about pay cuts). When operating under the Industrial Relations Acts 1969–1990, the Rights Commissioners follow their own procedures and adopt their own practices, since that legislation does not give guidelines on how the potential outcomes of cases are to

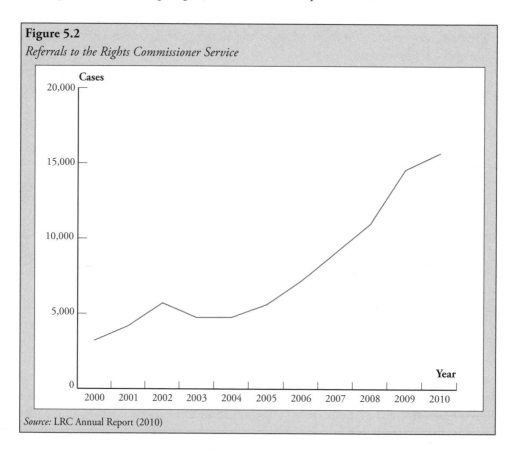

Figure 5.2

Referrals to the Rights Commissioner Service

Source: LRC Annual Report (2010)

be decided. Like the Labour Court, Rights Commissioners have less discretion with cases under individual employment law because of the need to apply the criteria of the relevant legislation (Commission of Inquiry on Industrial Relations 1981; O'Leary 2000). A study of referrals to the Rights Commissioners in 2006 showed that 70 per cent did not result in a recommendation or decision, since these were settled before or during the hearing or were withdrawn. Hann and Teague (2008) argue that this reflects the problem-solving nature of the service. There appears to be a high level of satisfaction with the Rights Commissioners, which has persisted over time (Cashell 2010; Kelly 1989a; Wallace 1982). Cashell (2010: 72) attributes this to the fact that the service is 'a simple, informal, lawyer-free institution where ordinary people can settle their affairs amicably without expense, delay, technicality or "hassle"'.

REFORM OF INSTITUTIONS

While the services offered by the dispute resolution bodies have been praised by many users, they have also been the subject of some criticism. Much of this has related to operational inefficiencies: duplication of work across bodies; the significant time delays in cases being heard, with delays of up to eighty weeks; confusion amongst users as to which body is responsible for which case or dispute; and the increasing legalistic nature of some bodies (Bruton 2011; Sheehan 2011a; Teague and Doherty 2009). Various governments have commissioned reports on institutional reform but none were acted upon. In 2011 the Minister for Jobs, Enterprise and Innovation, Richard Bruton TD, announced a set of proposals on reforming the state dispute bodies with the aims of promoting harmonious workplaces and a culture of compliance with employment law; reducing the number of disputes within the workplace; delivering a responsive, user-friendly service; and delivering value for money (Department of Jobs, Enterprise and Innovation 2012). The first change was the creation of a new service in January 2012, the Workplace Relations Customer Service, which acts as a single point of contact for users of the dispute resolution bodies instead of users contacting each relevant body. It is intended that this service will provide one website covering all dispute resolution services information, rather than each body having a separate website (Department of Jobs, Enterprise and Innovation 2012). Second, a single complaints form has been introduced, replacing the thirty-three different forms that previously existed. The third and most significant change is the planned rationalisation of the current bodies into two: a Workplace Relations Commission (WRC) and the Labour Court.

The WRC will result from a merger of the activities of the National Employment Rights Authority (NERA), the LRC, the Equality Tribunal and the first-instance functions of the Employment Appeals Tribunal (see Chapter 6) and the Labour Court. The WRC will have the following services:

- Advisory and Information Service (AIS)
- Registration Service
- Conciliation and Early Resolution Service (CERS)
- Adjudication Service

- Compliance and Enforcement Service (CES)
- Corporate and Strategic Service (CSS) (Department of Jobs, Enterprise and Innovation 2012).

The CSS will be responsible for the financial and operational functions of the new system. The AIS will provide information to employers and employees (as NERA does currently) and it will continue many of the current LRC Advisory Service functions, such as drafting codes of practice and implementing the Frequent Users Initiative. The Registration Service will have 'overall responsibility for steering the case through the system and ensuring it is dealt with efficiently and effectively' (Department of Jobs, Enterprise and Innovation 2012: 15). The CES will incorporate the current functions of NERA, i.e. the inspection and enforcement of employment law. Labour Inspectors currently working in NERA will be renamed Compliance Officers in CES. New functions of Compliance Officers include the power to submit an enforcement complaint against an employer to the Labour Court, and to issue fines against employers for certain breaches of law. The CERS will offer conciliation (currently offered by the LRC) as well as an early resolution service with the aim of assisting parties to reach agreement on a voluntary basis and without the need for adjudication. It is envisaged that agreements made between employers and employees in early resolution will be binding and enforceable by the civil courts.

Where a case is submitted for adjudication, all complaints will be heard and adjudicated in private in the first instance by one person in the WRC. Any appeal of a WRC adjudicator's decision will have to be submitted to the Labour Court within forty-two days. The Labour Court will be expanded, with four divisions, and it will incorporate the current appellate functions of the EAT ('appellate' meaning the hearing of appeals of decisions made by other bodies). It is planned that there will be a six-month time limit on the submission of complaints and there will be time limits on the complaint process, from making a complaint to getting a decision (Sheehan 2012a).

These are the most significant changes to the dispute institutions since the Industrial Relations Act 1990 and some aspects have been the subject of criticism. Teague and Doherty (2012: 18) argue that the new system (with early resolution, registration and adjudication) will not be as simple as intended and could trigger 'a new form of confusion and claim shopping, especially in cases involving multiple claims'. They label the plans regarding the Early Resolution Service (ERS) as 'astonishing' because it appears that it will be staffed by 'desk-based claims administrators' who will seek to mediate disputes over the phone and via e-mail (Teague and Doherty 2012: 18). They note that there is 'no reliable evidence that suggests that administrative/desk based mediation is successful' (Teague and Doherty 2012: 18). Similarly, a report approved by EAT members criticises the plan to have adjudication in the hands of 'lone civil servants with no expertise in industry or law' (Sheehan 2012b: 2). The report says that training would not substitute for the qualifications, skills and knowledge needed for the job and argued that this aspect of reform plans would 'bring the reform process into disrepute and give rise to a major increase in judicial reviews' (Sheehan 2012b: 2). The report argues that in the case of unfair dismissals cases, they should not be heard by a single person but by a tripartite body. It also questions the constitutionality of one of the reform proposals that the Labour Court would have the power to decide on whether a case was meritorious enough to be appealed, something which we noted earlier that the Labour Court had sought (Sheehan 2012b). The report also suggests that some aspects of the reforms could be in breach of international charters, specifically that the proposal for private hearings breaches the European Charter of Fundamental Rights and that if some complaints are not heard by a judge or legally qualified person other than at final appeal, this could breach the Charter of Fundamental Rights of the EU (Sheehan 2012b).

Teague and Doherty (2012) argue that the new WRC adjudicators should have experience as an industrial relations or HR practitioner rather than have 'a strong legal background providing a pure adjudication process'. Conversely, the Members of the Employment Bar Association said that 'despite the fact that individual employment disputes such as unfair dismissal rank among the most serious matters that individuals will ever litigate, the proposal suggests that all of these matters will be determined, at first instance and on appeal, by bodies where the adjudicators will have no requirement whatsoever that they be qualified in law' (Wall 2012a). However, Minister Bruton said the plan to have a single trained adjudicator will not change and said 'in any reform agenda you will have people who have done very well out of the existing system and they will throw up reasons why you should not change it' (Wall 2012a).

There is general consensus that reform of the state bodies is necessary, and while many of the current reform plans have been welcomed, there are still issues of concern. First, while many of the current types of disputes resolution processes (e.g. conciliation and adjudication) will remain, it is not clear who will staff these. Second, the Labour Court, which has traditionally been an industrial relations forum, will now have to adjust to incorporate the EAT's rights-based functions. While the reform plans indicate that the expanded Labour Court will not have civil court procedures, it is difficult to see how legalism can be reduced, given that a criticism of the EAT has been that it is over-legalistic. We have already noted the difficulties highlighted by the Labour Court in dealing with individual employment law issues. Third, the reform plans suggest an applicant fee might be introduced, but this has not yet been determined. IBEC had called for a fee to prevent 'dispute shopping' and 'frivolous' claims (Sheehan 2011b). However, there is also a danger that low-paid workers or those in financial difficulty in the recession will be deterred from making legitimate claims. Fourth, while the new structures may increase efficiencies, they are unlikely to change the trend of the state having to increasingly deal with large numbers of individual cases on employment law. In this regard, Teague (2009) contrasts the Irish system with an alternative system in Sweden, where there is a focus on dealing with disputes on a collective basis. Teague (2009: 517) notes that in Sweden 'there has been no discernible shift towards the individualisation of dispute resolution: any individualisation that has occurred has been within the framework of collective institutions'.

DISPUTE RESOLUTION IN THE PUBLIC SECTOR

The state is the main employer in the country, with some 339,400 public service employees and a further 52,900 employed in semi-state bodies in 2011 (CSO 2012). The public sector is highly unionised, with 87 per cent of workplaces having a trade union presence and an estimated 68.7 per cent of employees being a trade union member (O'Connell *et al.* 2010). Since higher union density is found internationally across public sectors, it is likely that there is an underlying reason for this. Dealing with large groups of employees through collective (as distinct from individual) bargaining offers substantial advantages to state employers and governments. While public sector industrial relations have been of particular concern since the foundation of the state, the relative importance of public sector industrial relations has grown in recent years. Among the factors driving this are the diverging union density rates between public and private sectors; a concern with quality of the delivery of public services and increased efficiencies; the impact of privatisation or part-sale of former state companies such as Eircom and Aer Lingus; increased competition; and the series of pay deals through the national wage agreements, benchmarking and the Croke Park Agreement. While recognising the differences between the public and private sectors, Cox and Hughes (1989: 99) suggest it would be inappropriate to view public sector industrial relations as inherently different.

There is, however, one distinctive area – the provision for third-party institutions – embodied in a range of internal conciliation and arbitration (C&A) schemes. McCarthy (1984: 35) writes that the exclusion of some public servants from access to the Labour Court appeared to have been based on the grounds 'that their inclusion might lead them to take a view of their relationship with their employer, the government, which would be excessively and improperly adversarial in character'. The government eventually conceded a C&A for civil servants on a temporary basis in 1950, which was made permanent in 1955. This was followed by schemes for teachers, Gardaí and officers of local authorities, health boards and vocational educational committees. The 'conciliation' stage generally consists of a conciliation council, involving equal numbers of staff (employee) and official (employer) representatives. Issues that are not resolved may proceed to arbitration, provided they are arbitrable under the terms of the particular scheme. All of the schemes provide for an arbitration board with representatives of the official and staff sides. The boards are chaired by a jointly agreed independent chairperson appointed by government, usually eminent senior counsels (McGinley 1997: 244). The finding of the board is sent to the Minister for Finance and the other appropriate ministers, who have one month to approve the report or submit it to the government. Under the local authority and health board schemes, the management or staff side have the option of rejecting the decision at arbitration. In the other schemes, an award can only be refused by moving a Dáil motion to reject or amend it. This course of action is rare but it has happened on two occasions: in 1953 and 1986. Since the late 1990s, employers and unions in some areas of the public service have agreed to abandon their C&A in favour of using the Labour Court/LRC, e.g. the health service, local authorities, Teachers' Union of Ireland (TUI) and academic staff of institutes of technology. These developments are hardly surprising given what Frawley (2002: 15) notes as the more flexible and pragmatic approach of the LRC and Labour Court compared to the inflexibility of C&A schemes.

WAGE-SETTING INSTITUTIONS

Joint Industrial Councils (JICs) and Joint Labour Committees (JLCs)

While collective bargaining at an industry level is common in many western European countries (e.g. Germany), most collective bargaining (negotiations on pay and conditions between an employer and employee representatives) in Ireland occurs at the level of the organisation. Collective bargaining at an industry level means that every employer in the same industry would pay the same wages to its employees. In Ireland, the only industry-level bargaining that occurs is through JICs, in which employer and employee representatives and an independent chairperson voluntarily negotiate pay and conditions for all employees in a certain industrial sector. JICs may be registered with the Labour Court and there are three currently registered: the Boot and Shoe Industry of Ireland, Dublin Wholesale Fruit and Vegetable Trade and the Construction Industry. There are also two unregistered JICs for Electrical Contracting and State Industrial Employees (Labour Court Annual Report 2010). When employer and employee representatives on a JIC agree pay and conditions, they register the agreement with the Labour Court and this Registered Employment Agreement (REA) then becomes legally binding on the whole industry. There were five REAs in 2011 for the following sectors: construction, electrical contracting, overhead powerline contractors, printing industry and drapery, footwear and allied trades (Labour Court Annual Report 2010). As noted in Chapter 4, the benefit to employers of having legally binding pay and conditions for a whole industry is that it prevents employers competing with each other on the basis of paying lower wages. Also, individual employers do not have to negotiate with their employees over pay, since it is already determined for the industry.

Joint Labour Committees are statutory bodies established under the Industrial Relations Act 1946, which set legally binding minimum pay and conditions of employment for certain employments. Like JICs, JLCs are comprised of employer and employee representatives and an independent chairperson. Unlike JICs, JLCs are generally created to protect vulnerable workers in employments where there is low pay and poor collective bargaining, typically as a result of low unionisation levels. Employer and employee representatives on each JLC negotiate on minimum pay and conditions of employment and they submit proposals to the Labour Court. Once approved, the minimum wage rates and conditions of employment become legally binding through an Employment Regulation Order (ERO) and these are enforced by NERA, which employs labour inspectors to check that workplaces are paying the correct rates. In 2011 there were thirteen JLCs, mostly covering services sector employments, e.g. hotels, retail, catering, contract cleaning and security. This means that employees working in these sectors have their minimum pay regulated by the relevant JLC and not by the national minimum wage (NMW). O'Sullivan and Wallace (2011) found that the minimum pay rates set by JLCs were often higher than the NMW, and until 2011 JLCs also set overtime pay rates and conditions, e.g. sick pay schemes. There was a major expansion in the number of employees covered by JLCs because of the increase in the number of people employed in services sector jobs. By 2007, it was estimated that 168,000 workers were covered by JLCs in comparison with only 65,000 in the late 1980s (see Figure 5.3). The wage rates set by JLCs are generally much lower than those set by JICs.

Figure 5.3
Number of Workers Covered by JLC System, 1926–2007

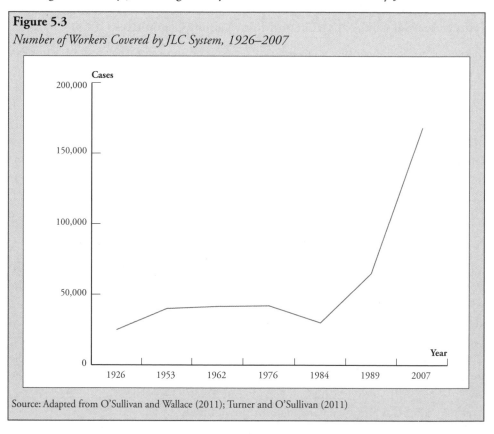

Source: Adapted from O'Sullivan and Wallace (2011); Turner and O'Sullivan (2011)

Challenges to JLCs and JICs

Up until the late 2000s, JICs and JLCs existed with little public policy attention or controversy. Any criticisms of them were generally dealt with by negotiation between employer organisations and trade unions sitting on the bodies themselves, or through social partnership. However, this pattern has changed with a series of legal cases taken against JLCs and JICs by employers, often by new employer bodies. In 2008, electrical contracting employers initiated High Court action to overturn an electrical contracting REA. The employers argued that the REA was agreed by parties that were not representative of the industry, something which the Industrial Relations Act 1946 requires (Higgins 2010a). However, the High Court dismissed the case in 2010, concluding that the employers took the case too late and that that the parties were representative of the industry at the time the REA was first registered. One of the employer groups, the National Electrical Contractor Trade Association (NECTA), has since launched an appeal of this decision with the Supreme Court (Higgins 2012d). Not all employers have been opposed to the REA. Indeed, many large employers supported it because they believed it provided protection from low-cost contractors from outside the state (Higgins 2011a). Up until late 2010, the employer bodies that were represented on the JIC – the Electrical Contractors' Association (ECA) and the Association of Electrical Contractors Ireland (AECI) – had supported it. However, in December 2011 they jointly gave notice to the Labour Court of their intention to cancel the electrical REA. The AECI argued that the REA cannot be policed properly and it was therefore of little value to legitimate contractors (Higgins 2010b). Despite the application to cancel the REA, the ECA has since engaged in negotiations with the electrical trade union, the TEEU, on new pay rates in the REA. The AECI has responded angrily to this development, saying that the ECA went behind its back (Higgins 2012b).

In the construction sector, the main employer body, the Construction Industry Federation (CIF), threatened to seek cancellation of the REA in 2010 if the trade unions did not agree to a pay cut in the REA wage rates. The CIF had sought a 20 per cent reduction in pay rates but the dispute was referred to the Labour Court, which recommended a 7.5 per cent reduction. While the CIF said this reduction was not enough, it remained a party to the REA because it provided protection from competitors from outside Ireland (Higgins 2010c). Trade unions later agreed to the lower pay rates. In 2012, the CIF sought a further 20 per cent pay cut and this is awaiting a Labour Court recommendation (Higgins 2012a). Thus, larger employer bodies in certain sectors view industry-level wage-setting institutions as beneficial to them as long as the collective agreements can be enforced to prevent wage undercutting and as long as they deem the REA wage rates to be reasonable.

The JLC system has had a similarly tumultuous few years as the JICs. Two High Court cases against JLCs were taken by a number of employers supported by the Irish Hotels Federation (IHF) and the Quick Service Food Alliance (QSFA). In 2007, a hotel employer and the IHF initiated a legal case but it was later settled out of court. A 2008 case launched by a fast-food employer and the QSFA went to full conclusion. In both cases, the employers argued that the JLC, in hotels and catering respectively, was unconstitutional because it set legally binding regulations, which, according to the Irish Constitution, only the Oireachtas (Parliament) has the authority to do. In June 2011 the High Court found in favour of the QSFA and deemed that the JLC was unconstitutional. Since the outcome of that case, other employers have brought legal challenges to the JLCs on the grounds that they are not covered by them, e.g. Coolmore Stud, Ballydoyle Stud and a Topaz service station (Farrelly 2011b; Higgins 2011b).

At the same time as the legal cases were being processed, Ireland fell deeper into an economic recession and this influenced the pressures on JLCs. In the context of the recession, employer bodies argued in the media and to government that the JLC system should be abolished because the minimum pay rates they set were 'costing jobs' (Sweeney and O'Brien 2011; Turner and O'Sullivan 2011; Wall 2011a). Employers were particularly critical of the JLCs' ability to set not just minimum basic pay rates but also minimum overtime rates and premiums for working on Sundays. Much of this criticism came about because of improved enforcement of EROs. When NERA was created by the government in 2007 and there were increased numbers of labour inspectors employed, the number of inspections of workplaces rose and more instances of noncompliance of EROs were found. For example, in 2008 NERA found that 73 per cent of catering workplaces it inspected were non-complaint with EROs and employment law (O'Sullivan and Royle forthcoming). A further development occurred in 2010 when, as part of Ireland's financial bailout by the IMF/EU/ECB, the government agreed to review the JIC and JLC systems because the implication was that these institutions might be acting as a barrier to employment. The subsequent review concluded that both systems should be retained but radically reformed (Duffy and Walsh 2011). This report, the lobbying of employers and the High Court decision that a JLC was unconstitutional culminated in the Fine Gael–Labour Party government introducing new legislation on JLCs and JICs, which provided that both systems would be retained but reformed.

The Industrial Relations (Amendment) Act 2012 provides that JLCs would no longer have the power to set premium rates for Sunday working, which may mean a loss of earnings for some employees since these premium rates used to be set at time-and-a-third or double-time. Under the Act, employers will be able to apply to the Labour Court to pay sub-minimum pay rates where they are in financial difficulty. This 'inability to pay' provision is available under the NMW legislation and was available under social partnership agreements but was previously resisted (in the case of JLCs) by the Labour Party when there was a similar proposal in the 1980s. Another significant provision in the Act is that employer and employee representatives on JLCs will have to consider a range of issues when deciding new minimum pay and conditions. These issues include the legitimate interests of employers and workers, the legitimate financial and commercial interests of employers, unemployment levels, wage levels in comparable sectors and wage levels in competitor EU countries. In relation to JICs, the 2012 Act provides that the terms of REAs can be changed without necessarily obtaining the consent of all parties to the agreement and the legislation clarifies when an REA may be cancelled.

While the proposed legislation will retain both systems, there are significant changes for JLCs in particular, with reduced powers and a more complicated decision-making process. It remains to be seen what effects this will have on employees' pay.

A key feature of the development of wage-setting systems is the difference of opinion held by different employer organisations with regard to minimum pay mechanisms. In regard to JLCs, many employer organisations have indicated they want the system abolished. However, since the JLC High Court decision, IBEC and a number of employers in contract cleaning have negotiated with trade unions to create a new JIC and REA for the sector (Higgins 2012c). Similarly, trade unions and IBEC and three other employer bodies in the security industry had negotiated a draft new REA. In electrical contracting, the ECA has negotiated a proposed new REA with trade unions despite its own earlier application to cancel it. Thus, employers in some sectors see benefits to negotiating with trade unions in order to have legally binding pay. This can help to raise industry standards and prevent a so-called 'race to the bottom', whereby employers compete with each other by paying lower wages. It could also be argued that the threats by some bodies like the ECA and the CIF to cancel REAs are negotiating tactics used in order to achieve their real goal of negotiating reduced pay rates with unions.

CONCLUDING COMMENTS

This chapter has reviewed the role of key institutions in employment relations. Bodies such as the Labour Court, LRC and Rights Commissioners perform a necessary function of helping employers and employees to resolve disputes. However, the ad hoc evolution of the dispute resolution system has led to complexity, which the proposed reforms aim to address. There are also significant changes proposed for the minimum wage institutions, JLCs and JICs. These are in response to the sustained efforts to abolish the bodies and to do so through a series of High Court cases – two new developments in Irish industrial relations. In addition, these challenges have come from new employer bodies that have not had the experience (or perhaps the desire) to negotiate with trade unions.

CHAPTER 6

Individual Employment Law

INTRODUCTION

The principal purpose of labour law is to regulate, to support and to restrain the power of management and the power of organised labour (Kahn-Freund 1977). The process of legislative intervention in the employment relationship can be traced back as far as the 1349 Ordinance of Labourers, when wage ceilings were imposed on both artisans and labourers in the 'Black Death' era of severe labour shortages. In recent years, there have been significant developments in the area of individual employment law. The various legislative initiatives may be viewed as a countervailing force attempting to redress the unequal bargaining power of the individual vis-à-vis the employing organisation. Of course, at the root of the employment relationship is the common law contract of employment, with its power to command and duty to obey. Although management still retain the power to 'hire and fire', this prerogative has been considerably restrained by a plethora of legislative initiatives taken primarily since the mid-1970s – often in response to Ireland's membership of the European Community or Union. In an attempt to cover the most relevant aspects of 'individual' employment law, this chapter reviews the contract of employment, dismissal, equality, health and safety, and redundancy legislation. It also summarises other statutes of particular relevance to industrial relations at work.

THE CONTRACT OF EMPLOYMENT

The contract of employment is the legal basis of the employment relationship and is central to the interpretation and application of statutory rights. As with the basic law of contract, it requires that there be (1) an offer from the employer, which is accepted by the employee, (2) consideration (or remuneration) from the employer for work done and (3) an intention to create a legal relationship. The contract may be concluded on an oral or written basis. However, under the Terms of Employment (Information) Act 1994, any employee who has one month's service is entitled (within two months of taking up employment) to a written statement of his/her basic terms and conditions of employment. A complaint lies to a Rights Commissioner in the event of failure to comply with the Act's provisions.

Common law attempts to distinguish between a contract *of* service (i.e. with an employee) and a contract *for* service (i.e. with an independent contractor). This is of some relevance given that it is only an 'employee' who can avail of the protection afforded under labour law. Case law indicates that three tests may be applied to differentiate between these contract types:

1. Control: Can the employer tell the employee what to do and how to do it?

2. Integration: Is the employee's work integrated into the business or is it a case of the independent contractor working for the business?

3. Multiple: What is the nature of the entire arrangement between the employer and the worker? This would be reflected in answers to questions such as:

   - Are there wages, sick and holiday pay? Who pays them?
   - Are income tax and social security deducted under the PAYE and PRSI systems respectively by the employer?
   - Does the worker share in the profits/losses?
   - Who provides the tools and equipment for the job?
   - Are there specific provisions relating to termination?
   - Is the employer entitled to exclusive service?
   - Is it a genuine case of self-employment or is there an attempt to avoid protective legislation?

Wedderburn (1986) has concluded that the variety of legal 'tests' have splintered in the hands of the judiciary and it is 'not practicable to lay down precise tests' or a 'hard and fast list'. He suggested that most courts now appear to apply the 'elephant test' for the employee, i.e. an animal that is difficult to define but easy to recognise when you see it! However, in the landmark decision of *Henry Denny and Sons (Ireland)* v. *The Minister for Social Welfare (1998)*, the Irish Supreme Court provided a measure of clarity on this issue and sent out a strong message to employers that despite the stated nature of the relationship, a court will look at the reality of the arrangement. The Denny case considered the social insurance status of a supermarket demonstrator whose contract very clearly stated that she was providing her services as an independent contractor. However, the courts held that she was an employee. Justice Keane stated that:

> While each case must be determined in the light of its particular facts and circumstances, in general a person will be regarded as providing his or her services under a contract of service and not as an independent contractor where he or she is performing those services for another person and not for himself or herself. (http://www.bailii.org/ie/cases/IESC/1997/9.html)

The Employment Status Group (2000), set up under the Programme for Prosperity and Fairness in 2000, issued a Code of Practice to assist individuals in determining their status. Though not legally binding, it is helpful and persuasive in distinguishing employees from independent contractors. The code emphasises that it is important that the job as a whole is looked at and that the reality of the relationship be considered. The overriding consideration or test stipulated is whether the person performing the work does so 'as a person in business on his or her own account' (2012, www.welfare. ie). The code also sets out specific criteria that are relevant to such determinations. With the advent of the economic recession, the sensitive subject of the unilateral variation of the contract of employment has surfaced. However, case precedent indicates that such variation(s) may give rise to:

- a claim of constructive dismissal under the Unfair Dismissals Acts;
- a claim under the Payment of Wages Act 1991 in respect of unlawful deductions;
- a claim for damages under common law; or
- a dispute under Industrial Relations legislation or processes.

Case law also confirms that *clear communication* in any move to change terms and conditions of employment and/or make staff redundant is crucial (McMahon 2011).

DISMISSAL AND THE LAW

The Unfair Dismissals Act 1977 was an important development in Irish labour law, with considerable consequences for the workplace. Though there are specific exceptions under its provisions, once an 'employee' has been continuously employed for one year, he/she has a right to claim unfair dismissal. An aggrieved employee may bring their case before either a Rights Commissioner or the Employment Appeals Tribunal (EAT) within six months of the date of dismissal. Under the 1993 amending Act, either the Tribunal or the Rights Commissioner may extend this time limit by six months in exceptional circumstances. The option of going directly to the Tribunal applies in the event of either party objecting in writing to a Rights Commissioner hearing. Either party may appeal the EAT's decision to the Circuit Court within six weeks from the date on which the determination is communicated to the parties. Should an employer fail to carry out a determination, an employee can instigate enforcement proceedings in the Circuit Court. Of course, if the employee has taken the matter to the Labour Court under the Industrial Relations Acts 1946–1990 or has instituted proceedings for damages at common law for wrongful dismissal, he/she would not also be entitled to redress under the Act.

Certain categories of employee are not covered under the enactments. The full list of exclusions is contained in the 1977 Act (as amended). The main excluded categories are:

- persons employed in the Defence Forces and Gardaí;
- FÁS trainees who are not employed;
- officers of VECs; and
- officers of the Health Service Executive (though temporary officers are not excluded).

The Act provides that a dismissal will automatically be deemed to be unfair if it can be attributed to:

- trade union membership or activities (including industrial action);
- religious or political opinion;
- involvement in civil or criminal legal proceedings against the employer;
- race or colour;
- sexual orientation;

- age;
- being a member of the Travelling community;
- pregnancy or matters connected with pregnancy;
- the exercise of maternity, adoptive leave or holiday entitlements;
- the exercise of entitlements under the National Minimum Wage Act 2000; or
- the exercise of rights under the Carer's Leave Act 2001.

The burden of proof in dismissal cases normally resides with the employer. However, the employee must show that he/she is actually covered by the Act's provisions and that a dismissal actually took place. In general, employers bear the brunt of the Act's regulatory force in so far as the onus of responsibility is on them to show that they have acted reasonably. The EAT evaluates the employer's (re)action and sanction with a view to determining whether it lies within the range of responses that a 'reasonable' employer might make. A common determinant of the Tribunal's decisions on the status of a dismissal is whether the employer followed fair and proper procedures prior to the dismissal. This requirement of procedural fairness is rooted in the common law concept of 'natural justice' and in the provisions of the 1937 Constitution. In addition, the Code of Practice on Grievance and Disciplinary Procedures (Statutory Instrument 146/2000) issued by the LRC provides a clear rationale for the adoption of such procedures and is admissible in proceedings. Related to this, the four basic obligations in regard to disciplinary procedural arrangements identified from case law by Fennell and Lynch (1993: 230–1) are:

- **Investigation:** An inadequate investigation of the situation on the part of the employer may give rise to a dismissal being deemed unfair.
- **Hearing:** The employer must put the relevant case to the employee, thus allowing him/her to respond. A refusal to allow representation at such meetings is likely to render the dismissal unfair.
- **Warning:** Prior to dismissal for misconduct or poor performance the employee should generally be given a series of warnings, thus providing him/her with an opportunity to improve.
- **Proportionate penalties:** A dismissal will be adjudged to be unfair where the employer is seen to over-react, that is, if a lesser penalty would have been more appropriate in the circumstances.

The normal reaction of the EAT to a failure to follow fair procedures (especially those laid down in a collective agreement or written disciplinary procedure) is to adjudge the dismissal to be unfair (see Chapter 7). However, the extent of the contribution on the employee's part to the circumstances resulting in the dismissal will be taken into account in deciding the appropriate remedy. Consequently, even if the Tribunal concludes that a dismissal was unfair, it might consider it appropriate to make up to a 100 per cent deduction from the compensation to which the employee would otherwise be entitled. It is also notable that the Circuit Court has concluded that an otherwise 'fair dismissal' does not automatically become unfair due to its procedural defects (Madden and Kerr

1996). Nevertheless, a direct result of this 'procedural fairness' factor is that there have been widespread changes in organisations' procedures.

Fair Dismissal

Those areas where a dismissal may be justified can largely (but not exclusively) be categorised under the following headings: (1) conduct, (2) capability/competence and (3) redundancy.

Conduct

This may take the form of a single act of gross misconduct or a series of such minor acts where the employee disregards relevant warnings. Dismissal arising out of alleged employee gross misconduct is one of the most common case types coming before a Rights Commissioner or the EAT. A fair dismissal under this heading normally occurs where the essential employer–employee relationship of trust is undermined. It generally applies to matters of abuse of sick leave, substance or alcohol abuse, criminal convictions, dishonesty, disobedience, breach of the duty of loyalty and fidelity, and violence or intimidation (see Madden and Kerr 1996). However, the EAT has not established any objective standard of 'unacceptable conduct' that justifies dismissal. Instead, it opts to evaluate the dismissal decision on the grounds of 'reasonableness' given the particular circumstances of each case. Consequently, one cannot construct a comprehensive and rigid checklist of conduct types that will be adjudged by the EAT to be unacceptable and warrant dismissal. The 'reasonableness' parameters inside which it will evaluate each case relate to the nature and extent of the investigation undertaken prior to the dismissal and the conclusion reached on the basis of the information yielded. Accordingly, the employer is obliged to carry out a fair and full investigation while adhering to the aforementioned principles of natural justice. It is also relevant under this heading that 'off-duty' conduct – where it has implications for the employer – may be adjudged by both the EAT and the courts to constitute grounds for fair dismissal.

Capability/Competence/Qualifications

Dismissal pertaining to the capability, competence or qualifications of the employee relating to work of the kind which he/she was employed to do may be justified. Of course, these 'driven' dismissals often require the employer to advise the employee in advance of the relevant failure, thus enabling him/her to improve. Competence-related dismissals tend to arise where the employee is alleged to demonstrate sub-standard work. Capability-related dismissals normally surface under the guise of attendance at work. Employees who are persistently late or fail to attend work regularly are commonly adjudged by the EAT to be incapable of performing the work they were employed to do. Indeed, even in those cases of persistent or extensive absence due to illness, the furnishing of medical certification may not protect an employee from a dismissal where the employer has satisfied him/herself that a return to work is not imminent. Medical certification can even provide conclusive proof that an employee is not capable of undertaking their work. Related to this, it is also notable that the Employment Equality Acts 1998–2011 (see below) have implications for employers considering dismissal on the grounds of incapability due to long-term absence. That is, treating a person with a particular disability the same as everyone else is not enough to comply with the law. Hence, when faced with such scenarios, prior to taking any precipitative action, employers need to establish whether (1) the long-term absentee has a disability, (2) disability is causing the absence, (3) prognosis is that the employee will/will not return to work and (4) provision of any special treatment or facilities can be provided that would address the attendance problem.

Redundancy

Dismissals on the grounds of redundancy usually constitute fair dismissals. Accordingly, dismissal attributed to the employer ceasing business, reducing workforce size or no longer requiring the employee's kind of work is not unfair. The onus of proving that a genuine redundancy situation exists resides with the employer and the claimant can question the validity of the redundancy. The employer is precluded from using arbitrary criteria when selecting staff for redundancy, although he/she may successfully plead special reasons for departing from an agreed or traditional procedure. Employers also need to be careful that in carrying out the selection for redundancy, fair procedures are followed (McMahon 2011).

Any Other Substantial Reason

The 'any other substantial reason' heading has been a 'catch all' category and can include issues such as damage to the employer's business or failure to conform to certain behavioural norms during one's private life, as in *Flynn* v. *Sister Mary Anne Power and the Sisters of the Holy Faith (1985)*.

Constructive Dismissal

The term 'constructive dismissal' relates to those cases where the employee terminates their contract on account of the employer's conduct. For example, an employee would be entitled to terminate the contract where the employer's conduct constitutes a significant breach of the contract or in the event of the employer indicating that he/she no longer intends to be bound by one or more of its essential terms, e.g. refusal to pay the employee's wages. The reasonableness of an employee in refusing to accept changes in the terms or conditions of employment will be considered by the EAT in the light of the circumstances and of good industrial relations. However, the onus of proof that there was an act or omission on the employer's part constituting a breach of contract resides with the employee. Case law precedent has led some to conclude that the concept of constructive dismissal is somewhat meaningless, as the relevant criteria to be applied remain unclear (von Prondzynski 1989). What is clear is that each case will turn on its own facts and that a hasty decision to resign on the employee's part, without attempting in some way to resolve the problem, can make it difficult to discharge the onus of proof that is upon them.

Unfair Dismissal Remedies

In 2010 and 2011 the EAT had 2,157 and 2,107 unfair dismissal cases respectively referred to it – the overwhelming majority of which were direct claims. The EAT disposed of 1,599 such claims during 2011, constituting a 32 per cent increase (on 1,210) in 2010 (EAT Annual Report 2011). Notably, the EAT's Annual Report for 2011 points out that during the early years of Ireland's economic recession, the total number of cases referred to it annually had increased three-fold (to a high of 9,458 in 2009) (EAT Annual Report 2011). This peak figure dropped slightly in 2010, with a further (but lesser) drop in 2011. However, this contrasts sharply with the average number of pre-recession annual referrals that had plateaued at around 3,500 (EAT Annual Report 2011). This has impacted significantly on waiting periods for hearings, now running at over seventy-five weeks nationally.

The Act provides for three remedial options in the event of a dismissal being deemed to have been unfair: reinstatement, re-engagement and compensation. Reinstatement enables the employee to resume in the same position on the same contractual terms as those applying prior to the dismissal event. A practical implication of this award is that the dismissal is effectively deemed never to have occurred. Accordingly, the relevant back-pay will be awarded, the employee's seniority maintained and pension rights restored. Furthermore, if there have been any changes in the interim in the terms and conditions of employment that would have been applicable to that employee they must also now be enforced, e.g. pay rise. Reinstatement is only awarded where the employee is adjudged not to have contributed to the dismissal in any way.

Re-engagement entitles the employee to resume in the same or in a reasonably suitable different position, on contractual terms which are deemed reasonable in light of prevailing circumstances. Such awards do not normally date back to the date of dismissal. As a result, though the unfairly dismissed employee's continuity of service is not affected, the period elapsing between the dismissal and the re-engagement effectively constitutes suspension without pay. When deciding between a reinstatement or a re-engagement award, the EAT tends to take account of the extent, if any, to which the employee contributed to the unfair dismissal.

Financial compensation is the most common remedial option. This may be a maximum of 104 weeks' net remuneration (including bonus payments) in respect of the employment from which the employee was dismissed. The size of payment is determined by taking into account the estimated future loss, pension loss and the present loss of remuneration (from the date of dismissal to the date of hearing) incurred by the employee. Earnings since dismissal, where applicable, are deducted and there is an onus on an applicant to seek to mitigate their loss, but social welfare payments are not deducted. An employee incurring no loss can be awarded compensation up to a maximum of four weeks' remuneration.

Compensation awards may be reduced where it is adjudged that the employee contributed to their own dismissal or that the employee failed to take adequate steps to secure alternative employment following dismissal. In 2011 the EAT awarded compensation amounting to €6,100,173 in 338 cases – yielding an average compensation award of €18,048 (compared with €16,064 in 2010). Reinstatement was ordered in six cases and re-engagement was ordered in seven cases (compared with six and three respectively in 2010).

The EAT selects whichever remedy it deems appropriate in the particular circumstances. Although the EAT elicits the views of the parties to the case, it may still choose to overlook same and issue a different remedy than that preferred. According to Madden and Kerr (1996: 456) the factors which appear to drive this decision are:

> … the poor nature of the relationship between the parties, the fact that the employee has made serious allegations about the employer, the fact that the employee is not fit to return to work, [and] the fact that changes in the work situation means that no suitable job is available.

Where the EAT issues a reinstatement or re-engagement award, it would appear to assume that the relationship between the parties is not beyond repair. However, Fennell and Lynch's (1993) review indicates that re-employment is ordered where the employer acted extremely badly or the claimant is in great hardship.

Unfair Dismissals Acts 1977–2007 in Perspective

While employer organisations have chided the alleged impact on job creation of such legislative impositions, this allegation is strongly contested (Department of Labour 1986b). Some even argue that the dismissal enactments have had major beneficial consequences for the conduct of industrial relations in the country. According to Murphy (1989: 251):

> The Act has been a considerable success and has contributed to more effective management in notoriously problematic areas of management decision making … in many areas of personnel administration and disciplinary control … [it] has strengthened collective bargaining at workplace level by creating a closer harmony between employer and trade union views of what constitutes a fair dismissal.

Browne (1994) paints a less optimistic view of the legislation, with a number of negative findings for trade unions and workers emerging from her empirical research. She found an association between occupational status and success, whereupon 'claimants from higher occupational grades have a greater success rate at the EAT than claimants from lower occupational grades' (Browne 1994: 195). Unions, she found, coped poorly with the legalism of the EAT, while employers 'put trust and faith behind the law' (Browne 1994). Workers taking cases were also at a significant disadvantage because of the costs of legal representation and the advantages this conferred on employers. Browne (1994:

204) also argues that the juridification of the employment relationship, inherent in this process, has 'individualised conflict, marginalised collective bargaining and made the role of the shop steward less relevant than previously'.

THE EMPLOYMENT APPEALS TRIBUNAL (EAT)

The EAT is the main institution for adjudicating on individual employment law. It was initially established under section 39 of the Redundancy Payments Act 1967 as the Redundancy Appeals Tribunal to adjudicate on claims for statutory redundancy payment. The Minimum Notice and Terms of Employment Act 1973 extended the Tribunal's functions to adjudicating on claims for statutory minimum notice. The Tribunal was re-titled the EAT under the terms of the Unfair Dismissals Act 1977. Since then the EAT has been given further responsibility for adjudicating on a wide range of employment legislation (albeit not cases under equality legislation). The EAT also hears appeals from the decisions of Rights Commissioners under various individual employment legislative provisions.

EAT Usage, Case Processing and Operations

The number of cases referred to the EAT has varied over time. During the early years of the economic recession the number of cases referred to the EAT annually increased three-fold (to a peak of 9,458 in 2009). This figure dropped slightly to 8,778 in 2010 and there was a further but lesser drop to 8,458 in 2011. In stark comparison, only 1,410 referrals were made in 1978, while the average number of annual referrals before the recession had plateaued at around 3,500. The increase may also be explained by the increased range of legislation enacted, trends in the labour market and a more litigious workforce – since more people interact with employment relations issues as 'legal subjects' (i.e. individuals) as opposed to being in membership of a collective institution (e.g. a trade union) (Sheehan 2008a). Applications to the EAT are made on a Workplace Relations Complaints Form. In presenting a case a party may make an opening statement, call witnesses, cross-examine any witnesses called by any other party, give evidence and address the EAT at the close of the evidence. Cases are usually held in public. Each division of the EAT is separately constituted and determinations are not subject to precedents set in other divisions. However, they are subject to precedents on points of law established in higher courts. The decision of the EAT (called a 'determination') can be given at the close of the hearing but more usually it is issued some time later in written form. Appeals against EAT determinations are heard by either the Circuit Court or the High Court, depending on the legislation involved. For example, in the case of the Unfair Dismissals Acts 1977–2007 appeals may be made to the Circuit Court within six weeks, where such cases are heard *de novo* (i.e. with a full re-hearing). In 2011 approximately 128 such cases were appealed to the Circuit Court. Of these, forty were upheld, nine adjourned, nineteen struck out, three withdrawn and fifty-seven were pending (no information was available in respect of the remaining cases).

Appeals in relation to the other Acts (such as redundancy, protection of employees, minimum notice and part-time workers) are referred to the High Court. In these cases, the EAT is the final arbiter of the 'facts of the case', as appeals are only on a 'point of law'. In 2010 and 2011 only three and four such cases respectively were lodged with the High Court. Should an employer fail to carry out the terms of a determination, proceedings may be taken by the Minister for Jobs, Enterprise and Innovation to the Circuit Court in order to ensure compliance. In principle the decisions of the EAT are legally binding on an employer – subject, of course, to an appeal option.

In contrast with the Labour Court, the EAT is more legalistic in its composition and operation. The chairman of the EAT must, under statute, be a barrister of seven years' standing and (though not a requirement) the vice-chairmen tend to be legal practitioners. The EAT consists of a chairman, forty-six vice-chairmen and a panel of eighty-two other members: forty-one nominated by the ICTU and forty-one by organisations representative of employers. The EAT operates in divisions consisting of a chairperson or vice-chairperson and one member from the trade union and employer sides. Forde (1991: 23) notes that EAT proceedings are subject to the principles of 'constitutional' or 'natural justice' and in the past it has come under criticism for being excessively legalistic. Fennell and Lynch (1993: 309) describe the EAT's approach as 'legalistic, individualistic, rights based, heavily reliant on common law notions of fair procedure and assessment of reasonableness'.

The EAT attempts to reduce the degree of legalism and has drawn attention to the fact that it was introduced to 'provide a speedy, and relatively informal means for the resolution of disputes' and though 'empowered to take evidence on oath' the Tribunal endeavours to limit such usage (Moffatt 2006). However, whether this attempted minimisation of legalism is being realised is dubious. Indeed, Sheehan's (2008a: 25) research review noted the strong presence of the legal profession in the EAT process and the increasing formality of proceedings, as the Tribunal tends to act 'judicially' and 'scrupulously' in accord with the legislation. In 2011, 3,068 employees had representation (378 by trade unions, 1,998 by legal representatives and 692 by other persons) under the various enactments or combination thereof, compared with 2,524 employers (121 by employer associations, 1,729 by legal representatives and 674 by other persons). This illustrates the continued dominance of EAT hearings by the legal profession.

Despite the pressures towards greater legalism, the EAT's hearings are not adjudged to be a 'court of law' in the strictest sense – though from the users' perspective the Tribunal is regarded as the most legalistic and formal of all the public employment dispute resolution agencies. Sheehan (2008a: 26) also notes in his research review that the EAT is worthy of praise for the 'highly proficient and fair manner' in which it goes about its business. His research review also highlights the fact that 56 per cent of claims before the Tribunal fail, i.e. 44 per cent were successful – with an average award of €7,110. However, there is considerable variation in this ratio under the various Acts. For example, those taken under the 'dismissal' heading are most likely to succeed (82 per cent of cases that claimed unfair dismissal on the ground of improper procedure succeed). In contrast, 84.4 per cent of cases taken under the Organisation of Working Time Act 1997 failed.

EMPLOYMENT EQUALITY AND THE LAW

As with many of the legislative initiatives pertaining to employment matters, the introduction of equality legislation was primarily prompted by Ireland's membership of the European Community (EC) and the necessity to comply with Community Directives. Initial equality legislation was focused largely on gender. The Anti-Discrimination (Pay) Act 1974 and the Employment Equality Act 1977 were passed to implement the equal pay and equal treatment directives respectively. The subsequent consolidation of these two measures into one Act – the Employment Equality Act 1998 – has significantly altered and broadened the law in this area. Likewise, the Maternity (Protection of Employees) Act 1981 gave way to the Maternity Protection Act 1994 in order to give effect to the so-called 'Pregnant Workers' Directive of 1992.

Equal Pay and Employment Equality

The Employment Equality Acts 1998–2004 enable a claim to be made where the complainant is alleging he/she is performing equal work but is being paid less on grounds of sex, marital status, family status, sexual orientation, religion, age, disability, race or membership of the Travelling community (i.e. the 'nine grounds'). For the purposes of an equal pay claim, pay is interpreted as basic wages together with all direct and indirect financial benefits and incentives (excluding pension benefits). The person or persons claiming – group claims are common – must compare themselves with an actual comparator. The complainant must also satisfy certain conditions. He/she must be:

- working under a contract of service;
- working for the same or an associated employer; and
- performing 'like work' with the comparator, i.e. either (a) his/her work is identical, (b) job differences are insignificant in relation to the job as a whole or (c) his/her work is 'equal in value' in terms of criteria such as responsibility, skill, physical or mental effort.

If the complainant can establish these requirements, the onus shifts to the employer to show that there are grounds other than gender (or any of the aforementioned grounds) for the difference in the respective rates of pay. Standard grounds in this respect include qualifications, experience, service or grading.

The Employment Equality Acts 1998 and 2004 are also designed to protect against discrimination (on the grounds specified above) in relation to access to employment; terms and conditions of employment; access to promotion and training schemes, benefits, facilities and services; and treatment in relation to dismissal. They also make it unlawful to victimise an employee for exercising his/her rights under the legislation. Unlawful discrimination can take place on a direct or indirect basis. Direct discrimination occurs where a person is treated less favourably than a person with or without the relevant characteristic (gender, age, disability, etc.) is (or would be) treated in similar circumstances. For example, claims in relation to discrimination at the recruitment and selection stage are common and often revolve around alleged discriminatory questions or treatment at interview, e.g. asking only women questions in relation to childminding responsibilities (McMahon 2001).

The definitions of indirect discrimination were reshaped in the 1998 Act to take into account the decision of the Supreme Court in the *Nathan* v. *Bailey Gibson Ltd* case and European Union (EU) definitions (Moffatt 2006). Basically, indirect discrimination involves an apparently neutral practice or requirement that effectively serves to discriminate against a particular category because fewer of its members are able to comply with it. The practice or requirement must not be objectively justifiable for the employment in question. For example, a minimum height requirement for a job where height was not a relevant factor might operate to indirectly discriminate against women as a group as opposed to men.

Redress Routes

Under the 1998 Act, the Equality Authority is charged with providing information on the legislation and advising potential complainants, as well as taking proceedings on someone's behalf where it is not reasonable to expect the person in question to take a case themselves. It is also empowered to conduct enquiries and to issue non-discrimination notices and, ultimately, to apply for an injunction in the Circuit or High Court to prevent discrimination continuing. Furthermore, the Authority can provide legal assistance to claimants taking cases under the Employment Equality Acts where such cases are considered to be of strategic importance. In 2011 the government announced plans to merge the Equality Authority with the Human Rights Commission and form the Human Rights and Equality Commission.

Under the provisions of the 1998 enactment, Equality Officers were transferred from the Labour Relations Commission to the Office of the Director of Equality Investigations (ODEI), which is now called the Equality Tribunal. The Director of Equality Investigations may award up to three years' arrears of equal pay or compensation of up to 104 weeks' remuneration in equal treatment cases (or €12,700 where the claimant was not in receipt of remuneration). The Labour Court has the same powers, with an additional facility to order reinstatement or re-engagement (with or without compensation) in dismissal cases. Potential appeals lie from the Director or Equality Tribunal to the Labour Court, and from there to the Circuit Court. The Circuit Court may also enforce decisions of the Director or the Labour Court and points of law may be referred to the High Court. Cases may be referred to the Equality Tribunal within six months of the act of alleged discrimination occurring.

The Equality Tribunal notes that a case cannot be referred to it if a court has begun hearing a case by the complainant regarding the same issue. Conversely, a complainant who has referred a case to the Equality Tribunal cannot recover damages through court proceedings regarding the same issue once the Tribunal has begun an investigation of their complaint or if it has been settled by mediation. The Equality Officers and the Labour Court remain in their existing roles under the 1998 enactment.

Before the 2004 Act, all claims (except those taken directly to the Circuit Court) began at the Equality Tribunal. This excluded *dismissal* cases, which were heard by the

Labour Court at first instance. In cases of gender discrimination only, a claimant can refer the matter directly to the Circuit Court. The 2004 Act amendments provide for all cases, including dismissals, to commence before the Equality Tribunal, with an appeal for a full rehearing to the Labour Court, subject to the gender provision. That is, gender-based complaints or claims in relation to the infringement of the equal pay or equal treatment directives may be brought directly to the Circuit Court.

The Process of Referring an Equality Case

When investigating a case, the Tribunal's Equality Officer considers the evidence presented by the parties and consequently issues a written decision, which must be published. Should discrimination be found to have taken place, the Equality Officer can make an order for redress. This can include compensation, equal pay, arrears for equal pay, equal treatment or an order for a particular course of action to be taken. The decisions are binding and enforceable. Decisions of cases taken under the Employment Equality Acts may be appealed to the Labour Court within forty-two days. The Labour Court dealt with eighty-eight and seventy-four such referrals in 2010 and 2009 respectively (2012, www.labourcourt.ie). When the Equality Tribunal was established there were only about 100 claims (e.g. in 2000) and virtually all concerned gender and work. Since then, there has been a significant rise (to 906 and 821 overall referrals in 2009 and 2010 respectively) in the Tribunal's workload (Equality Tribunal Annual Report 2010). In 2010 these claims arose under all of the aforementioned nine grounds – with race, multiple grounds, disability, age and gender claims predominant. Amounts totalling over €1 million (excluding equal pay and pay arrears, etc.) were awarded in compensation where discrimination was found, constituting an average award of €17,775.

Mediation

An alternative to investigation is mediation. The 1998 enactment provides for the establishment of a mediation service staffed by Equality Mediation Officers (or mediators). It also provides that: 'if at any time after a case has been referred to the Director … it appears to the Director that the case is one which could be resolved by mediation, the Director shall refer the case for mediation to an equality mediation officer'. Hence, if the Director of Equality Investigations feels a case could be resolved by mediation, they can request the parties involved to consider using it. It is notable that mediation cannot take place if either party objects. Alternatively, the Employment Equality Act allows the Labour Court to either conduct mediation itself (in cases referred to it) or to refer a case to the Director for mediation.

If an agreement is reached at the end of the mediation process, the Mediation Officer draws up the terms of the agreement. Once signed by the parties, these terms become legally binding and may be enforced through the Circuit Court. Should a case remain unresolved after mediation, the complainant may resubmit the complaint to the Director for investigation. The option of mediation appears to have a number of advantages, including that of being considerably quicker than an investigation before an Equality

Officer. Since developing the service in 2000, it is now well established, with about one-quarter of the Tribunal's cases going to mediation and the majority of these concluding in agreement (sixty-four equality-related cases reached agreement via the mediation service in 2010 and thirty-six further cases were closed at mediation) (Equality Tribunal Annual Report 2010: 8). A 2009 customer survey gave an overwhelming endorsement to the Tribunal's mediation service, indicating that it does make a difference and its decisions are valued 'as being clear and reasoned and bringing the possibility of closure to a dispute' (Equality Tribunal Annual Report 2009: 4) During 2010 the Tribunal again received positive feedback from clients, with satisfaction ratings rising by 5 per cent on average over the 2004 results. Overall almost 91 per cent of respondents expressed satisfaction with the mediation service, while 92 per cent expressed satisfaction with the mediator(s), noting that they had shown fairness to both sides and helped create a calm atmosphere enabling the mediation process (Equality Tribunal Mediation Review 2010: 3).

MATERNITY LAW

Under the Maternity Protection Acts 1994–2004 female employees are entitled to a period of paid maternity leave of at least eighteen weeks, with an additional right to eight weeks' further unpaid leave. The employer concerned must be notified in writing at least four weeks prior to the expected 'confinement' and a medical certificate establishing the fact of pregnancy must be supplied. In addition to this leave period, there is a right to time off – without loss of pay – for antenatal and postnatal medical visits. This entitlement is dependent on the provision of both medical evidence of pregnancy and the appropriate notification to the employer concerned. There is no qualifying service or minimum weekly working hours requirement to secure the right. The employee can choose the exact dates of the maternity leave but the period should cover the four weeks prior to and post confinement. While on paid maternity leave, the employee's employment rights are preserved. She is entitled to return to her job after the birth, provided she notifies the employer of her intentions in writing at least four working weeks in advance of the envisaged date of return. The EAT or a Rights Commissioner may extend the time for giving the notification where there are 'reasonable grounds' for the failure or delay in providing it. The 1994 Act also introduced a potential right to 'health and safety leave' from work for pregnant workers, workers who are breastfeeding or who have recently given birth. In addition, if a doctor certifies that night work is unsuitable and the worker cannot be moved to day work, she may become entitled to such leave. Disputes as to leave entitlements are heard by a Rights Commissioner with an appeal to the EAT. There were six cases referred to the EAT in both 2009 and 2010 and two in 2011 under the maternity legislation.

HEALTH AND SAFETY AT WORK

Over the past thirty years, the subject of health and safety has shot up the list of HRM priorities in Ireland. This prioritisation has been propelled by the enactment of comprehensive and detailed health and safety legislation and extensively supplemented by case law precedents. Related to these facts is the reality that many Irish employers have awoken to the priority now accorded health and safety matters as a result of a series of court awards in the area (Butler 2007). This dimension has become even more pronounced since 2004, with the establishment of the Personal Injuries Assessment Board (PIAB), whose role includes the assessment of compensation due to an injured person where those injuries arise from workplace accidents.

Prior to the establishment of the PIAB, employees suffering personal injuries could issue proceedings (depending on the potential size of the claim) in the District Court, Circuit Court or High Court. Successful plaintiffs were awarded the majority (if not all) costs. In an attempt to reduce such costs (and employers' premium payments), the insurance industry and employers sought reform of the system and this culminated in the establishment of the PIAB. Garavan (2002) claims that with the eventual recognition of the immensity of such costs to employers – and the prospect of reduced costs through safer and healthier work environments and practices – it was apparent that more proactive safety management practices were emerging in many Irish workplaces. In this regard, the enactment of the Safety, Health and Welfare at Work Act 1989 was also relevant. However, in 2007, 2008, 2009 and 2010 the number of fatal injuries at work stood at sixty-seven, fifty-seven, forty-three and forty-eight respectively. Of course, these figures do not capture a host of other relevant considerations, such as accidents and dangerous occurrences at work; health and safety-related absenteeism; and the prevalence of bullying, harassment, victimisation and stress at the workplace. Thus, while health and safety may have more priority, it remains problematic.

Common and Statute Law

Under common law, the Irish courts have decided that employers are obliged to exercise reasonable care towards employees in relation to health and safety matters. The implications of common law are that employers must:

- provide a safe system of work;
- ensure the provision of competent fellow workers;
- provide safety equipment and effective supervision; and
- provide a safe place of work.

The provision of a safe system of work obliges the employer to show that the system provided is at least in accord with the general practice of that trade. Accordingly, an employer would not be responsible solely because an accident occurred in the course of the job; some element of negligence has to be involved. The failure to employ competent fellow workers (including subordinates and supervisors) may, but rarely does, constitute the basis of a claim. Nevertheless, the employer may be found liable for the careless action of one employee which causes injury to another employee (i.e. vicarious liability). The common law obligation to provide proper safety equipment (for the purpose of avoiding staff exposure to risk and injury) includes a requirement that management take reasonable steps (up to and including disciplinary action) to ensure the use of that equipment.

The provision of a safe place of work requires that the workplace be organised in the interests of health and safety. This obligation also extends to a customer's premises. Consequently, if workers are injured while working on a customer's premises they may successfully claim against their own employer.

In recent years, the employer's duty to provide a safe workplace (hitherto confined to reducing risks to the physical health of the employee) has been extended to one's psychological wellbeing. Several court decisions have established the obligation on employers to prevent foreseeable risk from stress in work and numerous successful claims have also been brought in relation to bullying and harassment at work (McMahon 2009a). Notably, the aforementioned Employment Equality Acts 1998–2004 provide a redress route for those scenarios where harassment (under one or more of the nine grounds) is alleged.

The main legislation in this area is the Safety, Health and Welfare at Work Act 2005, which repealed and replaced the aforementioned Safety, Health and Welfare at Work Act 1989. Almost all of the specific health and safety laws that apply generally to all employments are contained in the Safety, Health and Welfare at Work (General Application) Regulations 2007. The 2005 enactment applies to all employers, employees (including fixed-term and temporary employees) and self-employed people at work. The Act sets out the rights and obligations of both employers and employees and (most consequentially) provides for substantial fines and penalties for breaches of the health and safety legislation. Related to this, it specifies the employer's duties and how they can maintain appropriate levels of health and safety through general protective and preventative techniques. These techniques include 'risk assessments', 'safety statements', employing a 'competent person' in the area, safety representatives, consultation obligations, protection for employees and safety representatives against penalisation (or victimisation), and administrative obligations. The Act also outlines the process for developing regulations, guidance and codes of practice and describes the role and function of the Health and Safety Authority (HSA), which serves as the national statutory body with responsibility for enforcing the law, promoting and encouraging accident prevention and providing information and advice to all relevant parties. The enactment also outlines various offences that may arise and their corresponding penalties, setting down the maximum fine for such offences and the potential personal liability of an organisation's directors and senior executives. The Act is also appended by several *schedules* that detail miscellaneous information (including the General Principles of Prevention), all of which are legally enforceable.

The profile of the topic has also been raised as a result of the work of the Health and Safety Authority (HSA). In 2010 it conducted a total of 16,714 inspections and investigations and in 9 per cent of inspections (where employers were unwilling to meet the legal requirements), formal enforcement actions to ensure compliance were taken (2012, www.hsa.ie). In the same year, twenty-seven prosecutions were completed successfully and a further twenty-three files were sent to the Director of

Public Prosecutions (DPP) for direction, while the Authority issued 914 'Improvement Notices' (for eliminating identified risks) and 599 'Prohibition Notices' (barring the usage of certain equipment or processes).

ORGANISATION OF WORKING TIME

As a result of the necessity to implement an EU measure – the Working Time Directive – the area of working hours and holidays is codified in one piece of legislation: the Organisation of Working Time Act 1997. Some of its salient features provide for:

- maximum average working week of forty-eight hours, over a reference period of four, six or twelve months, depending on the category of worker;
- minimum rest breaks of fifteen minutes per 4.5 hours worked and thirty minutes per six hours worked;
- minimum rest period of eleven consecutive hours per twenty-four hours;
- minimum weekly consecutive rest period of a total of thirty-five hours (twenty-four hours plus eleven hours' daily rest) in seven days; or a total of fifty-nine hours (forty-eight hours plus eleven hours' daily rest) in fourteen days;
- minimum annual leave entitlements of four weeks for full-time workers and 8 per cent of hours worked in the case of part-time or casual employees;
- entitlement to a premium payment or paid time off in lieu for Sunday work (JLCs no longer set Sunday premium rates; a new code of practice on Sunday working is being prepared by the LRC);
- entitlement to a minimum payment should a worker be engaged on a zero-hour contract and not be provided with any or the requisite amount of work; and
- special restrictions on hours worked at night, in particular night work involving particular hazards.

Complaints under this Act are made to a Rights Commissioner, with a right of appeal to the Labour Court. The Labour Court dealt with 279 and 289 such cases in 2010 and 2009 respectively (Labour Court Annual Reports 2009, 2010).

Table 6.1
Summary of Other Select Employment Legislation in Ireland

Act	Scope
Adoptive Leave Acts 1995–2005	Rights to leave from work in the event of adoption
Data Protection Acts 1988–2003	Access to and accuracy of (personal) automated/computer and manual/paper files
Parental Leave Acts 1998–2006	Rights to leave from work for both parents from the birth or adoption of a child. Also provides for force majeure leave where, for urgent family reasons, the immediate presence of the employee is indispensible owing to an injury or illness of a close family member.
National Minimum Wage Act 2000	Introduces a minimum wage depending on age and experience of employee
Carer's Leave Act 2001	Rights to leave from work to care for a person in need of full-time care and attention
EU Directive on Temporary Agency Work 2008/104/EC	Equal treatment of agency workers vis-à-vis regular workers

Young People at Work

The Protection of Young Persons (Employment) Act 1996 prohibits the employment of children younger than sixteen years of age. However, a child over fourteen years of age may be permitted to do light, non-industrial work during school holidays provided it is not harmful to health, development or schooling. The Act sets limits to the working hours of young people and provides for minimum rest intervals and the prohibition of night work. There is minimal activity at the EAT under this Act, with only one appeal (against a Rights Commissioner recommendation) to the EAT over the period 2008 to 2011.

Minimum Notice Law

In the absence of a specific term in the contract of employment dealing with the issue of notice, the Minimum Notice and Terms of Employment Acts 1973–2005 entitle employees to a minimum period (or to accept pay in lieu) of notice prior to dismissal. Employees with between thirteen weeks' and two years' continuous service are entitled to one week's notice; thereafter, entitlements increase on a gradual basis up to a maximum notice of eight weeks where an employee has service of fifteen or more years. An employer is also entitled to at least one week's notice from an employee with thirteen or more weeks' service. There is considerable activity under this Act, with 2,118 and 2,070 such cases referred to the EAT under this legislation in 2010 and 2011 respectively (EAT Annual Reports 2010, 2011).

TERMS OF EMPLOYMENT

Under the Terms of Employment (Information) Acts 1994–2001 an employer is obliged to furnish any employee who has one month's continuous service with a written statement outlining their terms of employment. There is a direct method of complaint for an aggrieved employee to a Rights Commissioner. The information required in the statement includes:

- names of employer and employee and the address of the employer in the state;
- the place of work and the employee's job title and nature of work;
- the date of commencement of employment;
- details of pay, including overtime, commission and bonus and the methods of calculating them;
- whether pay is to be weekly, monthly or otherwise;
- conditions about hours of work, including details of breaks and provision in relation to overtime and holiday entitlements;
- sick pay arrangements and pension schemes, if any; and
- periods of notice or, if the contract of employment is for a fixed time, the date when the contract expires.

There were 277 and 264 such cases referred to the EAT under this legislation in 2009 and 2010 respectively (EAT Annual Report 2009, 2010).

WAGE PAYMENT LAW

Under the Payment of Wages Act 1991, seven legal wage-payment methods are provided for, including payment by cheque, bank draft, credit transfer or similar method, postal order and cash. The circumstances in which deductions, in particular those relating to acts or omissions of the employee, can legally be made from wages and payments are specified in the enactment. Effectively, deductions must be provided for in the contract (or other written form), the employee must be made aware in advance that a deduction will be made and the deduction must be reasonable in relation to the employee's wages. In the event of a dispute, the initial claim is made to a Rights Commissioner with a right of appeal to the Tribunal. A total of 316 and 478 cases were referred to the Tribunal under this enactment in 2010 and 2011 respectively (EAT Annual Report 2010, 2011).

PART-TIME AND FIXED-TERM LAW

Arising from the growth of the secondary labour market and the peripheral workforce, protective legislation for part-time workers came into operation in 1991. This was replaced by the Protection of Employees (Part-time Work) Act 2001, which was introduced as a result of the EU Framework Directive on Part-time Work. This extended the protection of employment legislation to all part-time workers regardless of the number of hours worked per week. It entitles part-time workers to *pro rata* treatment with comparable full-time colleagues in relation to conditions of employment such as pay and annual leave. Complaints under this Act are made to a Rights Commissioner with a right of appeal to the Labour Court. The Labour Court dealt with ten and seven referrals under the Act in 2010 and 2009 respectively (Labour Court Annual Report 2009, 2010). A similar directive on the rights of fixed-term contract workers was enacted via the Protection of Employees (Fixed-term Work) Act 2003, which protects fixed-term employees by ensuring that they cannot be treated less favourably than comparable permanent workers and that employers cannot continually renew fixed-term contracts. The Labour Court dealt with forty-five and thirty-three referrals under the Act in 2010 and 2009 respectively (Labour Court Annual Report 2009, 2010).

PENSIONS PROVISIONS

Under the Pensions Acts 1990–2009 a range of provisions were made, including:

- the establishment of a Pensions Board to monitor and supervise the new requirements under the Act;
- the compulsory preservation of pension entitlements for employees who change employments;
- the introduction of a minimum funding standard for certain funded schemes;
- arrangements for the disclosure of information to scheme members;
- clarification of the duties and responsibilities of scheme trustees; and
- implementation of the principle of equal treatment for men and women in occupational benefit schemes.

The Pensions (Amendment) Act 2002 provides for the introduction of a framework for Personal Retirement Savings Accounts (PRSAs) and their associated tax reliefs and arrangements and a Pensions Ombudsman was established under its remit. In 2011 two directors of a construction firm were jailed for pension offences – the first time employers had ever been imprisoned for such offences in Ireland. At the same time, the Irish Pensions Board revealed that it was investigating 192 employers in the sector on suspicion of failing to pay over pension contributions deducted from employees (see www.rte.ie/news/2011/0927/pensions-business.html).

DATA PROTECTION LAW

The Data Protection Acts 1988–2003 entitle individuals to establish the existence of automated and manual/paper-based personal data, to have access to such data in relation to them and to have inaccurate data rectified or erased. The Acts also oblige the data controller (i.e. the organisation that uses such personal data) to adhere to a number of obligations associated with the accuracy, relevance and use of such data. Furthermore, a Data Protection Commissioner is provided with a legal basis for intervening where an individual complains that the principles have not been observed. The relevant principles provided for in the Acts are that:

- the data controller fairly obtains and processes the data;
- the data be factually accurate and, where necessary, up to date;
- the data is kept for one or more specified and lawful purposes;
- the data shall not be used or disclosed in any manner incompatible with the specified and lawful purposes;
- the data retained be attainable, relevant and not excessive in relation to the specified and lawful purposes;
- the personal data shall not be kept for longer than is necessary for the specified and lawful purposes; and
- appropriate security measures should be taken by data controllers and processors against unauthorised access to or attention, disclosure or destruction of the data, and against its accidental destruction or loss.

Furthermore, under the 1998 Freedom of Information Act, one has the right of access to official records held by government departments or other specified public bodies. This includes the right to have personal information held corrected or updated and the right to be given reasons for decisions taken by public bodies that affect one. This legislative initiative has been deployed by job applicants and interviewees to gain access to the reasons for their failure either to be shortlisted or successful at interview (McMahon 2001).

REDUNDANCY PAYMENTS LEGISLATION

The Redundancy Payments Acts 1967–2007 apply to workers with at least 104 weeks' continuous service and who have not reached retirement age. Under the Redundancy Acts, employees are entitled to two weeks' pay per year of service plus one week's lump sum. The calculation of a week's pay is subject to a statutory ceiling of €600. In addition to statutory redundancy entitlements, redundancy pay may be enhanced through collective or individual bargaining arrangements. There are a large number of disputes under this legislation. The EAT dealt with 2,951 and 2,598 referrals under this legislation in 2010 and 2011 respectively (EAT Annual Reports 2010, 2011).

PROTECTION OF EMPLOYMENT ACTS 1977–2007

Where collective redundancies arise, the provisions of the Protection of Employment Acts 1977–2007 apply. These require the employer to supply the employees' representatives with specific information regarding the proposed redundancies and to consult with those representatives at least thirty days before the first dismissal takes place in order to see if they can be lessened or avoided. Collective redundancies are defined as dismissals involving a certain number of employees (depending on the total number of employees) in any period of thirty consecutive days. The employer is also obliged to advise the Minister at least thirty days in advance of the first dismissal. Under this legislation, an offence may be prosecuted by the relevant Minister. There was only one such case before the Labour Court over the period 2009 to 2010, where the Minister sought an opinion on collective redundancies.

PROTECTION OF EMPLOYEES (EMPLOYERS' INSOLVENCY) ACTS 1984–2004

The Protection of Employees (Employers' Insolvency) Acts 1984–2004 protect certain outstanding entitlements relating to employees' pay in the event of their employers becoming insolvent. Subject to certain limits and conditions, monies due to employees in a range of situations may be paid by the Department of Social Protection out of the Social Insurance Fund. These can include:

- arrears of pay (including arrears of pay due under an Employment Regulation Order);
- holiday and sick pay;
- entitlements under the minimum notice and terms of employment, employment equality and unfair dismissals legislation; and
- court orders in respect of wages, holiday pay or damages at common law for wrongful dismissal.

The Insolvency Payments Scheme also protects employees' outstanding contributions to occupational pension schemes, which an employer may have deducted from wages but not paid into the schemes. Unpaid contributions to an occupational pension scheme due from the employer may also be paid from the Social Insurance Fund, subject to certain limits. The scheme applies to outstanding pension contributions for up to a year prior to the date of insolvency. The EAT dealt with eleven and five referrals under this legislation in 2009 and 2010 respectively (EAT Annual Reports 2009, 2010).

TRANSFER OF UNDERTAKINGS REGULATIONS

The European Communities (Protection of Employees on Transfer of Undertakings) Regulations 2003 are designed to protect employees' jobs in the event of a change in their employer's identity, where the business in question resumes its activities having been sold as a going concern. Subject to the employer's right to effect redundancies for economic, technical or organisational reasons involving changes in the workforce, employees are entitled to continue working under the same terms of employment with service and contractual rights maintained. Employee pension rights – aside from those provided for by social welfare legislation – do not transfer to the new employment. However, where there is a pension scheme in operation in the original employer's business at the time of the transfer, the legislation provides that:

- if the scheme is an occupational pension scheme covered by the Pension Acts, then the protections given by that legislation apply; and
- in the case of other pension schemes, the new employer must ensure that rights are protected.

Both the outgoing and incoming employers are also obliged to keep employees informed of developments. An employee whose rights are infringed under the legislation, resulting in dismissal, may bring an unfair dismissal claim to a Rights Commissioner or the EAT. A total of forty-four and twenty-one cases were referred to the Tribunal under this enactment in 2011 and 2010 respectively (EAT Annual Reports 2010, 2011).

INSTITUTIONAL INITIATIVES AND REVISIONS

Of particular relevance to the matter of (compliance with) employment legislation, the National Employment Rights Authority (NERA) was established under the Social Partnership Agreement 'Towards 2016'. Its role is to achieve a national culture of employment rights compliance, which it endeavours to do via the provision of information to employees and employers, monitoring employment conditions through its inspection services and enforcing compliance and seeking redress. In 2010 NERA concluded 7,164 workplace inspections (compared with 8,859 in 2009). It focuses particularly on matters of compliance in respect of the national minimum wage, the Protection of Young Persons and Employment Permit enactments, together with adherence to the provisions of prevailing Employment Regulation Orders and Registered Employment Agreements (http://www.employmentrights.ie/en/). NERA and other state dispute resolution bodies, including the Rights Commissioners, EAT and the Equality Tribunal, are undergoing a process of reform (see Chapter 5).

CONCLUDING COMMENTS

Due to advances in the labour law arena, the relationship between employer and employee has been transformed over the last forty years in the Republic of Ireland. Almost every facet of the employment relationship (from recruitment to retirement) is now regulated to some extent by statute law. Such law, together with the decisions of the courts and tribunals, impacts on all aspects of the workplace relationship. Case precedents surface on an ongoing basis from a wide range of state-provided dispute resolution agencies, including the Labour Court, the LRC, the Equality Tribunal and the EAT, as well as the ordinary civil courts. This chapter gives students an introduction to the principal areas of employment law affecting Ireland's workplace – with a summary of other select employment legislation included in Table 6.1 – as it attempts to explain one of the most consequential and complicated areas that both parties must deal with, i.e. their obligations and entitlements under employment law.

CHAPTER 7

Collective and Individual Workplace Procedures

INTRODUCTION

This chapter examines the regulation of industrial relations at the workplace. Such regulation is extensively governed by procedures either jointly agreed between union and management or unilaterally determined normally by management. The procedural regulation of workplace relations has its genesis in collective bargaining, which originated in the second half of the nineteenth century with the purpose of regulating relations between unions, their members and employers. Its aim was to introduce norms in order to limit disputes. As Webb and Webb (1897) pointed out, it was part of union efforts to provide a 'common rule' promoting equitable treatment of workers. These collective procedures have also influenced procedural regulation in non-union companies, notably in the areas of discipline and grievance. Apart from their collective origins, there are two other influences on the development of workplace procedures. These are the perspectives offered by organisational psychologists/organisational behaviourists and, most importantly, the growth in legal regulation from the 1970s onwards. This chapter explores the nature of collective agreements, the arrangements for procedural regulation at the workplace, practical prescriptions for dealing with individual workplace disputes and the skills necessary to effectively deal with such issues.

THE NATURE OF COLLECTIVE AGREEMENTS

Collective agreements are commonly used to regulate relations in unionised companies; they are the obvious and standard outcome of a collective bargaining process. Indeed, the International Labour Organization (ILO) deems collective bargaining 'to be the activity or process leading up to the conclusion of a collective agreement' (Gernigon *et al.* 2000). Collective agreements arose in order to regulate relationships between management and unions and they have a long history dating back to the late nineteenth century (Pelling 1976). The contents of collective agreements can be divided into *substantive* and *procedural* terms. Substantive terms are concerned with terms and conditions of employment. Examples of substantive terms include wage rates, overtime and shift work rates, hours of work, holiday entitlements and pension arrangements. In contrast, procedural terms lay down the rules for regulating the relationship between the parties and how substantive terms are agreed and changed. Examples of procedural terms are union recognition and negotiating rights, management's right to manage and the ways in which employees can contest management decisions. Procedural terms are normally contained in an overarching agreement – a procedure agreement (or procedural agreement).

Procedure agreements differ in their contents across organisations. Some procedure agreements are short and concise, while others are long and detailed. Agreements may be quite general, or technical and specific (even quasi legalistic) in terms of how they are drafted and worded. The content of procedure agreements also varies widely, although there are usually common elements. They usually contain initial clauses dealing with union recognition and negotiating rights, the competence of both parties and provisions for dealing with disputes when they arise. In the area of individual disputes, procedure agreements will usually contain specific sections dealing with disciplinary and grievance issues. Nowadays, they may also cover individual issues such as equality, health and safety, and bullying and harassment. However, even in unionised companies these will sometimes be specified in a company rule book.

Disputes procedures are a central part of any procedure agreement. They are most important in collective disputes, but they also cover individual issues. Disputes procedures will invariably contain a peace clause. This will normally specify a requirement for local negotiations and referral to third parties, up to and including the Labour Court (or other specified body), in advance of industrial action by either union or management. Individual disputes often require employees to use internal disciplinary and grievance procedures prior to referral to a third party. They may also include arrangements for workers to provide continued emergency and maintenance services in the event of a strike.

On some occasions a disputes procedure may extend to a no-strike clause. Some no-strike clauses have been inserted in agreements in return for a pay increase and these are designed to last for the duration of the agreement only. In rarer cases, no-strike clauses are designed to be a permanent part of the arrangements between the parties. In such cases some alternative mechanism for the resolution of disputes needs to be specified, e.g. binding arbitration. In the public sector there is provision for arbitration under the public sector conciliation and arbitration schemes. Under a number of such schemes, the government can only refuse to pay an arbitrator's award if it places a motion before the Dáil and that is passed. However, the prohibition on strike action applies only to a minority of public servants covered by these schemes, notably the members of An Garda Síochána.

A key issue in the operation of dispute procedures has been the maintenance or otherwise of the status quo while the dispute is in progress. Pluralist writers have generally considered that the onus is on the side seeking change to maintain the status quo until procedures are exhausted. The principle of maintenance of the status quo has been narrowed by the development of functional flexibility in the 1980s. This requires employees to be flexible between tasks, thereby limiting the range of issues over which a status quo requirement applies. Despite this, observation of the status quo can apply as part of the normal requirement on management in unionised companies to negotiate on change. It is common in collective agreements that individual employees are required to accept change and work under protest while appealing a management instruction. However, there are limits to changes that can be required. Arbitrary alterations to an individual's contract can fall foul of unfair dismissals legislation and, depending on the nature of the change, amount to constructive dismissal (see Chapter 6). The Croke Park Agreement 2010–2014 provides that where employees contest a change in working arrangements covered by the provisions of the agreement, they must operate the change pending the outcome of a binding arbitration procedure (Croke Park Agreement 2010).

Workplace Collective Agreements and the Law

Collective agreements are generally not considered to be legally enforceable. The Commission of Inquiry on Industrial Relations (1981: 214) noted that this reflects the view that collective bargaining – not the law – should be the primary source of regulation in the employment relationship. The main legal reason for the lack of enforceability of collective agreements is that the courts consider they are entered into 'without an intention to create legal relations'. A further reason for the general lack of legal enforceability is that neither a trade union nor a union official are normally considered to have a right 'agency' to conclude agreements on behalf of members (Wallace 1989). Agency is a situation where a person or organisation can conclude legally binding agreements on behalf of an individual or organisation. Agency can exist in limited circumstances, most notably when the number of employees is 'small and definite and the matters dealt with are confined solely to that group' (Kerr and Whyte 1985: 161).

Some collective agreements are legally binding, most notably those registered by the parties with the Labour Court. Even non-binding collective agreements can have legal effect. For instance, the substantive terms of a collective agreement can become legally enforceable through the principle of 'incorporation'. Incorporation describes a process whereby an action permanently alters the contract of employment. Thus, when an employer pays a wage increase provided for in a collective agreement this can become a contractual entitlement that can only be altered with the employee's agreement. Similarly, a wage reduction specified in a collective agreement can permanently alter the contract of employment, not through the terms of the agreement but by the acceptance of the reduction by the employee (Kerr and Whyte 1985).

The legal principle of 'incorporation' does not generally apply to the procedural elements of an agreement. Nonetheless, procedures covering individual issues such as grievances, discipline, bullying and harassment can also have legal effect. Third parties with legal competence (such as the EAT, the Labour Court, the Equality Tribunal as well as the courts) may look at workplace procedures in much the same way that the rules of the road would be regarded in the event of a car accident. It is common to see an individual win an unfair dismissals case because the rules of procedural and natural justice have not been complied with, e.g. if the employee was not allowed representation during the disciplinary process, if they were not adequately informed of the charge against them or if they were not allowed an opportunity to respond to any charge.

The absence of legal enforceability should not be taken to mean that collective agreements are unimportant. They are considered to be 'binding in honour' and the parties to industrial relations set much store by them. A practitioner who fails to honour agreements can very quickly find their reputation severely damaged. Furthermore, third parties such as the LRC or Labour Court are likely to pay careful attention to claims that a dispute is covered by the terms of an agreement that has been freely entered into. Perhaps the most instructive illustration of a willingness to honour an agreement has been the stated intention by the Fine Gael–Labour Party coalition government to honour the Croke Park Agreement on the basis that it is essential to honour agreements in industrial relations. Tánaiste Eamon Gilmore pointed out the importance of this by saying: 'If you make an agreement, you keep the agreement, and there's a good reason for that. Because if you break an agreement, the people you make it with are unlikely to reach agreement with you again' (RTÉ 2012). However, this has not precluded a review of the agreement in the Croke Park extension process, which indicates the considerable flexibility that attaches to collective agreements in comparison with legal contracts.

EVOLUTION OF WORKPLACE DISCIPLINARY AND GRIEVANCE PROCEDURES

Torrington and Hall (1998: 538) describe discipline as the 'regulation of human activity to produce a controlled performance'. This definition draws attention to the essence of discipline as an exercise in control. That exercise of control involves the use of power by one party to the employment relationship (the employer) over the other (the employee), a feature of industrial relations emphasised by radical writers (Fox 1974). A grievance procedure, on the other hand, is 'an operational mechanism which defines, and may limit, the exercise of managerial authority and power through establishing a formal regulatory framework for handling specified issues' (Salamon 1998: 533). In effect, it is explicitly designed to limit managerial control.

The nature of industrial organisation creates the need for disciplinary measures and also gives rise to grievances. Industrial organisations need employees to attend on time, conform to certain behaviour and meet standards of performance, and discipline is one way of seeking to ensure these are delivered. Likewise, employees will typically have expectations of equitable and fair treatment in employment and an entitlement to bring grievances to management's attention and have them addressed. Both discipline and grievances are thus an integral aspect of the employment relationship and in part represent an expression of conflict in that relationship.

Historically, conflict over discipline was dealt with at the sole discretion of management. This discretion was enshrined in the common law system which, unlike other contracts, did not regard disputes arising out of the contract of employment as being subject to legal adjudication. This was known as 'employment at will'. The most notable aspect of employment at will was that an employee could be dismissed for any reason or none. Trade unions came to fill the vacuum created by the absence of the law. With collective solidarity, they sought to counterbalance the right of employers to unilaterally impose discipline (Cole 1913). By the 1920s, disciplinary procedures had been developed in some employments (notably public ones) that laid down rules and procedures for disciplinary action (Flanders 1956). Such disciplinary procedures were not entirely detached from the law, but borrowed procedural aspects from common law notions of due process and natural justice. Thus, in general, unions did not seek to contest management's right to impose discipline but imposed requirements on how discipline was to be carried out.

Since it developed over time, the procedural regulation of discipline and grievance was haphazard and sporadic. Flanders (1956: 320) notes that 'in many industries the employers' power "to hire and fire" is limited, if at all, only by the restraint imposed by the fear of "trouble"'. This absence of formal regulation at the level of the workplace was highlighted by the UK Donovan Commission, which argued there was a need to put in place workplace procedures for the regulation of industrial relations (Donovan 1968). The Commission's approach was based on the pluralist notion of management regaining power by sharing it. The Donovan recommendation had a major effect on workplace industrial relations in Ireland and, led by the new personnel management professionals, procedural regulation grew substantially (especially in manufacturing industry) from the late 1960s (Wallace 1989). Such collectively developed rules also came to influence rules for handling discipline and grievance in non-union companies with the introduction of procedures paralleling those in unionised companies (Wallace 1989). An example of the contents of a typical disciplinary procedure is shown in Table 7.1.

Table 7.1

Typical Contents of a Disciplinary Procedure

- Indication of conduct and other issues that may lead to disciplinary action
- Provision for a formal pre-disciplinary counselling phase in the case of lesser issues
- Employee is entitled to know the complaint
- Requirement for a full investigation
- Entitlement of employee to representation by shop steward, union official or fellow employee
- Manager hearing the case should not have a personal conflict of interest
- Employee is entitled to challenge any evidence/allegations
- Provision of graded penalties for lesser issues (e.g. conduct, performance); usually an oral warning, written warning(s) and final written warning
- Provision for support action by management to assist improved performance/conduct, e.g. training, use of employee assistance programme
- A step-back provision where, after a defined time period, a warning reverts to the stage below it (i.e. a final written warning becomes a written warning, a written warning becomes an oral warning)
- Removal of warnings from the employee's record following a specified time period
- In cases of alleged gross misconduct, provision for suspension with pay to allow for an investigation
- Provision for suspension/reassignment of duties/dismissal for a first offence for major issues of gross misconduct or persistent failure to address lesser issues
- An appeal to senior management
- Provision for referral to a third party in the event that disciplinary action is challenged; this may be absent from disciplinary procedure in a non-union company but in the event of dismissal is, of course, an option for a former employee

---

MANAGEMENT APPROACHES

In addition to the influence of collective procedures in non-union companies, there is a distinctly managerial influence on such arrangements. This owes much to the work of organisational psychologists and organisational behaviourists, particularly in the US. These approaches are described under the heading of 'corrective' or 'positive' approaches to discipline. The most significant development in management approaches to discipline in Ireland is the *corrective approach*, which appears in the textbooks from at least the 1970s and is widely espoused nowadays. This is contrasted with the *punitive, coercive* or *negative* approaches (Fenley 1998; Hawkins 1982; Osigweh and Hutchison 1989, 1990; Wheeler 1976). The corrective approach can be seen as an attempt to mask the power and control aspects of discipline.

The terms 'corrective' or 'positive' are used quite loosely in differing texts. In some texts, the corrective approach is advocated as an employee-centred approach to discipline; in others, it merely involves a stepped procedure as developed in corrective approaches. What is identified as a corrective approach in various texts can fall anywhere along a spectrum and these are outlined in Table 7.2. At one end of this spectrum, 'corrective' may mean little more than the issuing of a series or oral, written and final written warnings. The employee is given an opportunity to improve but there may be little engagement with the issues that have led to the poor performance or behavioural issue. The aim may be to achieve improvement but the punitive element of the warnings is to the fore. In effect, it can be viewed as a bureaucratic exercise designed to comply with legal requirements of due process (see Variant A in Table 7.2). A corrective approach can be more developed and involve an employee-centred, mutual problem-solving approach that this is referred to as a 'corrective' or 'positive' approach (see Variant B in Table 7.2). However, Variant B still makes provision for penalties and thus retains the punitive elements of Variant A.

Table 7.2
Corrective and Positive Approaches to Discipline

Corrective Approach Variant A	Corrective/Positive Approach Variant B	Positive Discipline Variant C
Basic Corrective Approach A series of warnings provided for, typically oral warning, written warning, final written warning, suspension and/or dismissal. Employee given an opportunity to improve, except in the case of gross misconduct where dismissal is specified for a first offence. Normally specified that corrective approach should not be punitive, but sanctions/penalties are invariably specified.	**Enhanced Corrective Approach** In addition to all features of corrective approach A, there is emphasis on using (i) a diagnostic and (ii) a joint problem-solving approach. (i) A diagnostic approach involves a review of why a problem has arisen, e.g. has employee been properly trained, are targets reasonable, is there another reason that may entail responsibility on the part of management? (ii) Joint problem solving between supervisor/manager and employee on how problem is to be resolved and how employee will meet management's requirements. Emphases on using counselling rather than penalties, but warnings are also provided for.	This approach uses the diagnostic and joint problem solving outlined in variant B. Employees are given a number of staged opportunities to improve. There is no provision for penalties. If an employee does not meet the employer's expectation and cannot commit to doing so, they are expected to voluntarily resign.

There is a separate positive approach, also referred to as a *counselling approach*. This is highly critical of the traditional corrective approach precisely because of punitive elements they contain (Riccucci 1988; Osigweh and Hutchinson 1989, 1990; Sherman and Lucia 1992). In the positive approach there is an absence of any provision for either warnings (either oral or written) or dismissal, with counselling being to the fore and the employee being given a number of opportunities to improve (see Variant C, Table 7.2). At the final stage, if they cannot meet the employer's expectation, employees are expected to voluntarily leave employment. In the US this approach is said to produce higher levels of satisfaction by those experiencing discipline (even in unionised companies); however, the research is extremely limited and the approach does not appear to be practised widely. It is not clear if it is used in a formal sense in any Irish employments. Indeed, there must be a real risk that the requirement on an employee to resign could be construed as constituting a form of constructive dismissal.

It is also worth noting that not all writers see punitive methods as dysfunctional. For instance, Arvey and Ivancevich (1980: 131) argue that 'punishment may be a very effective procedure in accomplishing behavioural change'. Salamon (1998) also suggests an occupational division in the approach to disciplinary warnings. He claims that warnings may have minimal effect on those in manual or lower clerical groups for whom there may be little if any career prospects. Thus, employees in manual grades may treat warnings in a cavalier fashion and 'play the system'. They may take their warnings up to the final warning stage and then wait for the step-back function to kick in, which will see warnings move back to the previous warning stage after a period. This may especially happen with attendance issues, whereby employees avoid the higher disciplinary sanctions by achieving good attendance until a warning has expired and is removed from their records.

By the early 1980s some texts had begun to advocate *preventive* discipline, whereby the culture of an organisation is designed to mitigate the need for discipline. This involves *autonomous discipline*, whereby teams regulate discipline or *self-discipline* and individuals are encouraged to take responsibility for their own performance (Strauss and Sayles 1980). Edwards (2005: 376–7) notes that self-discipline is still a form of control, being 'one aspect of the way in which control has to be negotiated'. There are some impressive examples of reductions in the use of discipline (and grievances) associated with responsible autonomy promoted by team-working, most notably in Rusal Aughinish – although there, the introduction of annual hours seemed to be the main casual variable (Wallace and Whyte 2008). Such developments suggest that the nature of work organisation may greatly influence employee performance and behaviour and may be more important than personal issues that are usually focused on by disciplinary procedures, whether of the traditional, corrective or positive variety.

Despite the claims for the positivity of management-led approaches to discipline, there is a degree of scepticism as to how these impact on workers. Saundry *et al.* (2011: 197) suggest that 'without the countervailing power offered by effective union representation, workplace discipline may be reduced to a stark exercise of managerial discretion'. They draw attention to the 'consistent survey evidence that links strong [trade union] organisation with lower rates of disciplinary sanctions and dismissals' (Saundry *et al.* 2011: 196). In fact, repeated surveys in the UK have found the imposition of discipline to be two and a half times lower in strongly unionised establishments. In addition, Saundry *et al.* (2011: 201) found that non-union organisations had 'less scope for resolving disciplinary disputes informally' and consequently had a greater reliance on procedure. Should a similar effect prevail in Ireland, this would moderate somewhat the pessimistic conclusions arising from Browne's (1994) findings that unions coped poorly with the law in dismissals cases. Also, if unions influence the disciplinary process in advance of dismissal, this would arguably be of much greater benefit to workers, since it would involve them keeping their job rather than having to challenge a dismissal – a far more difficult process.

Saundry *et al.* (2011: 204) reported that in cases of discipline in non-union companies, the use of 'non-union companions … did not necessarily help their colleague's case' and could get them 'into more trouble'. This was because they lacked the requisite skills and knowledge. In contrast, union involvement in the disciplinary process was positively perceived by managers in the study by Saundry *et al.* (2011). In weaker or non-unionised companies where they were accorded a representational role only, union involvement tended to be more adversarial (Saundry *et al.* 2011). Where union representation was seen as effective, it tended to be because they were able to persuade employees to own up and make a plea for mitigation, with that being 'often the most effective strategy' (Saundry *et al.* 2011). This suggests two main reasons for unions being positively perceived by managers. First, having a union test the case will make it less likely that it will be lost at a subsequent tribunal hearing. Second, the union can 'reality check' the employee – that involves bringing home the gravity of their situation to them and emphasising the need for compliance with management's requirements. This can make the warning system work more effectively, since there is a greater likelihood of subsequent improvement. Thus, generally it remains the case that management's right to determine and impose discipline is seldom challenged by unions.

Finally, it is worth noting that a 'more exacting approach to discipline, time-keeping and attendance' is evident with the onset of the current recession (Roche *et al.* 2011: 71). That being the case, the prescriptions advanced by the more managerial-centred corrective approaches may be the main casualty because it is likely that attention will still be paid to meeting legal requirements because of the potential consequence. It is also noted, however, that HR managers are concerned with delivering commitment and values of '"trust", "honesty", "transparency" and "fairness"' (Roche *et al.* 2011: 122). This suggests that the historical management considerations related to discipline have not disappeared.

LEGAL AND INSTITUTIONAL INFLUENCES PROMOTING PROCEDURAL REGULATION

Growing legal regulation has promoted greater formality in the handling of discipline and grievance issues in common law systems that previously eschewed legal intervention (Roche and Teague 2011; Saundry *et al.* 2011). As noted in Chapter 6, the Unfair Dismissals Act 1977 and Equality Acts of the 1970s were hugely important in promoting formal procedures. Roche and Teague (2011) note that this is a trend that has been accentuated by some fourteen pieces of legislation introduced since 1990. They argue that 'the growth of legislation on individual employment rights may impact on workplace conflict management procedures, as organisations seek to stay on the right side of the law' (Roche and Teague 2011: 439). Collective legislation has also been significant, with the Industrial Relations Act 1990 making provision for the publication of codes of practice. Under this legislation, since 2006 the LRC has published codes covering discipline, grievance and bullying; as has previously been noted, these codes can have legal implications. The absence of company procedures in areas such as discipline, bullying and harassment, or equality can make it difficult for an employer to defend a case to a third party. Equally, a failure on an employee's part to utilise internal company grievance procedures can lead to a case in these areas being lost by the employee irrespective of its substantive merits.

Table 7.3

Case Study

Banking on Discrimination

Mary McQuillan works in a bank. She marries a fellow employee in the same branch and on return from honeymoon is approached by her manager, who informs her she is being relocated to a branch twenty miles away, since it is the bank's policy that married employees cannot work in the same branch. She informs the manager that this is blatant discrimination and asks her why her husband is not the one to be moved. The manager does not answer the question, but says there is nothing he can do, since it is company policy. He tells Mary that she can take it up with corporate HR. Incensed, Mary immediately hands in her notice and some days later initiates a case under the Equality Acts 1998–2004 for constructive dismissal and discrimination on the grounds of gender and marital status.

Discussion Points

1   What are the potential strengths and weaknesses of Ms McQuillan's case?
2   What additional information might be necessary to have a more informed view of whether her case is likely to succeed or not?

Extent of Disciplinary and Grievance Procedures

Given the influences promoting the development of procedural regulation, it might be expected that such procedures would by now be almost universal. However, this is not the case. A study of 500 companies in Ireland found that only 60 per cent of organisations had formal written disciplinary and grievance procedures (Roche and Teague 2011). Written procedures for discipline and grievance were more likely to be found in the following organisations: unionised, medium/large size, manufacturing and foreign owned (Roche and Teague 2011). While the coverage of 60 per cent is reasonably widespread, it is far from universal and, given the legal and other pressures for procedural regulation discussed above, it requires some explanation. Research indicates a resistance by some managers to the formalisation involved in the procedural regulation of discipline and grievance. It has been pointed out that operational managers (as distinct from human resource managers) would prefer to avoid procedures and favour a pragmatic and informal approach to disciplinary issues (Jones and Saundry 2011). Although such preferences may have some effect on the way procedures operate within organisations, it is doubtful it determines the presence or absence of procedures.

Table 7.4
A Typology of Workplace Conflict Management Systems

Workplace Conflict Management System	Percentage (%)
Minimal conflict management system	41
Traditional industrial relations conflict management system	30
A high level of usage of ADR practices, combined with formal, written, stepwise conflict management practices	25
Hybrid ADR conflict management system	5
Source: Adapted from Roche and Teague (2011: 447)	

Labour market pressures are a more likely cause of the non-universal diffusion of disciplinary and grievance procedures. These pressures seem to be pulling workplace conflict management systems in different directions. Roche and Teague (2011: 438) point to the growth in knowledge-based workers – a development which may promote the adoption of 'innovative ADR-style conflict management practices', 'ADR' referring to alternative dispute resolution. Roche and Teague also note an opposite influence, due to the expansion in relatively low-wage and low-skilled jobs. They suggest that this may have led to 'a significant number of employees … working in organisations where even traditional workplace conflict management practices are absent' (Roche and Teague 2011: 438). In addition, there is the possibility of a hybrid between the traditional and innovative. This has led the authors to advance a four-way typology which they found was borne out by the results of their survey of 500 organisations (Table 7.4). Most notable is the finding that a majority (54 per cent) of the minimal conflict management group appeared to favour a largely improvised approach to managing workplace conflict, although even in this group 37 per cent still had formal, written, stepwise procedures.

ALTERNATIVE CONFLICT MANAGEMENT SYSTEMS

Table 7.5
Conflict Management Practices

Type of Conflict	Conventional Approach	ADR Approach
Conflict involving individuals	• Formal written grievance and disciplinary procedures	• Open-door policies • 'Speak up' systems • Ombudsmen • External and internal mediators • Review panels of managers and peers • Employee advocates • Arbitration
Conflict involving groups	• Formal written procedures • Resort at final stage (when deadlocked) to state agencies, e.g. LRC	• Assisted bargaining/mediation • Brainstorming • Interest-based bargaining • Private arbitration • Intensive communications surrounding change management
Source: Teague *et al.* (2012)		

Table 7.6

Case Study*

ADR: Assisted Bargaining in Hirem Recruitment PLC

Mary has been working for a non-union recruitment agency called Hirem for four years. She has become very experienced and has direct contact with a wide range of clients. The company has had a high labour turnover and Mary is, in fact, the longest-serving employee. Realising her value, Mary negotiates a substantial salary increase, hinting that if it were not forthcoming she would leave. She also gets agreement for the employment of an assistant, since she has been working extremely long hours. One day Mary comes across a note. It is addressed to Mary's direct manager and it is in the handwriting of the general manager. This note indicates that the general manager considers that Mary has become too independent in her work, has too many direct contacts with clients and that there is a risk she will leave and take clients with her. The note also says that her recent salary increase (she now earns €30,000 per annum) has made it too expensive to continue to employ her. The note indicates that it is not possible to replace her at present, but that the new assistant will take over her job in six months and preparations can then be made for her dismissal.

Mary is shocked at this note and decides to photocopy it. She continues to work and, after four months, her immediate manager begins to make a number of complaints. This is done over a two-month period. At the end of this period, the manager sends for her and indicates that her work is not satisfactory and she is to be made redundant. Mary informs the company that she has proof that the real reason for her dismissal is quite different. She hands her manager a copy of the general manager's note. Mary informs the company that she feels she has been 'bullied and harassed' and that this has caused her substantial stress. She says that she cannot continue to work with the company, but she expects a 'handsome package' to leave. The manager informs Mary that the note she copied was confidential and that copying any confidential material is a matter for disciplinary action.

Following further discussion, the manager indicates that she will accept Mary's resignation and will make a goodwill payment of €2,000 to 'dispose of the matter'. Mary rejects this as 'totally inadequate' and indicates that she 'will sue' and 'take a case for unfair dismissal'. The company indicates that they are prepared to 'negotiate' further. Mary asks to have her solicitor negotiate on her behalf but the company say they would prefer 'to keep the law out of it at this stage'. Mary proposes instead using an expert negotiator from Alternative Dispute Resolution PLC to negotiate on her behalf. The general manager agrees to this and a negotiating meeting is set up. Due to prior commitments of both parties, it is agreed that this meeting will last no longer than an hour and that if agreement is not reached, the parties 'will go their separate ways'.

* This case study can be used for analysis, discussion or role-play negotiation. Guidelines for using the case study are available for lecturers on the Gill & Macmillan website (www.gillmacmillan.ie).

ADR practices grew in the US in the 1980s as an alternative to processing disputes in civil courts. ADR practices aim to resolve disputes and improve future relationships. Examples of ADR practices and comparison to traditional methods are provided in Table 7.5. A variety of factors can affect the extent to which ADR is used, e.g. firm size, firm type, whether the firm is unionised or non-unionised, if the company is a MNC and the demographics of the workforce (Teague *et al.* 2012). The most common ADR mechanism is that of open-door policies. A recent study found that these are present in

53 per cent of companies, but there is a low incidence of other ADR practices (Teague *et al.* 2012). Of the firms surveyed, 40 per cent had formal written procedures for dealing with disputes involving groups of employees, 30 per cent used intensive formal communications regarding impending change, 20 per cent used external experts to assist in negotiations and 31 per cent used brainstorming and problem-solving techniques (Teague *et al.* 2012: 14). Overall, the evidence suggests that ADR is not diffusing on any widespread basis in Ireland (Teague *et al.* 2012). The case study of Hirem Recruitment (in Table 7.6) illustrates an assisted bargaining ADR case in a non-union setting. It provides a good opportunity for role-play or class discussion.

BULLYING AND HARASSMENT

There has been a major growth in attention to the bullying and harassment aspects of interpersonal conflicts in recent years; they are some of the most complex issues for managers to deal with. Bullying is repeated inappropriate behaviour that can reasonably be regarded as undermining the individual's right to dignity at work (LRC 2006). Unlike bullying, which is repeated behaviour, harassment and sexual harassment can include a one-off incidence. They are defined as behaviour which is unwelcome to the employee and could reasonably be regarded as offensive, humiliating or intimidating (Equality Authority 2002). Bullying and harassment can be perpetrated by an individual's colleagues, customers or clients and they are often alleged to be perpetrated by an individual's supervisor or manager (Hutchinson *et al.* 2008).

Early research on bullying focused on the personalities of the victim and the bully in order to explain why bullying occurred. However, many authors have cautioned against this and have focused on the culture, power and hierarchy of the organisation and external factors in order to explain bullying (MacMahon *et al.* 2009). For example, it has been argued that organisations with 'destructive' leadership can trigger or sustain bullying behaviour by management not intervening when bullying behaviours occur (Einarsen and Skogstad 1996; Salin 2008; Skogstad *et al.* 2007). Thus, bullying can become institutionalised where it is ignored or accepted (MacMahon *et al.* 2009). In reference to our earlier discussion on power, it has been argued that the imbalance of power between the possible victim and perpetrator can 'provide fertile soil for bullying' (Salin 2003: 1218).

A significant difficulty in addressing bullying in the workplace is the fact that it is rarely reported by victims. However, this does not mean that employers can ignore the issue, since bullying can have serious consequences for an individual's health and wellbeing as well as for the organisation (Kelly 2006; MacMahon *et al.* 2009; O'Connell *et al.* 2007). Health and safety legislation requires employers to provide a safe place to work and equality legislation states that they must take all reasonably practicable steps to prevent and address harassment. A number of codes of practice have been produced to guide employers on bullying and harassment procedures, e.g. by the Health and Safety Authority, the LRC and the Equality Authority. These codes of practice advocate that an employer should develop a bullying and harassment policy and that this should be communicated to all staff as well as customers/clients. These codes provide that should a bullying or harassment incident be alleged to have occurred, the individual could be encouraged to use an informal process whereby they alert the perpetrator to their inappropriate behaviour. If this does not resolve the issue, then provision needs to be made for the use of a formal complaints procedure where an individual can make a written complaint and the employer carries out an investigation into the issue. The case study in Table 7.7 offers an opportunity for class discussion of issues involved in a case of alleged bullying.

Table 7.7

Case Study*

The Allegation

Lisa worked as a cleaner in a large factory for five years. In February, she was notified that management and the union had agreed to introduce a new morning shift of 6am–2pm. The cleaners were not consulted about the change and were unhappy with it but didn't do anything about the issue. A few weeks into the new shift, Lisa approached her manager and told him that the new shift was unsuitable for her as she had to get her children ready for school. The manager agreed to reduce the number of weekday shifts she had and to put her on Sunday shifts, which Lisa was happy about as they were paid at double time. Following this, she experienced changes in her colleagues' behaviour towards her. She felt excluded from conversations and she felt that her colleagues were whispering and laughing at her. On one occasion, a colleague spilled a drink on a floor Lisa had just cleaned – Lisa felt this was deliberate. Lisa's supervisor told her that Lisa's work was getting sloppy and that she was stupid. Following this, Lisa met the HR manager and told her about what was happening. She also met with the company occupational health nurse, who believed that Lisa was severely anxious and stressed. Lisa took a month off work. However, when she returned, she felt that the bullying continued and she submitted a formal bullying complaint.

Discussion Points

1   Discuss how this case illustrates difficulties (a) for an employee who feels bullied and (b) for an organisation faced with an allegation of bulling.
2   If you were the HR manager, what steps would you take regarding the bullying complaint?

HANDLING GRIEVANCES AND DISCIPLINE

Prescriptive texts often present discipline, grievance and other individual employment relations issues in non-problematic terms, but there are many considerations other than procedures which may impact on dealing with them. Despite the elaborate procedural norms that characterise disciplinary and grievance administration, many of the underlying concepts are quite subjective. Of particular note are concepts such as 'reasonableness', 'fairness' and 'consistency'. As far back as the 1950s, Gouldner (1954) noted that workers had an indulgency expectation, believing that procedures would be implemented in 'an indulgent' way, i.e. that the full force of procedures would not be used. Thus, custom and practice have a particularly strong influence on the operation of formal rules. Edwards (2005: 384) points out that 'any manager sticking to the letter of the rule book might well be surprised not merely by the workers' reactions but also by line managers, who have negotiated a form of workplace equilibrium that turns on rules in practice'. It would also be wrong to imagine that managers have a gung ho attitude to discipline, with Jones and Saundry (2011: 263) reporting findings of a Chartered Institute for Personnel and Development (CIPD) UK survey that managers are 'often reluctant to deal with emerging disciplinary issues'.

The above caveats should be borne in mind for a nuanced understanding when considering the remainder of this chapter, which deals with prescriptive norms and practices for handling such issues in the workplace. A number of case studies are presented. These have been selected to reflect the real-world complexities that discipline, grievance and other workplace issues regularly bring to the fore. The case studies provide material for class discussion, debate and role-play.

Grievances

Prescriptive management texts claim that grievance procedures have a number of benefits. Grievance procedures provide an opportunity for an employee to 'voice' concerns, provide feedback to management, limit misunderstandings and disputes over what is appropriate, provide an avenue of communication and increase fairness and consistency (Hawkins 1979; Thomason 1984). In effect, they can be considered as a mechanism to match the expectations of an employer and employee. However, as in the case of discipline, the act of initiating a grievance can be influenced by the underlying power dynamic. It is not clear that employees will be comfortable initiating a grievance. They may feel it would draw undesirable attention to them and create difficulties with management.

It would be wrong to think that raising a formal grievance is the only way of dealing with an employee's grievance. Most employee concerns will be resolved informally through the normal 'give and take' that characterise workplaces. However, those that are unresolved may need to be processed through formal written procedures. The main aims of grievance procedures are to ensure that issues raised by employees are handled promptly and settled fairly at, or as near as possible to, their point of origin. Such aims are based on the premise that effectively operated grievance procedures limit the escalation of grievances into more serious disputes. Line management and employees/

Table 7.8

Management Checklist for Grievance Handling

- Management should make every effort to understand the nature of and the reasons for grievances.
- All levels of management should be aware of the potentially significant influence that grievance handling has on industrial relations and company performance generally.
- Companies should have a written policy that sets out an orderly and effective framework for handling employee grievances.
- Line management, particularly first-level supervision, should be aware of their key role in effective grievance handling.
- Managers need to be aware of the need for consistency and consider if a precedent is being set in resolving the grievance.

employee representatives handle the vast majority of workplace grievances and disputes at workplace level, so they need to be familiar with grievance procedures and have the skills to handle them. This is the case even where no written procedures exist and an informal approach is adopted by organisations. Summary guidelines for managers involved in grievance handling are outlined in Table 7.8.

A written grievance procedure will normally set out the requirements on employees and the employer in the event of a formal grievance and will outline the stages and approaches to be followed by managers and employees. In order to prevent grievance procedures being seen as a delaying tactic, it is recommended that they be handled promptly, with an employee receiving a response quickly. Grievance procedures will normally specify short time limits (usually only a few days) for each phase of the process. The standard elements of a grievance procedure are outlined in Table 7.9.

Table 7.9

Elements of a Typical Grievance Procedure

- Clear steps specifying the level at which a grievance should be raised.
- A requirement that the issue should be first discussed between employees and their immediate manager or supervisor.
- Provision for referral to higher levels of management if not resolved.
- Provision for a speedy response.
- Time limits to be specified for each stage of the procedure (if the issue is not dealt with in the specified time, the next stage of the procedure may be invoked).
- A right of employees to be represented by their trade union or an employee of their choice at the various stages of the procedure.
- Provision for referral to a third party if agreement cannot be reached 'in house' (this may be absent in non-union procedures but may still be an option for an employee).
- A 'peace clause', with both parties foregoing the use of industrial action prior to all stages of the agreed procedures being exhausted (this will not be present in non-union companies).

Discipline

Salamon (1998: 545) defines discipline as 'formal action taken by management against an individual who fails to conform to the rules established by management within the organisation'. Management will normally determine what are seen as acceptable rules and standards in areas such as employee performance, attendance and conduct at work. Inevitably situations will arise where employees are considered to have failed to have met expectations or, less commonly, where employees will wish to contest management rules and standards. Disciplinary procedures provide such a formal process. They serve to bring alleged offences to the notice of employees, indicate how employees can respond to such charges, identify the disciplinary action that may be taken and make clear the right of appeal. It is essential that any disciplinary hearing be preceded by a full investigation and that the hearing comply with the rules of natural justice.

If disciplinary action is justified, it can range from relatively minor and informal rebukes outside of formal discipline to more serious forms, e.g. formal warnings, suspension or dismissal. In issuing warnings, clarity is very important and a warning should specify the ways in which the employee's behaviour or performance was unsatisfactory, how that behaviour or performance can be improved, what the expected standard is and the consequences of not improving. Management are obliged to take any reasonable

---

Table 7.10

Case Study*

Furnworks Ltd

Bill Brennan has recently been appointed factory manager of Furnworks Ltd, a furniture company employing fifty people and located in the northwest. The company is not a member of an employer organisation and, while unionised, the union is not particularly active. In the past, the company has had a number of negative experiences with employment legislation. On taking up the position, the directors made it clear to Bill that although they wanted him to run a tight ship, they did not want to lose any more employment law cases. Bill's predecessor had left unexpectedly. Bill has heard through the grapevine that his predecessor had been 'encouraged to leave' because of the negative publicity associated with the loss of employment law cases – the directors had been embarrassed by local press coverage.

Three months after taking up employment, the factory supervisor, Tom Joyce, approaches Bill in connection with a problem that has arisen with an employee named Peter Turner. Peter has been with the company for eight years and Tom informs Bill that he 'has a history'. About a year ago, he was seen in a pub during working hours, being absent from his job without permission. When Turner point-blank denied he had been in the pub on the day in question, Tom Joyce felt he could not take any action. This was because the person who informed the company was not prepared to make a formal statement to that effect. About four weeks ago, Peter Turner was involved in a lifting incident after which he complained he had hurt his back. Subsequently, he went on sick leave and submitted several sick certificates from his local doctor to the effect that he was unable to work due to a back injury. The company has a sick pay scheme. In the written procedure agreement with the union, there is a stipulation that 'any abuse of the sick pay scheme will lead to instant dismissal'.

Last week Tom Joyce received information that Peter Turner was on a sun holiday in the Canary Islands. Peter Turner is known as a 'sun worshipper' because he takes so many sun holidays and always seems to have a suntan (his nickname is 'Ra' after the Egyptian sun god). Concerned that Turner would deny he had been on holiday, Tom Joyce found out when Turner was due to return, waited in the airport and secretly took a video of him coming out of the arrivals area. He was suitably dressed in colourful holiday gear and accompanied by his wife and three children. Tom Joyce informs Bill that he has had enough of Turner's antics and says: 'He has slipped up this time and either he goes or I go.' Tom goes on to indicate that he is holding a disciplinary hearing in the morning and 'will deal with the issue', if that is okay with Bill.

Discussion Points

1 Imagine that Bill is one of your personal friends. He knows you are doing a course in industrial relations. Bill rings you and asks you for advice on the Peter Turner situation. Advise Bill under the following headings:
   • Strengths of the case for the company
   • Weaknesses of the case for the company
   • The action you recommend Bill take in his role as factory manager
   • The range of all possible options available to Peter Turner in the event that he is dismissed.

*This case study can be used for analysis, discussion or role-play negotiation. Guidelines for using the case study are available for lecturers on the Gill & Macmillan website (www.gillmacmillan.ie).

Table 7.11

Case Study*

White Goods: White-collar Theft?

Your name is Joanna Mooney and six months ago you were appointed general manager of White Goods Distributor PLC. You were hired to shake up the company and make it more competitive. You have made it clear that you intend to be tough but fair. You have just discovered that Tom Mallon, a sales manager, has been taking traded-in fridges, washing machines, dishwashers and ovens (the property of the company). He refurbishes them and sells them on privately and keeps the money. You confront Tom and give him a chance to admit the offence but he denies any impropriety. He also admits he did not have permission for this activity. You have direct evidence from two people who have bought refurbished fridges. You feel that given Tom's position, his activity will inevitably reflect on the company and you are determined to put an end to this theft. You feel the company has been taken advantage of and you wonder what you should do. You are seriously considering Tom's dismissal.

^^*

Your name is Tom Mallon and you have been working as sales manager for White Goods Distributor PLC for twelve years. In an informal arrangement over the years, you have taken goods in good condition that were traded in to the company and you have refurbished them and sold them on privately. The company previously had to pay to dispose of them. Today you were confronted by the new general manager, Joanna Mooney – who makes no secret of being tough – and you were accused of stealing company property. You were totally shocked and did not know how to respond except to deny any impropriety. She asked you if you had permission to do this and you answered honestly that you did not. However, you don't see that as relevant, since it was well known that you did this and previous general managers never had a problem with it. Presumably they knew about the practice, even though you never had formal permission to do it. You are not in a union. You feel very vulnerable and wonder what you can do.

Discussion Points

1   How should Joanna Mooney proceed if she wishes to discipline Tom Mallon?
2   What options does Tom have should disciplinary action be initiated against him?
3   What factors in the above account might justify or not justify disciplinary action?
4   In your opinion, is dismissal justified? If yes, why? If no, why not?
5   What additional factors might an investigation uncover which might justify or not justify dismissal?

*This case study can be used for analysis, discussion or role-play negotiation. Guidelines for using the case study are available for lecturers on the Gill & Macmillan website (www.gillmacmillan.ie).

measures that might facilitate improvement, e.g. extra training. Of course, improvement may not ensue and suspension, dismissal or demotion may result where repeat minor issues remain unresolved. The Furnworks case study (Table 7.10) is designed to illustrate some of the intricacies of applying disciplinary action in practice. This case can be used for class discussion and analysis.

It is a common misconception that disciplinary action requires a series of progressively escalating warnings. In fact, it is normally specified that in the case of gross misconduct, options such as suspension, dismissal or relocation to other duties may be applied for a first offence. It is important to appreciate that offences that warrant dismissal for a first offence in one organisational setting may not merit dismissal in another. This is especially the case in the 'grey area' of fighting and substance abuse, for example. Being drunk on the job might, depending on the circumstances, merit dismissal, but in another context it might be handled by an employee being referred to a company employee assistance programme. This would especially apply if this was the first time an employee had exhibited this behaviour. In relation to fighting at work, while this was traditionally seen as falling in a grey area, the requirements of modern health and safety legislation may mean management nowadays take a stricter view of such instances. There are certain offences where dismissal will invariably be justified. Theft is the most obvious of these, although an employer must be able to establish that the theft took place and that the employee was involved. Employers are only required to establish facts on the balance of probability – not beyond a reasonable doubt. Nonetheless this is not always unproblematic, especially where white-collar managerial employees are involved. The parties involved may perceive the same events quite differently, even in the case of alleged theft. This is illustrated in the White Goods case study (see Table 7.11.)

The Interview Process

Any discipline or grievance situation and many bullying and harassment situations will require an interview to be conducted and records retained. If handled well, interviews can contribute to a successful resolution of the dispute, and if the dispute is unresolved, a good interview can strengthen management's case in front of a third party. If handled badly, the issue can escalate and lead to difficulties when third parties become involved. It is important to understand that any interview is, in effect, a negotiation and that the principles of negotiations apply. In particular, the approach used in an interview will inevitably fall into one or more of a number of styles which are outlined and briefly explained in Table 7.12. A style or choice of style may often happen unconsciously and many of the approaches that can be used are sub-optimal or negative. The following discussion outlines the merits and demerits of possible approaches.

A 'frank and friendly' manner may work in straightforward situations but is unlikely to be effective where there is a fundamental difference between the parties. In negotiation terms, it is an accommodation approach and means the supervisor/manager is placing a low priority on the organisation's concerns and a higher priority on the employee's concerns. If the employee is also accommodating in their attitude, then it may work. If the employee is not accommodating, the 'frank and friendly' approach is unlikely to work. The 'tell and listen' approach may also work. However, it places no obligations on the other party to come up with solutions and as a result, the employee may deploy an avoidance strategy and not really address the issues subsequently. The 'tell and sell' approach is a power-based approach and it is, in fact, implicit in the nature of progressive warnings – i.e. 'If improvement does not happen, then your job is at risk!' The approach does not require the employee to be part of generating solutions and this may result in them having little commitment to any 'selling' in which the supervisor/

manager has engaged. It may also create resentment in the employee. The 'sweet and sour' style is generally considered unethical and can land a company in legal difficulties, since it is inherently based on a contradictory approach within management to the issue. Intimidation involves the use of threats, which is clearly unethical and can lead to accusations of bullying and harassment.

Table 7.12

Possible Approaches to Grievance and Disciplinary Interviewing

- **Frank and friendly:** Inform the person of the problem in an open and friendly way.
- **Tell and listen:** Inform the person of the problem and then listen sympathetically.
- **Tell and sell:** Inform the person of the problem and tell them of the consequences if they do not take a particular course of action.
- **Sweet and sour:** Issue dealt with by two people from the one side; one adopts a hard approach and the other a 'softer' approach. The aim is to manipulate the other party into agreeing to the 'softer' settlement.
- **Intimidation:** Use of threats.
- **Joint problem solving:** Both sides explore the problem from their differing perspectives, search for mutually agreeable solutions and agree a solution and action plan for implementation.

The recommended best practice approach to conducting grievance and disciplinary interviews is the 'joint problem-solving' approach (Table 7.13). The conceptual basis for joint problem solving is that it attempts to remove or limit the 'power' dimension in the interview process. It is implicitly based on the presumption that joint problem solving is a superior way of addressing discipline and grievance issues. The professional body for human resources, the Institute for Personnel Management (the forerunner of the CIPD), has advocated such an approach and there are undoubted advantages to its use. A joint problem-solving approach requires assertiveness on the part of the interviewer but also active involvement on the part of the employee, who should be engaged in suggesting solutions. Solutions advanced by either the supervisor/manager or employee should then be evaluated on their merits.

The implementation of a problem-solving approach to either grievance or disciplinary administration may be difficult for a number of reasons. First, it requires special skills and is likely to require training to be implemented successfully. Second, it may be unpopular with supervisors/managers, who may see it as limiting their traditional role and making unreasonable demands on them. Third, there may be a desire to meet legal requirements rather than enact a truly problem-solving approach. This may manifest itself by having managers/supervisors focus on ensuring that procedures are complied with in a technical way rather than seeking to identify mutually agreed solutions to issues. Fourth, an employee may be reluctant to engage in a problem-solving approach or may feel threatened because of the punitive nature of discipline. Finally, employees can be very emotional when they have a grievance or are faced with disciplinary action and as a result may find it difficult to address an issue in a problem-solving way even where supervisors or managers try to use such an approach.

Despite these reservations, the joint problem-solving approach represents the ideal in handling individual issues and actually appears to have substantial benefits for supervisors and managers who are adept at it. Wichert (2002: 169) notes that 'the better a person is as a listener, the more likely he or she is to rise rapidly up the organisation hierarchy'. She goes on to note that managers overestimate their listening skills and are unaware of how employees view them. Training has been found to increase employees' ratings of the effectiveness of management's listening skills, suggesting 'it might be a good investment in managers' (Wichert 2002: 169).

Table 7.13

Joint Problem-solving Approach

Elements
- **Non-directive, open-minded interviewing:** Questioning and active listening are required.
- **Establishing the issue from the employee perspective:** Employee's interests must be addressed.
- **Stating the issue from the employer perspective:** Supervisor/manager must show assertiveness.
- **Problem-solving aspect:** Employee is invited to suggest solutions. The solutions are evaluated with reference to objective, mutually agreed standards.
- **Implementing:** Employee must meet company's needs; employer must meet employee's needs.

Dangers
- **Employer may not engage with the process:** Supervisor/manager may be unconvinced at the effectiveness of this method and may believe that it concedes too much power. They may also lack the skills and understanding necessary to execute the method effectively.
- **Employee may not engage with the process:** Employee may be reluctant to be open about issues. They may regard this method as mere manipulation on the manager's part.

RECORDKEEPING: ADMINISTRATIVE AND LEGAL CONSIDERATIONS

As with the outcome of all negotiations, keeping accurate records on grievance and disciplinary matters is essential. Since equality and unfair dismissals legislation places the burden of proof primarily on the employer, they must be able to back up reasons for discipline with adequate documentary evidence. The keeping of records is equally important for an employee in the event that an issue proceeds to a third party. Contemporaneous records of events will be more reliable and will have greater credence than memory and they will be especially important where events are contested. In addition to their usefulness at third-party hearings, records also provide data on the extent and nature of discipline and grievances in the organisation and can highlight areas to be addressed beyond the personal.

While recordkeeping is an important dimension of grievance handling, it should not be allowed to distract from the primary purpose. An overemphasis on recording all details may create excessive red tape and cause frustration among employees. The details that need to be retained will vary according to the level that an issue has reached.

Some organisations require that grievances entering the procedure after the first stage must be served in writing with details of the issue and the employee(s) concerned. This is designed to help clarify the exact nature of the claim or grievance and it can help to avoid misunderstandings. In grievance cases, clear reasons for any decisions taken should be recorded and retained.

At the counselling interview in the disciplinary process, a brief note of the issue, the individual concerned, the date and the nature of the discussion will suffice. At verbal and written warning and all subsequent stages, records should be more elaborate. Written records are especially important at, and after, the final warning stage in disciplinary cases and if a grievance is unresolved internally. In discipline cases there needs to be a record that the employee was informed of the seriousness of the issue and that future offences could result in dismissal. A copy that has been signed by the employee (as evidence that they received and understood the letter) should be placed on their personal file. A copy should also be given to the employee's trade union (if they are a member) and to the manager(s) involved.

CONCLUDING COMMENTS

Workplace procedures are now widespread and represent an established way of handling both collective and individual conflict. They are important whether employees are in a unionised or non-union employment. Surprisingly, procedures are not universal. Their absence in an organisation can cause problems should a dispute proceed to a third party. The requirements of procedural and natural justice will apply whether formal procedures are in place or not. In implementing procedures it is desirable that managers and supervisors have an appropriate skill set. Employees must remember that procedures place obligations on them as well as giving them rights.

CHAPTER 8

The Management of Industrial Relations

INTRODUCTION

In this chapter the main approaches to the management of industrial relations and associated contextual considerations are explained and reviewed. This is done despite the fact that many organisations do not make any deliberate strategic choices in this area. That is, their approach may be described as reactive, opportunist or 'fire-fighting', as they concentrate their strategic decision making on 'primary' business issues such as investment, divestment and production (Boxall and Purcell 2007). In contrast, some organisations do take a strategic approach to industrial relations matters (Guest 1987; Kochan *et al.* 1986). Thus, approaches to the management of industrial relations vary along a continuum from 'incidentalism', characterised by little or no strategic decision-making, to a more deliberate and considered approach.

Across such a span, this chapter addresses:

- the relevant ever-changing economic, market and organisational contexts within which entities devise and adapt their HRM and industrial relations styles, policies and practices; and
- the range of possible management styles in industrial relations and the variety and nature of influences thereon.

CONTEXTUAL INFLUENCES: EXTERNAL AND INTERNAL

In order to identify and explain variations in management approaches in industrial relations it is necessary to examine the interplay of a diverse range of external and internal factors (Gunnigle *et al.* 2011). For example, it is argued that changes in environmental conditions affect decisions on business strategy and ultimately industrial relations. These decisions are conditioned by various factors (including managerial values) and constrained by historical and current practices in industrial relations.

The *external environment* exerts a major influence on organisational decision making. It is widely acknowledged that a recessionary economic environment, increased product market competition, advances in technology and changes in the composition and operation of labour markets significantly change the context of enterprise-level industrial relations (Roche *et al.* 2011; Sparrow and Hiltrop 1994). For example, the severe recession experienced after the demise of the Celtic Tiger era in Ireland significantly altered HRM and industrial relations priorities and pursuits (Gunnigle *et al.* 2012). In this respect it is acknowledged that such downswings generally:

> … affect the conduct of employment relations. They do this by inclining employers towards more market-responsive postures that may involve downsizing and more

flexible employment arrangements, less investment in training and development and general restructuring activities that may weaken internal labour markets and assured career progression. (Roche *et al.* 2011: 221)

Associated with this, the national workplace survey undertaken by the National Centre for Partnership and Performance (see O'Connell *et al.* 2010) confirms that given their job security fears, most staff are prepared to facilitate change and to work harder to enable organisations to survive. In addition to the impact of the international economic recession, increased competitiveness has resulted from factors such as wider market competition attributed to late industrial starters (e.g. Singapore), greater liberalisation of trade due to developments under the General Agreement on Tariffs and Trade (GATT) and the impact of the Economic and Monetary Union (EMU). Piore and Sabel (1984) argue that these developments represent a new industrial revolution, incorporating a major restructuring of the capitalist order. In this vein, Marshall (1992) suggests that to an increasing extent, an enterprise's commercial viability depends on its ability to effectively restructure in the face of greater global competition and the fragmentation of mass markets. There have been major changes in the goods and services produced, the ways in which they are produced, their cost and the mode of their delivery to market. Inevitably, these developments directly or indirectly impact on the nature of enterprise-level industrial relations, prompting management initiatives that serve to alter hitherto traditional approaches to workforce management.

A key feature of the changing economic context is the *globalisation of competition*. This is a significant driver of change (at various levels). It entails greater access to new markets and the threat of increased product market competition. It is characterised by the closer integration of locations around the world into a single international market and the functional integration of internationally dispersed business activities. 'Globalisation' has significant industrial relations implications, since organisations 'benchmark' their activities and costs against international 'best practice'. This process prompts accusations of an 'international race to the bottom' (in respect of wages and employment terms and conditions) and 'social dumping', since entities may relocate to jurisdictions with lower wages and lower levels of employment rights/regulation (Blyton and Turnbull 2004). This is relevant in the Irish context, e.g. the Dell Computers decision to relocate manufacturing operations from Ireland to Poland in 2009 with the loss of almost 2,000 jobs. On the positive side, trade liberalisation provides greater opportunities to develop and access new markets. However, in order to capitalise on such opportunities, employers often have to improve their performance in areas such as unit production costs, delivery times and customer support. This in turn forces regular reviews of industrial relations, with potential implications for issues such as wage rates, labour flexibility/adaptability and job security.

Associated with globalisation is the impact of a greater *intensification of competition*. In addition to traditional sources of competition from countries such as the US and Japan, the competitive threat from countries such as Singapore, South Korea, China, India and Mexico is increasingly evident. Many of these jurisdictions combine a low cost base with strong performance on dimensions such as productivity and labour skills. Nearer home, many eastern and central European countries have undergone restructuring and provide stiff competition as a result of their low cost base, industrial tradition and an educational system with a strong technical and scientific foundation (Gunnigle and McGuire 2001). As a result, employees may experience job insecurity where their employer is operating in a competitive market, with the emergence of new processes, products and/or services threatening the old status quo.

Management Responses

In responding to such challenges, organisations have followed two broad strategies:

- rationalisation, including wage cuts and freezes, redundancies, contracting out or selling 'non-core' activities and 'de-layering' (Gunnigle *et al.* 2011 and Roche *et al.* 2011); and
- increased merger, acquisition and strategic alliance activities (Sparrow and Hiltrop 1994).

A common element to these responses is an increased focus on improving workforce management at the enterprise level, i.e. seeking productivity improvements and reduced labour costs. Related strategies can include the increased use of atypical employment patterns, task flexibility initiatives and improved performance management systems (McMahon 2009b). These revisions bring into focus the role of management in securing changed industrial relations in a manner that serves to enhance enterprise-level performance or 'the bottom line' (Gunnigle 1998b).

An organisation's performance in its *product/service market(s)* can have the most significant influence on strategic decision-making and management approaches or styles in industrial relations. For example, organisations operating from a strong product/market position through high market share or increasing demand have greater scope to adopt sophisticated HRM policies, e.g. offering bonus pay, attractive benefits and training and development. In turn, this may contribute to a more co-operative industrial relations climate. In contrast, firms operating under high levels of market pressure (contracting market share, high levels of price competition, etc.) will have less scope for choice and will be forced to adopt a more traditional 'cost and labour control' approach. In turn, this may contribute to a more adversarial industrial relations climate. Clearly the nature of a firm's product/service market is a key contextual factor influencing the choice of competitive strategy, with important implications for management approaches to industrial relations.

Kochan *et al.* (1986) provide a broad model of the impact of product/market change on strategic decision making and industrial relations. This helps explain how changes in the product/service market lead to strategic choice decisions at different levels of the organisation, namely:

- the long-term strategy formulation at the top;
- HRM/industrial relations policy in the middle; and
- workplace and individual organisation relationships at the shop floor level.

From this model, one can appreciate how a product/market change leads to a variety of business decisions with profound industrial relations implications. One such decision is to relocate across jurisdictions and/or to a non-union greenfield site. Related to this, Roche (2007a) explains that the insistence of many US MNCs on avoiding trade unions is largely attributable to a perception that product and process dynamism in fast-changing and turbulent product markets would be seriously compromised by engaging in time-consuming collective bargaining. Evaluating the impact of increased product/market competition, Kochan *et al.* (1986: 65) explain:

> When competition increases, the initial decision a firm must make is whether it wants to remain active in that line of business and compete in the new environment or withdraw and reallocate its capital resources to other opportunities. If the firm decides to remain in the market, the next decision it must make is whether to compete on the basis of low prices (costs) and high volume or to seek out more specialised market niches that will support a price premium. The central IR effect of this increased sensitivity to prices and costs is that firms shift their priorities away from maintaining labour peace to controlling labour costs, streamlining work rules (so as to increase manufacturing efficiency) and promoting productivity. The pressure to control or lower costs is especially intense if a firm attempts to compete across all segments of its product market on the basis of low prices and high volume.

The relevance of the product/service market was sharply underlined by a former director of British Airways, warning that HR requires a 'transformation' as it is not up to speed with the commercial reality of business, as 'customers are now in control – forever' (Special Correspondent 2008).

Public policy (the government's influence) is particularly important in explaining variations in national industrial relations systems and in the nature and extent of local or enterprise-level practices. For example, the revised approach of Ireland's industrial development agencies towards trade union recognition for MNC newcomers from the early 1980s heralded a significant rise in the incidence and extent of non-union establishments (Gunnigle 1995a; McGovern 1989). Likewise, the anti-union policies of successive Conservative governments in the UK during the 1980s gave legitimacy and support to 'macho' management practices that often undermined trade unions. At another consequential level, the influence of the EU (via a series of Directives) on almost all day-to-day staff–management interactions at the workplace is extensive, primarily in the protective labour law arena. Poole (1986) identifies the role of government or centralised control as a key constraining influence on managerial prerogative/discretion in decision making. That is, the greater the level of centralised control (corporatism), the more limited the scope for employers to develop industrial relations approaches or styles that undermine pluralist principles. Conversely, low levels of such regulation in industrial relations allow management greater discretion, rendering more likely the emergence of industrial relations approaches that diverge from the traditional pluralist–adversarial model.

As noted in Chapter 1, *technology* is another key external environmental factor affecting managerial approaches or styles in industrial relations (Beer *et al.* 1984). It impinges on a range of issues related to industrial relations, e.g. cost structure, job security, up-skilling, de-skilling, demarcation lines and reward systems. Marchington (1982) suggests that in labour-intensive sectors, where labour costs are high and market competition intense, organisations may adopt 'harder' approaches to HRM and industrial relations, characterised by high levels of work intensity and worker surveillance. However, in capital-intensive sectors, where labour costs constitute a small proportion of total costs, organisations may have greater scope to adopt 'softer' or more benign management approaches to HRM and industrial relations. The 'soft' approach places an emphasis on achieving high-trust relations between management and employees via initiatives designed to increase employee satisfaction, involvement and motivation. From an industrial relations perspective, advances in technology can impact on relative bargaining power positions, whether it be to strengthen the employer's position (with communications technology producing global markets and relocation opportunities) or the employee's position (in jobs requiring sizeable human capital or education/training/skills in capital-intensive settings).

The *labour market* represents an especially important contextual influence on industrial relations, specifically in relation to recruitment, training and development, and reward systems. For example, high unemployment conditions affect the power balance in labour–management relations, facilitating more authoritarian forms of management decision making. Such conditions also facilitate increased 'atypical' work patterns, job insecurity, lower pay, displacement, 'race to the bottom' initiatives and decreased union power and density. Workers and trade unions may be forced to accept less favourable levels of pay and working conditions. A notable development in the Irish labour market in this regard is the growth in the services sector. This has exerted a drag effect on union membership and recognition levels due to the fact that union density is generally low in this sector, particularly in private services such as domestic service, contract cleaning and hospitality. In contrast, low unemployment puts the focus on the attraction and retention of labour. This was especially evident at the height of the Celtic Tiger, where tight labour market conditions exerted upward pressure on wages, with the balance of power in collective bargaining tipping towards workers and trade unions.

While an organisation's external context serves to influence and guide management decisions on industrial relations, the factors in the organisation's *internal environment* are what determine unique organisational responses to the external environment. Such factors include managerial ideology, business strategy and organisation size and structure.

Management ideology and values incorporate the deeply held beliefs of senior management that serve to guide decisions on various aspects of workforce management (Gunnigle 1995a; Purcell 1987). In relation to managerial values, Kochan *et al.* (1986: 14) argue that these have a tremendous impact on industrial relations styles and strategies, acting as a 'lens' through which 'managerial decision makers weigh their options for responding to cues from the external environment'. Hence, options that are inconsistent with accepted values are discounted or not consciously considered. The impact of such ideologies is considered in detail later in this chapter in the context of managerial frames of reference and management styles in industrial relations.

Organisation structure and size are key internal factors impacting on management approaches to industrial relations. In relation to organisation structure, Purcell (1992) argues that senior (corporate) management in highly diversified organisations are primarily concerned with financial issues. As a consequence, HRM considerations (including industrial relations) are not a concern of corporate decision making, but rather an operational concern for management at the business unit level. A corollary of this argument is that organisations with a highly diversified product range are more likely to adopt differing HRM and industrial relations approaches and practices suited to the needs of constituent divisions and establishments. By comparison, 'core business' organisations with a narrow product range are more likely to integrate HRM issues into strategic planning. Daniels (2006: 18) presents three basic categories of organisational structure, which have particular implications for the employment relationship: functional, divisional and matrix.

- **Functional:** This applies to a structure whereby employees are grouped according to the type of work they do, i.e. by function. Limitations of this commonly used structure are that employees only have a partial view of the organisation's goals, are less likely to be innovative and work in an environment with poor horizontal co-ordination (i.e. poor co-ordination across functions) (Duncan 1979).

- **Divisional:** This applies to a structure where employees are grouped via product/ service markets. For example, the Virgin group has a number of different product lines, including an airline, a mobile phone company and financial products, so it is logical for Virgin to group employees according to the division in which they work. Likewise, Coca-Cola has a presence in over 200 countries and opts to structure its sales and marketing on a divisional basis by country. This enables it to market the product differently across various jurisdictions. Bank of America employs this structure via their retail, commercial, investment and asset management arms. Although this structure may be more efficient for the management of industrial relations, according to Duncan (1979), it is jeopardised by the prospect of poor co-ordination across product/service lines.

- **Matrix:** This structure endeavours to overcome weaknesses in the 'functional' and 'divisional' structural approaches by locating employees in a functional group and division that reflects their area of expertise. For example, all engineers may be in one engineering department and report to an engineering manager, but these same engineers may be assigned to different projects and report to a different engineering or project manager while working on that project. Therefore, each engineer may have to work under several managers in order to get their job done. Where the emphasis is on specific projects, it can enable empowerment and virtual teams to the advantage of customer service and delivery speed. Under this arrangement, working relationships are constantly changing. As Daniels (2006: 17) explains, one might be assigned to different products for varying durations, with the result that relationships become fragmented and fail to fully develop. Furthermore, employees are responsible to two managers (i.e. the divisional and functional manager) and this can lead to split loyalties and confusion.

In an era with extensive use of subcontracting, agency workers and virtual teams, Daniels's conclusion (2006: 18) that under these structures the term 'employee relations' becomes confusing is apt. The term indicates a relationship between an employee and the employer. However, within organisations there are ranges of relationships:

> ... concentrating our examination of employee relations solely on the relationship between employee and employer is a limited approach. If we do conclude that the focus is solely on the relationship between the employer and the employee, then we have to acknowledge that it is not always easy to identify who the 'employer' is.

Focusing on the industrial relations implications of an organisation's size, numerous studies have noted that trade union recognition and the presence of a specialised HR function are positively correlated with size. In the Irish context, Gunnigle and Brady (1984) found that management in smaller organisations tend to veer towards a unitarist frame of reference (see below) and adopt less formality in industrial relations than their counterparts in larger organisations (MacMahon 2002; Wallace 1982).

With regard to the impact of strategic decision making, *competitive strategy* is concerned with achieving sustainable competitive advantage in a particular industry or segment, e.g. through price or quality. Hence, management take steps to configure their HRM/industrial relations policies and practices in a manner that aids the implementation of the chosen competitive strategy. The main thrust of the debate on competitive strategy and HRM/industrial relations is the notion that organisations should seek to achieve 'fit' between them. That is, if an organisation is to successfully pursue a particular competitive strategy, it must adopt and implement a complementary set of HRM/industrial relations approaches. Related to this, it is argued that organisations will experience severe problems in strategy implementation if it is not effectively linked with appropriate HRM/industrial relations policy choices (Fombrun 1986). Porter (1990) identifies three different competitive strategies with specific implications for HRM and industrial relations. First, there is the 'low-cost leadership strategy', which is characterised by a strong central authority, close supervision and limited employee empowerment. Second, there is the 'unique product/service differentiation strategy', warranting significant levels of employee involvement and creativity. The third 'focus strategy' entails concentration on a specific market or buyer group and encourages employees to develop customer loyalty and a focus on specific areas of activity, which some employees may find dull and uninspiring due to its narrow orientation.

TOWARDS STRATEGIC INDUSTRIAL RELATIONS?

From the foregoing environmental analysis, we can see how business strategy, product/market context and choice of competitive strategy can have important knock-on effects on HRM and industrial relations. Given the argument that management are increasingly recognising that improved utilisation of the organisation's workforce can have a significant impact on competitive advantage, this is most pertinent (Guest 1987). A useful analysis of this topic is provided by Wood and Peccei (1990), who differentiate between 'strategic HRM' (i.e. where HR and industrial relations issues are fully integrated into the strategic planning process) and 'business-led HRM' (i.e. where such issues are linked to the commercial imperatives of the organisation). Differences in these approaches lie in the level of strategic consideration of HRM and industrial relations issues. In relation to 'strategic HRM', industrial relations issues are integral to strategic planning and form part of the organisation's long-term business strategy. From the alternate 'business-led' perspective, policies and practices are very much a lower order strategic activity, linked to higher order strategic decisions in areas such as product development or market penetration. As noted earlier, the traditional perception advanced by Purcell (1992) is that strategic decision making in organisations largely focuses on 'primary' business issues such as finance, while any attention devoted to industrial relations issues is secondary and somewhat incidental. At the other extreme, some organisations incorporate HRM and industrial relations considerations into their strategic decision-making processes, taking well thought-out strategic decisions relating thereto.

Collings and Wood (2009) emphasise the centrality of employment/industrial relations to organisational competitiveness, while Dibben *et al.* (2011: 308) posit that in the face of increasing investor and customer mobility, technological change and economic and political uncertainty, it is 'all the more important' that employment relations be 'managed in a strategic way' to 'impact on the broader organisational context'. As delineated by Gennard and Judge (2010: 235), the bottom line on this theme is that:

> The key is to develop an employment relations strategy that is responsive to the needs of the organisation, that can provide an overall sense of purpose to the employment relations professional and assist employees to understand where they are going, how they are going to get there, why certain things are happening and, most importantly, the contribution they are expected to make towards achieving the organisational goals.

In the face of an economic depression and associated job insecurity fears, this theme has gained added impetus in many organisations in the form of 'employee engagement' initiatives. This aspiration is being 'heavily marketed by human resource consulting firms' advising as to 'how it can be created and leveraged' (Macey and Schneider 2008: 3). As the Chartered Institute of Personnel and Development (2006: 9) note, it is 'something of a vogue word, eclipsing commitment and motivation' in the literature. Directly related to this initiative in the new economic context is the finding by Roche *et al.* (2011: 105) that:

> More than any other single theme, participants quite consistently stressed that, in their eyes, intensive communications with employees and unions were a critical aspect of managing pay and headcount reductions effectively, as, more generally, of managing HR in recessionary conditions ... direct communications was the priority concern ...

In practice, the idea of the strategic integration of HRM/industrial relations at the extremes of 'total' or 'absent' is inadequate, although Roche (2007a) speculates that there has been a 'new dawn' for HRM in Ireland in recent years. He claims that this has been prompted by a new macro-level appreciation of the economic importance of investment in human assets, which in turn has been translated into revised approaches to people management matters that are more closely aligned with, or dependent on, business strategies and pressures. However, while the management of HRM and industrial relations in Ireland may be more strategically aligned with business strategies and conditions, this does not appear to have translated into the advent on any wide scale of the so-called 'high-performance HRM model' (Roche 2007a). This is pertinent given that a subsequent Irish study found that 'strategic HRM' as a dimension of high-performance work systems is positively correlated with productivity increases and greater levels of innovation (Guthrie *et al.* 2009). In an Economic and Social Research Institute (ESRI) study, Watson *et al.* (2010: 16) found that organisations benefit most (with better business outcomes) by adopting 'coherent bundles of employment practices'. The relevance of this theme also surfaced in research by Heffernan *et al.* (2008: 3), which found that the best-performing firms are 'those that apply sophisticated HRM to the vast majority of their workforce'.

With regard to the impact of the recession on HRM, there are contrasting views, with:

> … some suggesting that the recession will throw into question the viability of already existing employment models, others suggesting that high-commitment HR policies are likely to come to the fore during the downturn, and still others suggesting that the recession will not have a huge lasting or disjunctive impact on HR either way. (Roche *et al.* 2011: 45)

HRM IMPLICATIONS FOR THE MANAGEMENT OF INDUSTRIAL RELATIONS

In evaluating the implications of HRM for industrial relations, it is clear that there are challenges to collective bargaining and trade unions (Guest 1987; Storey 1992). In essence, these challenges entail a reduced emphasis on collective bargaining and management–trade union interactions largely through trade union avoidance. In this regard it is notable that the term 'union substitution' appears to have achieved widespread notoriety as a result of its association with non-union greenfield sites in the US (Gunnigle *et al.* 2009). Roche and Turner (1998) argue that a union substitution strategy is most likely to emerge in larger firms that operate in the more profitable sectors of the economy. In such instances, firms have the financial wherewithal to provide pay levels, employment conditions and the general working environment necessary to underpin such a strategy. Indeed, since the 1970s in Ireland there has been a significant growth in non-union approaches, particularly among US-owned firms (Gunnigle *et al.* 2001). Undoubtedly, some of these firms (e.g. IBM and Intel) have adopted a 'union substitution' strategy, involving the adoption of HRM policies designed to eliminate employees' need for collective representation (Dundon 2002). In order to successfully implement a union substitution strategy, employers usually need to ensure that most of the benefits associated with union recognition still accrue in the non-union environment. While a union substitution strategy is commonly associated with large multinational subsidiaries, Blyton and Turnbull (1994: 252) broaden the analysis, pointing out that the majority of non-union firms 'do not need nor could the majority afford' to implement such a substitution strategy.

From the employer's perspective, there are advantages and disadvantages to union recognition. There has been much academic focus on the impact of unionisation on organisational performance and specifically on issues such as profit levels, labour productivity and return on investment (Huselid 1995). In evaluating this literature, Roche and Turner (1998) find the results regarding the impact of unionisation on productivity to be inconclusive; however, they argue that the evidence from the manufacturing sector (particularly in the US) indicates that unionisation serves to reduce profitability. Hence, it is argued that non-union firms may have a sound economic rationale for pursuing a union avoidance or substitution strategy. It must be noted, however, that there are also potential costs associated with such a strategy. Flood and Toner (1997) have identified a number of disadvantages associated with both union substitution and recognition strategies (see Table 8.1).

Table 8.1
Disadvantages of Union Substitution and Union Recognition

Disadvantages of Union Substitution	Disadvantages of Union Recognition
• Need to provide pay and employment conditions at least on a par with those in similar unionised companies • Management reluctant to enforce discipline • Absence of adequate structure to deal with grievances (particularly collective issues) • Fear of unionisation is a constant concern • Supervisors are monitored too closely • Management in non-union firms must work harder at communications • Need for expensive, well-resourced personnel function	• Unions make changes in work organisation more difficult • Unions give rise to demarcation problems and impose restrictions on production • Unions impose higher manning levels • Unions protect unsatisfactory workers • Unions inhibit individual reward systems • Unions promote an adversarial IR climate and can cause industrial action • Unions encourage the pursuit of trivial grievances • Unions make communication with employees more difficult

Source: Flood and Toner (1997)

The disadvantages associated with union substitution are categorised by Flood and Toner (1997) as a 'catch 22' situation, whereby firms pursuing a union substitution strategy cannot take advantage of their non-union status. For example, by reducing pay and diluting employment conditions or disciplining/dismissing unsatisfactory workers, there is the fear that such action will lead to union recognition. This leads the authors to conclude that the major advantages of union substitution lie not in clear economic 'cost-benefit' criteria, but rather in allowing the firm greater scope to develop a unitary company culture and to foster 'warm personal relations' between management and employees. Accordingly, it is worth noting that there has been a substantial growth in non-union approaches in Ireland since the early 1980s. Having said this, Turner's (1993) analysis found few significant differences between union and non-union firms in the use of HRM practices.

MANAGEMENT VALUES, FRAMES OF REFERENCE AND MANAGEMENT STYLES IN INDUSTRIAL RELATIONS

All organisations are characterised by particular values and philosophies with respect to industrial relations. In some organisations these values may be explicit, as demonstrated in statements of corporate mission or philosophy. In others, they may be implicit and inferred from management practice in areas such as supervisory style, pay levels or communications. Of particular significance is the suggestion that managerial opposition to pluralism (see Chapter 1) and unionisation in particular is characteristic of the value system of managers from the US. Certain HRM approaches, which emphasise individual freedom and initiative, direct communications and merit-based rewards, are very much in line with this value system (Jacoby 1997; Kochan *et al.* 1986). This interpretation is significant for Ireland, since our economy is heavily dependent on foreign direct investment, much of which comes from the US.

Analyses of the management of industrial relations are largely preoccupied with the product of such values and ideologies as manifested in 'styles' and 'frames of reference'. The practical impact of such 'styles' is noted in Hutchinson and Purcell's (2003) finding that the behaviour of front-line management has a direct impact on employee commitment, motivation and satisfaction, with a poor relationship frequently the key reason for staff resignations and the manager's control orientation determining whether the manager–employee relationship breaks down.

Fox (1966) explained that management's approach to industrial relations is largely determined by the *frame of reference* they adopt since this determines how they expect people to behave and how managers believe they should behave (beliefs and values). This also determines management reactions to actual behaviour (management practice) and shapes the methods they choose when trying to change the behaviour of people at work (strategies/policies). The two main frames identified in Chapter 1 were unitarism and pluralism, although in practice, management may well adopt different approaches in different situations and/or change their approaches over time.

Rollinson (1993: 92) describes management styles in industrial relations as 'management's overall approach to handling the relationship between the organisation and its employees'. As noted, this is a dynamic process that can be refined and changed over time and (as detailed earlier) it is particularly vulnerable to the impact of environmental change. Although employer organisations play an important role in industrial relations, individual employers are primarily responsible for the development and implementation of their own style and associated policies and practices. The link between ownership and the legitimacy of managerial authority is also a critical characteristic of organisational life. Despite the fact that management are responsible to other interest groups, such as employees and their trade unions, they exercise considerable power (as manifested in their 'style') by virtue of their capacity to take strategic decisions on behalf of the owners' interests.

On the 'management style' theme, Purcell (1987) draws attention to the fact that employers' policies and practices cannot be wholly explained by structural variables such as size, product markets and technology. Accordingly, he identifies strategic choice, as exercised by senior management, as a key factor in explaining differences in management styles. Management can use their power to make strategic choices in respect of industrial relations matters, albeit within the all-important constraint of environmental factors (Marchington and Parker 1990: 99).

Furthermore, management can take strategic decisions that directly and indirectly influence industrial relations matters. For example, the impact is direct where company management decide not to recognise trade unions in a new greenfield start-up. The industrial relations implications are more indirect where, for example, a product line is terminated (perhaps due to poor market performance) and the consequent redundancies may detrimentally affect industrial relations. Table 8.2 provides a sample list of strategic decisions that will impact on dimensions of industrial relations.

Table 8.2
Indicative Strategic Decisions Impacting on Industrial Relations

Decisions	Impact on Industrial Relations
Location of plant	Influences labour supply, nature of labour force, labour costs, labour/employment law application and prospect of unionisation
Size of plant	Influences span of managerial control, communications, leadership/managerial style
Recruitment and selection	By deciding on the nature of the workforce (e.g. propensity of workers to join trade unions)
Training and development	Nature and extent of training and development can influence management and employee approaches and attitudes to industrial relations .
Union recognition	In a greenfield situation, management may be able to decide whether or not to deal with trade unions, which will have a significant impact on the subsequent nature of enterprise level-industrial relations.
Employer association	Deciding whether or not to join an employer association may influence subsequent industrial relations decisions (e.g. pay negotiations)
Procedural formalisation	The extent and nature of formalisation of industrial relations procedures will impact on enterprise-level industrial relations (e.g. grievance and dispute handling)
Use of HRM policies and practices	By introducing techniques such as performance appraisal or performance-related pay, management can limit the scope of trade unions

Table 8.3
Management Styles in Industrial Relations

Management Style	Characteristics
Traditionalist	'Orthodox unitarism': Opposes role for unions; little attention to employee needs
Sophisticated paternalist	Emphasises employee needs (training, pay, conditions, etc.); discourages unionisation; demands employee loyalty and commitment
Sophisticated modern	Accepts trade unions' role in specific areas; emphasises role of industrial relations procedures and consultative mechanisms Variations: (a) **Constitutionalists:** Emphasise codification of management–union relations through detailed collective agreements (b) **Consulters:** Collective bargaining established but management emphasises personal direct contact and problem solving, playing down a formal union role at workplace level
Standard modern	Pragmatic approach; unions' role accepted but no overall philosophy or strategy developed; 'fire-fighting' approach

Source: Adapted from Purcell and Sisson (1983)

Several commentators have attempted to develop categorisations of management styles in industrial relations in order to better illustrate and explain the differences in organisational approaches. However, Purcell and Sisson's (1983) five-fold categorisation of 'ideal-typical' management styles in industrial relations, which is based on differing management approaches to trade unions, collective bargaining, consultation and communications, is arguably seminal (see Table 8.3). However, despite the appeal of such categorisations, in reality it is hard to categorise management styles in industrial relations into clearly discernible 'ideal-typical' groupings (Deaton 1985; Gunnigle 1995b). Using data from over 1,400 UK organisations, Deaton (1985) sought to empirically evaluate the appropriateness of Purcell and Sisson's (1983) typology. He concluded that attempts to classify firms into a small number of ideal styles were problematic and that while the distinction between organisations that recognise trade unions and those that do not is crucial, it may not be possible to further subdivide styles in organisations where unions are recognised.

Likewise, when using more anecdotal evidence to examine variations in managerial styles in industrial relations, Poole (1986) found an array of hybrid styles, rather than any convergence towards particularly predominant patterns. As Daniels (2006) explains, one model with five categories could not hope to capture the complexities of the employment relationship, but the model does provide a spectrum of examples within each category. However, styles should not be rigidly interpreted. Likewise, Gunnigle *et al.* (2011: 323) conclude:

In practice, one finds that managers do not strictly adhere to one of these approaches but may adopt different approaches in different situations and/or change their approaches over time. Nevertheless the frames of reference approach provides a useful framework for evaluating management approaches to (industrial relations) at enterprise level.

THE MANAGEMENT OF INDUSTRIAL RELATIONS IN IRELAND

Based on this chapter's review of environmental influences on management styles in industrial relations and the key dimensions thereof, it is possible to propose a broad categorisation of such styles, drawing on the available Irish evidence. This categorisation is set out in Table 8.4 and it represents an attempt to apply the typology pioneered by Purcell and Sisson (1983) and Fox (1974). It identifies six 'ideal-typical' management styles, with differences derived from variations in, *inter alia*, the strategic significance that management attributes to industrial relations, and management approaches to collective employee representation as manifested through management practices in areas such as communications, reward systems and the role of the specialist HRM function.

While this typology is indicative of the predominant styles adopted by Irish-based organisations, in practice one often finds overlap in these styles within organisations. Given the caveats outlined above (i.e. the limitations of 'ideal-typical' categorisations) and reflecting on the Irish scenario, a most notable feature of the typology relates to the 'soft HRM', 'hard HRM' and 'dualist' styles. These styles are significant because they indicate a planned and co-ordinated approach to industrial relations management, in contrast with the other styles, which are more indicative of the 'incidentalist' approach.

Table 8.4

Typology of Management Styles in Industrial Relations in Ireland

Anti-union Style

Organisations in this category are characterised by a commodity view of labour. Manifestations of this approach include a preoccupation with retaining managerial prerogative, rejection of any role for trade unions or other modes of collective representation, little or no attention to HR/industrial relations except where absolutely necessary, a low-level HR function (at best), absence of procedures for communicating or consulting with employees, and authoritarian management control. The available research evidence suggests that 'anti-union' styles are predominantly confined to smaller indigenous entities managed in the classic 'small firm/ entrepreneurial' mode and also among some foreign-owned firms.

Paternalist Style

With this style, top management prioritise the need to 'look after' employees, being benevolent and welfare oriented. However, the management approach is essentially unitarist. Little attention is paid to deploying systems or procedures for employee representation, involvement or development. Opinions adjudged to be divergent from those of management are considered to be indicative of disloyalty and potentially damaging. Indeed, the paternalist style may incorporate a high level of management complacency about the perceived closeness of management and employee interests and expectations. HRM policy manifestations include a caring supervisory style but also a work system that limits employee involvement and discretion, limited communication mechanisms and a low-level HR function whose role is of an administrative support nature.

Traditional Industrial Relations Style

The 'traditional industrial relations' style is characterised by adversarial industrial relations and primary reliance on collective bargaining. Management–union/multi-union relations may be formalised through procedural agreements dealing with relations between the parties and encompassing issues such as union recognition (including closed shop) and disciplinary, grievance and disputes procedures. Other manifestations of this style may include a bureaucratic organisation structure, job demarcation, a limited communications system and a 'contracts manager' HRM function whose primary role is to handle industrial relations (see Tyson and Fell 1986). In Ireland, it appears that this style is most common in the public sector and semi-state sector, and in larger, established, indigenous organisations and some MNCs (i.e. primarily those established prior to the 1980s).

'Soft' HRM Style

The 'soft' HRM style is characterised by a resource perspective of employees and a desire to create an organisational climate where employee needs are addressed and satisfied through positive employee-oriented policies designed in part to render collective representation unnecessary. This style often equates the 'union substitution' approach discussed above. Like the anti-union and paternalist styles (above), it is grounded in the unitarist perspective and is normally associated with a pronounced preference for non-union status. Manifestations of this style include competitive pay and employment conditions, extensive management–employee communications, direct employee involvement and procedures to promptly address grievance and disciplinary issues, together with a highly developed and influential HRM function. This approach appears to be most common in US-owned firms operating in high-technology sectors.

'Hard' HRM Style

With this style the focus is primarily on 'transaction costs'. The objective is to source and manage labour in as cheap and cost-effective a fashion as possible to ensure achievement of the organisation's 'bottom line' objectives. This style equates to what has been termed 'union suppression', incorporating low employment standards. It represents a marked contrast to the 'soft' HRM approach and may be found among some foreign-owned assembly and service firms, often operating in a subcontracting mode. Manifestations include use of 'atypical' employment forms to improve cost effectiveness and the application of performance management techniques in order to achieve high productivity.

Dualist Style

The 'dualist' style is characterised by an acceptance of the legitimacy of collective employee representation but is supplemented by a strong individualist orientation. Organisations adopting this style differ from 'soft' HRM in regard to union recognition and collective bargaining, but otherwise they pursue broadly similar policies. At workplace level, management seek to keep formality to a minimum. The management focus is on minimising the extent of collective bargaining, preferring direct dealings with employees. This style might be termed 'neo-pluralism' and it involves the use of selected HRM techniques, including sophisticated staff selection mechanisms, extensive direct communication with employees, performance-related pay systems and established collective bargaining procedures. Further characteristics can include extensive employee development, encouragement that employees deal directly with management on issues of concern, the training of line management in the area of industrial relations and a well-developed and influential HR function.

The 'traditional industrial relations' style (see Table 8.4) equates to the pluralist-adversarial model, which was historically the most pervasive in medium and large organisations in Ireland (Hillery 1994; Roche 1990). In contrast, the 'anti-union' and 'paternalist' styles reflect opposition to the pluralist model, as manifested through forthright attempts to curb or eliminate moves towards collective employee representation. It has been argued that these styles were confined to smaller organisations and that in the event of growth they would succumb in time to the 'traditional pluralist' model (Roche 1990). However, the available evidence indicates considerable change in enterprise-level industrial relations in Ireland. In terms of management styles, these developments are characterised by the increased adoption of HRM-based styles ('hard' or 'soft' variants). For example, there are clear indications of a strengthening of the unitarist ideology at greenfield site start-ups, greater opposition to union recognition, the emergence of a strong non-union sector and a continuing decline in union density.

A review of the literature on the historical development of the specialist personnel/ HR function in Ireland helps to illuminate our understanding on the evolution of management approaches or styles in industrial relations. This literature identifies industrial relations as traditionally the most significant area of activity (Gunnigle 1998b; O'Mahony 1964). This is largely due to the growth in influence of trade unions up to the early 1980s, with many larger employers engaging specialist 'personnel' managers to deal with industrial relations matters (particularly collective bargaining and grievance/ discipline administration) at enterprise level. As Gunnigle (1998b: 4) notes:

> For the personnel function, industrial relations became the priority, with personnel practitioners vested with the responsibility to negotiate and police agreements. Industrial harmony was the objective and personnel specialists through their nego-tiating, interpersonal and procedural skills had responsibility for its achievement. This industrial relations emphasis helped position the personnel function in a more central management role, albeit a largely reactive one.

From rather humble origins, the specialist HR function developed to a stage where it became accepted as an integral part of the management structure of larger organisations charged with the establishment and maintenance of stable industrial relations. Often more reactive than strategic, this industrial relations orientation was significant: it served to define what HR work involved and it helped to position the function as an important component of the managerial infrastructure.

This role peaked in popularity in the 1970s, but by the early 1980s 'industrial relations orthodoxy' as the accepted model for the HR function had begun to unravel. The change can be traced to numerous sources, most particularly to increased competitive pressures on organisations. Contingency approaches became the order of the day, with the role of the HR function influenced by a variety of factors such as sector, managerial philosophy and market context. Elaborating on the trend, Roche and Gunnigle (1997: 445–6) point out that:

Never before has the analysis of industrial relations practices and policies been so closely tied to an appreciation of commercial and national and international political pressures. In the past, the worlds of industrial relations practitioners and academics alike tended to be much more introverted and preoccupied with the internal dynamics of industrial relations systems, agreements and procedures. The professional preoccupations and vocabularies of industrial relations experts tended to revolve around distinctly industrial relations themes: disputes and grievance procedures, anomalies in pay structures, productivity bargaining ... Currently, these concerns, though not altogether displaced, often take second place to such issues as company performance, the union's role in contributing to business success, mission statements and quality standards, business units, employment flexibility and so on.

The most widely accepted explanation of these changes is the aforementioned increasingly competitive nature of product and service markets. These pressures appear to create a 'flexibility imperative' whereby organisations have to be increasingly responsive to consumer demand on dimensions such as price, customer service and product quality. It is also significant that these competitive trends are increasingly penetrating the state sector because of the erosion of monopoly status as a result of EU-imposed pressures (see Hastings 2003). One example of a hitherto state-owned company grappling with a changing and more competitive environment is Aer Lingus. Deregulation in the airline industry left the company facing increased competition, particularly from low-cost airlines (notably Ryanair and EasyJet). Resultant restructuring has led to significant changes in employee numbers, employment patterns and reward systems. However, McGovern *et al.* (2007: 288) warn against an overdue emphasis on the 'marketisation' view of transformation in industrial relations as being unduly influenced by misconstruing as structural change 'an unduly severe downswing in the economy that had involved short-term turbulence'.

Although the industrial relations aspect remains an important part of the work of the specialist HR function, we have witnessed a considerable reorientation in its role in many organisations. This involves a broadening of its remit so that other core areas of HR activity (beyond industrial relations) are given greater priority, e.g. training and development, performance management and an increased role in more generic management initiatives (Heraty *et al.* 1994). In some organisations this change has led to a greater strategic role for the HR function, involving the development of closer linkages between business strategy and HR/industrial relations practice (Sheehan 2002). Specifically, Roche *et al.* (2011: 42) find that the impact of the post-2007 recession on industrial relations has resulted in:

> ... fairly widespread incidence of pay reductions and freezes, which distinguishes this recession from the last serious business downturn in Ireland during the 1980s ... in some instances the recession has triggered greater co-operation between trade unions and management while in other cases established co-operative relations have been frayed by the downturn.

Given that different management styles in industrial relations are significantly reflected in enterprise-level approaches to collective employee representation, it is noteworthy that although union de-recognition has not emerged to any great extent in Ireland, what is often termed 'union marginalisation' (i.e. reducing the impact of trade unions in enterprise-level industrial relations) has surfaced in the economic downturn and arguably beforehand. Roche *et al.* (2011: 228) record the perception amongst the trade union community and suggest:

> ... a pattern where employers and HR managers sought to bypass unions and implement change unilaterally. They also sought to rescind or ignore collective agreements and to change the established rules of collective bargaining and industrial relations. Union officials were of the view that their role was often only to rubber stamp decisions already made.

Concluding Comments

This chapter has considered management approaches to industrial relations and the various contextual influences impacting thereon. This review suggests that many organisations do not make not make any deliberate strategic choices with regard to industrial relations, but rather adopt somewhat more reactive and ad hoc approaches. However, we also present evidence that some organisations employ more strategic approaches and the characteristics of such approaches or styles have been outlined. We have placed considerable focus on management approaches to collective employee representation (and particularly trade union recognition and avoidance), how this has changed over time in Ireland and the impact of the global financial crisis on industrial relations, management–trade union interactions and enterprise industrial relations more generally.

CHAPTER 9

The Nature of Industrial Conflict

INTRODUCTION

Industrial conflict is one of the most emotive aspects of industrial relations and it often makes headlines in the media. Inevitably, media commentary is driven by the immediate concerns of those involved – management, workers, government and consumers – with the causes of disputes being rehearsed from differing perspectives. The media also frequently pronounce implicitly on the 'rights' and 'wrongs' of disputes. They sometimes seem to become actors in the particular dispute and influence its direction and even its outcome. For example, the Association of Secondary Teachers of Ireland (ASTI) received cold treatment in the media in their dispute with the Department of Education over their attempts to opt out of benchmarking in the early 2000s. In contrast, Vita Cortex workers, who occupied their former place of employment from December 2011 to May 2012, received widespread sympathetic media treatment in spite of the fact that occupations are illegal. Industrial conflict also has wider societal considerations beyond the immediate workplace. The ways in which societies choose to allow, disallow or regulate industrial conflict have major implications for the nature of society. It is a mark of democratic societies that collective industrial conflict is allowed but that institutions are provided to moderate such conflict. However, the ways in which this is done will vary greatly from country to country. This chapter explores the dimensions of industrial conflict, both collective and individual, in order to provide a more nuanced and deeper understanding of its nature.

IDENTIFYING CONFLICT

At a very basic level the identification of what constitutes conflict is an issue for critical examination. The most obvious form of industrial conflict is that between employers and workers. However, industrial conflict is not confined to such disputes but is arguably inherent in the nature of industrial competition (Dahrendorf 1959). Some of the most bruising examples of conflict take place between businesses (e.g. disputes over patents involving Samsung and Apple) or between companies and governments (e.g. Microsoft and the US government). Closer to home, the dispute between the Quinn family and the Irish Bank Resolution Corporation (formerly Anglo Irish Bank) is a graphic example of conflict between corporate entities. Commercial disputes are normally dealt with through the courts. Industrial action has wider societal dimensions and it is not always appropriate to legal adjudication and not always capable of being contained within legal systems.

NATURE AND FORMS OF INDUSTRIAL ACTION

Classifying Conflict

Given the difficulties in defining industrial conflict, industrial relations scholars have drawn attention to the diverse forms that it can take. They point out that conflict can be collective or individual, organised or unorganised (spontaneous) and it may occur between workers and management, between workers themselves or between managers themselves (Jackson 1991). Conflict can also be inherent in the employment relationship but it can remain unexpressed – this is known as latent conflict. Industrial action, on the other hand, is the manifest expression of conflict. The possibility that conflict can be latent implies that an absence of conflict cannot automatically be considered a 'good thing'. Conflict may not be expressed because management 'buy out' conflict to the long-run detriment of the organisation, something industrial relations practitioners refer to as 'cheque book' industrial relations. Workers may be unable to express conflict because they have insufficient power resources at their disposal or it may be illegal and suppressed. The question might be asked as to why women did not strike over the years, given the evident discrimination against them in pay and other opportunities in the labour markets. It is not credible to argue that there were not potential grievances. The question arises as to how exactly these grievances were limited so that they did not end up in conflict. The reality is that the collective bargaining system institutionalised gender pay discrimination, with women generally receiving pay rises that were only 60 per cent of those of their male counterparts. In the early national agreements of the 1970s, increases were raised to 85 per cent of the male rates. It is notable that it was only with social mobilisation via the women's movement in the 1970s that women were able to press their case, and it wasn't until Ireland sought membership of the EEC that anti-discrimination pay legislation was introduced (see Chapter 6).

While it is difficult to define industrial conflict, collective industrial action is 'any temporary suspension of normal working arrangements which is initiated unilaterally by either employees (whether through their union or not), or management, with the aim of exerting pressure within the collective bargaining process' (Salamon 2000: 411). However, this definition is only one type of industrial conflict; industrial action can exist outside of collective conflict. Thus, two broad categories of industrial conflict can be recognised, as follows:

- explicit and organised collective industrial action; or
- unorganised and implicit individual industrial action (Jackson 1991; Salamon 1998).

The conceptual difference between the two forms of action is that individual unorganised action represents a 'withdrawal from the source of discontent' by individuals, while organised collective action is more likely to be a conscious strategy to change the situation that is the source of the discontent (Hyman 1989: 56).

Table 9.1 contains examples of the main forms of both individual and collective industrial action. Individual conflict such as absenteeism, labour turnover and dismissals are less visible forms of conflict. Even actions such as sabotage, theft, industrial espionage and passive non-cooperation can be expressions of individual conflict. Such unorganised or individual action by workers represents a largely spontaneous, reactive and random response to the employment relationship and generally does not involve any conscious strategy. The growth of disputes referred to the Employment Appeals Tribunal (EAT) in recent years (see Chapter 6) is an indication of quite a dramatic increase in individually based conflict in Ireland in the last ten years. The most common examples of organised industrial action arising from workers are strikes, go slows, overtime bans and non-cooperation. The lockout is a well-recognised form of collective management conflict, but there are other, less obvious forms arising from industrial restructuring, e.g. plant closures and relocation. Hebdon and Stern (1998: 204) note that measures such as 'arbitration' are also correctly viewed as expressions of conflict, with arbitration and strikes acting as direct substitutes. This is a variant on the notion that diplomacy is war by other means!

Individual Unorganised Conflict

While absenteeism and high labour turnover can be indicators of individual conflict, an inability to attend work due to illness or other such factors is not an indication of conflict. Absenteeism is determined by a range of factors including such things as the ability to attend work, the motivation to attend, family circumstances, gender, the level of social welfare provision and sick pay. This reservation aside, absenteeism and turnover rates can be affected by the nature of the job: a job that has low discretion and is unrewarding can lead to higher absenteeism or high levels of turnover. These are rightly regarded as expressions of conflict. Royle and Towers (2002) note that high levels of absenteeism in McDonald's are an expression of unorganised individual conflict against the McDonald's work system. Looking at the issue of turnover, employees may continue to work in what they consider unrewarding jobs because of high unemployment and the lack of an alternative choice – this is a form of unexpressed or latent individual conflict. Other individual forms of conflict can be subtle and virtually impossible to detect or measure. Employees may engage in passive non-cooperation, underperform or exhibit low-trust behaviour (Fox 1974). Such individual action may not even be conscious but it can have long-term effects on productivity and the employment relationship. Indeed, underperformance has been a common concern of management theorists since Taylor's development of scientific management (Rose 1977).

It is important to note that unorganised individual conflict also arises from the management side of industry. Examples include overly strict supervision, arbitrary discipline, bullying, victimisation, speed-ups, industrial accidents and unauthorised deductions of wages. Salamon (2000) notes that speed-ups, disciplinary action and unilateral changes to agreed working arrangements can be viewed as management-initiated conflict. Beynon's (1973) celebrated study of the Ford motor plant in Halewood in the UK (*Working for Ford*) paints a vivid picture of the reality of speed-ups as management-initiated conflict. He notes that 'production managers out to make a name for themselves' engaged in speed-ups, resulting in 'unofficial walkouts' (Beynon

Table 9.1

Forms of Industrial Action

- **Strike:** Collective in nature, involving temporary withdrawal of labour.
- **Lockout:** The most conspicuous form of organised industrial action instigated by employers, which involves preventing the workforce, or a proportion thereof, from attending work.
- **Withdrawal of co-operation:** Collective in nature, involving the withdrawal of representatives from joint institutions; strict interpretation of and rigorous adherence to procedures; absence of flexibility.
- **Work to rule:** Collective in nature, involving working only in accordance with the strict interpretation of written terms and conditions of employment, job description or other rules, such as those concerning safety or hygiene.
- **Overtime ban:** Collective in nature, involving refusal to work outside normal contractual hours of work.
- **Go slow:** Collective in nature, involving working at a lower than normal level of performance.
- **Work-in/sit-in:** Occupation of the workplace or section thereof; denial of access to management. This approach is often used to prevent movement of plant and equipment and is associated with plant closures. A recent example was its use in Vita Cortex in Cork.
- **Blacking of goods/services:** Refusing to handle goods or co-operate with services from a particular employer(s).
- **Unilateral management changes:** Changes to the agreed speed of work; work intensification; job insecurity; unilateral changes to terms of contract of employment by employer – if considered unreasonable by EAT, may constitute grounds for constructive dismissal.
- **Other management action:** Blacklisting of workers; harassment and intimidation; industrial accidents due to improper safety, speed-ups, etc.
- **Sabotage and industrial espionage:** Individual or collective in nature, involving conscious action to damage goods or equipment; illegitimate leaking of commercial information to competitors; distributing false, damaging information about an organisation.
- **Whistleblowing:** Unauthorised release of internal company information to the media, government or other source on commercial, health and safety or other matters. Generally individual but may be collective.
- **Pilfering and theft:** Individual in nature, involving stealing by employees, either from the organisation or customers; also unauthorised deductions of wages by management.
- **Absenteeism:** Generically defined as all absences from work other than authorised leave. It is estimated that only a small proportion of absenteeism may represent a form of industrial action. Where it does, it can represent an individualised response to perceived problems in the workplace.
- **Labour turnover:** High turnover can be an expression of underlying employee dissatisfaction. Only a proportion of labour turnover in organisations may represent a form of industrial action.
- **Motivational withdrawal:** Lack of trust; passive non-cooperation; low productivity.
- **Suicide:** Suicides in Renault and France Telecom have been individual responses to work stress. In Taiwan and China, there have been both individual incidences and threats of mass suicide in response to grievances over working conditions.

1973: 138). In order to ensure agreements on the speed of the line were observed, the management conceded to shop stewards the right to hold the key that locked the assembly line.

More recently the issue of job insecurity and work intensification associated with flexibility has been found to place stress on employees and affect their health and psychological wellbeing. Burchell *et al.* (2002: 2) note that intensification of work poses even greater problems – in terms of 'stress, psychological health and family tension'. Nolan (2002) points to the limitations of family-friendly policies. She notes that they have the capacity to limit the impact on employees, but that when organisations are under intense strain to perform 'the inclinations of managers to develop "family-friendly" policies diminishes' (Nolan 2002: 131). She also notes that such work intensification also limits the informal support provided by fellow team members and other employees. As Burchell *et al.* (2012) point out, such policies are not independent of the neo-liberal imperatives of economic competition.

A recent dramatic employee response to employer-initiated conflict has been employee suicide or the threat of suicide. Notable examples include the suicide of three executives of Renault in France who were dismissed following company accusations of industrial espionage (later proven to be false) that they had leaked details of its electric car to rivals and the suicide of workers in the Foxconn Plant in China, which manufactures components for high-profile companies including Apple, Hewlett-Packard and Dell (Brown 2012; Zhang 2012).

Collective Conflict

The 'fact' that the employment relationship may be characterised by conflict rarely gives rise to any public concern or comment, yet collective industrial action is commonly perceived as extremely negative and damaging. Rollinson (1993) identifies three principal reasons why it is seen in such negative terms:

- Industrial action (as initiated by workers) is normally vertical in nature and therefore challenges the legitimacy of management authority/prerogative in decision making.
- Industrial action tends to be highly visible, both within and outside the organisation, and it can involve large numbers of workers.
- The objective of industrial action tends to be misunderstood: such action is commonly seen as 'irrational' and/or dysfunctional, with most conflict situations viewed as being capable of resolution by discussions and negotiation, i.e. they should not result in industrial action.

Rollinson (1993: 252) suggests that the argument that industrial action is irrational/ dysfunctional is a fundamentally flawed perspective and that it is 'simply a rational extension of the negotiation process'. Indeed, collective bargaining requires the possibility of industrial action, since without that possibility there would be a much reduced incentive for either party to reach agreement during negotiations (Clegg 1975). In effect, the costs that industrial action may impose on both parties bring a reality to the negotiation process.

Organised collective conflict is generally associated solely with the existence of trade unions – a view that, while largely correct, is not fully accurate. The resistance of the Luddites to the new lace machines and factory production in the period 1811 to 1813 was notable for the fact that the opposition came from groups of workers who were not organised in the early trade unions or 'combinations', as they were then called (Darvall 1964). Furthermore, pre-existing collective conflict among unorganised workers can be a trigger for unionisation. While collective conflict is not necessarily confined to trade unions, it is uncommon to find unorganised workers engaging in formal collective action. In effect, trade unions provide an ordered mechanism for the expression and resolution of conflict. The main mechanism through which this is done is the process of collective bargaining, but strikes, go slows, bans on overtime or a work-to-rule are also measures that may be deployed. However, trade unions are moderating influences on industrial conflict, as emphasised by US sociologist C. Wright Mills (1948), who famously described trade union leaders as the 'managers of discontent'.

A major defect in much theorising about the causes of industrial action has been an insufficient attention to the role of employers and managers (Edwards 1992). The lockout is a commonly recognised but quite rare form of management-initiated organised conflict. Some employer conflict is masked as normal commercial activity. Plant closures, relocations and unilateral changes to terms and conditions of employment can constitute employer conflict. Salamon (2000: 421) notes that because of its permanency, plant closures or a threat of closure 'may be considered a more powerful sanction than the employees' temporary stoppage of work through strike action'. Conceptually these options increase an employer's BATNA (best alternative to a negotiated agreement; see Chapter 11) and they have become very important in modern industrial relations with the growth of multinational companies operating across state boundaries. Such companies often have a ready capacity to switch production (either temporarily or permanently) to limit the capacity of workers to take industrial action or to limit the effectiveness of industrial action if it occurs.

Even where unions are the clear initiators of collective conflict, this is almost invariably a reaction to management action or inaction. Salamon (2000: 424) notes that by passively resisting union demands or by unilaterally initiating change, management can 'place the onus on the employees or union to take direct industrial action'. Conceptually then, all collective industrial action should be viewed as joint industrial action in that both union and management will have decided to allow the action to proceed by making too few concessions to meet the demands of the other side or by demanding too much.

Crossover Between Individual and Collective Action

Not all conflict can be neatly divided into individual unorganised and collective organised forms. Even suicide has emerged as an expression of collective organised conflict, when up to 200 Chinese workers collectively threatened to jump from the top of the Foxconn dormitory in Wuhan in 2012. Their dispute was in pursuit of severance payments which they claimed had been promised following a decision to close the Xbox 360 assembly line (2012, www.independent.ie). So-called 'bossnapping' involves the kidnapping of managers and holding them overnight or for some hours. This occurred in several French plants in 2009 and included companies such as Sony, Caterpillar and 3M. The actions were carried out by groups of workers in order to enforce demands over redundancy. Thus, it involved conflict against individual managers but by organised groups of workers. Vahabi (2011) argues that bossnapping was used as an effective substitute for large strikes and that it worked because essentially the action had an implicit political intent, which saw the state recoil from taking legal action against what were clearly illegal acts. He argues:

> The recent state intervention to rescue and bail out banks was not accompanied by sanctions against employers who massively lay off workers ... But if the state that had previously given carrots to bankers had used sticks against the bossnappers, then it would have run a high risk of provoking another wave of strikes, as seen in November 2005. (Vahabi 2011: 91)

Individual conflict may be directly or inversely related to collective forms of actions, e.g. strikes. Wallace (1982) reported a direct relationship with turnover and strikes in the Limerick Ferenka plant – a highly strike-prone organisation that also had high turnover, with 44 per cent of employees leaving in one year. On the other hand, in the UK coal industry, Handy (1968) reported an inverse relationship between strikes and individual forms of conflict, e.g. absenteeism, labour wastage and industrial accidents. Thus, when strikes fell in the coal mines, accidents rose. This is explicable by the fact that a significant proportion of strikes in mining were over the issue of safety. Where workers felt they could not undertake strikes against dangerous conditions, this led to increased accidents. Where accidents substitute for strikes in this way, they are a manifestation of the costs of latent (unexpressed) industrial conflict. Thus, high employee discontent and high strikes can, depending on circumstances, be complements or substitutes for one another (Jackson 1991).

CONFLICT AND THE CONCEPTUAL FRAMEWORKS

As noted in Chapter 1, there are two broad conflicting assumptions as to the nature of industrial conflict. The first is a unitarist approach, which proceeds on the implicit assumption that conflict is frictional and is not a fundamental aspect of the employment relationship. The second is a range of pluralist approaches, which sees industrial conflict as being inherent in the employment relationship and/or the nature of society. Thus, the unitarist–pluralist dichotomy is a standard starting point for the analysis of conflict. This approach was introduced into the study of industrial relations by Alan Fox (1966) in a seminal working paper for the UK Donovan Commission 1965–1968. Unitarism and pluralism were presented under two headings, as:

- competing conceptual frameworks for viewing the industrial enterprise; and
- alternate employer approaches to the management of industrial relations.

Fox (1966) categorised unitarism as a view of the industrial enterprise in which there is one source of authority and one focus of loyalty. Organisations are viewed as essentially cohesive and harmonious units in which all members of the organisation (management and employees) have common interests and share common goals (Fox 1966; Marchington 1982).

In essence, unitarism views the industrial enterprise as a team. Implicit in the team view is the acceptance of a common goal by all members of the organisation. This means that there is no place for factions and that people 'accept their place'. Unitarism allows that differences of interest may arise at an individual or group level, but 'class' as a unit of analysis is not deployed and the possibility of class conflict is simply not recognised (Dahrendorf 1959). Conflict, when it does occur, is viewed as dysfunctional and the result of misunderstandings, the action of troublemakers, a breakdown in communications, lack of management leadership or other non-fundamental reasons, i.e. frictional factors.

In a unitarist perspective, industrial conflict is not seen as inevitable and a need for institutional arrangements to deal with conflict, even at a societal level, hardly arises. Appropriate management initiatives (e.g. effective communication, leadership and proper recruitment and selection) should be capable of either preventing conflict or resolving it when it arises. Trade unions are contradictorily viewed as either too powerful or no longer necessary. Marchington (1982: 38) points out that they are viewed as either achieving 'too much for their members in that they block change and inhibit efficiency or, conversely, as being irrelevant in that management is much more able than trade unions to identify and satisfy employees' needs'.

Fox (1966) contrasted unitarism with a pluralist conceptual framework that he considered offered a more realistic view of the industrial enterprise. This realism is based on the assertion that the employment relationship is characterised by different interests and as a result there is an inherent potential for conflict. In so far as there are shared goals within an organisation, these are instrumental: workers need to earn a living and the employers need workers to produce output. Factions and different groups are likely to emerge in organisations and these cannot be eliminated or integrated fully into the organisation. In resisting unionisation, long-term damage may be caused to industrial relations, since union recognition may only be achieved after a trial of strength, involving attempted dismissal of union activists (troublemakers), strikes or other industrial action.

Politicians and public policymakers in the UK largely disregarded the recommendations of the Donovan Commission and looked instead to legal reform based on the ill-fated Industrial Relations Act 1971 (Goldthorpe 1974). In contrast to its fate among politicians and public policymakers, the unitarist–pluralist analysis had a major impact on industrial relations practitioners and a seminal influence on academic analysis. The influence on practitioners has been explored in Chapter 7; in this chapter, we concentrate on the academic influence. Table 9.3 contains an outline of the unitarist–pluralist conceptual frameworks, together with the Marxist and radical approaches. Indeed, Marxist and radical approaches are properly considered to be pluralist explanations, since at a fundamental level pluralism simply means the acceptance of different interests. It is also important to note that Marxist and radical approaches are systems theories, since they see the individual constrained by the historical, economic and societal structures. They differ from Dunlop's systems theory in that they focus on issues of power and control in the employment relationship, whereas Dunlop gives greater attention to rules and institutions and is, therefore, more conservative. All systems approaches, however, envisage industrial relations actors as being greatly constrained and having only limited room for manoeuvre, although the extent of that room is a matter for debate (Hyman 1975).

Unitarism Developed

Human Relations

The various unitarist approaches have an underlying assumption that industrial conflict is frictional, not fundamental, and its elimination is within management control. Unitarism allows that differences of interest may arise at an individual or group level, but 'class' as a unit of analysis is not deployed and the possibility of class conflict is simply not recognised (Dahrendorf 1959). Implicit examples of unitarist ideology are found in the various human relations approaches, which originate with the work of Mayo in the 1920s (Mayo 1949; Rose 1977). Human relations was paradoxically a reaction to the class conflicts associated with the growth of mass production and the introduction of scientific management in the US in the early decades of the twentieth century. However, as Coser (1956: 24) points out, Mayo 'never considers the possibility that an industrial relations system might contain conflicting interests, as distinct from different attitudes or "logics"'.

To Mayo, management embodied the central purposes of society and all of his research was conducted to help management solve its problems (Coser 1956). In the human relations school, conflict is variously seen as a failure to meet the social needs of workers, incompatible personalities, overly strict supervision, the action of troublemakers or deviants, inadequate management or a breakdown in communications (Mayo 1949; Rose 1977; Scott and Homans 1947; Whyte 1951). According to Mayo (1949: 128), the elimination of conflict and different interests is merely a matter of 'intelligent organisation that takes careful account of all the group interests involved'. He envisages this being done by management deploying certain 'social skills' to ensure good communication and mutual understanding (Mayo 1949: 23, 191). Dahrendorf (1959: 111) points to the influence of popular writers on management, e.g. Drucker, who echo and adopt this implicit unitarist view that the individual must understand the goals and functions of the industrial enterprise as their goals and functions (Drucker 1950: 156–65).

A further significant omission in the human relations treatment of conflict is the systematic suppression of the evidence of both individual and collective conflict observed during the Hawthorne studies. Bramel and Friend (1981: 874), writing in *American Psychologist*, document these lapses: 'worker resistance to management was commonplace at Hawthorne (despite absence of a union), yet tended to be covered up in the popular writings of Mayo and Roethlisberger'. Mayo and Roethlisberger noted that management employed dismissals, threats, removal of breaks and increased hours of work. Restrictions of output among workers and a concern for the job security of fellow workers were also observed by the investigators but written off by them as irrational (Bramel and Friend 1981). Thus, Bramel and Friend (1981) go on to note that the very evidence uncovered in the Hawthorne studies contradicts the conflict-free view of the capitalist firm.

The Depression of the 1930s was not a fertile ground for the 'soft' policies advocated by the human relations school. Indeed, Rose (1977: 170) notes 'the rapid decay of the approach with the spread, and relative failure, of human relations training for supervisors'. The growing unionisation in the US following the introduction of Roosevelt's New Deal and the 1935 Wagner Act saw a move away from human relations (Rose 1977). Finally, the approach was subject to devastating critical academic assaults. Rose (1977: 171) writes that 'between 1946 and 1950 nearly all the conventional charges against the school were systematically pressed: neglect of unions; managerial bias; acceptance of manipulation; *inadequate treatment of industrial conflict*; failure to relate the factory to the wider social structure and fear of anomie'. The attacks culminated in the exposure of fatal methodological flaws in the Hawthorne studies and criticism of its neglect of 'economic factors' (Rose 1977: 172). Despite these defects, the human relations approach was to survive and evolve.

Neo-Human Relations and HRM

The development of the neo-human relations school post-World War II can also be seen as a reaction to the limitations of the earlier approach, particularly the neglect of financial rewards (Rose 1977). Maslow (1945) provided an explanation for conflict arising at an individual level. He identified a hierarchy of needs, with the implication that failure to meet the need at any level could lead to conflict (Maslow 1954). Thus, when basic needs were met, employees were identified as possessing a need for personal growth or self-actualisation. Meeting these needs could avoid conflict and lead to more productive and happier workers (Huczynski and Buchanan 1991). Herzberg (1968) introduced the distinction between satisfiers and dissatisfiers: poor pay may create dissatisfaction (and conflict) but good pay will not necessarily create satisfaction (absence of conflict). While the neo-human relations approach was influential in management circles in the 1960s and 1970s, it had little impact on the practice of industrial relations, not least because (like the earlier human relations approach) it sought to deal with conflict in an exclusively managerial framework excluding collective actors (Rose 1977).

The human resource management (HRM) approach to conflict is conceptually like its human relations predecessors, i.e. an implicitly unitarist framework. However, it is much more sophisticated than simple unitarism. It does not imply an absence of conflict but it retains the key feature of the earlier human relations approaches that conflict can be handled via appropriate management measures. The greater sophistication is inherent in the panoply of policies and measures that HRM can deploy. Teamworking, team briefings, merit pay, performance appraisal and a host of other techniques are indicative of an awareness of a highly developed need for planning in order to avoid conflict and ensure employees are motivated and productive – a possibility absent in Fox's (1966) sketch of unitarism.

Thus, unitarism has a degree of permanence as management's default or preferred approach to employment relations. Hence, Doherty and Teague's (2011) survey found that non-union organisations assume that management–employee interactions are based largely on 'trust and unity of interest', while workplace conflict is regarded as 'deviant'. This tallies with the unitarist perspective as outlined by (Fox 1966) that conflict is 'frictional' (due to incompatible personalities or things going wrong) and that it is as a result of poor 'communications', stupidity (in failing to appreciate common interests) or the work of agitators inciting the (otherwise content) majority.

It may be argued that HRM has had greater impact in tackling conflict than its conceptual predecessors. There is indeed evidence to support a substantial decrease in conflict (as measured by strikes and changes in workplace relations) since the early 1980s. However, the contribution of HRM to such a decrease is uncertain. Globalisation, the failure of state socialism as an alternative to capitalism, social partnership, neo-liberal economic policies and the decreased power of labour vis-à-vis capital are just some of a number of alternative causal variables for the reduction in conflict. Even if HRM has worked to reduce overt conflict, Edwards (1992: 363) argues it 'has not dissolved the bases of conflict' and it is crucial to understand where lines of tension remain.

Pluralism Developed

As with the unitarist-based academic explanations of conflict, there is a range of approaches to the analysis of conflict that can be classified under the banner of pluralism. Defined in this broad sense, pluralism simply means that the employment relationship is based on a 'plurality of interests'. All pluralist approaches share the proposition that to a greater or lesser degree, conflict is inherent in the employment relationship. It is not hard to sketch out a priori reasons why conflict might be a fundamental part of the employment relationship. Employers' needs for productivity, cost effectiveness and change can be at odds with workers' needs for job security, 'good pay' and rewarding work (Allen 1971; Hyman 1989; Huczynski and Buchanan 1991; Jackson 1987).

Indeed, such conflicts of interest are not just confined to the 'financial exchange' dimension but, in terms of pluralist analysis, are potentially inherent in other aspects of the employment relationship. The management of organisations requires the exercise of employer/managerial authority over employees on dimensions such as working time, work flow and task allocation (Morley *et al.* 2004; Reed 1989). Furthermore, the contract of employment is unlike most commercial contracts, i.e. specific on rewards but not on effort. Any and all of these factors hold the potential for conflict and are emphasised to a greater or lesser degree by differing pluralist approaches.

Here we focus on three pluralist approaches: (1) the institutional-pluralist, (2) the Marxist and (3) the radical approaches. Each of these brings insights into the nature of industrial conflict and provides a greater degree of sophistication to the research and analysis of conflict. As with the unitarist approaches, they do not provide definitive answers as to the cause of conflict, since there are fundamental differences between the various pluralist approaches.

Institutional Pluralism

Fox's original 1966 contribution is classified under the heading of institutional pluralism and is just one of a number of approaches that emphasise the role of institutions. Among other early writers in the institutional tradition are Allan Flanders, W.E.J. McCarthy and Hugh Clegg in the UK and John T. Dunlop, Clark Kerr, Arthur M. Ross and Paul T. Hartman in the US. Institutional approaches are considered functionalist in nature since although they see conflict as normal and inherent in the employment relationship, they regard it as being capable of being accommodated and controlled by institutional mechanisms (Goldthorpe 1974).

In institutional pluralism, temporary compromises (or collective agreements) help align the opposing aspirations of business to earn profits and increase productivity and efficiency with workers' demands for improved pay and working condition. As Dubin *et al.* (1954) explained, collective bargaining was the great social invention serving to institutionalise industrial conflict. That is, as the electoral process democratically institutionalised political conflict, collective bargaining created a dependable means for the resolution of industrial conflict. Salamon (2000) confirms this analysis, pointing out that conflict necessitates the establishment of acceptable procedures and institutions, serving to achieve collaboration via comprehensive and codified systems of negotiated regulation. Regulations or procedures manage an ongoing dynamic tension, which is sourced in conflicts of interest and loyalty (Rose 2001). In effect, institutional pluralism focuses on the organisations into which the differing interests tend to form and on the rules that regulate their relations (Dunlop 1958).

The focus on rules is very evident in the work of the UK Donovan Commission and its recommendations for institutional reform, which had an inherent institutional-pluralist perspective. This approach was also based on the tradition of voluntarism and aimed at developing workplace systems for channelling and resolving conflict. Fox (1966) noted that a pluralist view allowed for the development of appropriate procedures (notably disputes, grievance and disciplinary procedures) and including relevant social actors (e.g. shop stewards) in the processes of conflict resolution. In effect, by adopting a pluralist approach management can regain power by sharing it and the job of management is best seen as being that of balancing competing interests. While the distinction between unitarism and pluralism may seem to belong in the academic arena, it has long been recognised to have applicability to everyday industrial relations and it

---

Table 9.2

Case Study*

Perspectives on Conflict in a Medium-sized Enterprise

Clancy Transport is a medium-sized transport company in a town in Co. Kerry. The company is owned and managed by Tom Clancy, who built the company from the ground up having been a driver. The company maintains a garage for servicing the fleet. Tom has recently heard that a few disgruntled employees are unhappy with their pay and overtime payments. He is very surprised at this because he feels he has always treated his employees very well – like family, really. He operates an 'open-door policy' and sees no need for rules and procedures, since each person has to be handled differently. Over the years, he has had a number of approaches from a local union official saying that employees want to be represented by a union. The official refused to supply names and Tom shrugged off the approaches, telling her that he refused to entertain 'any involvement in his business by any outside body'. Tom talks to a few senior employees that he can trust. He asks them what is behind the current unrest and he hears that there are only a small number of employees involved. He concludes that they are just causing trouble and are showing no regard for the difficult financial pressures that the business is under at this time. As a result, he decides to 'ignore the gripes'. However, while investigating, he finds that some employees (not the same ones behind the gripes) are putting petrol in their own cars from the company fuel tank without signing for it. He allows employees to do this if they have a call out in lieu of overtime. He has always felt that this is a win-win, since they are not taxed on it. He discovers that three employees are filling up weekly. Tom is appalled at their action and feels betrayed. He calls in the three employees separately, telling them that he has clear proof of the theft and they have 'gone to town on a good thing'. He dismisses them without notice.

* * *

Mick Murphy has worked for Clancy Transport for six years. He thinks things are badly regulated, with pay below the norm for main car dealerships. Employees can be called in without notice at night or weekends to deal with breakdowns. There is no overtime or call-out pay for this, although employees do get a few gallons of petrol in lieu. Mick has bought a new house and is planning on getting married; he feels he should be paid the going rate for his work. Some mechanics are getting paid more than others but this is not widely known. Mick feels he can't do anything about this. While Tom Clancy says he operates an open-door policy, everyone knows you have to be careful what you say to him. Employees often say that it is 'Clancy's way or the highway'. Mick hears that three fellow employees are being sacked because Clancy said they were 'going to town on the petrol'. He thinks this is very unfair, since he knows these three employees are paid less than him, even though they are fully qualified.

Mick and a number of employees get together and join SIPTU. They tell the union official that they are going to strike. She insists that they do not do that. She explains that she will seek a meeting first thing on Monday with Tom Clancy in order to try to resolve issues and have the employees reinstated. Over the weekend, a number of employees get together and decide that there is 'no use in waiting' and that 'you need to strike when the iron is hot'. They decide they will picket the business. As a result, when Tom Clancy arrives to open on Monday at 9am, he finds himself confronted by four disgruntled employees picketing the premises and they stay there all day. At the same time, two employees arrive to picket Mr Clancy's home – but they do this without telling any of the other striking employees. Mrs Clancy is surprised and upset to see them there when she returns from taking her children to school.

Discussion Points

1 Through what implicit conceptual frameworks do Mr Clancy, Mr Murphy and the union official view the employment relationship? Give reasons for your answers.
2 If Mr Clancy asked you on Monday evening for advice on how he should handle the situation, what suggestions could you make? Give developed reasons for your recommendation and for your rejection of the other options.

*This case study can be used for analysis, discussion or role-play negotiation. Guidelines for using the case study are available for lecturers on the Gill & Macmillan website (www.gillmacmillan.ie).

underpins much of the procedural arrangements discussed in Chapter 7. The case study below provides an example of how the conceptual frameworks approach can be used to shed light on differing perspectives of conflict, allowing for an analysis without resort to the distortions thrown up by personal factors.

Jackson (1991) points out that there are options other than voluntarism arising from an institutional-pluralist approach. In Germany the systems of co-determination at works council and board level constitute a set of institutional arrangements designed to prevent rather than channel or resolve conflict (Jackson 1991). In the 1950s and 1960s, these worked effectively to allow the rationalisation of the coal industry in Germany without major conflict, something which stands in stark contrast to the UK experience in the 1970s and 1980s. Other European countries such as the Netherlands, France and Sweden have also evolved employee participation institutional arrangements of a less developed nature designed to prevent conflict (Ferner and Hyman 1998). Apart from limited provision for worker democracy in the state sector and European works councils in some companies, such co-determination provisions have not been a significant feature of the Irish system of industrial relations (see Chapter 12).

Marxism

The Marxist perspective sees conflict as being rooted in two factors – the nature of capitalist societies and the nature of work under capitalism. Capitalist society is divided into two main classes – the propertied (bourgeoisie) and labouring or working class (proletariat), with the former expropriating the latter through the extraction of surplus value from their labour. The hierarchical nature of society and the unequal nature of rewards, combined with the unrewarding and alienating nature of work under capitalism, causes conflict (Braverman 1974; Hyman 1975). These factors lead (or may lead) to the development of class consciousness among workers, with industrial conflict taking place along class lines between the proletariat and the bourgeoisie. In essence, Marx's class analysis is concerned with exploring the effects of common economic conditions leading to organised action (Dahrendorf 1959: 76).

Classical Marxism sees conflict as not just being inherent in the employment relationship but also as irreconcilable. It predicted that as capitalism matured, a growing and ever-impoverished working class would create the conditions for a working-class revolution. Industrial conflict is, therefore, part of a broader class-based conflict, with the potential to lead to revolution and the overthrow of capitalism. Surprisingly, there are also some similarities between the Marxist approaches and the human relations approaches: both identify unrewarding work, over-close supervision, etc. as leading to conflict. However, in the Marxist view the unrewarding nature of work is inherently bound up with capitalist production, whereas in the human relations tradition they are incidental occurrences requiring a technical fix by management.

Radicals

There is substantial crossover between Marxist and modern radical industrial relations academics, with the term being used interchangeably by some writers, e.g. Salamon

(2000). However, there are significant differences between classical Marxists and radicals and it is necessary to highlight some of these. The radical perspective is focused on the basic premise of an inequality in the employment relationship – capital is considered more powerful than labour (Fox 1974; Goldthorpe 1974). As with Marxism, there is a focus on the hierarchical nature of society, the unequal rewards and unrewarding work. The key difference is that the radical view does not approach the comprehensiveness or extremities of classical Marxist explanations. In fact the term 'radical' is an elastic one, stretching from social democrats through the so-called radical-pluralism of Alan Fox (1974) to neo-Marxists who analyse contemporary society using Marxist concepts in a non-doctrinaire way. This diverse group is united by an effort to understand the fundamental *root causes* of industrial conflict in a societal as well as an organisational context.

The development of a radical critique in the 1970s can in part be seen as a response to the growth in industrial conflict post-Donovan and the failure of the pluralist prescriptions to stem the tide of strikes, especially unofficial ones. It owes much to the work of Alan Fox, who revised his earlier pluralist analysis in a series of publications from 1973 onwards. In doing so, he focuses on the issues of power and control in the workplace (Fox 1974). While continuing to assert the superiority of pluralism over unitarism, he points to limitations in the pluralist approach and advocates a radical alternative interpretation for the existence of conflict. He writes that 'like the pluralist approach, it [the radical approach] emphasises the gross disparity of power between the employer and the individual employee' (Fox 1977: 141). He continues, 'unlike the pluralist, however, the radical does not see the collective organisation of employees as restoring the balance of power (or anything as yet approaching it) between the propertied and propertyless' (Fox 1977: 141). The need in pluralism to bind workers ever closer in procedures is seen by Fox as evidence of a low-trust relationship between those who manage and those who are managed. In essence, radicals point to the limits of institutional provisions where these are not underpinned by some degree of value consensus (Goldthorpe 1974).

Unlike classical Marxists, Fox (1974) does not anticipate any revolutionary change. He argues that the approach of many rank-and-file employees probably consists of low-key acceptance of the organisation's essential characteristics, accepting it without 'enthusiasm and commitment' (Fox 1977: 143). In essence, the industrial enterprise is divided into a 'them and us' mentality and involves control rather than commitment (D'Art and Turner 2002; Whelan 1982). In this scenario, conflict is institutionalised through collective bargaining but agreements may only be observed on the basis of expediency. Instead of advancing the proposition that revolution is inherent, or even inevitable, in the employment relationship, radical writers have been concerned to explain the limited extent of industrial conflict. Fox (1977: 142) argues that if workers go too far in challenging management power, privilege, values and objectives, they would face the combined power of employer and government, which 'would soon reveal where ultimate power lay'. Challenges are acceptable on a limited range of issues and the concessions workers achieve mean they have a stake in the system and have much to lose from going too far. Thus, the differences of interests in the employment

Table 9.3
Summary of Perspectives on Industrial Conflict

Unitarist Perspective
The basic unitarist position is a non-conscious and reactive one. Conflict is seen as an aberration that occurs because 'something has gone wrong'. Harmony and unity are seen as the natural state, with conflict being an abnormal phenomenon that occurs as a result of some failure in the normal functioning of the organisation (e.g. poor communications, bad management, a lack of management leadership or the work of 'troublemakers'). While viewing conflict as abnormal, the unitarist perspective also sees conflict as essentially negative and damaging to the normal harmonious, productive state of the organisation. Thus, conflict is viewed as something that can and should be avoided. Where it does occur, management should take appropriate steps to eradicate it, probably by addressing the alleged source (e.g. improve communications or organisational design, train managers or get rid of troublemakers). The role of collective representation hardly arises at an analytical level in unitarist perspectives, with trenchant opposition to union recognition being common at a practical management level.

Pluralist Perspective
The pluralist perspective views conflict as a naturally occurring phenomenon in organisations. It arises from the differing perspectives and interests of all the groups and individuals who make up the organisation. At an organisational level, the emphasis is on management to plan for and manage conflict. This can be done through the use of procedures and negotiating with representative bodies (e.g. trade unions). At a societal level, the role of the state is to provide institutional support for those engaged in trade unions in the form of provisions for conciliation, adjudication and arbitration on disputes. It may also provide for organs of worker participation (e.g. works councils). The pluralist perspective is also consistent with the view that conflict is not necessarily negative but can have beneficial effects. Efforts should therefore be concentrated on channelling conflict to limit damage and realise such organisational benefits.

Classical Marxist Perspective
Conflict in capitalist societies is seen as a symptom of the structural enmity that exists between capital and labour, employer and employee. Such enmity arises from the organisation of work in capitalist societies and the unequal distribution of power between the dominant establishment group that owns the means of production (employers, shareholders) and those whose labour is required to produce goods and services (workers). Therefore, conflict in organisations is simply a manifestation of broader class conflict in relation to the distribution of power in society and organisations themselves are simply a microcosm of a broader class conflict between the bourgeoisie (who control economic resources and political power) and the proletariat, with managers representing the interests of capital. In the Marxist perspective, conflict is seen as instigating revolutionary change designed to dismantle the capitalist system, redistribute power in favour of workers and the working class and ultimately achieve a classless society.

Radical Perspective
The radical perspective overlaps with Marxist analysis – it sees conflict as endemic in industrial societies, with a major cause being the unequal power distribution both in society and in organisations. Efforts by employers to organise work lead to a need for control, which tends to lead to compliance rather than commitment. Revolution or radical social change is not to be expected, since workers generally accept the system and their place in it. However, there are limitations to any efforts to contain conflict through institutions or procedural regulation. Workers may observe agreements on the basis of expedience. More recently, the complex interaction between conflict and co-operation and the mutual interdependence of managers and workers has been emphasised. HRM is seen as another form of control, leading to work intensification, stress and long working hours – the new forms of social conflict.

relationship may not even be 'synonymous with the use of overt collective industrial action' (Salamon 1998: 397). Later radical writers such as Edwards (1986) note that while the 'actors' involved in industrial relation have 'divergent wants', they also depend on each other and so need to co-operate across a range of issues. Thus, conflict and co-operation are integral parts of the employment relationship.

CONSIDERATION OF DIFFERING CONCEPTUAL FRAMEWORKS

The analysis above merely sketches the main elements of the various approaches, which require wider reading in order to explore them in greater depth. In this text, it is impossible to explore all schools of thought. For instance, Weber saw the growth of bureaucracy as having a major role in promoting conflict. In addition, some human relations writers have given attention to systems factors, notably the role of technology on the management of employees. In this view, certain technology promotes repetitive, unrewarding work, which is geared towards Taylorist work organisation (Woodward 1958). Such analysis was particularly identified with work in the automotive industry. However, it is not easy to identify a unidirectional link between conflict and technology. Blauner (1964) suggested that technology might initially lead to less rewarding work and increased conflict, but over time it would have a liberating effect and decrease conflict. Furthermore, neo-Marxists have challenged the notion that technology is an independent variable. They point out that technology that dehumanises work is introduced to lower the costs of labour and to increase profits.

While the various methods are at odds with one another, the debate surrounding the approaches and modern empirical research has led to a more nuanced understanding of conflict. Whatever its limitations, Fox's (1966) contribution remains one of the most insightful and influential works in industrial relations theorising. The prescriptions have been largely adopted and implemented in many unionised organisations, even though there are significant limitations on their ability to contain conflict. However, there is no guarantee that institutional arrangements that worked to prevent or resolve conflict in the past will continue to do so. Even if they work, there is no guarantee that they will continue to be highly regarded. Thus, there has been a move away from pluralism to unitarist approaches since the 1980s and it is now clear that unitarism has many more strings to its bow in informing managerial policies than in the 'straw man' model advanced by Fox in 1966.

The apparent historical inevitability of growing union density envisaged by Fox has been reversed and that union growth now appears to be the product of particular economic and social circumstances of the time – notably Keynesianism and full employment. The re-emergence of widespread unemployment from the 1970s, combined with globalisation, has changed the dynamic and has made unitarism attractive for many employers. Non-unionisation is now common in the private sector and a wide range of unitarist models for ordering employment relations is now common. These models range from the 'soft' human resource management approaches of Google or Intel to the 'hard' versions of Dell or Ryanair. Such approaches have been widely successful at using different approaches to managing people while limiting collective industrial relations conflict.

However, unitarism has serious defects at a theoretical and empirical level. Unitarism is not a theoretically self-aware approach, being merely an inherent and often unarticulated underlying assumption. Neither have unitarist-based approaches any capacity to deal with the wider social and political context. For example, they cannot explain the empirical differences in conflict between countries and across time periods. Scandinavian countries have combined high levels of unionisation together with generally low levels of strikes and economic prosperity. In order to analyse the reasons for this, one needs a perspective much wider than can be supplied by unitarist approaches such as the human relations one.

Contemporary Marxists have grappled with the failure of many of Marx's predictions to materialise. Some point to the extent to which capitalist societies reformed after the Great Depression of the 1930s, with Keynesian demand management policies and the welfare state ensuring the stability of such societies. Some claim that Marx predicted the *relative,* not *absolute* impoverishment of the working class, while others suggest that impoverishment has been staved off in the developed world due to the extension of capitalism to the developing world. Writing from a classical Marxist perspective, Arrighi (1990: 54) writes that 'in the past the tensions of capitalism could be eased by expansion of the system into new regions and that capitalism now operates on a truly global scale'.

The extensive strikes in Korea in the 1980s and 1990s are seen as evidence of the extension of traditional capital–labour conflicts to the newer economies in the developing world (Cho 1985; Edwards 1992; Salamon 2000). In this regard, the modern consumer electronic industry is seen as depending on exploitative working conditions in plants such as Foxconn, where extreme forms of labour conflicts (including, as previously noted, threats of mass suicide) have arisen. The death of nearly 300 workers in a factory fire in Karachi in September 2012 echoes historical experiences such as the infamous 1911 Triangle Shirtwaist Factory fire in New York City, which led to the death of 146 garment workers. In both cases, the workers were locked in with windows barred; as a result, they could not escape. This graphically illustrates the permanency of an extreme form of exploitative employment relationship which has not ceased to exist but has merely been geographically displaced. Such conditions are said to be widespread in Pakistan and they exist alongside other exploitative employment relationships such as child labour in the garment and sportswear industry. The Irish trade unions have taken an interest in the working conditions and trade union rights in developing countries, as demonstrated by the following extract from *The Irish Times.*

Table 9.4

Abuse of Sportswear Workers Highlighted

Irish Olympic athletes, sportspeople and parents buying children's runners have been urged to back an international campaign aimed at stopping abuse of workers in the sportswear industry. Factories in developing countries are 'breaking all the rules' to meet the unreasonable demands of massive sports corporations. These companies will reap particularly large profits during this Olympic year, Ms Kanjai Kaewchoo, president of the Thai Textile Garment and Leather Workers' Federation, told the ICTU women's conference in Galway yesterday. Ms Kaewchoo said that more than a million women in Thailand were employed in the sportswear industry and many are paid six cents a piece. Employees were regularly paid $3 a day to make $93 runners and could be forced to work up to forty-five extra hours a week – at the risk of losing their jobs. Apart from poor pay, sportswear manufacturing staff encountered backache and eye strain, while access to trade union membership was denied, she said. The Olympic Council of Ireland has been urged to back the Play Fair at the Olympics campaign, supported by ICTU, SIPTU and Oxfam Ireland (the website is www.fairolympics.org).

Source: Siggins (2004)

While a number of classical Marxist predictions have not been realised, the notion that industrial conflict arises from an inherent antagonism between capital and labour remains a powerful hypothesis to explain the permanence of such conflict, its underlying causes and periodic resurgence despite pluralist or managerial efforts at containment. Many industrial relations writers, neo-Marxists included, now regard the organisation of work in a capitalist society as a complex mix of conflict and co-operation. The simple zero-sum game inherent in classical Marxist analysis is mediated by the interdependence of employers and workers. Controlling workers is only one way of achieving effective work organisation (Grint 1991). Edwards (1992: 390) notes that 'there are aspects of new employment systems which benefit workers, and critical analysis does not imply that workers' and managers' interests are totally opposed'. The possibility of worker resistance to the introduction of new information technology, which was of much concern to the European Commission in the 1980s, now seems misplaced, since workers willingly embraced such technology.

Indeed, workers have an interest in effective management and management have an interest in tapping their workforce's initiative and creativity. While differences of interest may underlie the employment relationship, there are also strong imperatives that limit conflict and promote co-operation. Globalisation and international competition can heighten the need for collaborative arrangements in order to protect employment. This interdependence is evidenced by findings that workers and their representatives (shop stewards) prefer competent managers (Edwards 1992; Sturdy *et al.* 1992). In fact, this evidence is reciprocated in studies that reveal management have generally positive perceptions of the role played by shop stewards, findings which are at odds with the militant image in which shop stewards are sometimes portrayed (Ackers and Black 1992; Donovan 1968; Wallace 1982).

FUNCTIONS OF CONFLICT

While conflict may pose problems for society, organisations and workers, there is a strong tradition in social science that argues that conflict is functional. Coser (1956) has been an advocate for viewing conflict in a functional light and a strong critic of those who regard it as necessarily dysfunctional. Writing on US industrial relations, he notes that union organisation has frequently been accompanied by the organisation of employers into employer organisations, even to the extent that sometimes the employers have organised at the suggestion and with the help of the union (Coser 1956: 131). However, he is careful to note limitations to this functionality, with conservative employers seeing no need for an accommodation with unions and wishing to 'smash' them (Coser 1956: 130–1). This has arguably been the dominant trend in the US since the 1960s (Dunlop 1993).

Coser (1956) considered that conflict needed to be contained within communal bounds (trade unions and employer organisations being classic examples) and he disapproved of non-communal conflict. However, Dahrendorf (1959: 207) has suggested that Coser 'was too preoccupied with what he himself tends to call the "positive" or "integrative" functions of conflict'. Specific conflicts can, and do, take their own course and are not necessarily capable of being contained within 'the social structures which give rise to them' (Hyman 1989: 108). The demonstrations against globalisation in the early 1990s and early 2000s and those against austerity during the global financial crisis in Greece and other countries are indicative of conflict not contained within communal or institutional boundaries. In contrast, in Ireland discontent against austerity measures has largely been confined within the political and the industrial relations system.

Those who see conflict as functional oppose its suppression and warn of the dangers inherent in such a utopian venture. For example, Dahrendorf (1959: 224), a noted critic of Marxism, declares that 'effective suppression of conflict is in the long run impossible'. At a societal level, it is not hard to think of examples of failed attempts to contain, suppress or eliminate conflict. In former Communist countries such as Poland and the Soviet Union, free trade unions were not allowed and the primary function of those unions that did exist was to serve the needs of the state – or as it was known to be the 'transmission belts of the party'. This suppression of industrial conflict only led to greater upheavals eventually. Right-wing dictatorships have experienced similar developments, as exemplified by the collapse of apartheid in South Africa and the overthrow of the fascism of Franco in Spain, the fascism of Salazar in Portugal and the fall of the Pinochet regime in Chile.

Indeed, it is not difficult to find examples of collective conflict being functional. Many aspects of our current employment practice and regulation derive from former resolution of conflicts. The general provision for a forty-hour working week was established in the early to mid-1960s in a series of groundbreaking industrial disputes. This was subsequently reduced without overt conflict to 39 hours as part of the Programme for National Recovery (PNR) 1987–1991. Irish equality legislation of the 1970s arose in large part from European Community requirements, but its introduction was also a result of campaigning by the women's movement and the trade unions, which brought them into conflict with government and employers. The increase in the statutory redundancy provisions to two weeks' pay per year introduced in 2003 as part of the Sustaining Progress agreement first arose from union demands during a sit-in at Peerless Rugs in Athy, Co. Kildare and a strike in the Irish Glass Bottle Company in Dublin, both during 2002.

It is not just on the workers' side that one can identify examples of collective conflict being functional, as it has benefited both employers and government. In the 1980s a series of disputes in which unions were relatively unsuccessful led to greater flexibility in the Irish labour market, the reduction of traditional effort bargaining and union givebacks or concession bargaining (Wallace and Clifford 1998). Equally, the willingness of union members to accept the modest terms of the PNR in 1987 cannot be separated from these developments and the concern that Irish trade unions had at the negative strike outcomes for UK trade unions under Thatcherism (see Chapter 13). In effect, conflict exposes the actors in industrial relations to the reality of the shifting power balances and norms in employment relationships and the wider society.

THE DUAL FACE OF CONFLICT

In many situations conflict may have a *dual nature*, having both positive and negative aspects to it. When company closures occur, there are frequently harrowing interviews with employees who are traumatised by the immediate impact and express great anxiety for their future. The closure of Talk Talk in Waterford in September 2011 is a case in point. The negative personal aspects of this conflict are manifest, yet the alternative for an economy as a whole is the stagnation of state socialism. Faced with competition from low-cost countries, employers advocate 'moving up the value chain' (RTÉ interview with Brendan Butler, IBEC, September 2003). This is a functional strategic choice for an economy, but industrial restructuring can see a heavy price paid by workers because they often have sunken costs in their employment. This has been mitigated by the provision of enhanced redundancy payments and, where possible, the use of voluntary selection for redundancy within companies that continue to trade. Both of these are solutions that have been developed through the process of collective bargaining and are generally accepted.

In contrast to the practice in their home country, many US non-union multinationals pay redundancy terms well above the statutory minimum. In this way, employees in non-union companies enjoy benefits first negotiated by unionised employees – in effect, these companies might be considered to be in part 'crypto-unionised'. While enhanced redundancy terms are generally applied, in recent times there is evidence of the terms being more modest. The redundancy terms in Dell Limerick were much lower than the terms established in non-union companies like Digital and Wang in the 1980s. This trend has also been evident in the unionised sector, with the government insisting that Bank of Ireland reduce the redundancy pay-outs for bank employees from six weeks per year of service (plus statutory) to three weeks per year of service (plus statutory) when redundancies were being negotiated with the Irish Bank Officials Association (IBOA).

In addition, some companies have resisted any enhanced redundancy payments even where there was agreement on this in advance. The most notable recent example of the latter was the Vita Cortex dispute in the period 2011 to 2012.

Table 9.5

Case Study

Longer than the Dublin Lockout – The Vita Cortex Dispute

Thirty-two Vita Cortex workers in Cork were made redundant on 15 December 2011. The company did not pay statutory redundancy pay, claiming inability to pay. As such, the payment fell to be paid by the state social insurance fund. Workers were unhappy with the statutory payment and occupied the company's plant in a sit-in to enforce a claim for an enhanced payment of 2.9 weeks of service in total, the extra cost of which was estimated at around €372,000. They claimed they were entitled to this as part of an agreement which had seen this amount paid to workers previously made redundant. The workers occupied the plant over Christmas 2011 and drew support from the local community and a number of local businesses who supplied them with provisions. Many high-profile public figures, nationally and internationally, sent messages of support: Alex Ferguson, Mary Robinson, Katie Taylor, Christy Moore and Noam Chomsky. The company pointed out that there was no legal entitlement to the enhanced payment, that SIPTU had ignored the company's inability to pay and that the sit-in by the workers was 'unlawful' and 'unofficial'. Despite these points, the long service of the employees – some over forty years – and the dignified nature of the protest continued to garner widespread support. In January the employees were offered €1,500 per person to leave the plant – an offer which was seen as derisory – and subsequently the owner (not the company) Jack Ronan offered €180,000, which was also rejected. The dispute was the subject of unsuccessful LRC intervention and a recommendation made by a group of three mediators, led by Labour Court chairman Kevin Duffy, was rejected by the company. However, within days, and following direct negotiations between the parties, a confidential settlement was agreed. Following the settlement the SIPTU Manufacturing Division Organiser, Gerry McCormack, issued a statement: 'The workers are satisfied that these proposals, which were agreed following direct talks between SIPTU representatives and the owners of Vita Cortex earlier today in Cork, provide the basis for the full and final settlement of this dispute' (*Industrial Relations News* 2012: 1). Taoiseach Enda Kenny welcomed the settlement and praised the workers for their enormous 'dignity and fortitude' and said they 'deserved respect for their long years of committed and diligent service' (2012, www.rte.ie). The occupation ended on 24 May 2012 – 161 days after it began – after payment of the agreed enhanced redundancy terms had been made.

Discussion Points

1 What lessons does the above case have for managing redundancy situations?
2 Why might the employer not have used the law even if the dispute was illegal?
3 Why might the offers above have been made by the owners and not the company?

Source: Various *Industrial Relations News* articles, including IRN (2012); Roseingrave (2012); RTÉ (2012); <http://vitacortexworkers.wordpress.com/>.

CONCLUDING COMMENTS

Industrial conflict takes many differing forms, both individual and collective, which can impose personal, commercial and societal costs. It can be initiated by workers or management and it can be seen as being inherent in the nature of industry and business. There is evidence of greater pressure on workers from individual forms of employer-initiated conflict, e.g. work intensification and job insecurity associated with neo-liberal economic policies and HR policies of flexible working. However, conflict can also be functional and the ways in which societies allow and disallow conflict can have significant implications for the stability of those societies. Past conflicts have shaped major areas of work organisation in ways often unrealised. Trade unions and employer organisations have been instrumental in reaching accommodations on areas of differences between employers and workers and this has contributed to societal stability. However, such arrangements are now giving way to unilateral employer regulation only constrained by legal arrangements.

CHAPTER 10

Strikes and Lockouts as Forms of Organised Conflict

INTRODUCTION

Strikes are the most visible manifestation of industrial conflict. A strike can be defined as 'a temporary stoppage of work by a group of employees in order to express a grievance or enforce a demand' (Griffin 1939: 20). This longstanding definition emphasises that strikes are a temporary interruption in normal working. It also implies that strikes are rational actions, since they are undertaken to remedy a grievance or achieve a demand. Strike action is the most visible form of industrial action, but as already noted, they are far from the only form of conflict. Salamon (1998: 402) notes:

> ... the strike is often depicted as the ultimate and most favoured form of collective action in that, by stopping work and leaving the workplace, the employees clearly demonstrate both the importance of the issue in dispute and their solidarity.

Strike action, however, can involve considerable hardship for strikers through lost income and the risk of job loss. Thus, strikes can be a double-edged sword. If successful, a strike can strengthen a union's position, but a defeat can lead to decreased union membership and the marginalisation of the union members. Indeed, the resort to strike action can sometimes be an expression of weakness in workers' bargaining power rather than strength, something which Wallace and O'Shea (1987) found to be particularly the case in unofficial strikes.

Not all strikes are aimed against an employer. They can also take place because of disputes between unions (inter-union disputes) or because of disputes internal to the union (intra-union disputes). In Ireland, there were a small number of damaging intra-union and inter-union strikes in the 1960s and 1970s but these have been absent in recent years. Indeed, such strikes are no longer accorded legal protection as a result of the changes to the trade disputes law incorporated in the 1990 Industrial Relations Act. Strikes can also be targeted against government policy and general strikes such as these have become comparatively more common internationally in recent times. In co-ordinated market economies such as Ireland, Kelly and Hamann (2010: 11) see this as being linked to 'radical government intervention on an issue salient to union members; and union exclusion from policymaking in countries with strong corporatist traditions'. However, despite austerity, in Ireland there has been only one rather muted national public sector strike in recent years (in March 2009) (Teague and Donaghey 2012).

A lockout is the employer equivalent of a strike; however, no distinction is made between strikes and lockouts in published strike statistics. In some countries the lockout is illegal (e.g. France), while in others (e.g. Germany) it is legal. In Ireland, lockouts are legal but also rare and this may, in part, be due to the historical reverberations of the

1913 Dublin Lockout. However, as Stokke and Thörnqvist (2001) note, 'pure' lockouts are uncommon internationally: most lockouts are a response to strike action or the threat of strike action. Even in Germany, where the lockout is socially acceptable, it is seldom used by employers (Fuerstenberg 1987). Of course, the opposite can also be the case, with a strike being a disguised lockout that has been provoked by an employer in order to engineer a shut down.

HISTORICAL IMPORTANCE OF STRIKES

Historically, some strikes have been very influential and their outcome has set the tone for the industrial relations of an era. In many countries the establishment of trade union representation and recognition, especially among unskilled workers, was only achieved after successful strike action. The 1888 strike in Bryant & May by the London matchgirls presaged a rash of strike action over the following three years, along with the first widespread permanent unionisation of unskilled workers (Pelling 1976). As noted in Chapter 1, after the 1913 Dublin Lockout, union membership declined initially but resentment at the militant actions of the employers during the lockout, combined with the events of the 1916 Rising and the subsequent War of Independence, saw the membership in that union recover dramatically (Roche and Larragy 1986). These historical experiences contrast directly with the outcome of key conflicts since the 1980s. The loss of a number of strikes in the UK and the US in the early 1980s saw trade union influence and power recede. The most notable were the year-long National Union of Mineworker (NUM) strike in the UK in the period 1984 to 1985 and the Professional Air Traffic Controllers Organization (PATCO) strike in 1981 in the US. Unions also experienced unsuccessful outcomes to a number of strikes in the mid-1980s in Ireland, which was influential in trade unions embracing social partnership in 1987.

In addition to achieving industrial aims, strikes can mobilise collective interests in the broader social and political sphere. In France, strikes in 1936 and in 1968 led to major social and industrial changes. While strikes may express a popular desire for change, it is unusual for strikes to lead to revolutionary social change. A notable exception is the case of Poland dating from 1980 when martial law was used in an attempt to suppress the Polish Solidarity trade union (*Solidarność*). This attempted suppression was unsuccessful and led to major changes in Poland, which were to be influential in the eventual fall of state socialism throughout Eastern Europe in the early 1990s. The overthrow of these regimes and their replacement with capitalism systems contrasts with the role Marx envisaged for industrial conflict, where communism was predicted to replace capitalism.

Political strikes have also occurred in Ireland, although they do not constitute a legally recognised trade dispute and therefore are not protected by the immunities in the Industrial Relations Act 1990 (or its predecessor, the 1906 Trade Disputes Act). In the early 1980s there were a series of large-scale nationwide strikes against the disproportionate burden of taxation on PAYE workers. These were unsuccessful, with eventual tax reform concentrating on reducing the tax burden rather than redistributing it through a broadening of the tax base. A further notable example of a strike with political dimensions was the 1984–1987 strike by twelve Dunnes Stores workers, led by Mary Manning. This strike lasted for two and a half years and attained widespread international recognition. The workers refused to handle South African fruit in protest against apartheid in that country and they were dismissed as a result (2005, www.rte.ie). Such strikes are unusual, however, with most strikes being concerned with terms and conditions of employment.

STRIKE CAUSES

Recording the cause for a strike involves a degree of subjectivity, since this may be disputed by the parties. Although a strike cause may be disputed in any single strike, the overall distribution indicates clear differences in the extent to which potential areas of dispute contribute to strike activity. Table 10.1 contains details of the causes of strikes over the period 2003 to 2011. The top three contributors to the number of strikes are (1) wages, (2) engagement, dismissal and redundancy and (3) reorganisation, demarcation and transfers (in that order). The working days lost (WDL) figures are distorted by a single public sector strike over the imposition of the pension levy, thereby inflating the figure for pensions. In fact, that strike was over the effect the levy had on wages and could be considered to come under the wages category. An adjustment to take account of this would increase the WDL under the wages category to 77 per cent (not 22 per cent), thus making wages the overwhelming contributor to WDL.

Table 10.1

Causes of Strikes 2003–2011

	Number of Strikes	% Strikes	Number of WDL	% WDL
Wages	28	22.6	99,148	22.2
Engagement, dismissal, redundancy	36	29.0	26,530	5.9
Union representation, recognition	5	4.0	5,952	1.3
Agreements	6	4.9	7,322	1.6
Reorganisation, demarcation, transfers	20	16.1	23,110	5.2
Dispute over Labour Court recommendation	6	4.8	3,074	0.7
Failed negotiations	3	2.4	2,010	0.5
Pension	6	4.9	254,544	57.0
Hours of work	3	2.4	53	–
Other	10	8.1	24,422	5.5
Total	124		446,231	

Source: CSO
Note: Two strikes had more than one cause and we have counted their contribution to each cause. This results in the number of strikes and WDL being slightly inflated.

EXPLANATIONS FOR STRIKES

While the above data indicates that strikes generally occur over terms and conditions of employment, it does not provide any explanation for the trends over time. Strikes do not occur in a homogenous fashion. There are wide variations across countries, over time periods and between industries. As with theories of conflict, there is no one theory of strikes which can fully account for their incidence. Theories do, however, offer insights into the variables influencing strike activity and they point to the role of a number of factors that can influence the level and nature of strike activity. It is beyond the scope of this text to review all such approaches; instead, we focus on four particularly influential ones: (1) the role of industrialisation and the effect of institutions and collective bargaining, (2) economic factors as expressed by both the short-run business cycle and long waves, (3) industrial sector effects and (4) the impact of political economy, including the role of centralised collective bargaining. The aim is to give an insight into a number of leading theoretical and empirical approaches to explaining strike incidence as a prelude to examining the Irish strike record.

It is a truism that the movement of workers into large-scale factory production is the cause of the emergence of strike action. Early craft unions used strikes as a method to defend their craft, while unskilled workers used the strike weapon to gain union recognition and improve pay and conditions of employment. Battles for recognition were often bruising contests, with employers making frequent use of the lockout, especially where unskilled workers were involved. Ross and Hartman (1960) and Kerr *et al.* (1962) drew on these historical factors to construct an institutionalist explanation for strikes and their variation over time and between countries. They suggested that conflicts were especially intense between labour and capital in the early twentieth century, under the influence of syndicalist union policies and trenchant employer opposition to unionisation. As societies matured, these conflicts decreased; employers and unions came to accept each other, collective bargaining became established and more sophisticated and the state provided dispute resolution policies and procedures (Ross and Hartman 1960).

Ross and Hartman (1960) saw the development of industrial relations institutions, especially the growth of multi-employer bargaining and state intervention to assist dispute resolution, as having moderated 'primitive attitudes' to industrial action. Among the primitive aspects of industrial relations they identified was the nature of union movements, with communist-dominated and fragmented trade unions leading to higher strikes. On the other hand, they saw the rise of labour/social democratic parties in power decreasing strike activity. Controversially, they predicted the strike would wither away over time in certain societies, notably northern Europe (Ross and Hartman 1960). This prediction was confounded not just by the dramatic events in Europe in the 1960s and 1970s, which saw a widespread growth in strikes, but it was also undermined by the broadening of strikes in the 1960s to groups that had traditionally not been involved in strikes, e.g. white-collar workers (Crouch and Pizzorno 1978).

Despite the confounding of Ross and Hartman's prediction in the short term, it remains a persistent question as to whether industrial conflict is cyclical in nature or whether it will decline with the modernisation of economies and societies. It is salutary to note that even in the UK 'working days lost due to strikes remained at historically low levels from 1927 through to 1970' (Smith 2003: 206). Furthermore, the intensity of conflicts experienced prior to 1922 (as measured by violence on the part of the state, workers or employers) was generally not exceeded even in the strike-prone 1970s and 1980s in the UK (Kelly 1998). However, the recent demonstrations against austerity in Greece and other European countries indicate the capacity for continuing violence to erupt. In spite of this, it remains the case that in northern European states such events are not the norm. Indeed, a generally unacknowledged aspect of Irish strikes is that they are moderate and carried out according to generally understood rules of industrial relations. In developing countries, quite a different picture can still exist – as exemplified by the shooting dead of thirty-four miners by police during a goldmine strike in South Africa in August 2012.

Cyclical Explanations

In contrast to the institutional thesis of the withering away of the strike are explanations that suggest that strike action is cyclical. There are two variants of the cyclical approach: one based on the link between strikes and the *short-run* or Keynesian business cycle and the other based on variation in strikes over *long-run cycles* or Kondratieff waves (Edwards 1992; Kelly 1998). Analysis of the link between the short-run business cycle and strikes has heavily influenced economists' approach to the analysis of strikes. The analysis of such links dates back to at least the early 1920s (Jackson 1991). The key idea underlying the existence of such a link is that in good times the prospects for successful strikes are greater than when economic conditions are bad. Brannick *et al.* (1997: 299) write: 'obviously, unions are most likely to maximise their gains when business conditions are favourable'. It has also been suggested that revolt is most likely not when conditions of extreme misery exist, but when conditions are improving (Hoffer 2002). In seeking to test the link between strikes and the short-run business cycle, economists have linked strike action to the key macroeconomic variables: the rate of unemployment, changes in real or nominal wages, the rate of inflation and change in the profit ratio of organisations (Brannick *et al.* 1997; Edwards 1992). Thus, strikes should decrease as unemployment rises and should rise in line with inflation or profits. We will see later that the Irish strike record displays just such an effect up to the 1990s.

   While the economic analysis of strikes has a degree of utility in explaining strike incidence, there are a number of limitations. While a link between low unemployment and higher strikes is the most common economic variable to be tested, Brannick *et al.* (1997: 301) note that 'there is little consistent agreement as to the economic variables that influence strikes across countries'. Market forces are only one of a number of determinants of strike action and these can be counteracted by other factors, such as the nature and extent of unionisation (Shalev 1992) and the nature of collective bargaining (Clegg 1976). A further consideration is that certain sectors of the economy may be in a growth phase, even though the overall economy can be in decline; thus, any macroeconomic analysis needs to be supplemented with sectoral studies. Most critical for the economic approach is Paldam and Pederson's (1982) finding that the relationship between unemployment and strikes held in only one-third of seventeen countries examined for the period 1948 to 1975. Rigby and Aledo (2001) also note a lack of fit between unemployment and strikes and the rate of economic growth in Spain across the two decades of the 1980s and 1990s.

Kondratieff cycles, or long-wave theory, imply the periodic resurgence of strikes over historical time periods – not their withering away (Kelly 1998). Kondratieff waves are based on the claimed existence in capitalist economies of long-run business cycles of boom and depression, which are posited to occur across approximately fifty-year cycles. Strike incidence and intensity increase at the upswing of long waves as the economy prospers and as the prospects for success improve. They reach their highest point before or at the peak of the waves and continue at a lower level during the downswings as workers seek to protect and retain any gains achieved during the upswings (Edwards 1992; Kelly 1998). At the bottom of the cycle (during extended recessions or depressions), strikes continue but at a much lower level, largely due to the poor prospects for their success.

Kelly (1998) claims to identify a number of strike waves coinciding with the peaks and downswings of Kondratieff cycles. Reviewing a range of international empirical studies he writes, 'overall it can be argued that there are major strike waves towards the end of Kondratieff upswings (1860–1875, 1910–1920, 1968–1974) and minor strike waves towards Kondratieff downswings (1889–1893, 1935–1948)' (Kelly 1998: 89). Thus, there is a degree of evidence to support the Kondratieff hypothesis. There are, however, difficulties with empirical testing. First, the fifty-year cycle means that there has been only a limited timeframe in which to test for long-run cycles. Second, empirical testing also throws up anomalies (Edwards 1992). For example, within long-run cycles there will be variations caused by short-run business cycles, which can, and do, vary across countries. Finally, and most fundamentally, there is the general failure of strikes internationally to increase with the economic upswing of the 1990s, which has led to even neo-Marxists re-examining the withering away of the strike hypothesis (Edwards 1992).

Among the factors that Edwards (1992) suggests might account for the non-return to high strikes are economic restructuring, the greater power of capital, the extension of conflicts to the developing world and the expression of conflict in forms other than strikes, i.e. outside the industrial relations arena (Edwards 1992). Current evidence is equivocal in relation to the emergence of a strike wave in response to the financial crisis that emerged in 2008. Strike action has been most notable in Greece, Spain and France. In contrast, Ireland – one of the countries most affected by the crisis – has seen strike levels remain at a historic low.

Sectoral Factors

Strike levels vary across different industries. Some industries, such as mining and docking, have been noted to have high strike activity. In the case of Ireland, Brannick *et al.* (1997: 315) note that from 1922 to 1992 'the mining and turf sector has produced more strikes and work-days lost per employee than any other sector [and] the agriculture forestry and fishing sector … rarely experiences strike activity'. The question arises as to what accounts for this phenomenon. Kerr and Siegel (1954) attempted to explain the inter-industry propensity to strike based on the characteristics of the job and the nature of the workers. They examined the relative strike rankings of industries in eleven countries and posited a two-factor explanation to account for the common rankings they found.

Industries characterised by hard jobs – which attract tough, combative workers, living in isolated mass communities – have high strike proneness (e.g. mining and docking). Industries characterised by easy or skilled work performed in pleasant surroundings – whose workers are integrated into the wider community – will attract more submissive men or women and will have low strike proneness (e.g. railroad and agriculture).

While giving an insight into extremes of strike occurrence in some industries, the theory has been criticised on a number of grounds, e.g. there are contradictory experiences in the same industries in different countries. In addition to this, the methodology used in the research was flawed: results that did not fit (e.g. the steel industry) were excluded and the empirical results did not justify the conclusions (Edwards 1977). The low strike proneness of certain industries (e.g. agriculture) can ignore counter examples. In Ireland, agriculture experienced widespread strikes and agitation in the period 1917 to 1923, which has been documented by the labour historian Emmet O'Connor (see O'Connor 1988). The portrayal of agricultural work by Kerr and Siegel (1954) seems oddly romantic, since not everyone shares the view that farm work is easy.

Kerr and Siegel's analysis also leads us to ask if the men were made hard and combative by their job or if they were this way to begin with. Thus, Edwards (1977: 564) notes that Kerr and Siegel ignored alternative explanations, notably the uncertainty caused by 'perpetual problems over the planning and organisation of work, and over-earnings when these are related to output' – a feature mining shared with casual dock-work at the time. Most pointedly, the theory pays inadequate attention to economic and political factors and management action. Edwards (1992: 563) draws attention to Rimlinger's (1959) suggestion that in Britain it was the failure to counteract the mining environment with 'paternalism or state intervention which occurred elsewhere, leading to a legacy of conflict and bitterness'.

Political Factors and Collective Bargaining

Political economy explanations of strikes came to the fore in the 1970s with the development of neo-corporatist theories. Edwards (1992: 366) notes this approach sought to address the question: 'Why in particular have strike rates been low in Scandinavia and Germany and high in the US, Australia and France, for example, as well as in Britain?' This approach had been anticipated by the institutionalist explanation of Ross and Hartman (1960), which drew attention to the mitigating effect of labour and social democratic parties on strike levels. However, there is an important difference between their explanation and the later political economy explanations. The latter focuses not only on the institutional aspects of social democratic parties in power, but the political exchange dimension between capital and labour.

The reasoning behind the political economy approaches is that strikes impose high costs on workers and trade unions, and they can better achieve their aims through a labour party, which they control and which is sympathetic to them. It is suggested that neo-corporatist countries are more governable and stable in their industrial relations for a number of reasons. Collective bargaining is carried on centrally and this accords trade unions and employer organisations a monopoly position in representing the interests of workers and employers. The centralised nature of collective bargaining limits workplace conflict. Trade unions exchange industrial action for political action and pursue a higher social wage instead of using their industrial muscle to achieve higher money wages. Employer-initiated conflict is reduced by the capacity of employer organisations to bind members in collective agreements or by the general applicability of such agreements through the extension of agreements (Kelly 2003).

The political economy approach has been particularly useful in drawing attention to the differences in strikes between differing countries and the need to be aware of the wider political and social context; however, it has a number of limitations (Edwards 1992). Franzosi (1989) notes that political economic theories are 'labour movement theories' and that they focus on the role of labour, paying insufficient attention to the role of employers or the state. Taking the latter point, there are limits to which even labour governments can meet the expectations of labour, as exemplified by the socialist government of Françoise Mitterrand in France in the 1980s. Furthermore, the accession of labour or social democratic parties to power does not necessarily lead to lower strikes, since there are a number of counterfactual examples, e.g. Australia (late 1940s and early 1970s) and the UK (1978 to 1979, the 'winter of discontent'). More pointedly, since the 1980s, neo-liberal policies have been associated with dramatic reductions in strike levels, notably from 1985 onwards, during the period of the Conservative Thatcher government in the UK but also in the US under Ronald Reagan. Such reductions in strikes have involved government exclusion of unions rather than any involvement in political trade-offs.

The foregoing review draws attention to the crucial role played by institutional, economic, structural and political factors. The approaches reviewed are most useful in drawing attention to structural underpinnings of strikes, for which unitarist-type explanations cannot account. Thus, diagnoses based on unitarist notions such as bad communications, troublemakers or bad management (the conceptual equivalent of troublemakers) provide no explanation of why strikes should vary across countries, industries and over time. It is not credible to argue that strike-prone industries or countries are related to poorer communications and attract more troublemakers or bad managers. Undoubtedly such factors may be present in strikes, but they are more properly regarded as symptoms rather than causes of industrial conflict.

MEASUREMENT OF STRIKES

Information on strikes is the only data collected internationally on industrial conflict. Before looking at strike statistics, it is necessary to discuss two general problems that arise in relation to their compilation. These are the issue of *completeness* and *reliability* of strike data. Completeness relates to the extent to which statistics include all strikes. Different countries have adopted differing criteria for strikes to be included in their published statistics. This means that comparisons across countries are affected, something which particularly affects the statistic on the number of strikes.

In Ireland there is a low threshold for recording strikes – with strikes being counted once they last at least a half day or involve a minimum of ten working days lost. In contrast, some countries have much higher thresholds for their figures, most notably the US, which only counts strikes involving more than 1,000 workers. Furthermore, some countries do not count strikes in the public sector, e.g. Belgium, France, Greece and Portugal (Gall 1999). These inconsistencies make the inter-country comparisons of strikes somewhat suspect, but if the data is regularly collected within a country, trends over time can be more reliably examined. However, it is common for information on strikes in many developing countries to be inconsistently collected. Data is missing for some years and this makes comparisons across time difficult, if not impossible (Wallace and O'Sullivan 2006).

The second problem with strike statistics is one of *reliability*. Reliability is determined by the extent to which the strikes within the defined criteria are actually recorded and the extent of either under-reporting or over-reporting (Brannick and Kelly 1982). Under-reporting is the main problem. It is likely to affect the statistics for the number of strikes so that it appears smaller, while short strikes are more likely to be missed than larger and longer ones (Kelly and Brannick 1989). This means that the WDL statistic is least affected by problems of reliability. The number of workers involved is also likely to be less reliable than WDL, since this statistic can be affected by variations in numbers involved over the duration of a strike.

Strike Indices

It is standard practice to collect information on the number of strikes (*frequency*), the number of workers involved (*breadth*), the *duration* of the strike, *WDL* and the causes of strikes. We have already dealt with the causes of strikes and will now examine the other four attributes.

Strike frequency is simply the number of stoppages in a defined time period. The number of strikes is a measure used in many econometric studies of strikes and has been espoused as giving an indication of the general impact of strikes on management and the economy (Kelly and Brannick 1989). However, it is subject to the limitation that it gives equal weight to large and small strikes (Turner 1969). It is also the index with the greatest reliability problems due to two factors: the different criteria used by different countries for the inclusion of strikes and the likelihood that many smaller strikes that meet the definition for inclusion may not be counted.

Strike breadth is measured by the number of workers involved (WI) in strikes. It gives an indication of the size of strikes but it can be open to error if the numbers involved vary during a strike.

The third index is *strike duration*, which refers to the length of strikes in days and can reflect differing strike 'cultures' across countries. For instance, French strikes have traditionally been short due to the absence of strike pay in trade unions and the fact that strikes can be demonstration strikes with a political purpose. Traditionally, Irish strikes were quite long and this was taken as an indication of employer and union intransigence.

The final measure of strikes is *WDL*, which is calculated by multiplying the number of workers involved by the strike duration. In making comparisons across countries or sectors, WDL should be standardised for the level of employment. This is done by dividing the number of working days lost by the numbers in employment. As this is a measure of the impact of strikes, if not actual costs, it is considered the most informative indicator of the pattern of strike activity. However, it is necessary to be aware that the WDL index is affected by a small number of large strikes. Kelly and Brannick (1983: 69) note that 'the Irish strike pattern is extremely sensitive to this comparatively small number of large strikes'. This feature of Irish strikes has continued to the present, with only two strikes (2.5 per cent of the total) accounting for 75 per cent of all WDL in the period 2003 to 2011.

TRENDS IN IRISH STRIKE STATISTICS

Only a small proportion of all employments have experienced strike action in any one year. The number of recorded strikes in Ireland has exceeded 200 in only one year (1974), with 219 strikes. The number of strikes has only exceeded 100 in thirty of the years since 1922. There have been thirty-eight years in which the level of strikes has been between fifty and 100 (Figure 10.1). The number of strikes has been under fifty in only twenty-three years, twenty-one of which have occurred since the commencement of social partnership agreements in 1987; this trend becomes particularly marked in the 2000s. In looking at the variation over time, the evidence from the three strike indices in Figures 10.1, 10.2 and 10.3 indicate certain periods of higher and lower

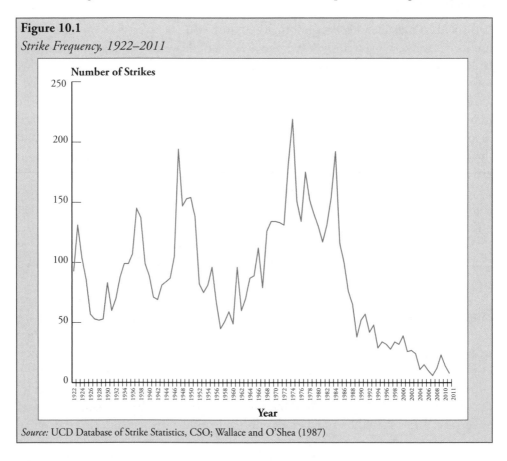

Figure 10.1
Strike Frequency, 1922–2011

Source: UCD Database of Strike Statistics, CSO; Wallace and O'Shea (1987)

Figure 10.2

Workers Involved in Strike Activity, 1922–2011

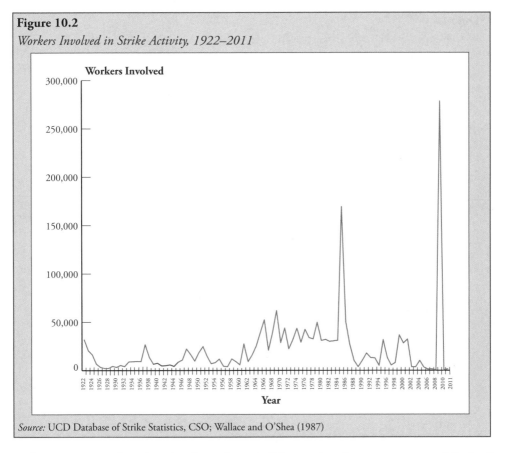

Source: UCD Database of Strike Statistics, CSO; Wallace and O'Shea (1987)

strike activity, combined with a large degree of fluctuation from year to year. Much of this movement, at least up to the 1990s, can be linked to economic factors. Two main economic influences can be identified: the cyclical explanations discussed earlier and industrial restructuring linked to the role of industrial policy.

Brannick *et al.* (1997: 310) emphasise that all three indices of strike activity over the period 1922 to 1995 are 'broadly pro cyclical with respect to economic changes'. This means that strike activity (most notably as represented by the frequency and WDL indices) rose and fell roughly in line with the short-run business cycle. There was a decline in strikes in the 1920s, which coincided with a period of recession and stagnation (Brannick *et al.* 1997). This was followed by an increase in strike levels during the 1930s, which corresponded to a period of increased industrialisation (with 1937 being the year with the largest number of WDL up to now). Thereafter there was a decline in strike activity, coinciding with World War II and the Wages Standstill Order, which, because of the restrictions on wage increases, made strikes over wages largely impractical.

The general increase in the frequency and WDL indices from 1945 to 1952 follow on the austerity of the war years and the removal of the Wages Standstill Order. This represented an effort by workers to restore losses in earnings, which had declined dramatically since 1939. From 1952 the economic depression of the 1950s (when the Irish economy was out of sync with the rest of northern Europe) saw both large-scale emigration and increased unemployment, which led to a decline in strike activity. The

Figure 10.3

Working Days Lost Through Strike Activity, 1922–2011

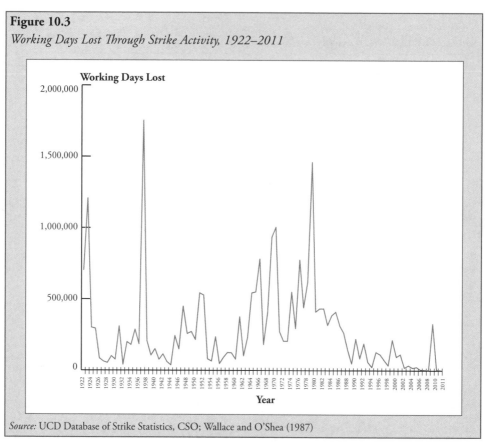

Source: UCD Database of Strike Statistics, CSO; Wallace and O'Shea (1987)

growth in economic activity in the 1960s was accompanied by a return to a higher level of strike activity, which reached a peak in the late 1970s. Although there was a decline thereafter, up to the mid-1980s the indices remained at relatively high levels by historical norms.

International and Industrial Policy Influences on Strike Trends

In addition to the short-run pro-cyclical economic influences outlined above, Irish strikes were influenced by international developments and industrial development policy. The years 1922 to 1924 coincided with the end of an earlier international strike wave. The rise in strikes in Ireland in the 1960s coincided with the Kondratieff wave, which Kelly (1998) identifies as lasting from 1968 to 1974. While part of an international trend, the Irish strike wave starts well before 1968 and lasts well beyond 1974. It is possible to suggest special reasons for this departure from the international strike wave of the late 1960s and early 1970s with a simplified narrative reading, as follows. After the 1950s, depression wages were low and the increase in economic activity led to increases in strike activity as workers sought to gain improvements in their terms and conditions of employment. The buoyant economy of the 1960s led to low levels of unemployment and increased the prospects of a successful outcome to a strike. This, combined with rising inflation and the decentralised nature of collective bargaining based on comparability with open-ended agreements (see Chapter 13), led to increased strike activity as measured by the three indices. These strikes led to significant improvements for workers, notably in terms of the introduction of the forty-hour week in 1964 and increased pay.

The successes achieved emboldened workers and led to union growth and this coincided with the international strike wave starting around 1968. Efforts at reforming collective bargaining with the introduction of national wage agreements led to some fall-off in the strike indices in the early 1970s, but this was only temporary. The second half of the 1970s saw strike activity increase, coinciding with historically high levels of inflation but still relatively low (although increasing) levels of unemployment. The early to mid-1980s saw a severe downturn in the Irish economy associated with the second oil crisis, and as a result employers sought concessions or 'givebacks' from employees. This led to a series of defensive strikes, as predicted by long-wave theory, which were generally unsuccessful. Following this lack of success, strike activity declined.

The influence of cyclical factors at a macro level masks the influence of the role of industrial development and industrial restructuring in the 1960s to 1980s. A seminal paper by Kelly and Brannick (1988) disentangles the strike record of British, Irish and US companies in three separate time periods: 1960 to 1969, 1970 to 1979 and 1980 to 1984. In the period 1961 to 1969, British companies in Ireland had the lowest strike record of the three groups, with US companies having the highest strike record. This changed dramatically in the period 1970 to 1977, with British companies becoming the most strike prone, and strike activity declining in US companies in the 1970s and reaching a low level in the 1980s. Kelly and Brannick (1988: 45) locate the reason for this change in the 'disjunctive impact' of industrial policy, which opened up the country's economy. They point especially to the effect of the Anglo-Irish Free Trade Area Agreement (AIFTA) of 1965, which required a progressive reduction in protective tariffs of 10 per cent per annum up to 1975.

British companies had been set up behind high tariff barriers and concentrated on supplying the Irish market, with little of their production being exported. These were exposed to competition by the progressive removal of the trade barriers in the 1970s. This led to 'a sharp disjuncture in the traditional relationship between the companies and their employees' and higher levels of strike activity (Kelly and Brannick, 1988: 52). These pressures led to 'slimming down policies' and 'new tougher stances by managements' (Kelly and Brannick, 1988: 52). The picture that emerges from Kelly and Brannick's research is one of employees and managers bearing the price of industrial adaptation. It is clear from these findings that the increased strike activity in British companies in the 1970s is a symptom of industrial change and the dislocation this causes. This finding is destructive of the notion that the industrial conflict was caused by 'troublemakers' or indeed its intellectual equivalent – 'bad managers'.

A CONSIDERATION OF CURRENT STRIKE LEVELS

Public and Private Sectors

Strike activity in the public and private sectors over the period 1960 to 2011 is illustrated in Table 10.2. This data indicates that the private sector was the source of most strike activity, as measured by all three indices, during the decades of the 1960s and 1970s. However, this might be expected – since employment was greater in the private sector. There has been a decline in the proportion of strikes accounted for by the private sector, from 80 per cent in the 1970s to 66 per cent since 2003. The drop in workers involved in the private sector is much greater – down from 76 per cent in the 1970s to only 6 per cent over the years 2003 to 2011. The public sector indices for WI and WDL are, however, greatly inflated by the 2009 one-day strike in protest at the government pension levy. This accounted for some 237,000 WDL with an involvement of over 265,000 workers – the vast bulk of public sector WDL and WI over the period 2003 to 2011. When the average length of strikes (strike duration) is examined, a different pattern emerges and strike duration continues to be longer in the private sector: six days on average, compared to just over one day in the public sector. Both of these are significantly reduced over the period 1990 to 1995, when the average length of public and private sector strikes was six and a half days and twenty-one days respectively (Brannick *et al.* 1997). Thus, there has been a considerable change in the character of strikes over recent years, with a reduction in strike duration being a major contributor to the overall reduction in WDL.

Table 10.2						
Proportion of Strike Activity in the Public Sector and Private Sector, 1960–2011						
	Strike Frequency (%)		**Workers Involved (%)**		**Working Days Lost (%)**	
Year	**Public Sector**	**Private Sector**	**Public Sector**	**Private Sector**	**Public Sector**	**Private Sector**
1960–1969	17.9	82.1	36.3	63.7	23.3	76.7
1970–1979	18.3	81.7	32.5	67.5	37.8	60.2
1980–1989	29.1	70.9	68.9	31.1	37.7	62.3
1990–1995	47.0	53.0	61.0	39.0	27.0	73.0
1996–2002	45.1	54.9	75.0	25.0	58.7	41.3
2003–2011	34.0	66.0	94.0	6.0	74.0	26.0
Source: 1960–1995 data from Brannick *et al.* (1997); 1996–2011 data supplied directly from the CSO						

Official and Unofficial Strikes

Strikes may be official or unofficial. Official strikes are defined as strikes that are 'sanctioned by the relevant union authority'; unofficial strikes do not have such sanction (Wallace and O'Shea 1987: 2). Unofficial strikes are distinguished from unconstitutional strikes, which are strikes in breach of procedures – not strikes in breach of the Constitution! The utility of the distinction between official and unofficial has long been questioned. Brannick and Kelly (1983: 10) found that among union officials there was substantial variation in what was considered an unofficial strike. In some instances a strike may not be made official because the union did not know of the strike; it would involve payment of strike pay, which the union could not afford; or it may be official at one level of the union but not at another level (Jackson 1982). In addition, strikes that start as unofficial may subsequently be made official.

During the years 1976 to 1979, unofficial strikes averaged 67 per cent of the total. This has fallen to an all-time low of only 19 per cent since 2000 (Table 10.3). Looking at the distribution of WDL, we see a similar if somewhat less dramatic decrease. In the late 1970s, unofficial strikes accounted for almost 16 per cent of total WDL. This increased to 19 per cent in the 1980s but has averaged just 7 per cent since then. Unofficial strikes are of much shorter duration and have much fewer workers involved – in the period 2003 to 2011 they accounted for only 3.5 per cent of workers involved in strikes. Thus, it is evident that there are substantial differences between the nature of official and unofficial strikes. Even within unofficial strikes there are different categories. Wallace and O'Shea (1987) found that longer unofficial strikes tended to be more like official strikes because they had perceived collective validity by the workers. In contrast, unofficial strikes without such perceived validity (so-called 'cowboy strikes') tended to be of very short duration – only one or two days.

Wallace and O'Shea (1987) report that of the forty-seven case studies of unofficial strikes they studied, the majority were reactive in nature, sparked off by a particular event at workplace level. Typical reactive events included the dismissal or suspension of a worker, unilateral changes in work practices or alleged management breach of procedures. In Ireland, unofficial strikes tend to be subject to considerable opprobrium and state institutions have had a general policy of not involving themselves in meetings to resolve unofficial strikes until work is resumed. Despite the general militant image of unofficial strikes, the evidence is that even in the early 1980s, they were generally a weak weapon for workers (Wallace and O'Shea 1987). This may account in part for their dramatic decline relative to official strikes, although the greater role of employment law (particularly the Unfair Dismissals Acts 1977–2007) is also likely to be a contributory factor.

Table 10.3
Summary of Official and Unofficial Strike Activity, 1976–2011

Year	Unofficial Strikes (As a Percentage of All Strikes)	WDL in Unofficial Strikes (As a Percentage of All Strikes)
1976–1979	66.8	15.5
1980–1989	42.1	19.3
1990–1999	27.4	6.8
2000–2011	18.7	7.4

Source: Wallace and O'Shea (1987); Department of Enterprise, Trade and Employment; CSO

National and International Influences on Recent Irish Strike Activity

Up to about 1993 the narrative in Ireland is largely consistent with a pro-cyclical hypothesis; however, there is no upswing in strike activity with the economic boom of the Celtic Tiger years as the former pro-cyclical relationship breaks down. The reasons for this disjuncture are a matter of debate, with the two main factors being identified as the partnership in industrial relations and the general reduction in strikes internationally. A disjuncture in Irish strike levels is already evident from the mid- to late 1980s, with fewer than sixty strikes in each year since 1988. This provides prima facie evidence for what Thomas et al. (2003: 36) identify as 'a peace dividend' attaching to Irish centralised agreements, which commenced in 1987. Thomas et al. see this dividend as being driven by union leaders who have sought to move away from 'an overtly adversarial style of industrial relations which had contributed little to the wider political objectives of the movement particularly in relation to achieving a more equitable and just society' (Thomas et al. 2003: 36). Allowing for the substantial growth in employment from the 1990s, this indicates an even greater level of reduction in strike activity than the absolute figures (Thomas et al. 2003). However, many of the new jobs are in private services – a sector in which union density and strikes have traditionally been lower. As such, there is clear evidence of a structural contribution to the lowered strike activity from the shift to a services-based economy over and beyond any partnership effect.

Turning to the international evidence, it is clear that there has been a dramatic reduction in strike incidence internationally since the 1980s (Kelly and Hamann 2010; Wallace and O'Sullivan 2006). The question arises as to whether the dramatic decline in Irish strike incidence is merely a reflection of this common trend or whether it is due to internal factors, most notably social partnership agreements of 1987 to 2008. Overall the evidence is somewhat equivocal and there seems to be room for both domestic and international influences at work. Focusing on the EU, Thomas et al. (2003: 42) claim that 'while there has been an overall decline in strike activity within the EU, the decline in industrial action within Ireland has been one of the sharpest'.

Looking at the rank order of WDL per 1,000 employees across nineteen developed countries, something of a mixed picture emerges (Table 10.4). The Irish position only changed marginally for much of the social partnership period. It was fifth highest in 1981 to 1985, it fell to seventh highest in the period 1991 to 1995, but then it returned to fifth highest in the period 1996 to 2000. This led Wallace and O'Sullivan (2002) to express surprise at the limited evidence that international comparisons provide for a larger reduction due to Irish social partnership. The latest date for which five-year data is available does, however, show a substantial drop in the Irish position, down to only eleventh highest out of the nineteen countries over the period 2001 to 2005. This represents a change of six places over the period 1981 to 1985 and does indeed indicate a sharp reduction in the placing of Ireland in a strike league of developed economies. In addition, Ireland is only marginally above the UK and Norway.

Despite this recent reduction, the evidence is still somewhat equivocal. It is noticeable that the UK has experienced an equivalent drop in strike activity with an entirely different market control approach – the opposite of social partnership (see Chapter 13). There has also been no return to high strike levels following the demise of social partnership in 2009. Nationally, it may also be the case that fundamental structural and attitudinal factors have worked to reduce strike activity and that these would have had an effect independent of social partnership. Within the unionised private sector, companies are open to international competitive pressures, more mobile internationally and can switch production between different plants within groups. Finally, many employees now have mortgages and other financial commitments, which previous generations of workers did not have, and that may act as a brake on strike action.

The strongest argument in favour of a strong social partnership effect is the break in the previous pro-cyclical strike trend and it may be improbable that this would have happened without a domestic initiative such as the partnership agreements. The strong growth of the Celtic Tiger years would have placed workers in a position to achieve favourable outcomes to strike action. Thomas *et al.* (2003: 36) point out that the relatively low level of conflict was secured and sustained by the continual striving of the social partners 'through a series of dense personalised networks and an array of informal, formal and ad hoc institutions'.

It is likely that a complex interaction between social partnership, national structural and behavioural factors and wider international developments exists. Thomas *et al.* (2003: 45) suggest that 'the shared understanding of the interdependent mechanism within Ireland's small open economy allied to the "cold wind" of reality generated by the intensification of international competition'. This, they suggest, has 'changed the

Table 10.4

International Comparison of Annual Average WDL per 1,000 employees, 1981–2005

Country	1981–1985	1986–1990	1991–1995	1996–2000	2001–2005
Australia	386	224	130	85	42
Austria	2	2	6	1	83
Belgium	n/a	(48)	32	21	71*
Canada	532	429	159	215	215
Denmark	306	41	45	296	35
Finland	326	410	218	56	78
France	78	111	94	68	72
Germany	52	5	17	2	3
Greece	516	6,316	1,148	29 (1996–1998)	87
Ireland	474 (fifth highest)	242 (sixth highest)	109 (seventh highest)	91 (fifth highest)	30 (eleventh highest)
Italy	774	315	183	76	71
Japan	10	5	(3)	1	0
Netherlands	24	13	33	4	12
Norway	58	142	62	134	29
Portugal	176	82	34	20	19
United Kingdom	440	137	24	21	27
Spain	584	602	469	182	171
Sweden	40	134	50	9	34
Switzerland	n/s	n/s	1	2	5

Source: 1981–1995 data from Brown *et al.* (1997); 1996–2000 data from Office for National Statistics (January 2003); 2000–2001 and 2003–2005 data from EIRO; 2002 data from ILO. There are some inconsistencies in the data sources.
Note: Brackets indicate averages based on incomplete data; n/a = not available; n/s = fewer than five days lost per 1,000; *= data only available for the first 6 months of 2009. Some figures are estimated.

terrain in which the labour market parties operate, particularly in relation to the private sector', making a wave of industrial militancy (reminiscent of the period 1965 to 1985) unlikely (Thomas *et al.* 2003: 45). In this view, Irish social partnership emerges as an Irish response to changing national and international circumstances.

The most marked feature of recent strike experience is the continued quiescence of Irish industrial relations under austerity and economic adjustment. One explanation for this quiescence is that practices that developed over the partnership years have continued to inform industrial relations practice in the austerity era (Sheehan 2011a). In the public sector the government has not performed a volte-face in relations with the social partners but has engaged in a slimmed down process of what is termed social dialogue which is not entirely different from social partnership (Sheehan 2011c). There has been an all too evident reluctance to strike on the part of workers. Teague and Donaghey (2012) draw attention to the lukewarm support for the ICTU national day of action in March 2009. Roche (2012c: 1) points to the limited nominal wage reductions in the private sector and the Croke Park Agreement in the public sector as accounting for the relative industrial peace. In particular, he sees the Croke Park Agreement as 'avoiding the industrial conflict, general strikes and chaos often observed in other bailout and indeed non-bailout countries like Italy, Spain, France and the UK' (Roche 2012c: 1).

CONCLUDING COMMENTS

No theory can explain the occurrence of any strike but it is clear that strike incidence and impact are affected by underlying structural factors. It is also clear that the nature of the political system and collective bargaining arrangements have effects on the extent and impact of strikes. Neo-corporatist systems tend to have low strike rates because of a political exchange between capital and labour. In Ireland in the 1960s the decentralised pay rounds were seen as being behind increased strike activity. However, this also coincided with a booming economy and an international strike wave. Thus, both the short-run and long-run economic waves are linked to the increase in strikes in the 1960s to the mid-1980s. An economic influence is also evident in an increase strike-proneness in British companies as a result of industrial restructuring consequent on the opening of the Irish economy following the Anglo-Irish Free Trade Area Agreement and entry to the EEC. Internationally, strike incidence and impact have declined greatly in most countries since the 1980s. In the Irish case, social partnership and other domestic changes, along with international developments, are likely to have contributed to a disjuncture in Irish strike experience, which is now at a historically low level. However, the contribution of each of these influences is unclear, since they are likely to be interrelated.

CHAPTER 11

Negotiations

INTRODUCTION

No more than becoming skilled in any other activity, negotiation in an industrial relations context requires study and practice. A common myth is the assertion that negotiation cannot be learned. Even an introduction can provide substantial benefits for industrial relations practitioners engaged in negotiations. Students and practitioners who fail to acquaint themselves with the basic elements of negotiation theory risk placing themselves at a substantial disadvantage in the negotiation process. Naturally, exposure to one chapter in a single text is insufficient to make someone a skilled negotiator – but even a basic understanding can significantly improve performance. One of the difficulties of modern negotiations textbooks is the fact that it can be a challenge to assimilate and apply the exhaustive prescriptions contained in them. A short review has its own merits in that it can simplify and highlight key points.

NEGOTIATION: CONCEPTS AND THEORY

Kennedy (1998: 11) defines negotiation as 'the process by which we search for the terms to obtain what we want from somebody who wants something from us'. The advantage of this definition is that it emphasises that negotiation is fundamentally an act of 'exchange', which is reached by a process of 'searching'. Thus, it is not essentially about persuasion or communication (although these are part of the process). Emphasising the exchange aspect of negotiation also draws attention to the idea that it requires movement: a negotiator can only attain some or all of *their* needs by being prepared to take into account some or all of the *other* party's needs. If this were not the case (i.e. if a negotiator could achieve their needs without taking account of the other party), there would be no need to negotiate. Since negotiation is a searching process, an ability to uncover the other party's needs is an essential part of the skilled negotiator's repertoire. Unskilled negotiators tend to focus excessively (and sometimes even exclusively) on their *own* needs and are less skilled at discovering the needs of the other party.

STRATEGIC CHOICE

Parties can pursue a number of strategic options in any negotiation. These options are often discussed under the heading of negotiation styles – but they can also be understood as choices that have to be made (Figure 11.1). Parties can choose to either negotiate or not negotiate (engage in *avoidance* behaviour). If they choose to negotiate, they can then choose a number of options. They can *accommodate*, which implies giving priority to the other party's outcomes; they can *compete*, which means seeking to maximise their own outcome; they can try to *collaborate*, which involves an attempt to simultaneously meet both parties' needs; or they can *compromise*. Compromise arises when each side is concerned about their own outcomes but neither side can achieve those ends without conceding to the other party some of what they would like to have. It should be noted that the above approaches represent extreme choices. Thus, negotiation can be approached with a greater or lesser degree of avoidance, accommodation, competition, collaboration or compromise.

Negotiation Choices

It is not uncommon for parties to adopt an approach by default and without conscious thought. This has the potential to be a serious mistake. Using a compromise strategy in a potential win-win (mutual gains) situation will 'leave value on the table'. A party that uses an accommodation approach when the outcomes are important to them will end up dissatisfied. For instance, a company that is in financial difficulty and avoids addressing this issue by conceding a too-high wage increase may further damage the company and cause the loss of employment. A union official who concedes to a company without adequately attempting to meet members' needs runs the risk of the union losing the support of its members and seeing members transfer to another union.

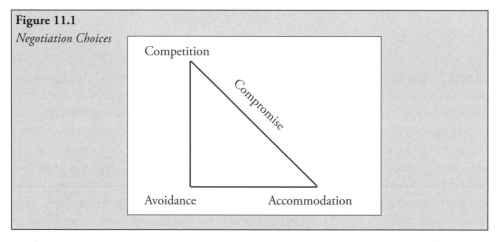

Figure 11.1
Negotiation Choices

Competition

Compromise

Avoidance   Accommodation

Avoidance

From a rational point of view, it is not always correct to negotiate. Entering into a negotiation process is justified when:

- we need something from someone or need someone's consent;
- the time and effort of negotiating are justified by the potential outcome; and
- the outcome is uncertain.

In certain industrial relations situations, the favoured option may be unilateral action. Ryanair has consistently refused to negotiate with trade unions and has been able to maintain that situation. Nowadays, this unitarist approach to management has been adopted by many other employers in Ireland. Equally for employees, refusal to undertake an order that has safety implications may be preferable to entering into negotiations.

The standard industrial relations prescription is to 'work under protest', but if this were to expose an employee to potential injury or loss of life, the risk may be considered too high. The existence of latent conflict is also indicative of an avoidance approach on the part of employees.

Accommodation

Accommodation is indicated when a party is more concerned about the other party's outcomes than its own. An accommodation approach was widely used by employers during Ireland's appearance in the World Cup in 2002. Production stopped in many companies and widespread arrangements were made for employees to watch games. The employers placed the 'relationship' aspect ahead of their legal entitlements under contract law to insist on 'performance'. It could be said that all negotiations involve the balancing of a range of factors, with relationships being particularly important in those interactions that are not 'one-off', e.g. employment relations situations. Sebenius (2001) calls attention to the error of focusing solely on price in negotiations to the exclusion of intangibles such as relationships. He suggests that 'most deals are 50 per cent emotion and 50 per cent economics' (Sebenius 2001: 89). This does not mean that negotiators can neglect the *hard* elements of negotiation such as price; rather, focusing solely on price is seldom sufficient in any complex negotiation, as is typical in industrial relations.

Table 11.1

Case Study

The 'Logic' of Accommodation

One party is given €100 to divide with another party as he/she likes; the second party can agree or disagree to any proposed arrangement. If the second party agrees, the €100 is divided in line with the first party's proposal; if not accepted, neither party gets anything.

Price logic would suggest that the first party should propose something like '€99 for me and €1 for you'. Although this is an extreme allocation, it still represents a position in which the second party gets something rather than nothing. Pure price negotiators confidently predict the other side will agree to the split. In laboratory experiments, however, most players turn down proposals that don't let them share in at least 35–40 per cent of the €100. This also holds true in laboratory-based experiments even when much larger stakes are involved and the amount forfeited is significant. While these rejections are 'irrational' on a pure price basis, studies show that when people feel a split is too unequal, they reject the offer as unfair, are offended by the process and perhaps try to teach the 'greedy' person a lesson.

If the first party is to get anything, they have to 'accommodate' to the second party with an offer well above that suggested by pure price-based logic.

Source: Adapted from Sebenius (2001)

Competition

Competitive bargaining is referred to as 'controlling' or 'power-centred' bargaining (Hiltrop and Udall 1995; Lewicki *et al.* 2010). Thus, the parties try to rely on their power position and to control the negotiation process and outcomes rather than solve problems.

A competing strategy may typically be encountered when a party has high concerns about their own outcomes and the other party has high concerns about theirs. This is often the case over items such as pay, hours of work, pensions and other such *substantive* aspects of industrial relations negotiations. Competition is characteristic of distributive bargaining, but an excessively competitive approach may prove counterproductive.

Collaboration

A collaboration strategy is indicated when mutual gains can potentially be generated. In this approach, both sides try to assist each other in gaining each other's desired outcome. A traditional aspect of collaborative bargaining can be seen in the productivity agreements of the 1960s and 1970s. A collaborative strategy is associated with a problem-solving approach. This is essential, since mutual gains are not always obvious and it may require considerable ingenuity to generate or discover them.

Compromise

Compromise involves the division of a resource. It is a distributive approach and involves 'cutting up the pie'. Sometimes practitioners may comment after a negotiation that it was a 'win-win outcome: we both compromised'. This is a misunderstanding because compromise negotiations involve a win-lose outcome: what one party gains, the other loses. Indeed, negotiators may have a preference for using compromise when dealing with the substantive elements of the employment relationship, e.g. pay.

In summary, it is important to stress that no single approach to negotiation is correct. Students who are new to negotiation theory tend to suggest that collaboration is superior, but that is not necessarily the case. Paradoxically, while espousing their attachment to collaboration, new negotiators find collaboration very difficult to *implement* in practice. However, if resources are fixed, collaboration may involve a long and costly search for a non-existent solution. Avoidance may be a preferred approach if an item is unimportant or if one's power position is such that the involvement of the other party is unnecessary

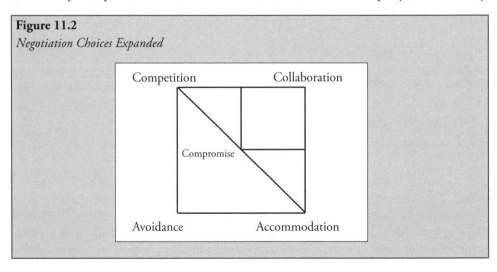

Figure 11.2
Negotiation Choices Expanded

Competition   Collaboration

Compromise

Avoidance   Accommodation

to reach one's desired outcome. Compromise may also be used where mutual gains do not exist or in the division of gains that have been generated.

Negotiations and Trust

Commentators frequently ascribe difficulties in industrial relations negotiations to a breakdown of trust. However, the issue of trust is not clear cut. It is simply incorrect to suggest that it is not possible to negotiate with a party one does not trust. People often have to negotiate with people they do not trust. Police officers regularly negotiate with criminals who it would be difficult (if not impossible) to trust. The presence of a high level of trust may facilitate integrative negotiations. However, Fisher *et al.* (1997) suggest that it is a mistake to either trust or not trust another party in a negotiation. They offer negotiators a way out of the trust dilemma by suggesting that negotiators should 'proceed independent of trust'. Thus, a party can take account of the revealed behaviour of the other party or objective protection can be built into any proposed agreement. Such measures are common, e.g. a warranty on a second-hand car is a practical example of objective protection.

Table 11.2

Case Study*

To Trust or Not to Trust?

TEX Engineering employs 500 employees, but due to competition it is forced to lay off 250 employees. A negotiating meeting is arranged at which the HR director announces to the union representing the workers that she wants to handle this in a constructive way and get away from the adversarial highball/lowball approach. She says the company wishes to deal with its employees in a fair way but there is a limit to what they will pay. Instead of starting low, then haggling and eventually going to the Labour Court, she is prepared to tell the union what is on offer. Pointing to her briefcase she says there is one-and-a-half weeks' pay per year of service 'in the bag' in addition to statutory redundancy entitlements. She says that the union can take this or drag negotiations out and go to the Labour Court, but 'that is all there is'. The HR director has a reputation for being a tough but honest negotiator.

Discussion Point

1   What kinds of issues should the union consider in evaluating the offer on the table?

*This case study can be used for analysis, discussion or role-play negotiation. Guidelines for using the case study are available for lecturers on the Gill & Macmillan website (www.gillmacmillan.ie).

Types of Bargaining

Distributive Bargaining

Distributive bargaining involves dividing up resources or issues and it is largely based on power. The difference between the opening positions of both parties sets the bargaining range. It is conventional for parties to have identified their opening position and intermediate position(s) – or realistic positions – to which they are prepared to move during a negotiation. If these positions prove insufficient to gain agreement, then they will have a fallback. A fallback is the least favourable offer they will accept from the other side in order to avoid breakdown and referral to a third party (Figure 11.3). Skilled negotiation should ensure a settlement if, *at a minimum*, the fallback positions of the parties overlap. If they do not overlap, then non-agreement will be the outcome – even with skilled negotiation. Fallback positions are best set with reference to the alternative available to a negotiator. Of course, parties may be unrealistic in setting a fallback position. It may be set too high (on the employee side) or too low (on the management side). Fallback positions established at the commencement of negotiations need to be kept under review in light of new information discovered during negotiations.

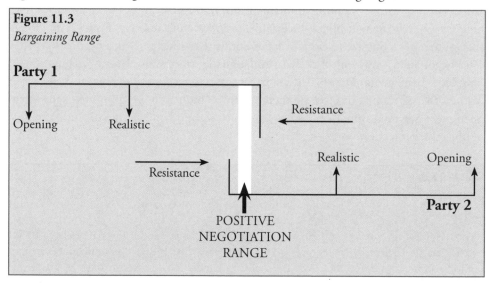

Figure 11.3
Bargaining Range

Party 1

Opening   Realistic   Resistance

Resistance   Realistic   Opening

Party 2

POSITIVE
NEGOTIATION
RANGE

The main objective of a negotiator in a distributive situation is to maximise the 'negotiator's surplus', i.e. the portion of the overlap between the two parties. The negotiator's surplus is the difference between the fallback position (sometimes called the resistance point) of parties 1 and 2 in Figure 11.3. The incentive to maximise the negotiator's surplus contains within it the potential to derail a negotiation. In attempting to maximise the negotiator's surplus, there is a strong temptation for negotiators to deploy hardball tactics. However, such tactics may make settlement more difficult, if the other party responds in kind and relationships are damaged.

Table 11.3
Case Study
The Negotiator's Surplus in Action

Due to the economic crisis, an employer organisation seeks a reduction in the pay of electricians. They are seeking 17 per cent but they will settle for 8 per cent. During its preparations for negotiation, the industry union that represents electricians decides it is willing to agree a 12 per cent reduction, but no more. Neither side is aware of the other's fallback. The eventual settlement is for an 11 per cent reduction. In this distributive example, the employer organisation has gained 75 per cent of the negotiator's surplus and the union 25 per cent.

Even where bargaining ranges overlap, there can be incentives for the parties not to reach agreement. In workplace negotiations, if management are of the view that any agreement reached with a union risks not being endorsed by the membership, they may keep offers in reserve to make an increased offer at conciliation at the LRC. They may even prefer not to move to a fallback position at conciliation, leaving room for a referral to the Labour Court. There is long-standing and repeated evidence of the existence of such an effect in Irish industrial relations, with a criticism of the parties' failure to engage in meaningful negotiations attracting comment from various Labour Court chairmen (Horgan 1989). Of course, if union negotiators suspect that management are keeping concessions in reserve, this creates an incentive for them to refer issues to the Labour Court in order to ensure they get the maximum that management are prepared to offer.

Integrative Bargaining

Integrative bargaining is characterised by an effort to address interests rather than positions in negotiations. The aim is to simultaneously meet the interests or needs of both parties. Lewicki *et al.* (2001: 94) define interests as 'the underlying concerns, needs, desires or fears that motivate a negotiator to take a particular position'. The notion of interests can sometimes be difficult to grasp and it may be easier to think in terms of addressing both parties' 'needs'. The central proposition in interest-based bargaining is that focusing on interests allows superior outcomes to be achieved for both parties. By contrast, focusing on positions (bargaining demands) can make it more difficult to gain agreement.

The notion that a focus on interests will aid the negotiation process is something of a paradox, since industrial relations theorists have identified differing interests as being at the root of employment conflict. However, the following example demonstrates how a focus on interests can work in a common Irish industrial relations situation. In a negotiation over restructuring, the position of workers might be no redundancies and no worsening of terms and conditions of employment. Their interests, on the other hand, might be a need for job security for the majority of workers, but with older workers being open to early retirement. It may only be possible to achieve job security (the union need) by improving competitiveness (meeting the employer's need), which may necessitate agreement to new work methods and a reduction in employee numbers through redundancies. The *position* (no worsening of terms and conditions of employment and no redundancies) must then give way in order to meet the underlying primary *need* of job security.

A key feature of pure integrative negotiations is the free sharing of all relevant information and an open exchange of ideas. A free flow of information is essential along with concerted efforts by both sides to understand the needs of the other party and a concern for meeting those needs. One method for developing ideas is brainstorming, where ideas are generated and then evaluated with reference to pre-established and mutually agreed criteria. Such criteria are usually of a broad nature, e.g. acceptability to the parties, workability and fairness. In the brainstorming process, all ideas are noted down and only those that meet the criteria are retained for further discussion and negotiation.

True integrative bargaining does not involve the parties setting ideal, realistic or fallback positions – these are characteristics of distributive bargaining. Nor does it involve concealing information that is material to the negotiations. Some negotiators may claim to be negotiating on a win-win basis, but they are actually attempting to manipulate the other party. A test of a party's true intentions is to see if the party making the claim of engaging in a win-win negotiation is sharing all relevant information and if adequate concern is being shown for the other party's needs. A negative answer to either of these questions indicates that a distributive approach is really being adopted.

Approaches to Integrative Bargaining

A particular form of integrative bargaining known as 'principled bargaining' or 'interest-based bargaining' has been popularised by Fisher and Ury (1986) in an influential book entitled *Getting to Yes*. The approach focuses on the following principles:

*   separate the people from the problem;
*   focus on interests, not positions;
*   invent options for mutual gain; and
*   insist on using objective criteria.

It should be noted that Fisher and Ury's approach only represents a partial theory of negotiation and that the principled approach has not displaced more traditional adversarial bargaining. Nonetheless, their approach is similar to other interest-based approaches. Integrative approaches, including those of Lewicki *et al.* (1999), identify a number of key steps in the integrative negotiation process:

*   identify and define the problem in a mutually acceptable way;
*   keep the statement of the problem to be addressed simple;
*   state the problem as a goal and identify the obstacles to reaching that goal;
*   depersonalise the problem; and
*   identify the needs of the other party.

Fisher *et al.* (1997) insist that adopting a principled-based approach is not an easy option and requires 'real toughness' on the part of negotiators. A negotiator should not abandon their critical faculties. They are entitled to, and should, rigorously test the propositions advanced by the other party and they must justify their demands on objective grounds.

The implementation of a principled-based approach can be quite challenging. In particular, it can be difficult to implement if only one party is committed to the process. There is a danger that the party attempting to operate in an integrative way will merely end up accommodating the party using a distributive approach. Nonetheless, Fisher *et al.* (1997) claim that a principled-based approach can even be adopted with distributive or difficult bargainers. They suggest that this should be done with the aim of bringing difficult negotiators to their senses – not to their knees! However, this can be quite difficult in practice.

Let us now examine some integrative negotiation techniques.

Table 11.4

Case Study
Partnership and Relationship Change – WILO Pumps

WILO Pumps Ltd (WPL) is a Limerick-based Irish subsidiary of the German-based WILOSALMSON Group, which specialises in the manufacture and marketing of central heating pumps primarily for the European market. Since 1996 WPL endured intense competition from sister plants to produce and supply its motors at very competitive prices, thereby forcing it to adopt a highly focused approach of cost reduction within an environment demanding high-quality standards. WPL's management expended much effort in focusing on many improvement initiatives over a five-year period. While definite progress was made, management perceived that the results did not give the return for the effort expended. Consequently, it was agreed that relationships between the maintenance team and management, which were extremely adversarial, would need to be drastically developed to ensure the long-term future of the plant. Discussions took place with the assistant general secretary of the Technical Electrical Engineering Union (TEEU) in Limerick. Critical outcomes of these discussions were the acceptance of each other's bona fides and the mutual acceptance of the principle of achieving a win-win outcome for all parties. With the assistance of an independent facilitator, it was agreed that the extended management team and the entire maintenance department would meet off-site to explore the possibility of a way forward. This joint session became the major turning point for the plant, since both parties realised they had far more common interests than the differences that divided them.

The group agreed to meet on a monthly basis over an eight-month period in order to develop their relationships, improve communication channels and work on partnership initiatives. As a result, management became much more attuned to the underlying needs of its employees in bringing about change. These needs included respect, involvement and trust – the real drivers of sustainable change. On the union side, a keen appreciation of the business needs of the company developed. This ultimately led to negotiated reductions in labour headcount (reductions of approximately 25 per cent), increased employee efficiencies of 60 per cent and 110 per cent in its two key departments, and a dramatically changed working environment where much greater levels of mutual respect and trust prevailed. The key to achieving these solutions was the systematic use of problem solving and mutual gains bargaining, with employees being an integral part of defining and producing mutually agreed solutions.

Within twelve months of these successful changes, the core motor manufacturing business of WPL was closed, resulting in a reduction of 85 per cent of the workforce. This was done for group strategic reasons that were outside the Limerick facility's control. Despite the trauma of the closure, the development of relationships within the plant had dramatically changed attitudes on both sides; these relationships survived the closure decision and created a supportive environment for everyone in dealing with the closure. Subsequently, members of management, union officials and shop stewards have made presentations to the partnership network on their experiences in effecting a change in relationships.

Source: Contributed by Brendan Lyons, former managing director, WILO Pumps
(see www.partnershiplearningnetwork.com for further discussion points on partnership).

MIXED MOTIVE NEGOTIATIONS

In the 1980s it became common among writers to categorise distributive bargaining in somewhat garish terms and compare it unfavourably with integrative bargaining. For instance, Fisher and Ury (1986) claim that it is the process of distributive bargaining that impedes effective conflict resolution – and that a principled bargaining approach is superior. If this were the case, it would be expected that principled negotiations would have displaced distributive approaches over time. There is, however, no evidence that this has happened: distributive bargaining remains a commonly used approach to negotiations. There has been a reaction to the somewhat evangelical promotion of integrative approaches. Thompson (2009: 41) points out that 'even in win-win negotiations the pie of resources created by negotiators eventually has to be sliced' and this involves distributive bargaining. Lewicki (2010: 103) concurs and suggests that 'purely integrative or purely distributive negotiation situations are rare'. Lewicki *et al.* (2010) refer to combinations of integrative and distributive bargaining as '*mixed motive*' bargaining and this type of negotiation is characteristic of most industrial relations situations. The capacity to manage the complexities involved in mixed motive bargaining is a key negotiation skill. Negotiators need to be able to handle both distributive and integrative elements of the bargaining process.

A useful way to approach mixed motive negotiations is to separate the two phases. The integrative element can be dealt with first by using problem-solving techniques and sharing information and the distributive element (agreeing on the distribution of the gains) can then be dealt with. Even within the distributive phase, the use of creative and integrative techniques has the capacity to ensure a greater prospect of success and to solidify the relationship between the parties. Conversely, the extensive use of hardball tactics may have the opposite effect. Thus, some of the key techniques that are described as integrative are also used during distributive bargaining by skilled negotiators. It must be emphasised that this does not include disclosing one's fallback position. A party that does this is unlikely to achieve any more than their fallback as a result, thereby foregoing any *negotiator's surplus* that is available. Let us now discuss the negotiation process in typical distributive and mixed motive bargaining.

THE NEGOTIATION PROCESS

Industrial relations negotiations tend to be highly ritualistic processes in which both parties engage in an elaborate game. Normally, the formal initiation of industrial relations negotiations begins with one party presenting a claim to the other. It is a convention of normal industrial relations that a claim, once served, will be the subject of negotiation. The Industrial Relations Act 1990 has encouraged the resolution of issues at local level; the conciliation service of the LRC may wish to see that real efforts have been made at local negotiations before they agree to intervene in a dispute.

The negotiating process can be divided into stages. These may be categorised as (1) preparation for negotiations, (2) bargaining and (3) post-negotiation follow-up action. It is useful to think of the bargaining process itself as being divided into three phases – a beginning, middle and end. Table 11.5 contains a checklist of items needing attention in the negotiation process.

Table 11.5

Checklist for Industrial Relations Negotiations

1 Preparation
- Make appropriate administrative arrangements
- Conduct relevant research
- Agree negotiating objectives
- Prioritise
- Check mandate
- Assess relative bargaining power
- Organise team

2 Bargaining
- Opening phase
  - Parties outline their case (expectation structuring)
  - Explore the other side's case
- Middle phase
  - Movement and solution-building
  - Exchange
- Closing phase
  - Final movements
  - Ensure clarity on agreement
  - Record agreement

or

  - Note areas of disagreement
  - Note subsequent action

-
- Referral to appropriate third party
- Option for industrial action

3 Post-negotiation
- Document agreement/disagreement
- Agree action plans
- Communicate
- Implement action plans
- Review

Stage 1: Preparation for Negotiations

Administrative Arrangements

Advance attention to the 'boring' administrative details is essential. An agenda should be agreed. The physical facilities should be appropriate. The venue should be spacious, free from interruptions and convenient. It should have appropriate seating and adjournment arrangements (non-intimidating break-out rooms) and back-up facilities (phone, fax, mobile phones, internet access, etc.). Many of these administrative details will be undertaken as a matter of course, but conscious and careful consideration should be given to them. While these issues may on occasion be non-contentious, it may be necessary to negotiate and agree on them in advance – this is known as 'negotiating the negotiation'. A willingness to do this shows concern for the other party and ensures they will be comfortable with any proposed arrangements. If a party is unhappy about an arrangement, the issue should be raised in advance. If a party becomes uncomfortable during the negotiations, it is best to address the issue as soon as possible. For example, if an off-site venue proves unsatisfactory because of noise, a change of venue can be sought. One should not continue in an environment in which one is uncomfortable.

Research

Many authors have stressed the importance of preparation for negotiations (Hawkins 1979; Hiltrop and Udall 1995; Lewicki *et al.* 2010; Thompson 2009). Adequate research is the key to good preparation: it helps to focus negotiations on facts rather than opinions or value judgements. All negotiators will at some time be faced with situations where they have not been able to prepare. Hiltrop and Udall (1995) strongly advise that when faced with this, negotiators should listen, ask questions for information and adjourn at an early opportunity. Such an approach is particularly recommended in grievance interviews because it prevents possible ill-considered responses by management to employee grievances.

Employer organisations and trade unions may have research departments. The LRC maintains an informative website and the Labour Court website enables parties to search previous cases. The EAT also publishes a summary of unfair dismissal cases and decisions. Preparatory research may require being aware of terms and conditions in comparable employment – the comparability criteria – and precedents. An evaluation of the knock-on effects of different potential outcomes of negotiations may also need to be conducted. While preparation is important, the evidence is that skilled negotiators do not spend more time in preparation than average negotiators, but they do spend more time considering how to use the information they have (www.huthwaite.co.uk).

Negotiating Objectives

The most important decision in preparing for a negotiation is for each party to identify *what* it wants to achieve; this can often be quite difficult. Not all elements within an organisation will have the same objectives and this can be particularly true of a trade union, where the aggregation of interests is essential. Any disagreements or differences should be aired and resolved in advance, otherwise they risk raising their head during negotiations with the other party. This resolution can only take place through intra-organisational negotiations in advance of meeting the other party and the difficulties of this should not be ignored. However, the same principles apply here as apply to general negotiation theory, with an even stronger emphasis on the benefits of an open, integrative approach.

Establishing bargaining objectives relative to one's interests is preferable to deciding on emotional or other grounds. This requires a critical examination of a case's strengths and weaknesses. Research shows that negotiators tend to be better able to evaluate weaknesses in the other party's case than weaknesses in their own. A technique to address this is to engage in perspective-taking – namely looking at things through the eyes of the other party. While this can be difficult to do honestly, role reversal exercises (where some members of one's negotiating team take on the role of the other party) can be helpful in achieving a realistic perspective of the other side's concerns and options. It is important to bear in mind that a party is more likely to achieve its objectives if it can make exchanges that enable the other party to meet its interests. Ignoring the other party's interests and thinking (cognition) is a serious mistake (Lewicki *et al.* 2010).

The Bargaining Mix and Prioritising

The bargaining mix refers to the items for discussion. It is essential to prioritise objectives in the bargaining mix in order to identify those items that can be traded. Negotiation conventions require that parties be prepared to move during negotiations and that trading is a superior form of movement to compromise. There are two conventional ways of prioritising. Parties can attach labels to items to classify them in decreasing order of importance, as follows:

- items they must get;
- items they intend to get; and
- items they would like to get.

Alternatively items can be labelled 1, 2, 3 and so on in decreasing order of priority. Using the first method, there is a great temptation to allot a large number of items to the 'must get' category. However, Kennedy (1998) points out that the more items one has to achieve from a bargaining mix, the lower one's power position is in a negotiation. This arises because one has fewer items to trade in return for concessions from the other party. However, many negotiators think the opposite is the case: that the more they define as 'must get', the higher their power position. This is a serious mistake that can impede agreement being reached even where the real interests of the parties lie in reaching a settlement (Kennedy 1998).

Objectives can be tangible (e.g. a reduction in wage costs) or intangible. The intangibles can be vitally important. For managers, they might include issues such as ensuring good relations with employees and their representatives. Bargaining objectives will vary according to the issue at hand. While parties should be clear on their walk-away position, flexible objectives are generally preferable to rigid ones because information uncovered during negotiations can alter the perception of one's interests.

Mandate

It is important that each party's objectives are clearly articulated and approved by constituents, particularly top management on the employer's side and trade union members/representatives on the union side. This helps to ensure that each negotiating team has a clear mandate. Failure to check and agree a mandate in advance runs the risk of something being agreed at the bargaining table only to be rejected when one or both parties return to their principals.

Bargaining Power

Bargaining power may be interpreted as the degree to which one party can achieve its negotiating goals despite the opposition of the other side. Relative bargaining power significantly influences the outcome of negotiations, with agreements likely to favour the party with the greatest bargaining power. The bargaining power of a party depends on a range of factors that are both external and internal to the negotiation process. Much power will be determined outside the bargaining process: by economic factors, the level of demand for a product, the skill possessed by workers and levels of unemployment. There is also a subjective element to bargaining power and there are measures that negotiators can influence.

In terms of preparation, two measures are essential in assessing one's power position. The first is to evaluate the relative strengths and weaknesses of one's own case. The second and most important measure is to pay attention to and to strengthen one's BATNA. A BATNA is a best alternative to a negotiated agreement, i.e. the best choice a negotiator has in preference to reaching an unfavourable agreement. A BATNA should not be confused with a fallback position (see example below). Disclosing one's fallback position, or reservation price, is never a good idea, but disclosing one's BATNA may be helpful if it is both strong and credible. The better a party's BATNA, the more negotiating power and leverage they have. Sebenius (2001) notes that even experienced negotiators frequently fail to pay attention to strengthening their BATNA.

Table 11.6

Distinguishing Between a Fallback and a BATNA

For someone negotiating to buy a house, a fallback position is the highest price the person is prepared to pay – say, €150,000. A BATNA, however, is the best alternative to not buying the house! It could be any one of the following: buying another house, renting, sharing accommodation, waiting for prices to fall or continuing to live at home.

Team Organisation

Conscious consideration should be given in advance to the selection of a negotiating team. The size and composition of the negotiating team may depend on the issues up for negotiation. In industrial relations it is inadvisable to enter negotiations with fewer than two people. Having at least two people provides a witness to what is said and can allow for greater objectivity. With more than two people, the question arises as to the optimum size. Increased numbers can give solidarity, ensure greater technical knowledge and aid planning. A greater number also allows the allocation of responsibilities in presenting the case, analysis of verbal and non-verbal responses, recordkeeping and consideration of the consequences of various settlement options and management responses (Nierenberg 1968). However, greater numbers increase the possibility of internal disagreement and the inclusion of less skilled/unskilled negotiators who may be more prone to making errors or who may be picked off by the other party. The size and composition of a team may be outside the control of the parties. For trade unions, large numbers of shop stewards may attend negotiations to ensure that the various constituents are fairly represented by the lead negotiator(s). In such situations, strict rules for making contributions can be laid out in advance to prevent someone making a point that would undermine a case.

Table 11.7
Case Study*
The Blinding Flash in Negotiations

A union has tabled a claim for pay parity with local authority employees for members employed by a private sector company with links to the local authority. The company is resisting the claim and produces figures to support its case. The union represents only 40 per cent of the employees. During negotiations, a shop steward notices that based on figures presented by the company, it could afford the pay increase if it was paid to unionised employees only.

Discussion Point

1 Should the shop steward make this point during negotiations? If so, why? If not, why not?

*This case study can be used for analysis, discussion or role-play negotiation. Guidelines for using the case study are available for lecturers on the Gill & Macmillan website (www.gillmacmillan.ie).

Irrespective of its size, a team needs to provide for three functions. These are:

- **Lead spokesperson:** The role of the chief representative is to present arguments, control strategy and tactics and make major on-the-spot decisions.
- **Observer/analyst:** Their role is to evaluate progress relative to objectives, spot key reactions, identify changes in approach and advise the chief negotiator.
- **Recorder:** This involves recording key points in negotiations and documenting the final agreement.

More vital than any allocation of roles is the way in which a team gels. During the negotiation process, team members should support the lead spokesperson without supplanting her/him. Team members should display empathy and be mutually supportive. A clarification or digression can be of enormous benefit to a team member under pressure or who has made an error. There are few situations in a negotiation that cannot be retrieved with an appropriate and *prompt* 'clarification' or 'amplification'.

Stage 2: Bargaining

Opening Phase

The opening phase involves each side setting out its case and seeking clarification from the other side. It is vitally important to be clear on all the items in the bargaining mix. The subsequent introduction of new demands is generally considered to be outside accepted negotiation conventions, but highly integrative negotiations may allow for a focus on identifying and exploring previously unidentified options. A key skill in the opening phase is the use of open questions that focus on what, how and why. However, Thompson (2009) notes that the most effective questioning is around exploring the other side's interests and articulating one's own interests. Interests are the reason for pursuing a negotiating objective. This involves exploring *why* the other side wishes something and explaining *why* something is being demanded. Following an initial outline of the issues, parties are likely to wish to adjourn to consider any new information and to consult with their principals and to check on their mandate. In particular, unions need to keep in touch with their members. In complex negotiations, the opening phase of a negotiation can be spread over many meetings.

A key activity identified by Walton and McKersie (1965) in the opening phase is that of *attitudinal structuring*. This involves attempts by either party to define the negotiation in terms favourable to them. This is done through the deployment of so-called *key commitments*, which are underlying arguments that aim to concentrate negotiations on one party's side of the case. Key commitments are not bargaining objectives. Bargaining objectives are concrete and can be traded, whereas key commitments are merely underlying arguments and can only be argued. In a situation where management want to introduce a pay pause, the bargaining objective is the pay pause and management's key commitments are to remain competitive and contain costs. Where a union is seeking a 5 per cent pay increase, this is their bargaining objective and its key commitments are to compensate for inflation and to reward employees for increased productivity. Viewed in this way, key commitments involve the exploration of interests – not the articulation of bargaining positions.

Research by the Huthwaite group has found that skilled negotiators deploy fewer arguments (key commitments) than less skilled negotiators (www.huthwaite.co.uk). The use of more and more arguments leads to the problem of *argument dilution*. Ever more arguments affect credibility and are easier to counter because they tend to be weaker. However, new negotiators tend to be drawn into this process when they find their initial arguments do not seem to be gaining acceptance. It is vital in the opening phase of distributive negotiations not to be fazed by an apparent rejection of one's concerns/key commitments.

Middle Phase

The middle phase involves further testing of the arguments advanced and exploration of the possible solutions. Identifying areas for movement and solution-building is a critical aspect of this process. Trading is a crucial part of the middle phase and is an inherently integrative technique that produces potentially superior outcomes to compromise. We now discuss some key processes involved in movement and solution-building.

Movement and Solution Building

Movement is a vital point in a negotiation and it is best approached as a trading process – not as the making of unreciprocated offers. Remember: once an offer is put on the table, negotiation conventions dictate that it cannot be removed unless the other party rejects it. Less skilled negotiators tend to blurt out offers without adequate preparation and without linking them to any requirement for concession by the other party. They do so in the expectation that having made a concession, the other side is then under an obligation to respond. This expectation is frequently disappointed. In fact, the other party may immediately indicate the offer is inadequate and demand further concessions. This happens because the person making the concession has made a fundamental mistake. They have inadvertently sent a signal that their negotiation style is one of accommodation and that they are likely to move again without the other party having to reciprocate.

Indicating Movement

When making movement, skilled negotiators tend to talk in terms of 'proposals', not offers. They talk about their proposal and show how it is designed to respond to the needs of the other party. For example: 'The reason we are making this proposal is because we have listened carefully to a number of points you've made. We feel a number of them have merit and we want to try to meet them within the limits of our mandate. In order to do this, we are proposing the following...' It is not a good idea to describe one's own proposals as 'fair', 'good', 'generous', etc., since such descriptions have been found to act as irritants to the other side (i.e. if they do not accept an offer described as fair, the implication is that *they* are not being fair). Offers can and should be justified by comparison to objective standards, such as the going rate in the industry, provisions in national agreements, previous Labour Court recommendations, etc.

Size of Offers

It is common for the initial movements to be large and for later movements to decrease in size. This is contrary to a hardball tactic of making small concessions initially. The benefit of a larger initial movement followed by subsequent smaller ones is that it signals decreasing room for movement to the other party without having to disclose one's fallback position in any way. More importantly, one can require greater concessions in return for a larger movement: a small concession may very well be reciprocated in kind, making progress difficult.

Trading

The essence of negotiation is trading. When making a proposal, it is best presented so as to incorporate something you want from the other party. This should be linked *directly* to any concession you intend making to the other party. A standard technique used by skilled negotiators is to make a concession *tentative* in the first instance and *conditional* on the other party agreeing to their demands. Consider phrases such as: 'If you were prepared to consider movement on X and Y, that would enable us to reconsider our position on A and B.' Phrasing an offer like this allows possible trades to be explored without committing oneself in advance. It is designed to see if the linkages you have made between issues are valued by the other side. If they are not, then they need not be pursued further and other options can be explored. If they are, then they can be 'firmed up'. Making proposals conditional has the dual advantage of identifying what a party wants in exchange and allowing a withdrawal of an offer if that exchange is not agreed. This is why making proposals conditional is so important.

Table 11.8

Exploring Trades – a Practical Example

'*If* the union can agree to a 10 per cent increase in productivity and to work reserve hours as required, then that *would* be sufficient for us to consider a significant move on the pension scheme and to make improvements to the sick pay scheme.'

Note that management have put their requirement *first* and their proposal is less specific than the demand from the other party. If the union is interested, they can ask: 'By how much do you propose to increase the pension and the sick pay scheme?' If the union does not agree to increased productivity, there is no obligation on management to leave the *conditional* offer on the sick pay scheme or pension on the table.

Responding to Proposals/Offers

In responding to offers, it is generally not a good idea to talk down or make little of an offer even if that offer is inadequate. A better response is to welcome the fact that an offer has been made and then to indicate how it would need to be improved in order to enable progress to be made. Put simply, effective negotiation involves opening doors rather than closing them. If a proposal is unacceptable, it may be possible to incorporate some element of the other party's offer in a counterproposal. However, care should be taken in making counterproposals – the research notes that skilled negotiators use much fewer counterproposals than average negotiators (www.huthwaite.co.uk). Immediate counterproposals are often weak because they tend to arrive at a time when the other party is concerned with *its* proposals and can be perceived as designed to block the other party's proposals. They can also signal an anxiety to concede, i.e. that one's negotiating style is one of accommodation.

Adjournments

Adjournments are useful for considering new information and reviewing progress. A good idea before adjourning is to ask the other party to consider/reflect on key issues you have raised. This should be immediately followed up after the adjournment by asking the other party if they have come up with any proposals to respond to the issues you raised. Using adjournments in this way can prevent negotiations getting 'stuck in a rut' or going around in circles. It is best not to use adjournments to release pressure and 'blow off steam'. Proper preparation can ensure that this is not necessary. Remember, the other party will be alert for non-verbal behaviour and inappropriate adjournments can inadvertently reveal a lot about one's position.

Closing Phase

This phase carries many traps for the unwary and can lead to major difficulties in implementation. Three tasks normally have to be undertaken in the closing phase: (1)

finalising the agreement, (2) noting issues for further negotiation and (3) recording details of any area of failure to agree. Offers and counteroffers may come rapidly in this phase after little has happened in the earlier phases. This is especially the case where parties have *unwisely* used a 'chicken tactic' – waiting until the last minute to make movement. In this situation, it is all too easy to lose sight of the cost or value of proposals – careful costing of proposals in advance will limit the prospect of errors and of a 'winner's curse' effect (see below). A further danger is that both parties will have different beliefs as to what *has* been agreed. Not infrequently this leads to subsequent accusations of bad faith on the part of one or both parties.

It is essential to slow down and proceed in a deliberate, considered manner in the closing phase. Each party should be clear on the substance and interpretation of any agreement. Active listening that involves paraphrasing and asking direct and leading questions to ensure mutual understanding is essential. Here is an example: 'So we are agreed on twenty-five redundancies to be on a voluntary basis. If insufficient employees opt for redundancy in order to make up these numbers, compulsory redundancies will take place on a LIFO (last in first out) basis.' Any review of an agreement should be clearly specified and agreed before the parties leave the negotiating table.

If agreement is not reached, it is normal in Irish industrial relations for the dispute to be referred to an appropriate third party – the LRC, Labour Court, etc. Disputes procedures normally specify that industrial action cannot be used by either party until these procedures have been exhausted.

Stage 3: Post-negotiation

Once the negotiations have been concluded, the parties involved will normally report back on the outcome. The way in which the agreement is communicated to employees should also be agreed on, as should decisions on any administrative obligations. Problems can arise not only in delivering to the other party what has been agreed, but in implementing all of the concessions made by the other party. Thus, details of implementation should be worked out and responsibilities clearly allocated within organisations.

Implementation of an agreement is the key post-negotiation consideration. Non-implementation can arise from bad faith negotiation but also from the 'winner's curse' effect. This is where one side leaves the table having reached an agreement but subsequently feel they could have got a better deal. This can lead to non-implementation or implementation in a way other than understood and can sour relations and permanently damage a negotiator's credibility. While it is desirable to review and assess the lessons learned from the negotiation experience, research by the Huthwaite group found this to be done infrequently.

Negotiation Techniques

We conclude this chapter with an examination of integrative and hardball negotiation techniques.

Integrative Techniques

As noted above, Fisher *et al.* (1997) suggest that interest-based negotiations involve real toughness. While the interpersonal interaction may be easier in integrative negotiations, such negotiations place considerable demands on the skill of the negotiator. The use of integrative techniques is not confined to pure integrative negotiations. They are also useful in mixed motive negotiations and can move the negotiations towards the integrative end of the spectrum. The deployment of such approaches has been demonstrated to increase the prospects of a successful outcome and to leave both parties feeling more satisfied with the process.

Enlarge the Pie

The most obvious integrative technique is to enlarge the 'pie'. This may be easier said than done. However, ingenuity can lead to one identifying ways in which this can be achieved. The use of productivity deals in the 1960s and 1970s involved increased productivity in return for higher wage increases. As with all integrative techniques, the technique of enlarging the pie needs to be evaluated against rigorous criteria. For example, by the early 1980s, management had become disenchanted with aspects of productivity bargaining, some of which failed to deliver any real productivity gains.

Negotiate on a Package Basis

Less effective negotiators negotiate on an item-by-item basis, especially when they are making 'offers'. They treat each item in a bargaining mix separately, moving through an agenda one item at a time. This is a mistake because it reduces negotiation on each item to a win-lose situation. While it may be somewhat more difficult to deal with a number of issues at a time, the prospects of a superior outcome are greatly increased by negotiating on a package basis. Lewicki *et al.* (2010) refer to this technique as 'log-rolling' because it increases the possibility of exchanges and reduces the need for compromise.

Prioritise and Then Trade

If a team has prioritised in advance, appropriate trade-offs are easier to identify and agree on. This tactic is typically an iterative process of trial and error and may require the parties to redefine problems by separating or unbundling issues – referred to as fractionating – in order to come up with a mutually acceptable package. The best possible situation is where each party can exchange their low-priority items for their high-priority items. Thompson (2009) points out that trade-offs work not because they build common ground, but because they exploit differences. It is somewhat counterintuitive to think that differences can promote agreement but this *is* the case.

Non-specific Compensation

Non-specific compensation can be used where a mandate is excessively restrictive. An example is where management is attempting to attract a job applicant but cannot meet their salary demand due to a wage cap. An offer to pay for educational courses or provide an enhanced job title or a company car does not affect the wage cap and may be considered. Of course, issues such as these may themselves have knock-on consequences and their use needs to be carefully considered. The issue of bankers' bonuses, which has been the subject of major controversy internationally since 2008, is an example of non-specific compensation designed to get around wage caps.

Cutting the Cost of Compliance

This involves reducing the cost to the other party of agreeing to your proposals. Cutting the costs for one party is a staple of industrial relations. For example, paying relocation expenses is standard when recruiting employees from abroad where the move would impose a cost on the individual.

'Finding a Bridge' Solution

When using this technique, both sides attempt to invent novel options that satisfy their interests. A classic example of this occurred during negotiations on the Partnership 2000 agreement. The employers' maximum offer was a 7 per cent basic pay increase (excluding the local bargaining clause) while ICTU said it would not accept less than 8 per cent – an apparent impasse. Agreement was reached on an overall 8 per cent increase through the novel use of phasing. The increase was structured so that the employees achieved an 8 per cent increase by the close of the agreement but the cost to the employers was 7 per cent over the period of the agreement – the circle was squared! The following industrial relations case study enables students to identify options to break an apparent deadlock in negotiations over redundancies. By developing such options, it should be possible to make a proposal that meets the needs of the employees while remaining within the mandate established by head office.

Table 11.9

Case Study

Redundancies in MSC Engineering PLC – Developing Options

You are a manager in MSC Engineering PLC. Due to a fall in orders, the company decides to make twenty-five of their sixty clerical, administrative and sales staff redundant. They consult their employees, as required under EU legislation. The employees take the news very badly and threaten strike action. Previous to this the union was not active, with only 20 per cent of the employees being union members. All except five employees now join and the union agrees to represent them. Faced with this difficulty, the company agrees to negotiate on the terms of the redundancy subject to the withdrawal of the threat of strike action. The union agrees to suspend any consideration of strike action pending the outcome of negotiations.

There is a good atmosphere to the negotiations at first and a series of issues are resolved, including workloads following the restructuring, outplacement assistance and pension arrangements that will maximise the value of any settlement by minimising tax liability. The issue of whether redundancies should be voluntary or on a LIFO (last in first out) or FIFO (first in first out) basis is not addressed prior to moving on to the major issue of enhanced redundancy payments. As a result of the positive progress, you and the other local managers are anxious that the union committee will accept and endorse any package in order to maintain a good working relationship following the restructuring and to ensure that there are limited negative 'survivor effects'.

Following this positive phase, the negotiations on the terms of the redundancy compensation become difficult and face breakdown. The company offers one week's pay per year of service (plus the statutory entitlement of two weeks per year of service plus one bonus week) with a cap on payments of €15,000. The union looks for five weeks per year of service (plus statutory) and rejects the company cap as 'derisory', suggesting a cap of €60,000. They point out that when three people left in 1996, the company paid four weeks per year of service (plus statutory) without any union involvement.

The union demand is reduced to four weeks (plus the statutory entitlement) during negotiations but the union negotiator indicates to you in an 'off the record' briefing that a settlement of three weeks (plus statutory) would be acceptable. However, she adds that the employees have indicated nothing less will be acceptable, although it is unimportant how this figure is arrived at. She also indicates that special provision will have to be made for employees with less than two years' service who would not be legally entitled to statutory redundancy payment.

Management in your French headquarters have given you an absolute instruction that you may not pay more than two weeks per year of service plus statutory. However, they add that if local management can find other ways of 'squaring the circle', they will not object. They leave it to you to finalise the negotiations with this in mind. The company pays employees' health insurance on an annual subscription basis starting in January of each year. All employees are entitled to a minimum of a month's notice on termination of employment; those with 10 years' service and over have higher entitlements in line with legislation. There are no company cars.

Service of Staff

Number of Years of Service	Number of Staff	Average Salary for Group (€)
15	2	40,000
12	4	37,000
10	6	35,000
8	6	33,000
5	4	32,000
3	4	30,000
2	5	27,000
Less than 2	12	25,000
Less than 1	17	22,000

Task
Break into groups of four or five, appoint a rapporteur, spend twenty minutes discussing the case and come up with options to break the deadlock. Record your options and report back.

Discussion Point

1 Are there any integrative options available?

* Guidelines for using this case study are available for lecturers on the Gill & Macmillan website (www.gillmacmillan.ie). The issue of selecting on the basis of suitability has been excluded from the case for reasons of simplicity.

Hardball Tactics

Research indicates that some negotiation hardball tactics are outside the accepted norm while others are regarded as 'part of the game'. Generally unacceptable hardball tactics include deliberate lying, refusing to accept reality and failure to implement agreements. These are examples of 'bad faith' tactics and are commonly viewed as unethical (Lewicki *et al.* 1999). A party that employs bad faith tactics risks losing its credibility as a negotiator and damaging the long-term relationship. This can be the worst possible outcome where there is an ongoing relationship and can be much more costly than any temporary gain.

Between the acceptable and unacceptable, some hardball tactics can be viewed as ethically 'questionable'. Numerous writers have noted the acceptability of hardball tactics is blurred and negotiators have to be prepared to deal with them (Lewicki *et al.* 1999; Ury 1992). Lewicki *et al.* (2010: 62) note that hardball tactics 'can do more harm than good in negotiations'. They point out 'each tactic involves risk for the person using it, including harm to reputation, lost deals, negative publicity and consequences of the other party's revenge' (Lewicki *et al.* 2010: 62). Risky hardball tactics include the use of chicken (waiting until the very end to make movement), intimidation, fait accompli (introducing unilateral change) and dead leg (asserting there is no room for movement). Such tactics may be encountered. In fact, questions on how to deal with difficult negotiators employing such tactics tend to be the most-asked questions at negotiation courses.

The most common acceptable hardball tactic is probably the highball/lowball example. This involves making either exaggerated high demands or low offers. There are some advantages to this technique. A high/low opening position provides room for movement and concessions. In addition, research indicates that where an exaggerated opening position is taken seriously by the other party, it exercises a strong influence on the outcome to the advantage of the side using it. Thompson (2009: 49) notes that the common perception that an extremely high or low opening offer may insult the other party 'is more apparent than real'. He goes on to note opening offers have a strong anchoring effect and they have an 'at least 0.85 correlation with final outcomes' – that is, an 85 per cent correlation! This indicates that dealing with a highball/lowball opening position is very difficult. One option is to respond in kind but probably the best response is to refuse to table a counter highball/lowball offer, explain why and indicate it will be necessary for the other party to substantially revise their offer/demand in order for the negotiations to make progress. There are also disadvantages to a highball/lowball tactic, since it can backfire on those who use it. The main disadvantage is that the other party may decide there is no point in negotiating and may move directly to their BATNA – this is the lost deal outcome!

CONCLUDING COMMENTS

The process of negotiation has been the subject of considerable theoretical development in recent years. This has provided valuable insights into the process of collective bargaining and individual interactions in employment relations. These insights have promoted a more sophisticated and informed approach to the process of negotiation, the main thrust of which has been the advantages of focusing on an interest-based approach. This approach promotes integrative strategies and techniques at the expense of distributive ones. However, there is no evidence of integrative bargaining replacing distributive approaches, and most negotiations tend to be a mixture of both integrative and distributive approaches. As a result, those involved in industrial relations negotiations, whether of a collective or individual type, need to have an understanding of both integrative and distributive techniques and be able to handle both.

CHAPTER 12

Employee Involvement, Employee Participation and Workplace Partnership

INTRODUCTION

The terms 'employee participation' and 'involvement' may be interpreted as incorporating any mechanisms designed to increase employee input into managerial decision making. They are terms that are frequently used interchangeably, but there are considerable distinctions that can be made. The concept of employee participation is based on the premise that people who work in an organisation should be entitled to influence decisions affecting them. It is sometimes seen as the political democratisation of the workplace, since it facilitates the redistribution of decision-making power away from management and towards employees (Chamberlain 1948; Schregle 1974; Thomason 1984).

The structure of industrial organisations, with the support of the legal and business systems, has traditionally placed decision-making power in the hands of employers. Notwithstanding the primacy accorded the employers' position, employee participation in organisational decision making has a long history and various initiatives have been taken to promote this end. These range from information sharing, through consultation with employees on certain issues, to joint decision making and even worker control. These initiatives may result in a variety of institutional arrangements to facilitate employee participation and involvement, e.g. suggestion schemes, quality circles, empowerment, joint consultative committees, works councils or board-level participation.

EMPLOYEE INVOLVEMENT AND PARTICIPATION

In analysing the subject of employee involvement and participation it is customary to make two major distinctions: the first is between direct and indirect participation and the second is between task-centred and power-centred participation (Dundon *et al.* 2008; Wilkinson *et al.* 2010).

Direct employee participation encompasses any initiatives that provide for employee involvement in and influence on decisions affecting their work and immediate work environment (Wilkinson and Dundon 2010). Employees are directly involved themselves. Such direct participation and involvement is usually introduced at management's behest and may take a variety of forms, such as briefing groups, quality circles, consultative meetings and teamworking. From the 1980s it was frequently introduced as part of change initiatives whereby management transferred responsibility to employees for a limited range of job-related decisions, e.g. working methods, recruitment of team members and task allocation.

In contrast, *indirect participation* is power centred and is often referred to as representative participation. It is an indirect form of employee influence in so far as employee views and input are articulated through the use of some form of collective employee representation, e.g. via works councils or company boards (Lavelle *et al.* 2010; Salamon 2000). Such employee representatives are usually elected or nominated by the workforce and thus carry a mandate to represent the interests and views of those workers. They do not act in a personal capacity but as a conduit through which the broader mass of workers can influence organisational decision making. Indirect participation is considered power centred because it is largely concerned with redistributing decision-making power. It seeks to reduce the extent of management prerogative and bring about greater employee influence in areas that have traditionally been the remit of senior management.

The distinction between task-based direct participation and power-centred indirect participation tends to mark off the respective positions of employer and trade union positions. Employers tend to favour task-centred participation while trade unions have generally sought to extend power-centred participation. However, on occasion some ambiguity has been evident in trade union postures. For example, certain trade unionists may oppose the appointment of worker directors (a form of indirect participation), fearing it may undermine the enterprise-level role of trade unions and collective bargaining. They may be especially concerned at the capacity of unions to take an independent position to oppose company policy if workers have been involved in the formulation of that policy, e.g. through board-level participation. Others view the appointment of worker directors as a positive development that introduces joint regulation in the enterprise, particularly in relation to higher-level strategic decisions.

The Dynamics of Employee Involvement and Participation

Many descriptions of employee participation tend to be 'elastic' in character and it is necessary to be more precise in outlining the principal components. Marchington and Wilkinson's (2000) analysis highlights the dynamic nature of employee involvement and participation and also 'deconstructs' its various components according to degree, form, level and range of subject matter.

Figure 12.1

Ladder of Involvement and Participation

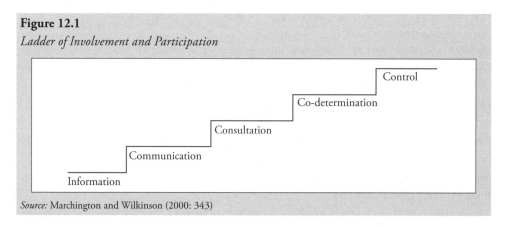

Source: Marchington and Wilkinson (2000: 343)

The *degree* of involvement and participation addresses the extent to which employees can influence management decisions, namely whether they are simply informed of changes, consulted or actually make decisions. This is demonstrated in Figure 12.1, which marks out a progression in the degree of participation rather than 'simply a move from zero participation to workers control' (Marchington and Wilkinson 2000: 342–3).

Second, there is the *level* at which such employee influence is exercised. This may occur at task, departmental, establishment or corporate level. Many developments at enterprise level in Ireland focus on increasing direct employee involvement at task level, namely in decisions that affect their immediate work role. However, we also find employee influence exercised at higher levels in the organisational hierarchy: at business unit level (through collective bargaining) or corporate level (through worker directors).

Third, we have the scope or *range* of subject matter. This dimension addresses the type and number of issues over which employees have the opportunity to influence decisions. The most commonly used categorisation in this respect is to differentiate between influence at the operational level and strategic level. Influence at the strategic level implies a capacity for employee input on the future nature and role of the organisation, while operational level covers more day-to-day matters (e.g. working arrangements and employee autonomy).

Fourth, there are variations in the *form* of participation: one may have involvement in structures or 'financial' or 'equity' participation. Financial involvement involves profit-sharing or gain-sharing schemes, whereby employees participate directly in the commercial success or failure of the organisation. Such schemes may allow workers to secure an equity share in their organisations. In such instances, financial rewards to employees are normally linked to some measure of corporate or establishment performance.

We now summarily outline the main ways in which workers or their representatives become involved in influencing decision making in organisations, namely through 'industrial democracy', 'participation' and 'employee involvement'. As noted earlier, while these terms are sometimes conflated or used interchangeably, it is possible to distinguish between these categories.

Industrial Democracy

Industrial democracy is generally understood to involve situations where workers exert primary control over organisational decision making. Salamon (2000: 370) describes industrial democracy as follows:

> Its central objective is the establishment of employee self-management within an organisation, whose ownership is vested in either the employees or the state and whose managerial function is exercised ultimately through a group, elected by the employees themselves, which has the authority over all decisions of the organisation, including the allocation of 'profits' between extra wages and reinvestment.

This approach is sometimes seen as the ultimate form of employee influence, involving a fundamental restructuring of control and power in industrial organisations towards employees.

Employee Participation

Salamon (2000: 371) argues that employee participation denotes a 'distinct evolutionary development', which is aimed at extending collective employee influence beyond the traditional remit of collective bargaining into 'much wider areas of organisational planning and decision making at both the operational and, more importantly, strategic level'. The collectivist element is a critical distinguishing characteristic of employee participation. This approach involves establishing and extending employee influence through representative structures such as trade unions, works councils or other forms of elected employee representation. Salamon (2000: 371) further notes the importance of power equality between capital and labour in giving effect to what he terms 'real' employee participation. Citing Pateman (1970), Salamon states that '"real" participation ideally requires both sides to have "equal power to determine the outcome of decisions"'. In the absence of such power equality, employees can only rely on management goodwill, i.e. its acceptance of and commitment to a participative philosophy or style of organisational management. There must be more than just the provision of information to employees or their representatives; there must be a genuine opportunity for employees to influence major strategic organisational decisions (Wilkinson *et al.* 2010).

Employee Involvement

Employee involvement embraces any means of increasing the direct involvement of workers in decisions affecting their work situation, e.g. work scheduling or quality monitoring. Salamon (2000: 372) notes that some of the more common mechanisms used to operationalise employee involvement (EI) include empowerment, teamworking, briefing groups and quality circles. He goes on to argue that employee involvement is generally introduced as a means of advancing management objectives:

> These measures have been introduced by management in order to optimise the utilisation of labour (in particular, to improve organisational quality and flexibility) and at the same time to secure the employee's identification with and commitment to the aims and needs of the organisation. Such measures may allow employees greater influence and control over decision making, but only in relation to their immediate work operations; hence the phrase sometimes used of 'task participation'. (Salamon 2000: 372)

The suggestion that employee involvement tends to be primarily management driven is also evident from Marchington and Wilkinson's (2000: 340) conclusion that 'more recent EI initiatives have been management sponsored and, not surprisingly, have reflected a management agenda concerned primarily with employee motivation and commitment to organisational objectives'. Similarly, Wilkinson's (1998: 1,720) analysis of the concept of employee 'empowerment' found that it largely focused on 'task-based involvement and attitudinal change' and did not incorporate any acknowledgement of 'workers having a right to a say'. Rather, it remained an employer (managerial) decision whether and how to empower employees. Wilkinson (1998: 1,720) also notes the potential variation in the extent of power that employees may be afforded under such schemes:

> Most [empowerment initiatives] are purposefully designed not to give workers a very significant role in decision making but rather to secure an enhanced employee contribution to the organisation with 'empowerment' taking place within the context of a strict management agenda. Empowerment schemes tend to be direct and based on individuals or small groups (usually the work group), a clear contrast with industrial democracy and participative schemes such as consultative committees which are collectivist and representative in nature.

The above distinctions reiterate the point that various approaches to employee involvement and participation can differ in regard to both the degree of employee influence on decision making and the level of institutional sophistication of the differing forms of employee influence. As we will see below, initial initiatives in the area of employee influence revolved around worker participation and industrial democracy. However, over recent decades there has been a significant shift in the employee influence debate towards more management-sponsored forms of employee influence. This has been accompanied by a move away from indirect (representative) forms of participation and towards a greater focus on the direct involvement of individual employees in decisions of immediate work relevance. We now proceed to review these developments.

INDIRECT EMPLOYEE INVOLVEMENT AND PARTICIPATION: DEBATES AND DEVELOPMENTS

The movement for worker influence in organisational decision making has its roots in early attempts to achieve worker control dating from the Industrial Revolution in the UK (Coates and Topham 1968). These initiatives were based on a rejection of an economic order rooted in capitalism and wage labour. The movement for workers' control and self-management highlights an important question – whether employee involvement should aim at achieving a changed economic order through redrawing the decision-making mechanisms within organisations or whether it should try to bring about greater employee participation within the current structure of industrial organisations. It is clear that most, if not all, recent developments follow the latter route. Hyman and Mason (1995: 8) observe that:

> Industrial democracy has little currency in contemporary market-driven economies where any worker or activist concern for industrial control has been fragmented and displaced by defensive struggles to retain individual employment and to protect employment rights.

A further 'big question' is whether promoting employee participation contributes to increasing employee influence. Salamon (2000: 398) argues that the appointment of worker directors is 'unlikely to affect significantly the power and decision making of senior management'. In the UK, the Bullock Committee Report found that some organisations had 'developed a de facto two-tier system' involving worker directors on the main board (Bullock 1977: 72). However, Salamon (2000) identified a number of other factors that serve to limit the extent to which worker directors can impact on management decision making, namely:

- infrequency of board meetings;
- exclusion of worker directors from other director and senior management meetings;
- main role of the board of directors is to formally endorse senior management proposals/decisions; and
- board-level decisions rely heavily on senior management for information.

A COMPARATIVE PERSPECTIVE

Developments aimed at increasing employee influence in organisational decision making have taken varying directions in different countries. With the demise of the early movements for workers' control, employee participation achieved its most concrete form through the extension of collective bargaining. More far-reaching developments took place in the post-World War II era, with various institutional arrangements developed to further employee participation, particularly in a number of continental European countries. While these developments fall considerably short of full industrial democracy, they entail institutional arrangements that provide for a degree of democratic input. This occurs within what Salamon (2000: 370) terms 'only a limited modification of the capitalist managerial authority system rather than a fundamental restructuring'. A classic example is the German system of co-determination involving the appointment of worker directors to the boards of firms employing more than 500 employees.

In the 1970s an extensive debate emerged on the desirability of extending representative participation, with a preference for a system along the German lines. The then West Germany had a strong tradition of representative participation dating back to the restructuring of the economy after World War II. This involves two pillars: co-determination and works councils. In structural terms, co-determination entails the appointment of worker directors to the main (supervisory) board of companies. Germany, like a number of other European countries, has a two-tier board structure: a supervisory board to deal with policy issues and a management board to deal with operational affairs. At workplace level, works councils provide for formal employee representation to facilitate consultation, discussion and information exchange between workers and management. In the German system, works councils are required to co-operate with management but are composed solely of workers.

The Debate in the UK

In the 1970s an extensive debate also took place in the UK. Like Ireland, the UK does not have any established tradition of worker directors and its company structure is based around a single (unitary) board of directors, as opposed to European two-tier systems. As the European debate intensified, a UK Committee of Inquiry, the Bullock Committee, was established to investigate the area of employee participation, with special reference to the issue of worker directors (Bullock 1977). The final report contained a majority proposal favouring the retention of the existing single board structure but proposed that boards of directors should be comprised of equal numbers of shareholder and employee representatives together with a smaller number of co-opted independent directors. However, employer representatives on the Bullock Committee vehemently opposed the idea of worker directors and produced a minority report that proposed a two-tier board structure with minority worker representation on supervisory boards only.

These conflicting positions are broadly representative of employer and labour positions in relation to worker representation at board level. Salamon (2000) notes the different perceptions between management and trade unions of the role of worker directors. Management tend to view the role of worker directors in terms of developing 'a "coalition" between employers and management' (Salamon 2000: 397). This is to be done by employee representatives making a positive contribution to the board and can involve articulating employee views, ensuring employee commitment to board-level decisions and by increasing employee awareness of the rationale for board-level decisions. We have already noted that while trade unions may favour worker directors, their attachment can be equivocal, as they may welcome input into decision making but may fear the effect on collective bargaining. The majority report of the Bullock Committee met with widespread employer opposition and was never acted upon. The election of a Conservative government led by Margaret Thatcher in 1979 effectively scuppered any further state initiatives in relation to worker directors.

EU Developments

During the 1970s and early 1980s, much of the debate on employee participation and involvement took place at the level of the European Economic Community, later to become the European Union (EU). In 1975 the European Commission produced a Green Paper on Employee Participation and Company Structure. While favouring a two-tier board system with worker directors on the supervisory board, the paper suggested that this was not the only option for extending employee participation, thus opening the opportunity for differing arrangements in differing countries. The first draft of the European Company Statute (1976) also proposed a two-tier board system along similar lines and further proposed that companies establish works councils and provide for the disclosure of certain types of company information. Despite extensive debate, few of these proposed measures came into effect on any widespread basis.

Works councils have a long-established tradition in many European countries, often enjoying legislative support and exerting considerable influence on the organisations in which they operate. Works councils are particularly associated with initiatives to extend employee participation in Germany and some other European countries since the end of World War II. As noted earlier, they represent a method of providing formal employee representation at workplace level to facilitate consultation and discussion of enterprise-related issues between workers and management. Their role is seen as primarily consultative and representing a broader range of employee opinion than trade unions alone.

This consultative role operates alongside collective bargaining. This approach incorporates a division between collective bargaining and works councils. This division was facilitated in countries such as Germany by the fact that collective bargaining on pay and related matters normally takes place at industry level, allowing works councils to become involved in 'non-pay' issues at workplace level.

Works councils in Europe are generally underpinned by statutes (such as the 1959 Works Council Act in Holland or the 1972 Works Constitution Act in Germany) which generally prescribe their specific role and nature. In reviewing developments in Europe (particularly Germany), Mills (1989) identifies four types of powers of works councils. First, there is the right to be informed on certain issues such as the current state and future prospects of the enterprise. Second, there is the right to be consulted on particular matters such as restructuring or collective redundancies. Third, there is the right to independently investigate certain matters, which generally involves a reciprocal obligation on management to co-operate in such investigations. Finally, there is the right of co-determination, which means that decisions cannot be made without the agreement of works councils. Such issues might include working hours, pay, and health and safety. The rights of works councils will vary somewhat between countries depending on the specific legislation. Based on the German experience, Mills (1989) categorises the issues over which works councils may have rights into economic and social issues. Economic issues relate to mergers/acquisitions, transfers, closure, expansion/contraction of operations, relocation, organisation structure, business trends and financial decisions. Social issues include redundancies/lay-offs, pay systems, training and development, pensions, profit distribution, holidays and health, safety and welfare.

More recently, additional concrete (if modest) developments have emerged at EU level in regard to indirect forms of involvement and participation. This has been done through the implementation of several directives. First was the European Works Councils Directive (EWC) (1994), second was the European Company Statute (ECS) in 2000 and third was the Employee Information and Consultation Directive 2002. Biagi *et al.* (2002: 37) note that the directive on EWCs is 'considered as an extremely important model which has made it possible to get the enactment of the European Company Statute firstly and later on the Directive on Information and Consultation rights in national undertakings'. In contrast to some other authors, Biagi *et al.* (2002: 37) take an essentially optimistic view of these new directives, suggesting they 'have re-opened an intensive debate on corporate governance, on employee involvement and on workers' participation'.

Although the EWC directive preceded the other two directives, we will consider the directive on the ECS first, followed by the Employee Information and Consultation directive. The developments in relation to works councils are dealt with later.

The ECS was agreed by the European Council in Nice in December 2000 and subsequently formally adopted by the EU's Council of Ministers on 8 October 2001. Keller (2002: 424) notes that the essential idea of an ECS is to enable the establishment of 'a unified management structure and reporting system to be governed by Community law instead of a large number of widely differing national laws'. A decision of a company to incorporate itself as a European company (known by the Latin term '*Societas Europaea*', or SE) is entirely voluntary. An SE can be created in any of four ways:

- merger of national companies from different member states;
- creation of a joint venture between companies (or other entities) in different member states;
- creation of an SE subsidiary of a national company; or
- conversion of a national company into an SE.

The directive came into effect on 8 October 2004 and provides for the involvement of workers' representatives on the company's supervisory board. EIRI Associates (2004: 15) note that:

> The participation arrangements only become activated if the company, before becoming a European company, already had participation arrangements in place under relevant national law. This also applies if a European company comes into existence through a merger or takeover if one of the merger partners or the company [being taken over] had participation arrangements in place.

Negotiations on the terms of the SE were especially difficult due to the above-mentioned factor. Member states with strong legislative provisions for worker participation feared that if there was no measure for employee participation present in the statute, 'many firms would use the new legislation to avoid stricter national rules on worker participation' (Higgins 2000a: 16). Furthermore, in member states without worker involvement provisions, there were concerns that the SE would lead to having such provisions being imposed on companies. The UK, Ireland and (especially) Spain were slow to agree to provisions for workers' board-level involvement. Under the statute, management and employees of the European company must jointly agree provisions for worker involvement: 'If an SE is being established, a special negotiating body (SNB) is to be set up, to agree the form of participation to apply' (Higgins 2001: 13). If no agreement can be reached, the standards set in the annex to the directive must be applied.

While the EWC directive is concerned with employee representation at a lower/plant level, covering 'tactical and operational issues of company management', the SE addresses employee involvement at strategic decision-making levels (Keller 2002: 425). Because this is where 'real' control lies, there have been lengthy debates about the statute's contents and introduction. For Ireland, the provisions of the ECS uphold the voluntarist nature of industrial relations because employee involvement in SEs is 'established by voluntary negotiations between social partners at the level of the individual company, instead of binding legislative action at EU level' (Keller 2002: 439). The consequence for employee representatives in SEs is that 'their negotiated rights of information and consultation will be rather weak – and their number limited in contrast to shareholders' (Keller 2002: 441).

Taking a more pessimistic view to that of Biagi *et al.* (2002), Keller believes that such involvement (as defined in the statute) will hardly reach the level of '"co-management" by co-decision in the strict sense of the term, which includes the option to make use of existing veto power in order to block unilateral decision by management' (Keller 2002: 442). Furthermore, Baglioni (2003: 344) points out that 'member states are assigned a major role and functions in applying the Directive'. Keller (2002: 434) argues that as a result the 'ECS will most likely lead to at least fifteen different (and in the future, after the so-called "eastern-enlargement", even considerably more), nationally modelled SEs – rather than to a single, relatively unified and standardised "European" model'. Thus, he claims, 'it is quite clear that the one-time goal of genuine "Europeanisation" of industrial relations will not be achieved' (Keller 2002: 441).

This pessimistic view contrasts that of Biagi *et al.* (2002), who see merit in the flexibility for applying the three directives. They write: 'after the EWC story we finally learnt that it is not possible to identify one single road in promoting employee involvement in various countries … In this context the old idea of harmonisation has been, if not dropped, at least reconsidered deeply.'

The prospects for success of the ECS are bound up with a range of factors, of which the provision for board-level worker representation is but one (arguably minor) element. Among other factors, Keller (2002: 435) identifies the potential disincentives which might arise from a common European tax policy (not yet created) against what the European Commission has argued are the 'huge' savings in transaction costs (administrative and legal costs among others).

The EU Employee Information and Consultation Directive (2002/14/EC), formally adopted in 2002, seeks 'to establish a general framework setting out minimum requirements for the right to information and consultation of employees in undertakings or establishments within the European Community'. Information and consultation is defined as taking place between the employer and employee representatives. The following general rights are specified in the directive:

- information on recent and probable development of the undertaking or the establishment's activities and economic situation;
- information and consultation on the situation, structure and probable development of employment within the undertaking and on any anticipatory measures envisaged in particular where there is a threat to employment; and
- information and consultation, with a view to reaching an agreement, on decisions likely to lead to substantial changes in work organisation or in contractual relations (Directive 2002/14/EC).

Developments in Ireland

Irish industrial relations came late to the employee involvement and participation debate. Kelly and Hourihan (1997: 405) note that 'the only opportunity to participate in Ireland was through the collective bargaining process'. By the mid-1960s, with the apparent success of the German model and the prospect of entry into the 'Common Market', interest had been aroused in the concept. In 1967 ICTU adopted a position in favour of promoting industrial democracy. In 1969 a study on industrial democracy by a joint committee of the then Federated Union of Employers and Confederation of Irish Industry (now IBEC) led to the Mulvey Report. Having examined industrial democracy in terms of employees sharing directly in the management of the enterprise, this report concluded that even in Germany there was no evidence to suggest that co-determination had in fact 'made any direct contribution to the sharing of managerial authority' (Department of Labour 1986c: 32–3) and maintained that the best way for employees to influence managerial decisions was through collective bargaining.

Board-level Participation

Meanwhile, developments at a European level dealing with both board-level participation and works councils, as discussed above, raised the possibility of the extension of European-type participation in Ireland. In the event, most activity in this sphere was confined to the state sector. In 1977 the Worker Participation (State Enterprises) Act was passed and this was subsequently augmented by the Worker Participation (State Enterprises) Act 1988. This legislation provided for the appointment of worker directors to the boards of seven semi-state companies: Bord na Móna, Córas Iompair Éireann (CIÉ), Electricity Supply Board (ESB), Aer Lingus, British and Irish Steam Packet Company Limited (B&I), Comhlucht Siúicre Éireann Teoranta (CSE) and Nitrigin Éireann Teoranta (NET). The 1988 Act extended board-level participation to include (among others) Aer Rianta, An Post, Bord Gáis, Bord Telecom Éireann, Irish Steel, the National Rehabilitation Board and the Voluntary Health Insurance Board (VHI).

The legislation requires that candidates for election as worker director must be nominated by a trade union or other body, such as a staff association or equivalent that is recognised for collective bargaining purposes in the organisation concerned. The electorate comprises full-time and regular part-time employees of the organisation (and subsidiaries in particular circumstances). Once elected, worker directors hold office for a four-year term and have equal status to other directors.

In an initial review of the operation of worker directors under the terms of the 1977 Act, Kelly (1989b) found that the experience had been broadly successful and concluded that employees held positive attitudes to board-level participation. He notes that management, though harbouring some reservations as to the role and contribution of worker directors, largely accepted their role. In a later evaluation, Kelly and Hourihan (1997) noted that the new worker directors quickly settled into their roles and encountered little difficulty in becoming involved in board-level activities. Kelly's (1989b) analysis did not find any major conflict between the role of worker directors and the operation of collective bargaining/trade unions in the organisations studied. He found that trade unions had largely dominated the participatory process:

> For all practical purposes the principal trade unions … control the worker director initiative. In the various elections the successful candidates have been trade union activists … Furthermore, the great majority of worker directors continue to hold some form of union office, which turned out to be an important linkpin in the maintenance of satisfactory relationships between the two power centres. Thus, from the outset the prospect of an alternative, parallel and possibly competing employee voice dissolved into insignificance, and to date there is no evidence that it is ever likely to become a divisive issue. (Kelly 1989b: 309)

Costello's (1983) study of the experience of worker directors in the seven state enterprises covered by the 1977 Act found that the exclusion of worker directors from more operational issues served to limit their influence. His analysis suggested that the impact of worker directors was primarily concentrated on broader corporate objectives, which effectively 'precluded worker directors from raising many of the issues which were of concern to the employees who had elected them' (Costello 1983: 57). 'Most of these issues were seen to fall within management's responsibility and attempts to raise them in the boardroom were invariably ruled out of order' (Costello 1983: 57). Murphy and Walsh's (1980) study considered the views of trade union officials and shop stewards on the role and effectiveness of worker directors. Shop stewards saw benefits in the role of worker directors but were generally sceptical of the capacity of worker directors to influence board-level decisions because of their minority position. Stewards generally saw themselves as a more effective means of resolving employee problems. Shop stewards also noted certain other problems, particularly in relation to the extent of feedback from worker directors. In contrast, worker directors saw themselves as placing considerable weight on the need to maintain strong links between their representative role and the collective bargaining system in the organisation (Murphy and Walsh 1980).

The views of trade union officials were somewhat more critical than shop stewards. Officials were particularly sceptical of the capacity of worker directors to contribute to significant improvements in industrial relations. In reviewing these study findings, Kelly and Hourihan (1997: 429) note that trade union officials were 'quick to mark a boundary separating collective bargaining issues from those concerning company policies'. Kelly and Hourihan (1997: 429) also note that there was no evidence of worker directors attempting to 'compete with, or compromise, the established workplace union organisation'. Possibly the most difficult issues for worker directors to address are those decisions which, from an employee perspective, are particularly unpalatable, e.g. redundancies or closures. In such circumstances, worker directors unsurprisingly 'adopt the expected trade union stance and register their opposition' (Kelly and Hourihan 1997: 429).

Privatisation has clearly had serious consequences for Irish worker directors. Among the first four organisations initially privatised (B&I, NET, CSE and Bord Telecom Éireann), one (B&I) immediately abolished the system of worker directors and two (NET and CSE) retained worker directors on a consultative board but 'all commercial, operational and policy decisions are taken by a second board' (O'Kelly and Compton 2003: 7). In the remaining organisation (Bord Telecom Éireann – now Eircom), the government removed all the worker directors in preparation for privatisation. Worker representation is now through the Employee Share Ownership Trust (ESOT), which has representatives on the Eircom board.

European Works Councils

Increasing employee participation over workplace issues represents a 'key tenet' of the Community Charter of Fundamental Social Rights, generally known as the 'Social Charter' (Blyton and Turnbull 1994). As a result of the Social Charter, the EU published a draft directive in 1991 proposing that companies with over 1,000 workers operating in two or more member states must establish a EWC. The role of EWCs is to supplement national structures to secure information and consultation rights for workers on transnational company matters. In Ireland this was given effect with the enactment of the Transnational Information and Consultation Act 1996. This Act provides for the establishment of a works council, or employee forum, in companies employing at least 1,000 workers across the EU and at least 150 workers in two EU member states.

In addressing the establishment of works councils, the Act outlines three ways in which 'transnational information and consultation' arrangements can be established (Kelly and Hourihan 1997).

1. Through pre-directive agreements on information and consultation concluded before the EU Directive came into force (September 1996).
2. After the Act came into force, moves to establish works councils may be initiated by employers or by 100 employees or their representatives. This approach requires the establishment of a 'special negotiating body' of employee representatives. This body then negotiates the establishment of a European employees' forum or works council with management.
3. If agreement is not reached, then employers must establish a EWC in line with the requirements of the 1996 Act. These requirements deal with a number of aspects of the EWC:
   • composition – a minimum of three and a maximum of thirty members, with membership proportional to the number of employees in each state;
   • frequency of EWC meetings (meeting with central management at least once a year); and
   • issues for consideration at such meetings. Issues specified include the state of the enterprise, business plans, employment and financial trends, organisation structure and organisation change/new working methods, transfers of production, mergers, cutbacks/closures and redundancy.

The legislation also provides for special meetings with management in 'exceptional circumstances' (such as closure, relocation or collective redundancies). The expenses of EWCs or their equivalent are to be borne by management. Employees who are members of works councils are entitled to reasonable paid time off to perform their works council functions and cannot be dismissed for performing their representative duties. The legislation deals with numerous other aspects relating to EWCs, such as voting and arbitration. An important employer concern in relation to works councils relates to the disclosure of commercially sensitive information. On this issue, the Irish legal context provides for the appointment of an independent arbitrator to deal with disputes over whether information being passed on or requested is commercially sensitive. Employees who disclose commercially sensitive information are subject to criminal sanctions.

Information and Consultation

The EU Information and Consultation Directive (2002/14/EC) was transposed into Irish law in July 2006 via the Employees (Provision of Information and Consultation) Act 2006. This meant that for the first time in Ireland there was statutory provision for employee information and consultation rights (with the exception of specific regulation relating to European Works Councils and consultation over collective redundancies and transfer of undertakings).

In transposing the directive into Irish law, the Employees (Provision of Information and Consultation) Act 2006 establishes a right to information and consultation in undertakings in Ireland with at least fifty employees. Dobbins (2009: 1) summarises the main features of the legislation as follows.

- The parties can develop customised 'pre-existing agreements'.
- Otherwise, a 10 per cent employee trigger mechanism is required for negotiations setting up an information and consultation structure (applications either directly to employer or to Labour Court in confidence), unless employers volunteer to introduce information and consultation (IC) arrangements.
- Trade unions are not the sole channel for employee representation.
- If a negotiated settlement is not possible, standard fallback rules provide for elected representative Information and Consultation Forums (along the lines of employee representative works councils).
- There is potential for employers to avail of direct forms of information and consultation to suit local circumstances, or a mix of direct and representative, so long as employees are agreeable.
- Provision for the Labour Court to issue binding determinations in instances of dispute/disagreement.

Dobbins (2009) argues that a controversial aspect of the legislation is the provision that negotiations on the establishment of an information and consultation structure must be triggered by workers themselves, unless an employer chooses to establish such a structure on a voluntary basis. Such a trigger mechanism must take the form of a written request from at least 10 per cent of employees in an undertaking, subject to a minimum of fifteen employees and a maximum of 100. Once such a request is submitted, the employer is required to enter into negotiations to agree an information and consultation procedure with employees or otherwise introduce the standard rules provided for in the legislation.

Another area of controversy identified by Dobbins (2009, 2011) is the provision for direct forms of information and consultation. For some time prior to its transposition, trade unions had long expressed their preference for independent and indirect trade union representation as the best way to enhance information and consultation with employees. However, the directive never envisaged that trade unions would be the sole channel for employee representation.

A definition of employee representatives is provided in section 6. It requires that they be employees of the undertaking, elected or appointed for the purposes of the Act and that the employer make suitable arrangements for the election or appointment of such employee representatives. In unionised firms where it is normal practice for employers to engage in collective bargaining with a trade union or excepted body representing 10 per cent or more of the employees in the undertaking, the legislation provides that employees who are union (or excepted body) members are entitled to elect or appoint from amongst their members one or more than one employees' representative.

Dobbins (2009: 2) also observes that the fallback or standard rules in the legislation provide what he terms are 'pretty strong "continental style" [information and consultation] provisions, in the form of an elected representative *employee forum* composed of not less than three or more than thirty elected/selected employees' representatives only, who shall be employees of the undertaking'. Under these standard rules employers are obliged to provide information and consultation on a range of issues, including probable developments in regard to the undertaking's activities and economic situation; the structure and probable development of employment within the undertaking and any anticipatory measures envisaged; and any decisions likely to lead to substantial changes in work organisation or contractual relations. Although the frequency with which an employee forum may meet on its own without an employer presence is subject to the employer's agreement, 'the employer may not unreasonably withhold consent to proposals made by employees or their representatives' (Employees (Provision of Information and Consultation) Act 2006). In addition, the employee forum is entitled to meet with the employer at least twice a year with the employer obliged to pay for the expenses of the forum, including those relating to members' participation.

DIRECT FORMS OF INVOLVEMENT AND PARTICIPATION: DEVELOPMENT AND DIFFUSION

Direct employee influence encompasses any initiatives designed to provide for personal involvement by employees, individually or as part of groups, in decisions affecting their jobs and/or immediate work environment. Such employee involvement may take a variety of forms, e.g. empowerment, briefing groups and teamworking. As noted earlier, direct involvement is generally instigated by management and is driven by managerial needs and objectives. Salamon (2000: 374) emphasises this point as follows:

> This strategy may be referred to as descending involvement, insofar as management invariably initiates the development for its own purposes (involvement is offered) and, as part of the change, may transfer authority and responsibility from itself to the employees for a limited range of work-related decisions (methods of working, allocation of tasks, maintenance of quality, etc.). However, the content of the process is confined largely to the implementation phase of operational decisions already made by management. This approach is intended to motivate the individual employee directly, to increase job satisfaction and to enhance the employee's sense of identification with the aims, objectives and decisions of the organisation (all of which have been determined by management).

Direct involvement tends to be quite an amorphous concept that may be used in organisations to describe a wide range of activities that vary considerably in their scope and impact on industrial relations practice. Direct involvement initiatives are principally confined to efforts at improving upward and downward communications, with limited provision for employee influence on the decision-making process (Dundon *et al.* 2008).

However, some direct involvement initiatives do impact on the decision-making process and it is this dimension of direct employee involvement that is of most interest from an industrial relations perspective. The terms most widely used to describe this approach are 'task involvement' or 'task participation'. Geary (1994: 637) notes:

> Task participation is defined as opportunities which management provides at workplace level for consultation with and/or delegation of responsibilities and authority for decision making to its subordinates either as individuals or as groups of employees relating to the immediate work task and/or working conditions.

Thus, task participation involves the devolution of greater control over work-related decisions to employees. Employees are encouraged to become more actively involved in influencing decisions, contributing their opinions and solving problems at the workplace level. Workers are required to assume greater responsibility for the general organisation and execution of work, while also being expected to concern themselves with broader enterprise objectives, e.g. improving productivity, controlling costs and general organisational efficiency:

> With TP [task participation], then, employees are granted more control over their immediate work situation and are invited to participate in decisions that relate to the organisation of work at the point of production. Thus, workers may influence the manner in which work is allocated, the scheduling of work and when to take breaks. They are also actively encouraged to seek solutions to problems and to make suggestions that will improve the organisation's efficiency. (Geary 1998: 3)

Sisson (1994) identifies two key forms of task participation. The first is *consultative participation*, whereby workers are given the opportunity to become involved in decisions and make their views known but are not involved in joint decision making. The second is *delegative participation*, whereby workers are empowered to make key decisions without the need for management approval.

Delegative participation means that individual workers assume greater autonomy in their work. Within the broad parameters of the debate on task participation, the growth of interest in teamworking emerges as a major theme with significant implications for industrial relations. The concept of teamworking has its traditional roots in movements designed to improve the quality of working life (Morley *et al.* 2004). While these early developments met with some support in countries such as the US and Scandinavia, they had little impact in Ireland (Geary 1996, 1999). In recent years there has been a significant increase in teamworking (with employers now the key instigators), often in pursuit of organisational change. This contrasts with earlier initiatives that were worker/ trade union driven and were designed to improve the quality of employees' working life. Teamworking is presented as an advanced form of delegative task participation, whereby workers make key decisions such as those concerning the selection of team members, selection of team leaders and the allocation of team roles and tasks. Geary (1996) argues that teamworking initiatives in Ireland have been few in number and largely efficiency driven rather than quality of work life/people driven. He further notes that Irish developments have largely involved 'tinkering at the margins' of existing work practices and are confined to a handful of foreign-owned companies. Although teamworking is somewhat more developed in some European countries, even there the developments seem modest, with some of the more significant progress being in the automotive sector, especially in Germany (Roth 1993; Womack *et al.* 1990). In evaluating the European experience of teamworking, Geary (1996) identifies five important issues.

1. **The regulation of teamwork:** The introduction of teamworking in Europe has been achieved more through agreement with employee representatives rather than via unilateral imposition. This is attributed to the strength of collective employee representation (especially works councils and trade union involvement in industry-wide bargaining) in countries such as Germany and Sweden, which have led the way in its introduction.

2. **The objectives of teamwork:** Achieving a balance between managerial goals of improved efficiency and worker goals of improved quality of work life is a critical issue in facilitating the successful introduction of teamworking. In particular, it appears that trade unions are more willing to engage in teamworking when it is not used solely, or primarily, to achieve managerial aims.

3. **Impact on working lives:** Teamworking has favoured skilled workers and the 'gender divide' has been left relatively untouched, i.e. a major divide remains with limited opportunities for women. However, some specialist categories of staff, such as engineers and accountants, have been transferred to line positions. Employers have not solely relied on persuasion to introduce teamworking, but rather 'more traditional forms' of management control have also been utilised, such as increased employee surveillance and more intense work schedules. Overall, increased skill and effort levels have been a common outcome of teamworking. A number of positive changes may be associated with teamworking, such as improved working conditions and job security, which can lead to productive efficiencies and encourage worker acceptance of teamworking.

4. **Teamwork and management support:** The European experience indicates that management commitment and support is an absolute prerequisite for the effective introduction of teamworking. If teamworking is introduced as an 'island solution' it has little chance of success, while line management 'indifference and resistance' is a key impediment to the effective introduction of teamworking.

5. **Integrating teamworking with HRM:** The European evidence indicates that teamworking is likely to be more successful where it is integrated with complementary

changes in other aspects of HR policy. In particular, a number of key policy changes are identified: a shift from individual-based pay to team-based pay, significant investment in training and development, and the maintenance of job security commitments.

Financial Participation

'Financial participation' is a generic term to describe mechanisms through which employees can gain some form of financial or equity share in their organisations through various profit-sharing, share-ownership or similar schemes. Financial participation is often seen as means of developing a sense of ownership among workers by giving them a stake in their organisation while also integrating employees more fully into the market economy. Indeed, increasing employee loyalty, commitment and morale through the closer identification of employee interests with those of the organisation is often a key objective of many schemes.

However, financial participation of itself will not normally allow for any significant increase in employee influence, since employees will generally represent a minority of the shareholders. Organisations such as the John Lewis Partnership in the UK and Donnelly Mirrors in Ireland have long been known for their policy of sharing profits with employees and other companies now offer share options or some other form of profit sharing, such as Irish Cement, Dell Computers and Abbott Laboratories.

Salamon (2000) identifies two major reasons for the developing interest in financial participation. First is an equity argument that workers should receive a share of the profits or other positive outcomes which they have helped to create. Second, such schemes encourage employee co-operation with management strategies to improve performance. Two broad forms of financial participation exist: the first is gain sharing or profit sharing and the second is employee share ownership.

Gain-sharing or profit-sharing arrangements essentially reward employees for improvements in organisation performance. While profit sharing is self-explanatory, gain sharing refers to arrangements where payments to workers are contingent on some measure of improvement in organisation performance other than profits. Commonly used measures are changes in levels of output or value added. However, gain-sharing arrangements may also be based on less obvious measures of performance, such as lower accident rates or scrap/rework levels. Gain-sharing arrangements are commonly linked to management attempts to instigate particular organisational change initiatives, often embracing attempts to increase employee involvement and commitment. We can identify a number of general objectives underlying such schemes (Armstrong and Stephens 2005):

- to encourage all employees to identify themselves more closely with the company by developing a common concern for its progress;
- to stimulate a greater interest among employees in the affairs of the company as a whole;
- to encourage better co-operation between management and employees;
- to recognise that employees of the company have a moral right to share in the profits they helped to produce;

- to demonstrate in practical terms the goodwill of the company to its employees; and
- to reward success in businesses where profitability is cyclical.

Such schemes have become particularly popular in the UK and the US and have been linked to corporate successes using such criteria as market share, profitability and quality.

The second form of financial participation is an employee share ownership plan (ESOP). ESOPs involve the allocation of a proportion of company shares to employees according to some agreed formula. In Ireland, the utilisation of employee share ownership has traditionally been quite low (Gunnigle *et al.* 2002). However, some growth was initially stimulated by the Finance Acts of 1982–1984, which provided a number of incentives to organisations and employees with respect to ESOPs. Subsequent government measures have tinkered with tax exemption limits, which impacts on the incentive value of such schemes. However, despite some growth in ESOPs in recent years, the overall scale is thought to remain quite modest (Gunnigle *et al.* 1997) and is confined to a relatively small number of organisations. Furthermore, in firms with share ownership schemes, these are generally seen as being most common at higher managerial levels.

Empirical Evidence

More recent data on the uptake of financial participation, teamworking and other forms of direct employee involvement in Ireland are available from the National Employee Workplace Survey and the National Employer Survey (NCPP 2009; further information is also available on the Gill & Macmillan website at www.gillmacmillan.ie). The 2009 Employee Workplace Survey provides data on the perspectives and experiences of more than 5,000 employees in the private and public sectors. Employees were asked about the type of information provided by senior management and the frequency of such provision (Tables 12.1 and 12.2). The findings indicate that a substantial proportion of

Table 12.1 *Frequency of Information Provision – Private Sector (%)*							
	The Level of Competition	**Plans to Develop New Products/ Services**	**Plans to Introduce New Technology**	**Plans to Re-organise the Company**	**Plans to Change Work Practices**	**Information on Sales, Profits, Market Share**	**Plans to Reduce Staff**
Regular basis	46.4	44.3	37.2	29.9	35.6	35.8	24.7
Occasionally	23.9	26.9	27.7	28.9	28.9	21.3	26.3
Hardly ever	29.6	21.9	26.1	31.0	27.2	42.9	34.5
Has not arisen	—	6.9	8.9	10.2	8.3	—	14.5
Total	**100.0**	**100.0**	**100.0**	**100.0**	**100.0**	**100.0**	**100.0**
Source: NCPP (2010)							

employees are not regularly provided with key business or work-related information. For example, less than half of private sector employees are regularly informed about the level of competition facing their firm and just over one-third of employees regularly receive information about plans to change work practices.

Table 12.2 *Frequency of Information Provision – Public Sector (%)*						
	The Budget of Your Organisation	Plans to Improve Services	Plans to Introduce New Technology	Plans to Re-Organise Delivery of Public Services	Plans to Change Work Practices	Plans to Reduce Staff
Regular basis	32.7	41.3	33.6	33.5	35.7	28.8
Occasionally	21.8	33.5	32.5	32.4	34.5	25.1
Hardly ever	45.5	22.9	27.7	27.5	23.9	35.7
Has not arisen	–	2.4	6.3	6.5	5.8	10.4
Total	**100.0**	**100.0**	**100.0**	**100.0**	**100.0**	**100.0**
Source: NCPP (2010)						

A useful source on financial participation and other aspects of information and consultation among MNCs in Ireland is the work of Lavelle *et al.* (2009). This study examined the incidence of three types of financial participation in MNCs, namely employee share ownership, profit sharing and share options (Lavelle *et al.* 2009; further information is also available on the Gill & Macmillan website at www.gillmacmillan. ie). This data suggests a reasonable take-up of all three forms of financial participation among both managerial and non-managerial employees, although these are clearly more common among managerial categories. We also find differences between foreign and Irish-owned MNCs regarding share options, which are used to a greater extent by foreign than Irish MNCs. US-owned MNCs were most likely to use all three forms of financial incentives, particularly employee share ownership.

This study also investigated the differing forms of communications found in MNCs in Ireland (Table 12.3); further information is also available on the Gill & Macmillan website at www.gillmacmillan.ie. The most commonly used communications mechanism was meetings between line managers and employees, followed by newsletters/email, systematic use of the 'management chain', company intranet, management meetings with total workforce, attitude/opinion surveys and suggestion schemes. While this study indicates a high level of utilisation of most communications mechanisms, regardless of nationality, Irish MNCs made least use of almost all communications mechanisms when compared to their foreign-owned counterparts. American companies were frequent users of attitude/opinion surveys, while Irish MNCs reported a substantially lower level of utilisation: one-third of Irish MNCs used attitude/opinion surveys, compared to three-quarters of foreign-owned MNCs. A broadly similar pattern emerges with regard to suggestion schemes.

Table 12.3
Communications Mechanisms in MNCs by Country of Origin (%)

Communication Mechanisms	Irish	UK	US	Europe	Rest
Meetings between line managers and employees	98	97	98	98	100
Newsletters/emails	89	91	94	97	100
Systematic use of management chain	70	91	87	87	87
Company intranet	67	76	85	76	86
Meetings management and whole workforce	64	76	90	63	79
Attitude/opinion surveys	33	71	84	59	93
Suggestion schemes	44	49	59	52	79

Source: Lavelle *et al.* (2009)

HIGH-PERFORMANCE WORK SYSTEMS, DIRECT INVOLVEMENT AND THE QUALITY OF WORK LIFE

The concept of high-performance work systems (HPWS) is closely associated with many of the new 'high-tech' companies that emerged in the US from the 1970s (e.g. Apple, Microsoft and Compaq). The essence of HPWS appears to lie in efforts to adopt a culture of continuous improvement and innovation at all levels in the organisation. This is to be achieved by a combination of work organisation and human resource management practices to sustain and develop this culture, particularly teamworking, quality consciousness and flexibility. It is argued that a specific characteristic of HPWS is a reliance on high levels of direct employee involvement in decision making (Lawler 1978, 1982). In evaluating the impact of HPWS, a significant issue is their effect on employees' work experience. It is particularly important to address the coupling of initiatives for direct employee involvement with the application of management techniques designed to improve quality and productivity, especially just in time (JIT) and statistical process control (SPC) systems. The introduction of these initiatives is generally rooted in the premise that increased direct employee involvement and autonomy is consistent with the use of JIT, SPC or related techniques. Indeed, the argument that direct employee involvement/autonomy complements the use of JIT and SPC is often a key selling point in encouraging employees (and trade unions where these are present) to co-operate in the introduction of such approaches. However, such a complementary beneficial dynamic may not necessarily exist.

In her seminal review of the implications of techniques such as JIT and SPC for employees, Klein (1989: 60) argued that such changes in production systems do not necessarily make for a more empowered workforce:

In Japan … where JIT and SPC have been used most comprehensively, employees are routinely organised into teams, but their involvement in workplace reform is typically restricted to suggestions for process improvement through structured quality control circles or *kaizen* groups. Individual Japanese workers have unprecedented responsibility. Yet it is hard to think of them exercising genuine autonomy, that is, in the sense of independent self-management.

Using examples from both the US and Japan, Klein found that increased pressures and constraints on workers were a common by-product of such manufacturing reforms. While allowing for greater employee involvement and autonomy than traditional assembly line systems, they are not conducive to the high levels of employee empowerment often thought to accompany a shift towards high-performance work systems. She observed:

> True, under JIT and SPC, employees become more self-managing than in a command and control factory. They investigate process improvements and monitor quality themselves; they consequently enjoy immediate, impartial feedback regarding their own performance ... They also gain a better understanding of all elements of the manufacturing process. On the other hand, the reform process that ushers in JIT and SPC is meant to eliminate all variations within production and therefore requires strict adherence to rigid methods and procedures. Within JIT, workers must meet set cycle times; with SPC, they must follow prescribed problem-solving methods. In their pure forms, then, JIT and SPC can turn workers into extensions of a system no less demanding than a busy assembly line. These systems can be very demanding on employees. (Klein 1989: 61)

This analysis challenges the thesis that HPWS necessarily contribute to an improved work experience for employees. In particular, Klein identified important aspects of the work experience that may regress or be lost as a result of reforms using SPC and JIT, namely:

- *individual autonomy* may be reduced due to the elimination of inventories under JIT, resulting in less slack or idle time which in turn limits the opportunity for workers to discuss issues, evaluate changes and make suggestions;
- *team autonomy* may be reduced because of the greater interdependency between groups due to the absence of buffer inventories, with resulting work pressures reducing the time available to consider broader changes in the work system; and
- *ability to influence* work methods may be reduced because SPC sets strict guidelines for working methods and procedures.

However, this analysis does not necessarily mean that HPWS incorporating JIT and SPC cannot positively impact on workers' job experience. Rather, it points to the fact that these techniques and systems may be applied in differing ways. Thus, the issue of management choice is important. Equally important can be the role of workers and trade unions in influencing management choice as to the nature of the deployment of these systems. It is plausible to argue that unfettered management prerogative in introducing so-called HPWS can contribute to a regression in employment conditions and employees' work experience. Klein (1989) argued that the key to improving employee involvement and autonomy when instigating HPWS is to provide for greater collaboration between teams and to allow greater opportunity for teams and individuals to propose and evaluate suggestions for changes in the work process and in the conduct of different jobs.

In other words, the application of new work systems is best facilitated through some combination of direct and indirect forms of employee involvement and participation. This echoes Geary's (1996, 1999) analysis based on the European collectivist experience. In such settings, he suggests that a critical issue in teamworking is the development of strategies for dealing with employee representatives/trade unions. Employers commonly object to the involvement of trade unions in work reorganisation and teamworking on the grounds that it is too time consuming and slows the process of organisational change. However, Geary points to the off-setting benefits of union involvement based on the European experience. First, trade unions/employee representatives have expertise that can benefit the process. Second, they can legitimise the 'necessity of proposed change' to their membership. An additional benefit is that such involvement forces management to integrate HR/industrial relations considerations more centrally than might otherwise be the case. Geary raises the critical question of how to involve employee representatives/ trade unions in the introduction of work reorganisation initiatives such as teamworking. Since, in the Irish and British context such changes were traditionally thrashed out in the collective bargaining arena, he questions whether new institutional arrangements need to be developed. In many of the European countries that have experimented with teamwork, there is an institutional separation between collective bargaining and the workplace. Thus, collective bargaining issues are frequently the remit of union–employer bargaining at industry level, while working arrangements tend to be dealt with through representative structures such as works councils in Germany and enterprise committees (*Comité d'enterprise*) in France. Turning specifically to the Irish context, Geary poses a series of questions on this dilemma:

- Can the introduction of teamworking be productively discussed through traditional 'adversarial' collective bargaining arrangements?
- Is there a need for works council-type arrangements?
- Are Irish managers ready for this type of joint regulation?
- Is it better if the structures used to inform employees are employee based and not strictly union based?

Clearly, many of these issues formed the nub of debates during the transposition of the EU Directive on Information and Consultation into Irish law, as discussed earlier (Dobbins 2009, 2011). More detailed analyses on the applications of HPWS has been co-ordinated by scholars at Dublin City University and the University of Limerick (see Armstrong *et al.* 2010; Guthrie *et al.* 2009, 2011; Liu *et al.* 2009; further information is also available on the Gill & Macmillan website at www.gillmacmillan.ie).

WORKPLACE PARTNERSHIP

Arguably the most significant development in Irish industrial relations over the last two decades was the sequence of national-level social partnership agreements, principally involving trade unions, employers and government, from 1987 to 2009 (see Chapter 13). While national-level social partnership had become well established by the mid-nineties there was a failure to replicate the consensus/partnership model at workplace level (i.e. create workplace partnership) despite numerous initiatives to this effect (Gunnigle 1998b; Roche 2007b, 2008a). Roche (1995: 5) observed that the Irish model of social partnership was somewhat narrow, involving only the top levels of union and employer bodies, and had not significantly impacted on developments in enterprise-level industrial relations. He described the Irish model as 'truncated' social partnership, inferring that employer–union relations at enterprise level continued to be characterised by adversarialism despite the existence of national-level partnership.

In traditionally voluntarist industrial relations systems such as in Ireland, workplace partnership tends to be characterised by a combination of indirect and direct employee participation and involvement initiatives. These include active co-operation between management and employee representatives including trade unions, teamworking and other direct involvement initiatives like suggestion schemes. They are supported by a variety of complementary HRM practices, including the use of a range of communications mechanisms, access to training and development and possibly commitments to employment tenure (Dobbins and Dundon 2011). Proponents of partnership often point to deficiencies in the adversarial industrial relations model, in particular the apparent dominance of distributive bargaining on short-term issues and its emphasis on dividing limited resources (Kochan and Osterman 1994; O'Donnell and O'Reardon 1996). It is suggested that this approach leads the parties to develop adversarial positions, believing that any gains can only be made by inflicting losses on the other party (Fisher *et al.* 1997; Kochan and Rubenstein 2000). Indeed, distributive bargaining reflects the very essence of the traditional pluralist-adversarial model: claims, offers, bluffs, threats, compromise, movement, agreement or conflict (see Chapter 11). In contrast, advocates of partnership at enterprise level posit that integrative/collaborative approaches represent a more attractive alternative, with their emphasis on exploring common ground and seeking solutions of mutual benefit for both employers and workers (Kochan and Osterman 1994). It is further argued that this new model allows both sides to break out of the traditional adversarial relationship through the adoption of a partnership model based on 'mutual gains' principles, as follows:

- employers recognise and facilitate worker and trade union involvement in strategic decision making;
- workers/trade unions commit themselves actively to productivity improvements;
- the gains of productivity improvements are shared between employers and workers; and
- productivity improvements do not result in redundancies, but rather employers actively seek new markets to keep workers gainfully employed.

In essence, the mutual gains argument on which workplace partnership is based is that workers and trade unions actively pursue with management solutions to business problems and appropriate work re-organisation in return for greater involvement in business decisions and in the process of work re-organisation. It is characterised by a strong emphasis on consensual decision making using integrative rather than distributive approaches in management–union interactions and negotiations.

The Characteristics of Workplace Partnership

In analysing the 'ideal-typical' characteristics of enterprise-level workplace partnership, Gunnigle (1998b) identifies three principal dimensions: strategic impact, role of trade unions/employee representatives and levels of institutional sophistication.

Employee and/or trade union involvement in the strategic decision-making process is probably the key element that characterises a highly developed 'strategic' workplace partnership approach. The focus on high-level strategic decisions is important and serves to differentiate 'strategic partnerships' from lower-level workplace partnerships that focus on operational-level decisions, such as those related to work organisation or quality. That is not to say that operational workplace issues cannot be a focus of strategic partnership arrangements, but rather to indicate that the 'strategic' element refers to partnership in making long-term strategic decisions that impact on the future nature and direction of the enterprise as a whole. As McKersie (2002: 111) notes, a critical feature of strategic partnership is union or employee involvement in key corporate decisions, with trade unions having the 'opportunity to challenge or confront management before a decision is made'.

Given the critical role played by the Irish trade union movement in national social partnership, unions are generally seen as an equally important facet of the development of workplace partnerships. Indeed, trade unions have played an important role in promoting the idea and providing an institutional stimulus for the introduction of workplace partnership arrangements (Dobbins and Gunnigle 2009; Roche 2008a). However, much of Ireland's industrial development has been led by foreign-owned firms, many of which are non-union. In the Irish non-union sector there are many organisations that claim to have well-developed management–employee partnerships. Many of these firms claim to deploy something along the lines of what have been labelled non-union 'high commitment systems' (Cutcher-Gershenfeld and Verma 1994). These inevitably have their roots in the US and place the primary focus on facilitating direct employee involvement in operational decision making at workplace level. However, it is often difficult to discern the existence and nature of such partnerships, since most accounts are based solely on a managerial perspective. As such, these cases present difficulties in evaluating the nature and extent of partnership.

Another critical dimension of effective workplace partnership concerns the extent to which there are well-developed institutional arrangements to facilitate a partnership approach. The non-union high commitment system relies primarily on direct employee involvement through teamworking and problem-solving groups – it does not normally involve formal representative structures (Cutcher-Gershenfeld and Verma 1994). However, in high-level workplace partnership (which provides for employee involvement in decision making), one would expect to find more formal structures. In unionised firms these structures normally exist in addition to established collective bargaining arrangements. For strategic partnership, one would expect to see provisions for union or worker representation at board level. An extract from a joint union/employer task force paper between Communications, Energy and Paper (CEP) Union and Bell (Canada) illustrates this point:

[Union-management partnerships need to] involve, through the corporate steering committee and other exchanges of information, appropriate union executives in planning, strategy, training, and policy formulation in areas such as quality, human resources planning, new technology, major product development and market changes, and strategic alliances with other telecommunications companies. (McKersie 1996: 1)

Another key distinction is that these partnerships are at the corporate level where key business decisions are made that affect the viability of the enterprise. To support well-developed partnership arrangements at the operational level, one might also expect to see the development of management–employee/union institutions to facilitate joint decision making. However, workplace partnership arrangements, particularly those of an operational nature, need not necessarily be underpinned by complementary institutional arrangements (Dobbins and Gunnigle 2009).

One can point to arrangements for periodic management–employee briefings where the focus is on information sharing and consultation. Such approaches do not normally provide for joint decision making. Management informs employees, discusses issues and considers employee or union opinion but retains prerogative in decision making.

It is possible to identify two additional and important components that may form part of workplace partnerships: gain sharing and job security commitments. As mentioned earlier, gain sharing broadly incorporates arrangements that reward workers for improvements in enterprise performance via profit sharing, share ownership or some other reward mechanism. Such schemes are critical in giving effect to an underlying principle of partnership, namely that the gains from improved performance are shared between employers and workers. In 1998 John O'Dowd, then director of the National Centre for Partnership, suggested that one of the key elements for successful workplace partnership is reasonable assurances of employment security so that employees will not be constrained by a sense of insecurity from making a significant contribution to organisational improvement. Although job security commitments are said to form part of the workplace partnership equation, there is little evidence of these being widespread (Wallace 1999). McCartney and Teague (2004) note that 'despite the use of innovative work practices, neither employer-volunteered job security pledges nor, more surprisingly, union-negotiated job ownership rights are particularly common'. The issue of job guarantees seems to have fallen into disrepute in the early 1980s when, faced with the downturn in the economy, such agreements proved illusory. Turlough O'Sullivan, then IBEC director general, said:

Management in companies have a clear view of optimum employment levels, and optimum manning levels, and therefore, they would not generally get into a negotiation where something other than optimum manning levels might ensue … The concept of building in an excess of fat, or whatever else you want to call it … to be fair, it's not something that trade unions here would push for. (Wallace 1999: 14)

Pressures for Workplace Partnership

In evaluating the pressures for workplace partnership one can identify a number of generic stimuli. First, the decline in trade union penetration has prompted the union movement to seek mechanisms to increase their legitimacy and representativeness at both enterprise and national level. Second, we have noted the increasingly competitive environment facing organisations. This has placed pressure on organisations to reconfigure their industrial relations policies in order to facilitate improved performance and productivity. Third, MNCs have promoted competition between branches and plants in differing countries as a corporate policy. Finally, there is the pressure of industrial restructuring. This arises from at least two sources: technological change, involving the rundown of older industries, and social dumping, involving the relocation of processes and even services (such as IT support) to low-cost locations.

In addressing these challenges, workers and management have on occasion been effectively thrown together to jointly try to stave off threats by increasing efficiency and containing or reducing labour costs. One way for unions to respond to these challenges is to seek to have an input in these changes rather than opposing them; in other words, to engage in collaborative bargaining. The same holds for management – they can attempt to force through unilateral change but this may be resisted and be destructive. It can also lead to the parties having to subsequently engage in negotiations, with the risk that the climate for such negotiations is damaged.

Since the mid-1990s national social partnership agreements in Ireland began to develop a more explicit focus on issues of employment and competitiveness. As part of the process for agreeing the Programme for Competitiveness and Work (1994), a Joint Declaration was issued by IBEC and ICTU that recognised the importance of increased employee involvement in addition to greater competitiveness for the effective development of the enterprise, increased job satisfaction, closer identification of employees with the organisation and a safe and healthy work environment. The union movement placed the development of workplace-level partnership to the fore in the next agreement, Partnership 2000, which explicitly sought to 'extend partnership arrangements at enterprise level' (Department of the Taoiseach 1997) and provided an explicit definition of partnership, as follows:

Partnership is an active relationship based on recognition of a common interest to secure the competitiveness, viability and prosperity of the enterprise. It involves a continuing commitment by employees to improvements in quality and efficiency; and the acceptance by employers of employees as stake holders with rights and interests to be considered in the context of major decisions affecting their employment. (Department of the Taoiseach 1997: 52)

The next agreement, the Programme for Prosperity and Fairness (PPF) 2000, sought to follow through on this agenda. IBEC and ICTU committed themselves 'to work together to develop guidelines to assist companies in embarking on and successfully putting in place partnership arrangements', including 'financial participation measures' (Department of the Taoiseach 2000: 15). The agreement enhanced the role of the

National Centre for Partnership, which was renamed the National Centre for Partnership and Performance (NCPP). Equally, the subsequent agreement (Sustaining Progress 2003) reaffirmed the 'commitments under previous national agreements' and declared 'that the National Centre for Partnership and Performance will play an increasing role in supporting this process' (Department of the Taoiseach 2003: 77) in conjunction with ICTU and IBEC.

These provisions in centralised agreements represented a concerted attempt to promote workplace partnership in Ireland. However, none of the agreements provided for any legislative requirement for partnership, which differs from countries where employee participation has taken root. As such there remains the moot question as to whether a system of partnership can be brought about through voluntary (centralised) agreements or whether legislation is required. Certainly the quite limited and patchy take-up of workplace partnership arrangements in Ireland suggests that such arrangements are unlikely to take root without stronger regulatory support.

The Diffusion of Workplace Partnership

There is a limited but growing body of empirical research that, either directly or indirectly, explores developments in workplace partnership. In this section we present

Table 12.4

Handling Workplace Change in Unionised Establishments

	How Change Is Handled (%)			
	Management Prerogative	Collective Bargaining	Partnership	Direct Involvement
Operational Issues				
Pay levels	17	62	11	10
Payment systems	21	40	18	22
New plant and technology	48	13	11	27
Working time	8	38	16	38
Work practices	13	25	20	41
Numbers employed	65	13	14	8
Employee involvement	26	14	14	46
Promotion structures and criteria	77	8	11	5
Strategic Issues				
New products/services	62	2	8	29
Setting business targets	71	3	3	23
Identifying ways of realising targets	47	4	8	41
Plans regarding mergers, acquisitions or divestments	92	1	2	6

Source: Roche and Geary (2002: 75)

a summary overview (further information is also available on the Gill & Macmillan website at www.gillmacmillan.ie).

Although a little dated, the UCD/ESRI Workplace Survey (Roche and Geary 2002) remains one of the most comprehensive sources of information on the diffusion of workplace partnership. This study investigated twelve key areas of workplace change, and where change had occurred it examined the predominant approach used by establishments to handle workplace change. This study looked at four optional approaches to handling change:

- management prerogative: change decisions made solely by management;
- traditional collective bargaining;
- partnership: engaging with trade unions to introduce change by consensus; and
- direct involvement: decided by management with the direct involvement of employees.

The data on workplace change in unionised establishments indicates that partnership approaches are very much the exception rather than the rule (Table 12.4). It also appears that where partnership is used, it occurs more in relation to operational rather than strategic issues. In contrast, we find much higher levels of utilisation of direct involvement in handling workplace change, both in relation to operational and strategic issues.

Looking at non-union establishments, we find even greater use of direct employee involvement, which occurs in relation to both strategic and operational issues (Table 12.5).

Table 12.5
Handling Workplace Change in Non-union Establishments

How Change Is Handled (%)		
	Management Prerogative	**Direct Involvement**
Operational Issues		
Pay levels	62	38
Payment systems	51	49
New plant and technology	52	48
Working time	20	80
Work practices	32	68
Numbers employed	33	67
Employee involvement	81	19
Promotion structures and criteria	76	24
Strategic Issues		
New products/services	56	44
Setting business targets	68	32
Identifying ways of realising targets	38	62
Plans regarding mergers, acquisitions or divestments	97	3
Source: Roche and Geary (1998)		

Nevertheless, management prerogative remains the most widely practised means of introducing workplace change and particularly so in regard to strategic issues. The study also looked at how employers hoped to handle future workplace change. Respondents in unionised establishments indicated a clear preference for partnership approaches or direct employee involvement rather than collective bargaining. This was especially strong with regard to operational matters. Respondents in non-union establishments revealed a strong preference for greater use of direct employee involvement.

An IBEC study in 2002 found that 22 per cent of companies surveyed operate a formal partnership arrangement (information direct from IBEC). Thirty-seven per cent of formal partnership arrangements were in unionised companies and 34 per cent in larger companies. They report that partnership is more likely to be found in the traditional manufacturing sector and least likely in the financial services sector. It is slightly more common in indigenous companies (26 per cent) than in foreign-owned companies (21 per cent). IBEC suggests that these figures disguise the high incidence of informal employee involvement arrangements (information direct from IBEC).

There is a close correspondence with 2003 and 2009 NCPP surveys. The most recent NCPP National Employer Survey, conducted in 2009, found that just 16 per cent of private sector employer respondents reported the presence of 'formal partnership committees' (equivalent to employee information and consultation bodies), with 34 per cent of employers reporting they have some 'informal' partnership arrangement (NCPP 2010). This is broadly equivalent to when a similar question was asked in the 2003 NCPP study.

However, when we look at the NCPP National Employee Survey also conducted in 2009, just one-fifth (21 per cent) of employees reported the presence of formal partnership institutions at their workplaces (see Table 12.6). The NCPP data indicates that partnership institutions are much more common in the public sector, where over 40 per cent of employees reported their presence, as compared to private sector organisations, where only 16 per cent reported their presence. The NCCP data indicate that just 4 per cent of employees are personally involved in such forms of employee representation. This is down from 6 per cent in 2003, indicating a decline in workplace partnership over the period. This may be due to a variety of factors, particularly the onset of the global financial crisis and its detrimental impact on employment, pay and other aspects of HRM (Gunnigle et al. 2013; Roche et al. 2011), plus the continuing decline in both trade union density and influence.

Summary data on the incidence of formal partnership institutions by sector and organisational size indicate that employees were more likely to be involved in formal partnership committees in large private sector firms or public sector organisations while employees working in hotels/restaurants, financial and other business activities, construction, and small firms were least likely to be thus involved.

More in-depth empirical evidence on direct and indirect forms of employee involvement and participation up to and including formal workplace partnership arrangements has been gathered by a team led by researchers at NUI Galway and Queens University, Belfast (Cullinane et al. 2012; Donaghey et al. 2011; Dundon et al. 2008; further information is available on the Gill & Macmillan website at www.gillmacmillan.ie). The specific issue

Table 12.6

Incidence of Partnership Institutions in the Workplace by Organisational Characteristics (Employee Respondents)

	Partnership in Work %	Involved in Partnership %
Public	40.9	7.8
Private	15.6	2.9
Other production	24.5	4.4
Construction	7.6	2.8
Wholesale and retail	13.9	3.0
Hotels and restaurants	5.0	1.7
Transport, storage, communication	33.9	5.1
Financial and other business activities	13.9	1.4
Public administration and defence	48.8	9.8
Education	26.4	5.0
Health	27.6	5.0
Other services	12.5	3.4
Size of Local Unit		
1–4	5.0	1.1
5–19	9.5	1.9
20–99	20.5	4.6
100 plus	36.6	6.4
Total	21.0	4.0

Source: National Centre for Partnership and Performance (2010a)

of workplace partnership in Ireland has been explored in recent work by Tony Dobbins, John Geary and Aurora Trif, among others (cf. Dobbins 2008, 2010; Dobbins and Dundon 2011; Dobbins and Gunnigle 2009; Geary 2008; Geary and Trif 2011).

CONCLUDING COMMENTS

This chapter has investigated the nature and extent of employee involvement and participation, with particular emphasis on the Irish context. We have identified a range of initiatives used in organisations to facilitate employee involvement and participation, their evolution over time and the regulatory environment underpinning such initiatives. We have also considered the issue of workplace partnership and reviewed research evidence on its diffusion in Ireland.

CHAPTER 13

National Collective Bargaining

INTRODUCTION

This chapter explores selected elements of collective bargaining theory before proceeding to examine the evolution of national bargaining and contemporary developments. As we have seen, collective bargaining is a mechanism to reconcile the divergent interests in the employment relationship. Its principal feature is that terms and conditions of employment are determined collectively, not individually. For a modern state, it has importance outside of the individual contract of employment, since wages and conditions of employment set under collective bargaining can have major impacts on public finances and the competitiveness of an economy. The outcomes from wage determination, whether through collective bargaining or otherwise, also affect income distribution within a society and contribute to the extent to which a society is more or less egalitarian. The national context for collective bargaining came to the fore in the 1970s and its importance was accentuated during the period of social partnership from 1987 to 2008. These agreements have been both credited with the economic success of the Celtic Tiger and blamed for the current economic crisis. Although formal social partnership agreements are no longer in place, the national level continues to have relevance (especially in the public sector) and the interactions between social actors during social partnership continue to influence current pay determination.

THEORETICAL OVERVIEW

There are a number of definitions of collective bargaining that stress different aspects of the process. Sidney and Beatrice Webb were the first to analyse the topic in detail. They saw collective bargaining as being the means unions used to achieve their objective of 'maintaining and improving the conditions of their members' working lives' (Webb and Webb 1897: 1). Flanders (1968) challenged the Webbs' definition, claiming that collective bargaining is primarily concerned with rule making. This perspective is reflected in the ILO (1973: 7) description of collective bargaining as involving 'the negotiation of an agreed set of rules to govern the terms of the employment relationship, as well as the relationship between the bargaining parties themselves'. While collective bargaining has more than economic aspects to it, arguably the pursuit of improvement of terms and conditions of employment (as set out by the Webbs) remains its *raison d'être* (Fox 1975).

Gunnigle and Flood (1990: 227) refer to collective bargaining as 'the process through which agreement on pay, working conditions, procedures and other negotiable issues are reached between organised employees and management representatives'. That collective bargaining is generally conducted with a view to reaching agreement does not exclude

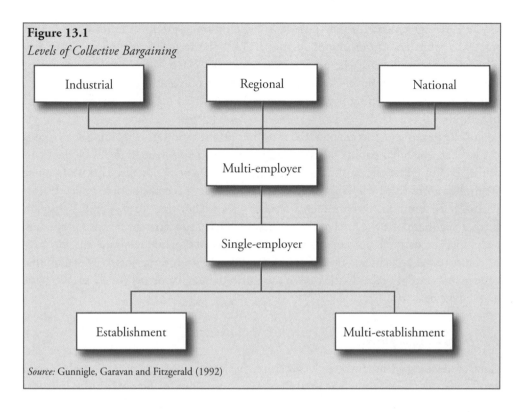

Figure 13.1
Levels of Collective Bargaining

Source: Gunnigle, Garavan and Fitzgerald (1992)

the possibility of the use of industrial action. Pluralists consider that collective bargaining redresses the disparity of power between capital and labour, although there is a vigorous debate in the industrial relations literature as to what extent this is achieved in practice (Clegg 1975, 1976; Fox 1974). Clegg (1975: 311) argues that the great advantage of collective bargaining is that compromise and agreement is the norm despite the absence of any assurance that compromise and agreement will result from every negotiation. He further contends that this element of pressure is vital to collective bargaining (Clegg 1976).

A key concept in examining collective bargaining is bargaining structure. This describes the framework in which negotiations between employers and organised workers take place (Parker *et al.* 1971). Bargaining structure has four aspects: bargaining form, bargaining scope, bargaining units and bargaining levels (Parker *et al.* 1971). Bargaining form describes the degree of formality of an agreement, which may vary from informal unwritten understandings to formal and comprehensive written agreements. Custom and practice can vary the application of collective agreements and can even be incorporated in the individual contract of employment (see Chapter 7). In general, the higher the bargaining level within an organisation, industry or country, the more likely it is that the degree of formality will be greater. Bargaining scope relates to the range of issues to be covered, which may be comprehensive or limited in range. A bargaining unit refers to the group of workers to be covered by a collective agreement. A bargaining unit may be narrow or wide, e.g. covering all fitters in a single company, all manual employees in an industry or all qualifying public sector workers (as is the case in the

Croke Park Agreement). It may involve a single union, a group of unions or, for that matter, a confederation of unions such as ICTU. The term 'bargaining unit' can also be applied to employers, where bargaining may take place with a single employer or with a number of employers – the latter is referred to as multi-employer bargaining. Multi-employer bargaining is generally associated with an industry, sector or national bargaining.

For the purpose of this chapter, the most important aspect of bargaining structure is the level at which bargaining takes place. It is useful to view bargaining as taking place at the level of either the workplace/enterprise, industry or nationally. This is of course a simplification, since bargaining can overlap and take place at multiple levels. In this regard, it is common for agreements reached at a higher level to be applied through further negotiation at the level of the workplace. Such a process can allow for individual adaptation of national agreements to local circumstances while retaining the integrity of the national agreement. However, it can also undermine the integrity of national agreement – most notably in the case of wage drift, which happened widely in the 1970s and will be discussed later.

Centralised Bargaining

Centralised bargaining involves negotiation between representatives of trade union confederations (ICTU in Ireland) and employer associations (primarily IBEC in Ireland). It has been typified by attempts to adopt a corporatist approach to collective bargaining. Corporatist arrangements, however, go beyond the mere level at which negotiations take place. They typically attempt to:

- integrate government intervention in collective bargaining so that negotiations become tripartite;
- establish a consensus on economic and social issues in pursuit of a 'national interest';
- promote a debate over broader issues, such as macroeconomic policy, industrial policy and employment promotion; and
- make provision for pay increases, typically taking account of broader issues such as rates of taxation and welfare provision.

Thus, centralised bargaining is inextricably bound up with a greater involvement by government in the industrial relations process than a simple voluntarist model implies, and corporatism extends this involvement. We now turn to examine corporatist theory and the role of the state in industrial relations.

Collective Bargaining and the Role of the State

While collective bargaining may take place at differing levels, a major factor determining which level dominates is the approach governments choose to adopt (Crouch 1982; Schmitter and Lehmbruch 1979). There are three broad options open to government. One is non-intervention, or what practitioners call 'free collective bargaining'. The term 'voluntarism' is sometimes used but it can cause confusion, since that term also describes minimal intervention by the law. A more formal and accurate term used to describe non-intervention in collective bargaining is 'liberal collectivism' (Palmer 1983). This refers to a situation where governments leave the regulation of industrial relations to unions and employer organisations. Roche (1989: 116) refers to this as an 'auxiliary' approach. He highlights the fact that Irish governments prior to the 1970s, while generally adopting a non-interventionist approach, did not abstain from efforts to influence employers and unions. However, these efforts were limited, with the most notable being frequent exhortations for the parties (invariably unions) to exercise wage restraint.

Liberal collectivism (free collective bargaining) came under pressure in Europe as a result of the success of Keynesian demand management policies employed in the aftermath of World War II. These policies were designed to prevent a recurrence of the economic dislocation of the Great Depression of the 1930s. Keynesian policies in the 1950s and 1960s led to unprecedented levels of 'full employment', which increased the power of organised labour. Employers could no longer rely on what Marx called the 'reserve army of the unemployed' to constrain the growth of wage rates. Initially governments addressed this by allowing a degree of inflation to maintain economic growth and full employment. However, by the 1960s, countries were beginning to experience 'stagflation', i.e. limited growth combined with growing inflation. Faced with this problem, governments had two alternatives to liberal collectivism: 'to move in the direction of greater state intervention in collective bargaining or to jettison the commitment to full employment' (Roche 1989: 116).

Table 13.1

Government Approaches to Collective Bargaining and Industrial Relations

	Collective Liberalism	Individual or Market Liberalism	Neo-corporatism
Role of Government in Collective Bargaining	• Non-intervention or at most auxiliary approach	• No direct intervention in industrial relations • Indirect intervention via market control	• Direct intervention with unions and employer organisations (social partnership)
Key Policy Measures	• Appeal to parties to behave responsibly • Reduce cost of labour via devaluation • Establish dispute resolution bodies	• Tighten monetary policy • Implement industrial restructuring • Impose legal restrictions on unions • Weaken the role of dispute resolution bodies	• Co-ordinate wage determination with economic and social policy • Strengthen the role of policy and research institutes • Strengthen dispute resolution bodies

Individual Liberalism

Jettisoning the commitment to full employment meant imposing 'discipline' on labour markets and curbing the power of organised labour, namely trade unions. This involved the adoption of an approach varyingly described in the industrial relations literature as 'individual liberalism' (Palmer 1983), 'market liberalism' (Rollinson 1993) or 'market control' (Roche 1989). The use of differing terms can be somewhat confusing, but they all represent the expression of a common laissez-faire neo-liberal economic philosophy that emphasises the primacy of markets. This is the principle underlying modern neo-classical economic theories – notably the monetarism of Milton Friedman, which became widely influential in the 1980s. In the neo-classical view, supply and demand is the ultimate arbitrator of the competing interests of capital and labour. Labour is a commodity to be bought or sold. Wage rates and terms and conditions of employment are to be determined by the market. Trade unions and collective bargaining are seen as distorting the market and governments should move to limit their influence.

In keeping with the laissez-faire doctrine, direct involvement by the state in industrial relations issues is to be avoided. Instead, indirect policies are to be applied. These include the restructuring of older uncompetitive industries and the adoption of a tight monetary policy. A tight monetary policy would mean that companies that conceded too-high wage increases in negotiations with unions would become uncompetitive and would fail. Such thinking informed the Thatcherite revolution in British industrial relations from 1979 onwards (Roche 1989). The economic restrictions were augmented by legislation rolling back the trade disputes immunities previously conferred on trade unions and placing successively tighter legal obligations on strike action. Initially, these legislative measures were promoted on the basis of enhancing union democracy but it quickly became apparent they had the aim of weakening trade unions.

Individual liberalism promises greater flexibility and superior economic performance, but as Crouch (1982) points out, it subordinates employees to the control and authority of the owner and promotes an employment relationship that is at best paternalistic and at worst exploitative. It is, in effect, unitarism at a state level. Although no Irish government has deployed a strategy of thoroughgoing market liberalism to date, it would be a mistake to suggest that market forces have not affected the nature of Irish industrial relations. The open nature of the Irish economy, globalisation and EU competition policy have been powerful forces in shaping the nature of collective bargaining (McDonough and Dundon 2010). This process of adaptation can be seen in the union 'givebacks' of the 1980s. They are also evident in the responses to market liberalisation and privatisation in the 1990s, such as union–management engagement with new forms of work organisation and attempts to develop workplace partnership (Hastings 2003). More tellingly, the economic crisis that has engulfed the state from 2008 has placed collective bargaining under considerable pressure; in much of private industry, it was effectively suspended after 2009 as most companies froze wages.

Corporatism

The origins of corporatism can be traced back to diverse sources, most notably the Social Christian tradition in the papal encyclical *Rerum Novarum* issued in 1893 by Pope Leo XIII. Corporatist ideas were (and are) opposed to notions of atomistic individual competition inherent in laissez-faire economic theories and the class conflict of Marxism. In contrast to classical economic theories, they recognised the legitimacy of collective organisations representing workers and employers. Corporatism was concerned with avoiding class conflict and it preached social harmony under organised and representative structures of workers and employers, co-ordinated by the state. These ideas continue to inform modern corporatist thinking.

The mass unemployment of the 1930s threatened the stability of the liberal democracies and led to the emergence of fascism in a number of European countries, notably Italy, Germany, Spain and Portugal. fascist countries turned to a form of state-led corporatism to produce 'social harmony'. In this type of corporatism, free trade unions were abolished or severely restricted and the state acted as the controlling influence in regulating labour management relations. In effect, dictatorship was extended to the labour market. Panitch (1979: 120) notes that the fascist states 'gave a rude answer to the question of how the social harmony trumpeted in theory would in fact come to replace the competition and class conflict of capitalist society'. It was no surprise that after 1945 there was a strong appreciation of the merits of independent trade unions and free collective bargaining as essential pillars of democracy acting as a brake on the excessive power of capital. In contrast, the associations with fascist authoritarianism led to the concept of corporatism being viewed in overwhelmingly negative and pejorative terms post-World War II (Panitch 1979; Schmitter 1979).

Neo-corporatism

By the 1970s political scientists and industrial relations scholars had begun to resurrect some corporatist ideas under the term of 'neo-corporatism', or new corporatism (Schmitter 1979). The re-examination of corporatist ideas was driven by the examples of a number of northern European states in the 1950s and 1960s, most notably Sweden. Sweden had strong trade unions with high union density and equally strong employer organisations. Collective bargaining played a major role in the Swedish economic model and there were none of the dire predictions inherent in neo-classical economic theory. In fact, the economy had enjoyed remarkable economic success and modernisation. Sweden also seemed to finesse the problems of stagflation that afflicted other European countries, notably the UK.

This was achieved through a 'political exchange', which involved unions exercising wage restraint in return for commitments from governments to pursue full employment and a high level of welfare provision. Management were allowed a largely free hand in the workplace and modernisation and technical innovation were embraced by trade unions. High taxation levels allowed the state to deliver enhanced standards of education, health, pension, housing and other entitlements, producing a high 'social wage' that compensated for wage restraint. There was also a large element of wage solidarity, with wage differentials being squeezed and overall income differentials being narrow. This led to lower levels of social and economic inequality than alternative models based on liberal ideas. Successful corporatist arrangements, as in Sweden, can be seen as being held together by a 'virtuous circle' of full employment and high welfare provisions, which had the effect of legitimating and reinforcing the unions' policies of wage restraint and government intervention (Roche 1989).

Differing Forms of Neo-corporatism

We can distinguish between different forms of corporatism: *social corporatism* as in Scandinavia and *liberal corporatism* as in Austria and the Netherlands (Pekkarinen *et al.* 1992). Social corporatism is based on a political and ideological analysis that perceives conflict as endemic to capital–labour relations and where compromise arises from a position of power on both sides. In this model, corporatism acts to institutionalise conflict as part of a democratic class struggle (Korpi 1983). In contrast, liberal corporatism is based on the view that there is essentially a commonality of interests between capital and labour (Pekkarinen *et al.* 1992). In liberal corporatism there is a gradual institutionalisation of a consensus, particularly between leaders rather than members of organisations. The management of economic adjustment and the sharing of burdens and rewards are controlled by the elites at the top of hierarchies of interest organisations. The gains go chiefly to insiders, reflecting the relative power of peak-level federations (unions such as ICTU and national employer organisations such as IBEC) and their member organisations. There is an absence of (or only weak commitment to) egalitarianism, resulting in the preservation of existing disparities in wealth and life chances (Turner and Wallace 2000).

Contemporary Corporatist Developments

The redistributive and solidaristic policies of social corporatism came under threat following the 1970s. In Sweden, the employers broke from the system that had previously been lauded and industry-level bargaining replaced national bargaining as the dominant wage determination mechanism. By the mid-1980s it appeared that neo-corporatism as a specific political and economic approach to economic management had declined in many European countries (Golden *et al.*1999). However, by the 1990s, corporatism had 'undergone an astonishingly lively and broad based revival' with the emergence of what are called national social pacts in a number of countries (Pochet and Fajertag 2000: 9). Social pacts involved centralised agreements between governments, trade union confederations and employer organisations. These social pacts have been analysed under the term 'competitive corporatism' and are attributed to increasing competition in a global market (Turner 2006; Turner and Wallace 2000). Competitive corporatism is a search for an alternative or 'third way' to the neo-liberal prescriptions of deregulated labour markets and reduced welfare (Ferner and Hyman 1998; Goetschy 2000). Teague and Donaghey (2009: 79) note that such pacts were associated with the introduction of the Economic and Monetary Union (EMU) and, unlike Irish social partnership, most proved unsustainable once the key motivation of EMU had been achieved and, as a result, collapsed.

Competitive corporatism is equivalent to liberal corporatism, as is evident from policy measures. Competitive or liberal corporatism represents an attempt to meet the demands for economic efficiency while promoting some equity or at least defending existing social protection systems (Rhodes 1998). Both involve greater flexibility in the labour market together with social security systems tailored more closely to the imperatives of competition. Labour market reforms are used to promote employment rather than government management of aggregate demand (Goetschy 2000). Rhodes (1998: 200) observes that competitive corporatism prioritises competitiveness and 'downplays the equity function of more traditional golden age forms of corporatism'. In effect the 'policies of competitive corporatism, for example, labour market deregulation and a reduction in corporate taxation, promotes increased inequality' (Turner and Wallace 2000: 4).

It should be noted that the distinctions made between liberal (or competitive) corporatism and social corporatism reflect ideal types and real-life examples tend to fall somewhere along a continuum between these two ideal types. For example, it is now recognised that Swedish neo-corporatism paid great attention to competitiveness. Moene and Wallerstein (1999: 234) note that 'the Nordic variety of corporatism was associated not with protectionism and monopolistic pricing, but with free trade and the subsequent need to remain competitive'. In evaluating any real-world corporatist system, the key question is not whether the example matches either of the ideal types, but which version the particular example most approximates. In this regard, differences in taxation policy and income distribution are crucial. Liberal corporatism is based on low taxation, which limits the redistributive capability of centralised agreements and government policy. This is an especially important consideration in evaluating where the Irish social partnership agreements lie along the corporatist continuum.

THE DEVELOPMENT OF IRISH COLLECTIVE BARGAINING

Collective bargaining is a relatively new concept, which arose out of the economic, political and social developments of the nineteenth century. Large-scale industrialisation led to a major growth in trade unionism and employer organisations. Craft unions, which were the main workers' organisations in Ireland up to the early 1900s, were the first to establish a degree of collective regulation of work. Only in the late 1880s (with 'new unionism' in the UK) did general workers achieve permanent unionisation. Large-scale new unionism came to Ireland in the first decade of the twentieth century with the founding of the ITGWU in 1909. A period of intense conflict ensued during the years 1910 to 1913. The lessons of the 1913 Dublin Lockout and the dislocation of the War of Independence saw both employers and unions change their approaches to industrial relations. Employers gradually abandoned their resistance to the new unionism and new unions in turn moved away from a militant syndicalism that sought the overthrow of capitalism through the use of the strike weapon. In effect, collective bargaining became the preferred alternative to damaging and recurring conflict for both parties. It would be wrong to think that the development of collective bargaining was confined to manual workers and large-scale conflict. White-collar workers from early days also sought to have collective regulation of their terms and conditions of employment. This was notable in teaching, banking and retail.

Early collective bargaining was dependent on the vagaries of the business cycle or the employer's goodwill: in times of depression or when there were competitive pressures, employers could resort to unilateral wage reductions (ILO 1960). Such action precipitated the general strike of 1926 in the UK. The period between the two world wars saw collective bargaining still in its infancy in this country. O'Brien (1989: 133) writes that 'while collective bargaining was extensive, it covered only a minority of all workers and it was uncoordinated and rather haphazard'. From the 1930s, public sector workers (such as teachers, civil servants and Gardaí) sought to achieve collective bargaining and to have supporting institutional arrangements for determining terms and conditions of employment established. These were only eventually put in place in the 1950s and 1960s with the establishment of the public sector conciliation and arbitrations schemes (see Chapter 5).

The onset of World War II brought a cessation to much collective bargaining. Wage determination was governed by the Wages Standstill Order (No. 83) of 1941, which limited wage increases. Prices rose steadily during the war period and this, combined with the wage restraints, led to a decline in purchasing power and a substantial erosion of living standards. Unsurprisingly, when the Wages Standstill Order was suspended at the end of the war, there were widespread claims for wage increases and this resulted in the initiation of a wage round system. This system, which lasted from 1946 to 1970, established collective bargaining as the dominant method for determining wages and conditions of employment in the Irish economy. It was also associated with a major growth in union density and an increased importance of employer organisations, most notably the FUE.

Table 13.2
Outline Profile of Wage Bargaining, 1922–2013

	Level of Bargaining	Number of Agreements	Name
Pre-1941	Haphazard and sporadic bargaining	No systematic number of agreements	None
1941–1946	National legal regulation	Wage increases restricted by law	Wages Standstill Order
1946–1970	Industry and local (some national element in four of these)	Twelve	Wage rounds
1970–1981	National supplemented by enterprise level	Seven	National wage agreements
		Two	National understandings
1982–1987	Enterprise-level and general public sector agreements	Varied in organisations: generally five (max. six)	Decentralised wage agreements
1987–2009	Centralised	Seven	Consensus/partnership agreements
2010–2013	Public sector national	One	Croke Park Agreement
	Private sector enterprise – minimal bargaining	One	IBEC–ICTU protocol on private sector

Wage Rounds, 1946–1970

Wage rounds involved a largely unplanned general upward movement of wages and salaries over a period of time which recurred at intervals (McCarthy *et al.* 1975). Four of the twelve wage rounds were the result of bipartite agreements negotiated between the FUE and ICTU at national level. This prefaced the development of national bargaining. The other eight were decentralised examples of free collective bargaining and were negotiated either 'at industry and trade or company level' (O'Brien 1989: 134). Craft workers were to the fore in the initiation of new wage rounds and this reflected their relative strength within the trade union movement of the time. The process of decentralised wage rounds involved *pattern bargaining*. Pattern bargaining involved bargaining groups who considered their wages were inadequate and felt that they had sufficient power to submit a claim on their employer. If negotiations were unsuccessful, a strike would ensue and the eventual wage increase agreed would then form a basis for other groups to seek to restore their earnings relative to that settlement. Thus, relativities between groups played a central part in determining wage increases. The terms of wage rounds were usually accepted quickly in industries, particularly if the Labour Court upheld a subsequent claim for restoration of a differential. However, the gaps between those who entered a round first and those entering later grew over time; by the late 1960s, the gap was over twenty-one months in some cases. Workers covered by later settlements tended to gain higher increases to compensate, although this depended on the type of work they did. Wage increases for women workers were generally of the order of 60 per cent of the male rate.

The wage round process became the subject of much criticism over time. As in other northern European countries, it was the relative prosperity of the 1960s that heightened government concern at the impact of collective bargaining (Hardiman 1988). Critics focused on the wage competition between bargaining groups and the sacredness of 'wage differentials' and sectional interest being pushed to the fore at the expense of the national interest (O'Brien 1989). Sectional wage bargaining was particularly prevalent in the craft sector, where the protection of relativities and differentials was deeply entrenched. Roche (1989: 116) argues that the wage rounds 'came to be identified by successive Irish governments as a significant contributor to economic problems, especially inflation'.

The main charge against wage rounds that they caused inflation is unproven. Neo-Keynesian economists saw wages as contributing to inflation – called wage push inflation. As such, they tended to favour government intervention in collective bargaining in order to constrain wage rises through corporatist-type arrangements. There was an undeniable and strong link between wage increases throughout the 1960s and 1970s, but such a correlation does not prove causality. Indeed, the rate of inflation was very influential in wage settlements. While inflation was increasing, workers saw themselves serving wage claims to chase inflation. Among neo-classical economists a consensus had emerged by the late 1970s that unions did not cause inflation, but rather increased unemployment (Hardiman 1988). By increasing wages above their market level, it was argued they made labour uncompetitive. However, Irish unemployment in 1969 at the end of the wage round system was only 4 per cent – effectively full employment. In terms of unemployment, therefore, there is little evidence that the outcomes from wage rounds were out of line with the underlying growth of the economy. Whatever about the economic arguments, criticisms of the wage round system increased with the heightened level of wage demands and the strike activity of the late 1960s. These created, in the words of Professor Charles McCarthy, an impression of a 'decade of upheaval' and presaged the demise of the wage round system (McCarthy 1973).

Centralised Wage Agreements, 1970–1981

The six-week-long maintenance craftsmen's dispute of 1969 crystallised government concern at the unregulated wage round system. That strike, and the wage increases resulting from it, represented a watershed in industrial relations and high wage demands for an emerging thirteenth round in 1970 prompted government action. In October 1970 the Fianna Fáil government published a Prices and Incomes Bill, which proposed to limit wage increases to 6 per cent until the end of 1971 (Dáil Debates 1970). Not unnaturally, unions were opposed to the bill but employers were also concerned at the idea of establishing a statutory system of wage determination. Indeed, it is doubtful if government really wished to take on this role. Allen (1997: 144) claims the bill 'was mainly a device by the Fianna Fáil Government to pressurise the union leaders into standing up against their own militants'.

The threat of legislation was effective and employers and unions entered negotiations under the auspices of a body called the Employer Labour Conference (ELC). This led to an agreement being reached that provided for a wage increase of some 14 per cent over eighteen months – well in excess of the 6 per cent mooted in the Prices and Incomes Bill (Breen *et al.* 1990). The increase was a reflection of the rising expectations of workers and the increasing rate of inflation, which was common to many Western economies at the time. It was an indication that the process of national bargaining could not be insulated from such expectations or external influences, an experience repeated in the early 2000s under social partnership. The agreement provided a model for six further national wage agreements spanning the years 1970 to 1978 and two national understandings.

The initial agreements were bipartite employer–union agreements with the government involvement confined to its role as a public sector employer. As the decade progressed, government became more involved in its role as government – a trend that culminated in the two national understandings in 1979 and 1980. These two agreements represented an attempt to establish a more developed form of neo-corporatism, taking account of a wide range of issues including welfare and taxation policy. The nine agreements set wage increases for unionised workers across the economy but the agreements also became a standard for wage increases in non-union employments. This represented an informal process of the 'extension of collective bargaining', which in a range of other western European countries is given effect through legal provision. Fogarty *et al.* (1981: 19) famously drew attention to this aspect of the process, saying national wage agreements were viewed as 'an award from Heaven or Dublin'. In the 1970s, collective bargaining was the main determinant of wage increases not just in the unionised sector, but in the Irish economy generally.

The Performance of Centralised Bargaining, 1970–1981

The centralised agreements were a much more structured system than the pay rounds. Pay was set in specific terms, the duration of the agreements was fixed and machinery was provided to deal with disputes arising out of the terms of the agreements and any anomalies. In terms of process, 'they had basically stabilised what had become a chaotic picture' (von Prondzynski 1992: 79). They enabled employers to project pay costs and also provided for an element of wage solidarity by giving minimum absolute levels of increases to lower-paid workers, which was designed to narrow wage differentials. The national wage agreements tended to be strongly supported by unions representing lower-paid workers with weak bargaining power, such as the Irish Union of Distributive Workers and Clerks (a forerunner of the current MANDATE trade union). During their existence, they were strongly supported by public commentators, with free collective bargaining being referred to in pejorative terms as 'a free for all' and often presented as an unrealistic and even on occasion a 'lunatic' option.

While they enjoyed strong support, over time opinions changed, especially among employers. This was because of a failure to deliver on implicit objectives. McCarthy (1977) identified the following objectives for centralised bargaining:

- control inflation;
- promote full employment;
- reduce industrial unrest;
- moderate income increases; and
- deliver relatively higher increases to lower-paid workers.

None of these objectives can be considered to have been met to any great degree, although this was far from being due to the process of centralised bargaining. International developments meant that any attempts to control inflation were certain to be stillborn. Fuelled by the oil crises of 1973/1974 and 1979/1980, inflation rose and fell precipitously during the 1970s, reaching around 20 per cent in both 1975 and 1981.

Employment grew over the period of the agreements but the labour force expanded at a greater rate, resulting in a rise in unemployment from 4 per cent in 1969 to 10.7 per cent by 1982 (Conniffe and Kennedy 1984; Hardiman 1988). There was some modest initial impact on industrial unrest with a decline in strike statistics under the early agreements. However, in the second half of the decade strikes and working days lost increased (see Chapter 10). Thus, the objective of reducing industrial unrest was not achieved. The agreements failed to moderate income increases. A complaint of workers was that the agreements did not place any constraints on increases in income generally and only restrained wages. From an employer perspective, the agreements failed to deliver the promised wage restraint. While national wage norms were specified in the agreements, free collective bargaining could still operate at enterprise level. Clauses in the agreements provided for above the norm (ATN) increases, which could be negotiated for higher productivity. These on occasion led to 'spurious productivity' deals in which wage increases were conceded but the productivity elements were not realised (Wallace 1982). The operation of these provisions led to substantial wage drift, i.e. increases above the national norm. Roche (2009: 192) argues that 'while employers and governments complained of the bad faith of union leaders, trade union members saw little reason to moderate their pay demands against a background of high inflation and an escalating income tax burden'. The growth in the tax burden saw many low-paid workers drawn into the tax net for the first time and this eroded the solidaristic element of the wage increases, which arguably had a greater impact than the traditionally highlighted restoration of differentials by more powerful groups of workers.

Not only do the national wage agreements of the 1970s have to be evaluated in the light of external influences on the economy, they must also be viewed against unwise pro-cyclical policies. The most damaging of these arose from the Fianna Fáil government elected in 1977, which sought full employment through a naïve Keynesianism involving the expansion of the public sector and simultaneously narrowed the tax base by abolishing rates on private dwellings (a property tax) and motor tax. The extensive welfare and social provisions associated with the agreements had to be paid from a narrow tax base. Arguably the most telling defect of the Irish experiment with corporatism in the 1970s was that it represented an attempt to transplant an egalitarian model into a country with an inegalitarian taxation system. Hardiman (1988: 102) notes that 'by the late 1970s almost 90 per cent of income tax came from the PAYE sector'. In the case of the trade unions, the inequities in the tax system were the subject of the large-scale tax marches. These had little effect, as the overall tax burden on wage and salary earners actually rose from 30 per cent in 1979 to 45 per cent in 1981. Figure 13.2 illustrates the tax wedge effect of increased taxation, where employers saw 'labour costs rising steeply while the net value of earnings increased but little' (Hardiman 1988: 99). The result was that the pay terms of the agreements worked against the interests of both employers *and* workers. However, it was employers who were the most dissatisfied with national agreements, chiefly because of their failure to deliver the promised wage restraint and industrial peace. Faced with a deepening recession prompted by the second oil crisis and unhappy

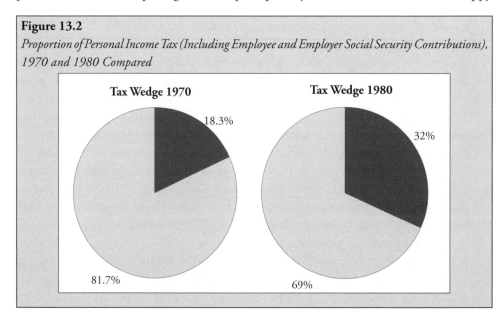

Figure 13.2
Proportion of Personal Income Tax (Including Employee and Employer Social Security Contributions), 1970 and 1980 Compared

at the levels of government spending and taxation, they only reluctantly agreed under extreme government pressure to be party to the second national understanding in 1980 and declined to enter a new one when that agreement terminated in 1982.

Decentralised Bargaining, 1982–1987

The second national understanding was followed by a period of decentralised bargaining which lasted from 1982 to 1987 and coincided with a long and deep recession. There was a reduction in the numbers at work due to redundancies, in excess of an average of 20,000 per annum. Unemployment rocketed from almost 9 per cent in 1981 to 18.1 per cent in 1986. In the private sector the focus of bargaining activity moved to enterprise level. There was no return to the industry bargaining prevalent in the 1960s, when some sixty industrial groups had been in existence (O'Brien 1989: 138). Viability and economic performance became the key criteria shaping wage increases as a 'new realism' was introduced into employer–employee relationships (Gunnigle *et al.* 1994). There was a major gain in wage competitiveness, as private sector unit wage costs rose by only 7 per cent between 1980 and 1985, compared with an average 37 per cent increase in competing countries (Hardiman 1988: 220). As can be seen from Table 13.3, the trend of wage increases decreased greatly in line with a reduction in the rate of inflation. Inflation was driven downward not only by the deflationary effects of the recession but also by disciplinary effects of the decision in 1979 to link the Irish punt to the European Exchange Rate Mechanism (ERM).

Table 13.3
Wage Increases and Inflation Compared, 1982–1987

Round	Average Cumulative Increase (%)	Average Length (Months)	Year	Inflation (%)
22	16.4	14.9	1982	17.1
23	10.9	13.5	1983	10.4
24	9.3	12.75	1984	8.6
25	6.8	12	1985	5.4
26	6.0	12	1986	3.9
27	4.5–6.5*	15.4*	1987	3.2

* Only a small number of agreements were concluded in the 27th round, which was overtaken by the Programme for National Recovery.
Source: McGinley (1989b); Department of Finance (2003).

At times the government attempted to impose a norm through pay guidelines but these were largely ignored by private sector negotiators. The FIE sought to shift collective bargaining away from the notion of a specific wage increase norm that would be extended generally via pattern bargaining and from the idea that wage rounds ought to follow each other automatically. Its position was that pay increases should be closely tied to what the individual firms could bear (Hardiman 1988). As a result, settlements varied widely across industries and some analysts questioned whether the wage round concept was at all applicable to the private sector between 1982 and 1987 (McGinley 1989b). The most visible aspect of employer assertiveness in the 1980s was concession bargaining. Concession bargaining involves 'union givebacks' such as wage cuts, reductions in terms and conditions of employment and accompanying productivity concessions. These were the reverse of the spurious productive deals of the 1970s. In addition, prominent employers such as the banks introduced two-tier employment systems, with new entrants being paid below the rate of established workers – these were termed 'yellow pack' and 'green pack' employment grades. Overall real disposable income was estimated to have fallen by between 8 and 10 per cent between 1980 and 1987 (Turner and D'Art 2000). While the adverse economic circumstances led to a much-weakened trade union movement, there was some lengthening of the union negotiating agenda. Non-wage issues took on a greater significance than before, with issues such as hours of work, bonuses, leave and general working conditions becoming part of the agenda (Incomes Data Service 1992).

THE RETURN TO CENTRALISED AGREEMENTS, 1987

The 1980s was a period of severe economic difficulties with a growing crisis in the public finances being especially marked. Three of the principal elements in current government expenditure are foreign debt service, social welfare and the public sector payroll. At the end of 1986 the debt/GNP ratio stood at over 120 per cent of GNP unemployment had reached some 17 per cent and, as a result, expenditure in social services had increased from 28.9 per cent of GNP in 1980 to 35.6 per cent in 1985 (NESC 1986). Early 1987 brought the election of a Fianna Fáil government with Charles Haughey TD as Taoiseach and Bertie Ahern TD as Minister for Labour. That government's economic strategy was to address public finances with a focus on tackling the public sector payroll. It saw a return to national bargaining as a potential mechanism to enable this to be achieved and invitations were issued to the employers and unions to enter negotiations. The name of the resultant agreement – the Programme for National Recovery (PNR) – reflected the economic circumstances in which the state found itself. Employer support was copper-fastened by the extremely modest wage increases of approximately 2.5 per cent per annum spread over thirty-nine months to January 1991. This was significantly lower than the trend then emerging under the twenty-seventh round, of about 4.5 per cent per annum. For trade unions the agreement delivered a one-hour reduction in the working week, to thirty-nine hours. It also held out the promise of giving them influence at national level and avoiding marginalisation, as had happened in the UK.

In addition to the pay terms, a number of broader policy objectives were set out. These included:

- the creation of a fiscal, exchange and monetary climate conducive to economic growth, including a commitment that the ratio of debt to GNP should be reduced;
- movement towards greater equity and fairness in the tax system;
- measures to generate employment opportunities; and
- a reduction of social inequalities.

These objectives differed from agreements of the 1970s in that they were expressed as specific targets and not as binding commitments. Over time, these elements expanded greatly in successive agreements – especially from 1997, when the voluntary pillar was added to negotiations. The PNR initiated a consensus approach to collective bargaining that in time became known as social partnership. Although called 'partnership', this does not mean that the negotiation process was purely integrative. There were many examples of distributive tactics such as 'sabre rattling', the use of bottom lines and preconditions in evidence. In effect, the process of negotiation conformed to a mixed motive model of negotiation (see Chapter 11).

Wage Terms of the Agreements

While the agreements dealt with a wide range of issues, as in all corporatist-type arrange-ments, the provisions for wage increases were determined centrally. The agreements can be divided into two broad groups. Five of the agreements had provision for more modest wage rises, while two – the Programme for Economic and Social Progress (PESP) and the Programme for Prosperity and Fairness (PPF) – contained wage increases of a higher order of magnitude. While the wage increases in Towards 2016 were modest in absolute terms, the increase of 6.5 per cent agreed in Phase 2 in 2008 proved to be out of line with the quickly changing developments in the economy. Not all the agreements were implemented as set down. In early 1992, lower than expected growth saw the government delay the agreed increases and pay them a year in arrears with full retrospection (von Prondzynski 1992). In 2001 the PPF was renegotiated when inflation exceeded the predicted 2.5 per cent per annum. This renegotiation was resisted by employers but they eventually agreed to a 2 per cent additional pay rise plus a 1 per cent 'lump sum' payment. Finally, although Phase 2 of Towards 2016 was agreed in September 2008, that agreement quickly unravelled in line with the deteriorating economic situation and was not implemented.

ATN and Local Bargaining Provisions

Employers were generally opposed to local-level bargaining, although two of the agreements contained a local bargaining clause – PESP (3 per cent) and Partnership 2000 (2 per cent). The latter 2 per cent was based on profit sharing and conditional on 'deepening partnership and securing commitment to competitiveness at the level of the enterprise' (Department of the Taoiseach 1997: 64). This increase was generally paid but did not lead to any deep and sustained workplace partnership (see Chapter 12). These aside, provisions for ATN were not a feature of the agreements. There is evidence of some wage drift but that appeared to be driven by underlying market conditions and tended to be concentrated on higher skill grades. Sheehan (2001: 24) notes that 'many companies have had to breach the agreement [Partnership 2000] to ensure they attract or retain and pay the growing rate for scarce labour'. In any event, the wage drift that did exist in the private sector did not lead to major employer complaints as in the 1970s.

Wage Tax Trade-offs

The central feature of the agreements was the trade union movement's exercise of wage restraint in return for reductions in personal income tax. This meant that real take-home pay increased at a rate greater than the nominal increases under the agreement. Employers also achieved substantial tax reductions on the corporate tax take, which was designed to encourage companies to locate in Ireland and to reward enterprise. Table 13.4 contains outline details of the wage and tax elements of the agreements. However, low personal tax was not a creation of social partnership but owed its origin to the political system (notably the influence of the Progressive Democrat Party, even before it entered government first in 1989). While low personal tax was a central part of partnership agreements, it cannot be considered a consensus policy, at least as applied from the election of the Fianna Fáil– Progressive Democrat government in 1997. David Begg, general secretary of ICTU, argues that that government's 'entire philosophy' was laid out in 2000 by the then Tánaiste, Mary Harney, in her 'Boston versus Berlin' speech. Begg pointed to the well-known speech, where:

> She spoke of a country 'that believes in the incentive power of low taxation … that believes in economic liberalisation … that believes in essential regulation, but not over-regulation'. (See Sheehan 2011e: 17)

Begg added:

> the policy of the Government that came to power in 1997 … [was that they] were hell bent on cutting taxes for the wealthy and deregulating whole swathes of the economy … It is a matter of public record that Congress opposed that decision. (Quoted in Sheehan 2011e: 17)

However, like other issues such as union recognition and the aim of higher wage increases for lower-paid workers, the low taxation model was not a deal breaker for the unions. Indeed, the wage restraint in return for tax concessions was the central mechanism driving the social partnership agreements and had underpinned the agreements before 1997. McDonough and Dundon (2011: 548) are highly critical of the after-effects of this policy, pointing out that it has left Ireland in a position where 'as a percentage of GDP, Irish taxation remains at a similar level to some of the poorer Eastern European Member States of the EU'. This low taxation rate was accompanied by a widening gap between high- and low-income earners in the years 1987 and 2005 (D'Art and Turner 2011; McDonough *et al.* 2009) and a drop in disposable income for the bottom 50 per cent of households, which fell from 25.25 per cent to 23.49 per cent in the years 1987 to 2007 (D'Art and Turner 2011; Social Justice Ireland 2009).

Trade Unions and Their Approaches to Partnership

Trade unions generally supported the agreements. From an early date, ICTU saw a consensus approach as holding out the possibility of the 'development of a modern

Table 13.4

Wage and Tax Elements of NWAs, 1987–2009

Programme	Years	Duration in Months	Tax Provisions	Wage Increases
Programme for National Recovery (PNR)	1987–1991	39 months (6-month pay pause to apply to the public sector)	• Reduction of IR£225m (IR£750 actually delivered), including increases in the PAYE allowance costing IR£70m • Widening of tax band and cut in tax rates to 30% and 53%	• 3% on the first IR£120 per week • 2% on the remaining weekly pay • Minimum IR£4 increase per week
Programme for Economic and Social Progress (PESP)	1991–1994	36 months	• Reduce bottom rate to 25% (only 27% achieved) plus 1% income levy added • Marginal relief rate of taxation reduced from 48% to 40%	• Year 1: 4% increase • Year 2: 3% increase* (+3% local (exceptional) bargaining clause) • Year 3: 3.75%
Programme for Competitiveness and Work (PCW)	1994–1997	36 months	• IR£900m tax cuts, reduction from 27% to 26% on standard rate • PRSI reduced by 1% • IR£100m cut in business tax and improvements for small firms	• Year 1: 2.5% increase • Year 2: 2.5% increase • Year 3: 2.5%
Partnership 2000 for Inclusion, Employment and Competitiveness	1997–2000	39 months	• IR£900m in tax reductions over 3 years • IR£100m cut in business tax, including reductions in corporation tax	• Year 1: 2.5% increase • Year 2: 2.25% increase* (+ 2% local bargaining clause) • Year 3: 1.5% first 9 months + 1% last 6 months
Programme for Prosperity and Fairness (PPF)	2000–2003	33 months (locally agreed pay pauses on last phase of agreement due to inability to pay)	• IR£1.2b in tax breaks: increase personal allowance by IR£800 to IR£5,500 and the PAYE allowance increased by IR£1,100 to IR£2,000 • Widening of the standard tax band: single earner from IR£17,000 to IR£20,000 and married from IR£28,000 to IR£29,000 • Reductions in the rates in which tax is levied to 42% and 20%	• Year 1: 5.5% increase • Year 2: 5.5% increase (+ 2% renegotiated) • Year 3: 4% increase final 9 months + 1% once-off lump sum
Sustaining Progress	2003–2006	1st phase: 18 months 2nd phase: 18 months 6-month pay pause for public sector	• Progress to be made on removing those on the minimum wage from the tax net • Aim to have 85% of taxpayers on standard rate	• 3% first 9 months • 2% next 6 months • 2% next 3 months • Min wage €7 an hour from 1 Feb 2004 • Mid-term review • 1.5% first 6 months • 1.5% second 6 months • 2.5% final 6 months
Towards 2016 Phase 1	2006–2008	27 months	None	• 3% first 6 months • 2% next 6 months • 2.5% next 6 months • 2.5% last 6 months plus extra 0.5% for workers paid less than €10.25 per hour in Phase 2
Towards 2016 Phase 2 (agreement discontinued in 2009)	2008–2009	36 months in 2 phases. 3-month pay pause for private sector; 11 months for public sector	None	• Pay pause 3 months • 3.5% next 6 months • 2.5% next 12 months (extra 0.5% for workers under €11.00 per hour)

Note: This table simplifies the provisions and the original agreements should be consulted for the full terms. In particular, the application of public sector pay increases varies from the norms above.

* Indicates the earliest date for payment of Local Bargaining Clauses.

Source: National Agreements 1987–2008

efficient low inflation economy ... with low levels of unemployment and high levels of social protection' (*Business and Finance* 1990). While generally supported, this did not mean that the agreements were immune from union criticism – quite the contrary. Among a range of issues that gave rise to complaints were the unfair sharing of the gains arising from economic success, social welfare cuts, the absence of provisions for union recognition, the continued tax burden on Pay as You Earn (PAYE) workers and a failure to extend partnership to the workplace. None of these issues, however, were to prove deal breakers. Teague and Donaghey (2012: 13) suggest that unions remained committed to the process for three main reasons: the 'logic of representation' was preferable to 'logic of mobilisation', real wage increases were higher than those achieved by most other workers in Europe and 'the employment boom effectively tied trade unions to social partnership, as it would have been widely deemed cavalier to have adopted any alternative strategy'.

Perhaps the most serious charge was that the agreements only provided limited pay solidarity for low-paid workers. Unions representing lower-paid workers, notably MANDATE and the Civil and Public Services Union (CPSU), opposed a number of the agreements – a reversal of the position in the 1970s. In 2010 John Douglas, general secretary of MANDATE, was critical of union negotiators across a number of partnership agreements for ignoring his union's call for flat rate increases (IRN 2010). However, majority union support was not in doubt as all the agreements were approved at special delegate congresses of ICTU. The outcomes of these ballots are contained in Table 13.5. It can be seen that as economic uncertainty set in in 2006 and the crisis of 2008 arrived, support increased greatly, with Phase 2 of Towards 2016 being carried by an unprecedented 88 per cent majority vote of delegates (Sheehan 2008b).

Table 13.5

Voting Results at ICTU Special Delegate Congresses on National Agreements

Agreement	For	Against
PNR	181	114
PESP	224	109
PCW	256	76
Partnership 2000	217	134
PPF	251	112
Sustaining Progress	195	147
Towards 2016 Phase 1	242	84
Towards 2016 Phase 2	305	36
Source: IRN (various editions)		

Employers and Their Approaches to Social Partnership

Private sector employers were also generally positive about social partnership. Writing on the Programme for Competitiveness and Work (PCW) agreement, Brian Geoghegan of IBEC argued that the national programme had delivered on jobs, kept inflation and interest rates low and delivered additional disposable income to an average employee (Geoghegan 1996). IBEC's main concerns were generally with the issues of competitiveness, levels of taxation and public expenditure. The main opposition from an employer side came from the Irish Small and Medium Enterprises Association (ISME), which claimed that centralised agreements placed unfair burdens on small firms. Such views were not representative of the broad body of employer opinion. In a survey of employer and union elites, Wallace *et al.* (1998) found that not a single employer or union respondent favoured a return to decentralised bargaining. As late as 2006, social partnership continued to have broad support from business leaders. A survey of chief executive officers (CEOs) reported that 82 per cent of them were of the view that social partnership remained necessary (Fitzgerald 2006).

Social Provision and Involvement of the Community and Voluntary Sector

The agreements contained a number of social provisions that increased in importance over time up to the Towards 2016 agreement in 2006, when the specific industrial relations issue of employment law compliance comes to the fore (Table 13.6). The community and voluntary sector was involved directly for the first time in the negotiation of the Partnership 2000 agreement in 1997. This was in response to criticisms that they had been excluded from negotiations and that it was insufficient to have the trade unions put forward points for this constituency, as traditionally had been the case. Groups such as the Irish National Organisation of the Unemployed (INOU), the National Youth Council, the Conference of Religious of Ireland (CORI) and Protestant Aid were among nineteen separate groups that made presentations as part of the process.

The involvement of the voluntary pillar was seen as a move to a new and more inclusive 'deliberative democracy' form of governance (O'Donnell and Thomas 2002). However, unions and employers continued to dominate proceedings and unsurprisingly the influence of the voluntary pillar was asymmetrical to that yielded by groups that represented economic interests (Larragy 2010; Stafford 2011). More importantly, few concrete policy initiatives emanated from the many working groups that were established (Hardiman 2006; Roche 2012b). Teague and Donaghey (2012: 5) argue that this 'calls into question the view of social partnership as a successful system of new governance'. In a rejection of the claims of deliberative governance, Roche (2012b: 21) points to 'the dismal failure of deliberation in the face of the advent of the current economic crisis' and a return 'to mainly distributive bargaining'.

In 2004 the government turned to addressing the perceived social deficit accompanying the Celtic Tiger. This had little to do with social partnership but was driven by the poor performance of Fianna Fáil in the local elections and European elections of that year, which was blamed on that party's shift to the right. This saw an expansion of welfare provision from a low base, leading to a series of redistributive budgets from 2004 (Roche 2012a). The Towards 2016 agreement was signed in 2006 and reflected these developments, including major action on employment rights. With the current economic crisis there has been a sharp retrenchment in this expansion of social measures. Roche (2012a: 31) argues this is not just a reflection of the economic crisis, but also reflects 'long-prevalent political attitudes favouring low taxes over collective consumption or redistribution'.

Table 13.6

Social Provisions of the NWAs, 1987–2008

Agreement	Key Social Provisions
PNR	• Emphasis on government policy on social equity with particular attention to health services, education and housing for the disadvantaged • Maintain value in social welfare benefits and where resources are available consider increases for those receiving the lowest payments
PESP	• Seven-year health programme to improve community-based services • Education initiatives at all levels
PCW	• PESP terms for social reform to be carried over • Particular attention to improving social welfare due to 1994 Budget provisions
Partnership 2000	• IR£525 million to be spent on social inclusion • Adoption of National Anti-Poverty Strategy (NAPS) • Particular attention to tackling unemployment
PPF	• Investment of IR£1.5 billion on social inclusion measures • Update and review NAPS and poverty-proofing arrangements • Establishment of Housing Forum to monitor supply and affordability of housing
Sustaining Progress	• Emphasis on dealing with poverty and promoting social inclusion under NAPS, especially pensioner poverty • Structural reform of the health service • Improving employment equality, especially gender inequality and treatment of persons with disabilities
Towards 2016	• Employment law compliance • Commitment to establish NERA

Source: Various national wage agreements

ECONOMIC DEVELOPMENTS AND CENTRALISED AGREEMENTS, 1987–2009

Over the period of centralised agreements since 1987, the Irish economy underwent a remarkable transformation, unprecedented economic success and a precipitous economic collapse. The economic trends can be broken down into four broad periods: a period of stabilisation from 1987 to 1993, a period of expansion and growth from 1994 to 2000, a somewhat rockier period from 2001 to 2006 and an emergent and eventual crisis from 2007 to 2009.

The *first period* was one of stabilisation and uncertainty. On the positive side, growth was maintained with an average real GNP growth of 4.2 per cent from 1988 to 1993 and the debt/GNP ratio saw a significant decline (Figure 13.3). Growth rates were almost three times higher than the EU average and more than twice the OECD average. Inflation stayed low but at a level higher than the average in the EU. Under the Programme for Economic and Social Progress (PESP) in the early 1990s, uncertainty emerged as the effects of the international downturn associated with the first Gulf War were felt. Interest rates rocketed to around 12–15 per cent until decreasing following the devaluation of the Irish punt in early 1993. The public sector pay bill proved difficult to rein in, growing over 27 per cent between 1990 and 1993. However, the main problem was unemployment. This remained stubbornly high and actually increased from 1990 to 1994 – a trend that masked a slight growth in overall employment (Figure 13.4).

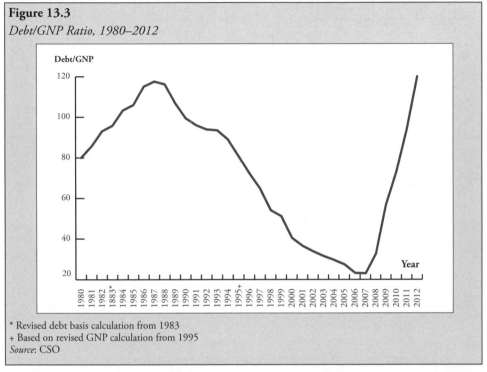

Figure 13.3
Debt/GNP Ratio, 1980–2012

* Revised debt basis calculation from 1983
\+ Based on revised GNP calculation from 1995
Source: CSO

The *second period* commencing around 1994 saw the economic fundamentals change dramatically and in an unanticipated way. Growth rates become extraordinary, budget surpluses become the norm (consistently outstripping predictions) and the debt/GNP ratio reduced to only 35 per cent by 2002. Real disposable income increased by 27 per cent between 1987 and 1998 – a contrast with the decline between 1980 and 1987 (Turner and D'Art 2000). Led by growth in the services sector, increased female participation rates and inward migration, there was dramatic employment growth accompanied by declining unemployment (Figures 13.4 and 13.5). By 2000, unemployment had reached 4.1 per cent and it was maintained around this level for a number of years, rising to only 4.5 per cent by 2007. There was even a transformation in the hitherto stubbornly high level of long-term unemployment, which fell from 9 per cent of the total labour force in 1994 to 2.3 per cent in 1999. Teague and Donaghey (2009: 58) argue strongly that the 'high levels of employment growth can be viewed as the Celtic Tiger's social dimension'.

These developments led to the Irish economy being accorded the sobriquet 'the Celtic Tiger'. Hardiman (2000: 292), writing of the period, notes 'real increases in disposable income were delivered, while keeping industrial conflict at low levels'. The general view is that the economic performance during this period marked a genuine productivity and competitiveness boom and was soundly based (Roche 2012b: 113–49). Employer benefits were relatively greater, with a large upward swing in the proportion of national income

Figure 13.4

Total Numbers Employed and Unemployed, 1983–2012 (ILO Definition)

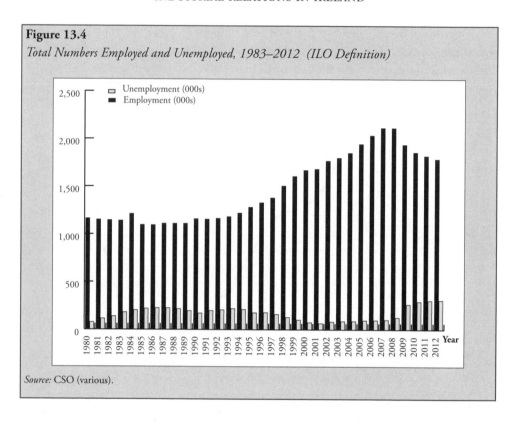

Source: CSO (various).

Figure 13.5

Unemployment Rate, 1987–2012

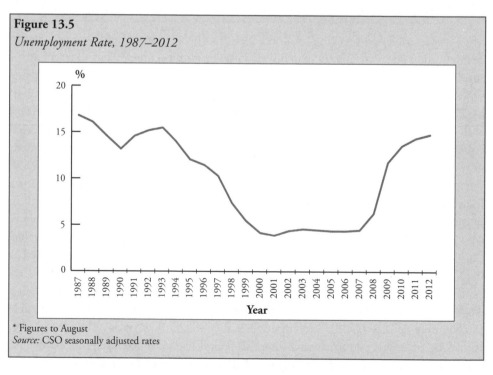

* Figures to August
Source: CSO seasonally adjusted rates

going to profits accompanied by a corresponding fall in the proportion going to wages. Teague and Donaghey (2009: 68) record that 'in comparative terms, the share of labour in national income was 54.2 per cent in 2001, while the EU average was 67.2 per cent'.

The *third period* from 2000 to 2006 saw most economic indicators continue to be comparatively healthy. Growth rates as measured by both GNP and GDP tapered off (Figures 13.6 and 13.7) but were still positive, employment continued to expand and unemployment remained low, hovering around 4 per cent. However, internationally, the bursting of the dotcom bubble and the aftermath of the 9/11 attack on the Twin Towers meant that the economy was entering a more unsettled period. IBEC had become concerned at 'the loss of competitiveness' and the rise in public sector expenditure (Sheehan 2004: 17). There was substance to these concerns, since 'from the early 2000s pay increases began to diverge from pay trends in Ireland's trading partners, and both pay and unit cost competitiveness declined' (Roche 2012a: 7). As in the 1960s and 1970s, pay pressure was driven by both rising expectations from a buoyant economy and rising inflation, which was also above the EU average from 2000 to 2003. In addition, the real rise in the cost of living was not captured by the Consumer Price Index as it did not include house price rises. The growth in house prices placed pressure on wages in both the public and private sphere.

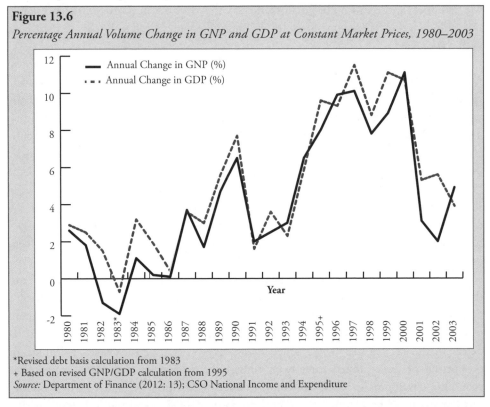

Figure 13.6

Percentage Annual Volume Change in GNP and GDP at Constant Market Prices, 1980–2003

*Revised debt basis calculation from 1983
+ Based on revised GNP/GDP calculation from 1995
Source: Department of Finance (2012: 13); CSO National Income and Expenditure

In the public sphere, inflationary pressure fed into the first benchmarking process in 2003, as the rather colourful argument was made that a married guard and nurse could not afford to buy a house together. The average 8.9 per cent increase emanating from benchmarking constituted a form of institutionalised wage drift via social partnership. Benchmarking, which was provided for under the Programme for Prosperity and Fairness (PPF), was meant to compare public with private sector pay. However, the process by which the increases were determined was opaque to say the least, since the bases of comparisons were not made public. A further concern for some trade unions was that it inflated the pay of higher-paid civil servants precisely because of the link to pay of comparator executives in the private sector. Jack O'Connor, general president of SIPTU, has said that 'top people in the private sector "have been awarding themselves multiples of what workers have received", a point entirely missed in media reports' (Sheehan 2007: 20). Thus, public sector pay for the higher-paid public servants was being determined not by solidaristic principles, but by market-led forces that had seen a huge increase in wage inequality since the early 1980s.

Neither did benchmarking deliver significantly on public sector reform – a point emphasised by Richard Bruton TD of Fine Gael in a radio interview in 2003 (RTÉ Radio 1, *News at One*, 29 November 2003). Defenders of the process have pointed out that the alternative was the unregulated comparability process and a failed attempt to replace that with grade restructuring reform (Sheehan 2011c). The second benchmarking report issued in January 2008 provided for overall increases of less than 1 per cent. Increases were confined mostly to higher-paid workers, with most public sector workers (notably nurses and teachers) receiving no increases, leading to widespread union disenchantment with the process.

The follow-up agreement to the PPF, Sustaining Progress, represented an attempt to restore stability but actually contributed to problems with wage increases, which were chasing the high cost of living. The looming crises in construction and internationally were to compromise any contribution centralised agreements could make to stability. The early part of the *fourth period* from 2006 to 2007 continued to be marked by confidence, with talk of a soft landing remaining the dominant economic discourse, even from bodies such as the Economic and Social Research Institute (ESRI) and the NESC. However, critical voices were increasingly warning of a property bubble and this was given immediacy with the crisis of the US sub-prime property market and the collapse in February 2008 of Lehman Brothers bank. By 2007 'construction accounted for 13 per cent of employment in 2007 compared with an average of about 8 per cent in the EU' (Roche 2012a: 12).

Soothing noises were made by the Financial Regulator and the Central Bank about the solidity of the Irish banks. In reality the Irish economy was on the brink of a precipice in which the very financial foundations of the state were at risk. The main problem was the exposure of the banks to property loans but there was also a structural defect in the tax regime, which relied excessively on transactions taxes, a significant proportion of them linked directly or indirectly to property. Instead of sustainable economic development based on sound financial principles, Ireland was in a boom–bust cycle, caused by unwise pro-cyclical domestic polices, a sectoral imbalance arising from the concentration on construction, huge levels of public and private debt and neo-liberal light touch regulation in the banking sector. Fatally, these were magnified by an emerging international financial crisis, making for the economic version of a 'perfect storm' that swept over the country in 2008 and 2009, the consequences of which will persist for many years.

The Economic Crisis 2008–2009 and Collective Bargaining

The economic dimensions of the crisis that has engulfed the country since 2008 are evident in the changes to annual GNP and GDP growth figures, as shown in Figure 13.7. GNP has fallen most as a result of the deflationary policies pursued to bring the deficit in public finances to a maximum of 3 per cent by 2015. This was accompanied by a startling rise in unemployment from 4.5 per cent in 2007 to over 13 per cent by 2009. It has grown to over 14 per cent since then, but this is a rate that seriously understates the employment effect, as large-scale emigration has recommenced and there has been a withdrawal of people from the labour market. Faced with a banking crisis in October 2008, the government decided to act as guarantor for all deposits and liabilities in Irish banks, thereby socialising bank debt and making it sovereign debt (Roche 2012a). The government believed that the banks had a liquidity problem but fatally they were on the brink of insolvency and this has led not to the 'cheapest bailout in history', but to some €70 billion being added to state debt. By 2010 the cost of borrowing on international capital markets had risen to unsustainable levels and the government found itself forced to apply for a rescue package to the EU/IMF/ECB troika. The consequent loss of

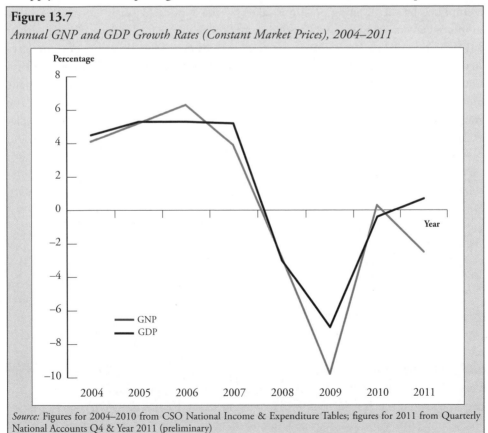

Figure 13.7

Annual GNP and GDP Growth Rates (Constant Market Prices), 2004–2011

Source: Figures for 2004–2010 from CSO National Income & Expenditure Tables; figures for 2011 from Quarterly National Accounts Q4 & Year 2011 (preliminary)

financial independence saw Irish budgetary policy and expenditure being directed and overseen by the troika. This rocked the political landscape and led to the decimation of the governing parties – Fianna Fáil and the Green Party – in the general election of February 2011 and their replacement with a Fine Gael–Labour coalition.

Teague and Donaghey (2012: 20) remark that the 'social partnership process was a bit player in the unfolding Irish economic crisis'. As with the demise of NWAs in the early 1980s, employer commitment first weakened 'about 2005 and evaporated with the onset of the recession' (Teague and Donaghey 2012: 20). As the crisis loomed unions became more attached to the process of social partnership (see Table 13.4, above). Despite growing questions among employers, an ambitious ten-year phased agreement called Towards 2016 was negotiated in 2006. A major concern of unions in both phases was to tackle the emergence of low standard practices by some employers – the so-called 'race to the bottom'. Phase 1 contained measures to protect labour standards and these were strengthened in Phase 2 (the Transitional Agreement) with the commitment to establish NERA. The Transitional Agreement agreed in September 2008 was concluded against all the odds. It contained provision for a 6 per cent pay increase (6.5 per cent for the lower-paid) over twenty-one months.

Faced with a looming budget, the government sought to revise the Transition Agreement in late 2009. The unions were prepared to make concessions but the talks broke down in December 2009 following internal Fianna Fáil disagreement. This was exemplified by the differing positions taken by the Taoiseach, Brian Cowen TD, who supported an emerging revised agreement, and the Minister for Finance, Brian Lenihan TD, who opposed it. The Minister for Finance's position prevailed as the government's 'need for immediate savings combined with fears that it faced acute political opposition from within the Fianna Fáil parliamentary party' (Roche 2012b: 130). The resultant breakdown was accompanied by a welter of recriminations from unions at the government action. Unilateral government measures now became the order of the day

Table 13.7
Main Unilateral Government Measures Affecting Earnings, 2009–2012

Universal Social Charge	• 2% on the first €10,036 • 4% on the next €5,980 • 7% on earnings above €16,011
Public sector pension levy, rate as of 1 May 2009 (introduced on 1 March and amended within two months, to lessen impact on lower-paid workers)	• Exempt on the first €15,000 • 5% between €15,000 and €20,000 • 10% between €20,000 and €60,000 • 10.5% above €60,000
Public sector wage reductions	• 5% on the first €30,000 • 7.5% on the next €40,000 • 10% on the next €55,000 • Above €125,000 cuts ranging from 8–15% (as recommended by the Review Body on Higher Remuneration in Public Sector) • 20% reduction in the case of the Taoiseach

Sources: www.per.gov.ie; O'Neill and Higgins (2010); www.revenue.ie

to achieve savings in public sector expenditure. Indeed, a public sector pension levy had already been introduced unilaterally earlier in 2009 and this was followed with public sector wage cuts (Table 13.7). A Universal Social Charge followed in 2010, which (along with the other measures) spelled the end of the low-tax model on which the wage restraint of Irish social partnership had been based.

Following the breakdown of talks with the government, IBEC formally withdrew from the agreement in December 2008. Its director general, Danny McCoy, commented at the time that 'the pay terms are wholly unsuited to our economic circumstances' (Sheehan 2010b). In truth the agreement was always likely to be unstable. As noted above, the CIF had declined to be a party to it and it had begun to unravel within months with only a minority of companies honouring the terms (Sheehan 2010b). Despite a mini pay round in 2011, for the most part collective bargaining over wage increases has atrophied in much of the private sector (Table 13.8). However, only a minority of private sector companies have introduced pay cuts, with most operating a pay freeze. Roche (2012a: 30) credits the absence of 'extensive and deep cuts in nominal pay levels' with the low level of industrial conflict in the private sector. A return to a pro-cyclical strike trend with low strike levels because of the depth of the recession and the limited prospect for successful strike action is also a possible reason.

Table 13.8
Outline of Collective Bargaining Arrangements, 2009–2014

Date/Arrangement	Main Terms
2009 Private sector: IBEC withdraws from Transitional Agreement 2008	Pay terms of Phase 2 effectively lapse. Results in: • Pay freeze in about 80% of companies • Pay reductions in about 10–20% of companies • Wide-scale redundancies and closures
March 2010 IBEC–ICTU protocol on private sector industrial relations	• Adhere to established collective agreements • Use state IR institutions to resolve disputes • Co-operation with ongoing change • Sustain employment • Local engagement
June 2010–2014 Croke Park Agreement covering public sector	• Pay freeze with no further pay reductions beyond those in 2009 and 2010 • Voluntary redundancies • Co-operation with modernisation redeployment
2011 Private sector: mini pay round	Limited local bargaining: • Low pay rises (around 2%) in export-led sector: pharmaceuticals, food and medical devices

Source: Various agreements

THE CROKE PARK AGREEMENT

The Croke Park Agreement was the result of an initiative brokered by the LRC under its chairperson, Kieran Mulvey, and the director of the Conciliation Service, Kevin Foley, which resulted in an agreement in the public sector up to 2014. It was approved by a two-thirds majority (1,894 votes to 986) of the Public Sector Committee of ICTU but only after intense internal union debate (Higgins 2010e). The key elements of the agreement were no further reductions in core pay in return for large-scale reductions in the number of employees and co-operation with change and restructuring. The agreement also implicitly means the unilateral government pay reductions of around 15 per cent on average 'have been formally acknowledged by the unions' (Sheehan 2010c: 20). The agreement provided that the pay reductions for those workers earning under €35,000 would be restored if savings were achieved. This, however, has been tacitly abandoned by the unions and now appears a dead letter.

The reduction in the numbers of employees was to be achieved through voluntary redundancies. Although criticised by some, this approach is consistent with the general approach to redundancies in the private sector. Provision was made for monitoring the delivery of the savings and a speedy dispute resolution mechanism. This even included a requirement that unions would co-operate with change in the event of any appeal – a direct reversal of the standard requirement for parties in negotiations to observe the status quo pending the outcome of negotiations (see Chapter 7). The agreement provides for an implementation body and this is chaired by P.J. Fitzpatrick. He has pointed out that it is not the role of 'the Implementation Body, to make decisions on the reforms that need to be made' (Fitzpatrick 2012: 6). Details of the work of the implementation body can be viewed at http://implementationbody.gov.ie/the-public-service-agreement-2010-2014/.

There has been considerable media discussion of the Croke Park Agreement, much of it critical. The coverage has been described as being 'very often unfair and in some cases factually incorrect' (Fitzpatrick 2012: 23). There have also been political tensions between Fine Gael and Labour over the agreement, with Labour being seen as protective of the agreement and elements of Fine Gael opposed. This opposition was exemplified by an open letter critical of the agreement signed by eight Fine Gael TDs (*Irish Examiner*, 15 October 2012). The main critical point is that given the scale of the crisis no area of public expenditure should be off limits for cuts, especially as the alternative is cuts to front-line services.

Some commentators called for the scrapping of the Croke Park Agreement but more informed critics argued not for its abandonment, but for either more effective use of the measures within it, limited interpretation of the commitment to retain pay levels or its renegotiation. The first point concerned the capacity of public sector management to realise the agreement's transformative potential. The second involved suggestions that the payment of annual increments be suspended or that allowances be cut. The debate on allowances and increments can be seen as falling between calls for renegotiation and more effective implementation, with P.J. Fitzpatrick pointing out that the agreement is silent on these (RTÉ Radio 1, *Morning Ireland*, 15 October 2012). The third point suggested that government should invoke clause 1.28, which provides that 'the implementation of this agreement is subject to no currently unforeseen budgetary situation'. It was claimed that this allowed for renegotiation because the growth projections on which the agreement was based have not been realised. However, it was pointed out by unions that the budgetary targets had been met and growth targets were not specified in the agreement. One of the strongest critics of the agreement has been Eddie Molloy, who has described it as 'convoluted, clubby industrial relations machinery' (Molloy 2012: 12).

Criticisms aside, Croke Park has also been defended on the basis of the industrial peace it has delivered and the major changes agreed. Roche (2012c: 1) notes that international audiences are impressed with the contribution of the Croke Park Agreement to the Irish response to the crisis and that they typically respond with: 'We could do with that type of framework here.' Brian Lucy (2012) has pointed out that the debate has lacked rationality because the assertions that 'private sector wages have fallen, public sector wages have not' are incorrect. The agreement has been strongly defended by P.J. Fitzpatrick, who, in his 2012 Countess Markievicz memorial lecture, pointed to 'some €810 million in sustainable pay bill savings … as well as some €678 million in non-pay savings – a total of €1.5 billion' having been achieved in the first two years (Fitzpatrick 2012: 13). He went on to note that:

> … there seems to be at times very unrealistic expectations of this Agreement. It cannot possibly be the solution for all of the ills the country faces … [However,] it provides a framework which can – and is – making an important contribution to the recovery effort by supporting the reduction in the cost and size of the public service and by enabling significant reform and increases in productivity. (Fitzpatrick 2012: 13)

Government ministers also defended the agreement and argued that it is delivering. Nonetheless, under intense media pressure and decreasing room for manoeuvre in meeting the targets set by the troika, in late 2012 the government acted on the renegotiation suggestion and sought to a review the agreement. This review was termed the Croke Park Extension and set about achieving further staff reductions and annual savings of €1 billion by 2015 (Wall 2012b). The formula envisaged was similar to the first agreement with pay being protected in return for savings elsewhere, although at the time of writing, these have not been specified by government negotiators. Unions indicated that agreement would be difficult to achieve and could not be at the expense of the lower-paid (Wall 2012b).

A RETROSPECTIVE ON CONTEMPORARY IRISH COLLECTIVE BARGAINING

Social partnership today gets a bad press from popular commentators, which contrasts with the almost universal approval it received at the height of the Celtic Tiger. In this way it is not dissimilar to the turnaround in commentators' views on centralised bargaining of the 1970s. During the national wage agreements (NWAs), they seemed to be the only way to order wage bargaining but were widely denounced as a failure when they ended. They did not prove to be the only way of doing business, since employers and unions quickly adapted to the dreaded 'free for all' of decentralised bargaining when it arrived in 1982. Indeed, the period 1982 to 1987 held few problems for employers as the recession of the 1980s moderated worker expectations and allowed businesses to adapt to a new reality. Similarly, with the current recession businesses face few problems from pay bargaining; unions, on the other hand, have many. Pay freezes combined with inflation mean that real wages have fallen in all sectors of the economy for the vast majority of workers. The fall in earnings for workers has been much greater than in the 1980s and in much of the economy these look set to continue. The fall in wages are accentuated by increases in taxation, notably the universal social charge and more workers being drawn into the tax net. High unemployment has again, as in the 1950s, weakened the bargaining power of unions. This is a viscous circle and reversal of the virtuous circle identified with social partnership in the 1990s.

The critique of social partnership is reflected in the debate on the Croke Park Agreement. Although the agreement was only reluctantly accepted by public sector unions, it is now projected as a special privilege protecting insiders. The public sector is the subject of sustained comment, which ICTU (2010) estimates is 90 per cent hostile to them. What is notable is that much of this commentary is led not by industrial correspondents but opinion writers and political correspondents, some of whom project social partnership as having been a takeover of the political system by the unions. Roche (2012b) considers that such arguments have little merit. He argues: 'political leaders showed themselves on occasion well capable of standing up to union demands or social partnership commitments, or of ignoring them, as Charlie McCreevy was to do from time to time' (Roche 2012b: 128). Teague and Donaghey (2012: 17) note that it was 'financialisation' and 'the speculative bubble ... causing disorderly economic behaviour' that was responsible for the economic crisis. This is an argument that hints at the limitations of the influence of social partnership. This appears similar to the experience of the NWAs of the 1970s in that many events were outside the control of the collective bargaining system. In effect, social partnership was more a follower than a shaper of the economic terrain – just as NWAs were before.

Unions seem bewildered by much of the negative commentary, given the adaptations they have made in the interests of national economic policy since 1987 and the moderate role they adopted in that time. For them, the crisis arose from the evils of neo-liberal policies that allowed the banks and developers to engage in casino capitalism and placed the country in peril. They see the socialisation of the debts arising from this activity as an affront. The suggestions of a takeover of the political system is particularly galling to them because social partnership did not deliver on greater social equality but 'retained' or 'accentuated' inequality and led to an unequal sharing of the benefits of economic growth.

Differences on social partnership in public discourse are largely reversed in the academic debate, where there is considerable criticism of the agreements precisely because they failed to deliver greater social equity. D'Art and Turner (2011) are highly critical of partnership, pointing to failures in the areas of trade union recognition, workplace democracy and trade union influence in national policy-making. McDonough and Dundon (2010) decry the growth in inequality that they argue accompanied social partnership. In contrast, Teague and Donaghey (2012) defend social partnership on the grounds of the employment creation and the likely ineffectiveness of the alternative of 'mobilisation' – industrial conflict. Roche (2012b) appears to favour a middle position, seeing the agreements as pragmatic settlements between employers and unions not greatly different from the traditional mix of distributive and co-operative industrial relations. In effect, a form of competitive corporatism adapted to the realities of the Irish situation (Roche 2012b).

For the moment, pragmatism continues to mark trade union approaches, as they persist with engagement with government despite their proposal for an economic solidarity pact having been rejected out of hand. The government now espouses a diluted form of social dialogue (Sheehan 2011c). Thus, the Oireachtas Library and Research Service (2011) notes: 'economic governance continues to rely heavily on the social partners and in particular, trade unions, to achieve goals'. The Croke Park Extension process is a manifestation of this, with the outcome of that process still in the balance at the time of going to press. Thus, collective bargaining continues to morph, adapt and change to the underlying economic and social situation much as it has done since the foundation of the state. However, the greatly weakened position of unions, the contraction of the domestic economy, weak consumer demand and the parlous state of the global economy all combine to present Irish collective bargaining with its sternest challenge to date.

CONCLUDING COMMENTS

Collective bargaining is a nineteenth-century creation that some regard as an undesirable development interfering with the free market, others see as contributing to democracy and still others see as preserving the status quo in society. Collective bargaining has been an economic and social reality, shaping Irish life most notably since the end of World War II. It is clear that while so doing it is greatly influenced by and responsive to the underlying economic circumstances of the day. This has seen various forms of collective bargaining come and go, changing from a wage round system to national agreements, back to wage rounds and to a long-lived partnership era. Today, collective bargaining is conducted against a backdrop of austerity and an economic crisis not seen since the 1950s. Opinions are sharply divided on the contribution it is making in the public sector to meeting the challenges posed by this crisis. In the private sector, the influence of collective bargaining is weakened not just by the economic crisis but by the decline in private sector union density.

Bibliography

Abbott, B. (2006) 'Determining the Significance of the Citizens' Advice Bureaux as an Industrial Relations Actor', *Employee Relations,* 28(5), 435–8.

Abbott, B., Heery, E. and Williams, S. (2011) 'Civil Society Organisations and the Exercise of Power in the Employment Relationship', *Employee Relations,* 34(1), 91–107.

Ackers, P. and Black, J. (1992) 'Watching the Detectives: Shop Stewards' Expectations of their Managers in the Age of Human Resource Management', in A. Sturdy, D. Knights and H. Willmott (eds.) *Skill and Consent: Contemporary Studies in the Labour Process.* London: Routledge.

Ahearne, A. (2010) 'Ireland's Economic Crisis: Implications for the Labour Market'. Lecture prepared for the 18th John Lovett Memorial Lecture Series. University of Limerick.

Allen, K. (1997) *Fianna Fáil and Irish Labour: 1926 to the Present.* London: Pluto Press.

Allen, V. (1971) *The Sociology of Industrial Relations.* London: Longman.

Armstrong, C.A., Flood, P.C., Guthrie, J., Liu, W., MacCurtain, S. and Mkamwa, T. (2010) 'Beyond High Performance Work Systems: The Impact of Including Diversity and Equality Management on Firm Performance', *Human Resource Management,* 49(6), 977–98.

Armstrong, M. and Stephens, T. (2005) *A Handbook of Employee Reward Management and Practice.* London: Kogan Page.

Arrighi, G. (1990) 'Marxist Century, American Century: The Making and the Remaking of the World's Labour Movement', *New Left Review,* 179, 29–64.

Arvey, R.D. and Ivancevich, J.M. (1980) 'Punishment in Organisations: A Review, Propositions and Research Suggestions', *Academy of Management Review,* 5(1), 123–32.

Auer, P. (2000) *Employment Revival in Europe: Labour Market Success in Austria, Denmark, Ireland and the Netherlands.* Geneva: International Labour Office.

Baccaro, L. (2008) *Labour, Globalization and Inequality: Are Trade Unions Still Redistributive?* Geneva: International Institute for Labour Studies.

Baccaro, L. and Simoni, M. (2004) 'The Irish Social Partnership and the "Celtic Tiger" Phenomenon', International Institute for Labour Studies, Discussion Paper (DP/154/2004), Decent Work Research Programme. Geneva: International Labour Organization.

Baglioni, G. (2003) 'Employee Involvement in the European Company Directive', *Transfer*, 9(2), 341–8.

Bain, G.S. and Price, R. (1983) 'Union Growth: Dimensions, Determinants and Destiny', in G.S. Bain (ed.) *Industrial Relations in Britain*. Oxford: Basil Blackwell.

Barnard, C. (2008) 'Social Dumping or Dumping Socialism?', *Cambridge Law Journal*, 67(2), 262–4.

Barnard, C. (2012) 'A Proportionate Response to Proportionality in the Field of Collective Action', *European Law Review*, 37(2), 117–35.

Barry, M. and Wilkinson, A. (2011) 'Reconceptualising Employer Associations Under Evolving Employment Relations: Countervailing Power Revisited', *Work, Employment and Society*, 25, 149–62.

Beaumont, P.B and Harris, R.I.D. (1991) 'Trade Union Recognition and Employment Contraction, 1980–1984', *British Journal of Industrial Relations*, 29(1), 49–58.

Beer, M., Spector, B., Lawrence, P.R., Quinn-Mills, D. and Walton, R.E. (1984) *Managing Human Assets: The Groundbreaking Harvard Business School Program*. New York: The Free Press/Macmillan.

Behrens, M., Hamann, K. and Hurd, R. (2004) 'Conceptualizing Labour Union Revitalization', in C. Frege and J. Kelly (eds.) *Varieties of Unionism: Strategies for Union Revitalization in a Globalizing Economy*. Oxford: Oxford University Press.

Bew, P., Hazelkorn, E. and Patterson, H. (1989) *The Dynamics of Irish Politics*. London: Lawrence and Wishart.

Beynon, H. (1973) *Working for Ford*. Harmondsworth: Penguin.

Biagi, M., Tiraboschi, M. and Rymkevitch, O. (2002) 'The "Europeanisation" of Industrial Relations: Evaluating the Quality of European Industrial Relations in a Global Context: a Literature Review'. Dublin: The European Foundation for the Improvement of Living and Working Conditions. <www.eurofound.ie/publications/files/EF0276EN.pdf>

Blanchflower, D.G. (2006) 'Cross-Country Study of Union Membership', Discussion Paper No. 2016. Bonn: Institute for the Study of Labor.

Blauner, R. (1964) *Alienation and Freedom*. Chicago: University of Chicago Press.

Blyton, P. and Turnbull, P. (1994) *The Dynamics of Employee Relations*. London: Macmillan.

Blyton, P. and Turnbull, P. (2004) *The Dynamics of Employee Relations*. Basingstoke: Palgrave Macmillan.

Bonner, K. (1989) 'Industrial Relations Reform', in Department of Industrial Relations, UCD (eds.) *Industrial Relations in Ireland: Contemporary Issues and Developments*. Dublin: University College Dublin.

Boyd, A. (1972) *The Rise of the Irish Trade Unions, 1729–1970.* Tralee: Anvil.

Boyd, A. (1984) *Have Trade Unions Failed the North?* Dublin: Mercier Press.

Boyle, J.W. (1988) *The Irish Labor Movement in the Nineteenth Century.* Washington, DC: The Catholic University of America Press.

Boxall, P. and Purcell, J. (2007) *Strategy and Human Resource Management* (2nd edn.). Basingstoke: Macmillan.

Bradley, D., Huber, E. and Moller, S. (2003) 'Distribution and Redistribution in Post-Industrial Democracies', *World Politics*, 55, 193–228.

Bramel, D. and Friend, R. (1981) 'Hawthorne, the Myth of the Docile Worker, and Class Bias in Psychology', *American Psychologist,* 36(8), 867–78.

Brannick, T. and Kelly, A. (1982) 'The Reliability and Validity of Irish Strike Data and Statistics', *Economic and Social Review*, 14, 249–58.

Brannick, T., Doyle, L. and Kelly, A. (1997) 'Industrial Conflict', in T.V. Murphy and W.K. Roche (eds.) *Irish Industrial Relations in Practice.* Dublin: Oak Tree Press.

Braverman, H. (1974) *Labor and Monopoly Capital: The Degradation of Work in the Twentieth Century.* New York: Monthly Review Press.

Breen, R., Hannon, D., Rottman, D. and Whelan, C. (1990) *Understanding Contemporary Ireland.* Dublin: Gill & Macmillan.

Brown, L. (2012) 'Renault Prepared for Staff Suicides over Spying Scandal', *France 24,* 13 October.

Brown, W. (1981) *The Changing Contours of British Industrial Relations: A Survey of Manufacturing Industry.* Oxford: Blackwell.

Brown, W., Deakin, S. and Ryan, P. (1997) 'The Effects of British Industrial Relations Legislation 1979–1997', *National Institute Economic Review*, 161, 69–83.

Browne, J. (1994) *The Juridification of the Employment Relationship.* Aldershot: Avebury.

Bruton, R. (2011) *Consultation on the Reform of the State's Employment Rights and Industrial Relations Structures and Procedures.* Dublin: Department of Jobs, Enterprise and Innovation.

Bullock, Lord (1977) *Report of the Committee of Inquiry on Industrial Democracy.* London: HMSO.

Burchell, B., Ladipo, D. and Wilkinson F. (eds.) (2002) *Job Insecurity and Work Intensification.* London: Routledge.

Business & Finance (1990) 'Leaders Try to Sell the New Realism and Tame the Market', *Business & Finance*, 25 October.

Butler, A. (2007) 'Enforcement Issues: Could It Be Me?', Health and Safety Management: Not Just A Slogan – Health and Safety Review Conference. Dublin: 24 May.

Cashell, M. (2010) *A History of the Rights Commissioner Service 1970–2010*. Dublin: Labour Relations Commission.

Central Statistics Office (CSO) (2010) *Quarterly National Household Survey Union Membership Quarter 2 2009*. Dublin: Central Statistics Office.

Central Statistics Office (CSO) (2012) *Quarterly National Household Survey Quarter 1 2012*. Dublin: Central Statistics Office.

Chamberlain, N.W. (1948) *The Union Challenge to Management Control*. New York: Harper.

Chartered Institute of Personnel and Development (2006) *Reflections on Employee Engagement*. London: Chartered Institute of Personnel and Development.

Cho, S.K. (1985) 'The Labour Process and Capital Mobility: The Limits of the New International Division of Labour', *Politics and Society*, 14(2), 185–222.

Clegg, H.A. (1975) 'Pluralism in Industrial Relations', *British Journal of Industrial Relations*, 13(3), 309–16.

Clegg, H.A. (1976) *Trade Unionism under Collective Bargaining: A Theory Based on Comparisons of Six Countries*. Oxford: Blackwell.

Coates, K. and Topham, A. (eds.) (1968) *Industrial Democracy in Great Britain*. London: McKibbon and Kee.

Cole, G.D.H. (1913) *The World of Labour: A Discussion of the Present and Future of Trade Unionism*. London: Fabian Research Department.

Collings, D.G., Gunnigle, P. and Morley, M. (2008) 'Between Boston and Berlin: American MNCs and the Shifting Contours of Industrial Relations in Ireland', *The International Journal of Human Resource Management*, 19(2), 242–63.

Collings, D. and Wood, G. (2009) *Human Resource Management: A Critical Approach*. London: Routledge.

Commission of Inquiry on Industrial Relations (1981) *Report of the Commission of Inquiry on Industrial Relations*. Dublin: Stationery Office.

Conniffe, D. and Kennedy, K.A. (1984) *Employment and Unemployment Policy for Ireland*. Dublin: ERSI.

Connolly, C. and Darlington, R. (2012) 'Radical Political Unionism in France and Britain: A Comparative Study of SUD-Rail and the RMT', *European Journal of Industrial Relations*, 18(3), 235–50.

Coser, L. (1956) *The Functions of Social Conflict*. London: Routledge & Kegan Paul.

Costello, M. (1983) 'Ireland's Experiment with Worker Directors', *Personnel Management*, October.

Cox, B. and Hughes, J. (1989) 'Industrial Relations in the Public Sector', in Department of Industrial Relations, UCD (eds.) *Industrial Relations in Ireland: Contemporary Issues and Developments*. Dublin: University College Dublin.

Crouch, C. (1982) *Trade Unions: The Logic of Collective Action*. London: Fontana.

Crouch, C. and Pizzorno, A. (1978) *The Resurgence of Class Conflict in Western Europe Since 1968: Vols I and II*. London: Macmillan.

Cullinane N., Donaghey, J., Dundon, T. and Dobbins, T. (2012) 'Different Rooms, Different Voices: Double-Breasting, Multi-Channel Representation and the Managerial Agenda', *The International Journal of Human Resource Management*, 23(2), 368–84.

Cutcher-Gershenfeld, J. and Verma, A. (1994) 'Joint Governance in North American Work-Places: A Glimpse of the Future or the End of an Era', *International Journal of Human Resource Management*, 5(3), 547–80.

Dahrendorf, R. (1959) *Class and Class Conflict in Industrial Society*. London: Routledge.

Dáil Éireann (1963–1990) *Dáil Debates Collections* (various). Dublin: Stationery Office.

Daniel, W. and Millward, N. (1983) *Workplace Industrial Relations in Britain: TheDE/ PSI/SSRC Survey*. London: Heinemann.

Daniels, K. (2006) *Employee Relations in an Organisational Context*. London: Chartered Institute of Personnel and Development.

D'Arcy, F.A. (1994) 'The Irish Trade Union Movement in the Nineteenth Century', in D. Nevin (ed.) *Trade Union Century*. Dublin: ICTU.

D'Art, D. and Turner, T. (2002) 'Corporatism in Ireland: A View from Below', in D. D'Art and T. Turner (eds.) *Irish Employment Relations in the New Economy*. Dublin: Blackhall Publishing.

D'Art, D. and Turner, T. (2005) 'Union Recognition and Partnership at Work: A New Legitimacy for Irish Trade Unions?' *Industrial Relations Journal*, 36, 121–39.

D'Art, D. and Turner, T. (2006a) 'New Working Arrangements: Changing the Nature of the Employment Relationship?', *The International Journal of Human Resource Management*, 17(3), 523–38.

D'Art, D. and Turner, T. (2006b) 'Union Organising, Union Recognition and Employer Opposition: Case Studies of the Irish Experience', *Irish Journal of Management*, 26(2), 165–84.

D'Art, D. and Turner, T. (2007a) 'Ireland in Breach of ILO Conventions on Freedom of Association', *Industrial Relations News*, 11, 21 March, 19–21.

D'Art, D. and Turner, T. (2007b) 'Trade Unions and Political Participation in the European Union: Still Providing a Democratic Dividend?', *British Journal of Industrial Relations,* 45(1), 103–36.

D'Art, D. and Turner, T. (2011) 'Irish Trade Unions Under Social Partnership: A Faustian Bargain?', *Industrial Relations Journal,* 42(2), 157–73.

Daly, B. and Docherty, M. (2010) *Principles of Irish Employment Law.* Dublin: Clarus Press.

Darvall, F.O. (1964) *Popular Disturbances and Public Order in Regency England.* London: Oxford University Press.

Deaton, D. (1985) 'Management Style and Large-Scale Survey Evidence', *Industrial Relations Journal,* 26(2), 67–71.

Department of Finance (2003) *Budgetary and Economic Statistics, January 2003.* Dublin: Department of Finance.

Department of Finance (2012) *Budgetary and Economic Statistics.* Dublin: Department of Finance, October.

Department of Jobs, Enterprise and Innovation (2012) *Blueprint to Deliver a World-Class Workplace Relations Service.* Dublin: Department of Jobs, Enterprise and Innovation.

Department of Labour (1986a) *Outline of Principal Proposals of Proposed New Trade Dispute and Industrial Relations Legislation.* Dublin: Department of Labour.

Department of Labour (1986b) *Perception of the Effect of Labour Legislation.* Dublin: Government Publications Office.

Department of Labour (1986c), *Report of the Advisory Committee on Worker Participation.* Dublin: Stationery Office.

Department of Labour (1991) A speech by the Minister for Labour prepared for the seminar on the Industrial Relations Act 1990, organised by the Irish Society for Labour Law. Dublin: 13 July.

Department of Public Expenditure and Reform (2010) *The Public Service Agreement 2012–2014 (Croke Park Agreement).* <http://per.gov.ie/wp-content/uploads/Public-Service-Agreement-2010-2014-Final-for-print-June-2010.pdf>

Department of the Taoiseach (1997) *Partnership 2000.* Dublin: Stationery Office.

Department of the Taoiseach (2000) *Programme for Prosperity and Fairness.* Dublin: Stationery Office.

Department of the Taoiseach (2003) *Sustaining Progress.* Dublin: Stationery Office.

Dibben, P., Klerck, G. and Wood, G. (2011) *Employment Relations: A Critical and International Approach.* London: Chartered Institute of Personnel and Development.

Dobbins, A. and Gunnigle, P. (2009) 'Can Voluntary Workplace Partnership Deliver Sustainable Mutual Gains?', *British Journal of Industrial Relations*, 47(3), 546–70.

Dobbins, T. (2003) 'SIPTU Targets "Low Hanging Fruit" in €700,000 Recruitment Drive', *Industrial Relations News,* 33, 4 September, 17–19.

Dobbins, T. (2004) 'Union Organising Drive in Security Sector Pay Some Dividends', *Industrial Relations News*, 10, 4 March, 13–14.

Dobbins, T. (2007) 'Apathy Reigns on Information and Consultation, Despite Minister's Move', *Industrial Relations Journal,* 12, 29 March, 3–4.

Dobbins, T. (2008) *Workplace Partnership in Practice: Securing Sustainable Mutual Gains at Waterford Glass and Aughinish Alumina?* Dublin: Liffey Press.

Dobbins, T. (2009) *The Impact of the Information and Consultation Directive on Industrial Relations — Ireland.* European Industrial Relations Observatory Online. <http://www.eurofound.europa.eu/eiro/studies/tn0710029s/ie0710029q.htm>

Dobbins, T. (2010) 'The Case for Beneficial Constraints: Why Permissive Voluntarism Impedes Workplace Cooperation in Ireland', *Economic and Industrial Democracy*, 31(4), 497–519.

Dobbins, T. (2011) *Final Questionnaire for EIRO CAR on 'The Effect of the Information and Consultation Directive on Industrial Relations in the EU Member States Five Years After Its Transposition – Ireland'.* European Industrial Relations Observatory Online. <http://www.eurofound.europa.eu/eiro/studies/tn1009029s/ie1009029q.htm>

Dobbins, T. and Dundon, T. (2011) 'Workplace Partnership and the Future Trajectory of Employment Relations within Liberal Market Economies', in K. Townsend and A. Wilkinson (eds.) *The Future of Employment Relations: New Paradigms, New Approaches.* London: Palgrave Macmillan.

Docherty, M. (2009) 'Representation, Bargaining and the Law: Where Next for the Unions', *Northern Ireland Legal Quarterly*, 60(4), 383–402.

Doherty, G.M. and O'Riordan, T.A. 'Dublin 1913 – Strike and Lockout'. Multitext Project in Irish History. Dublin: UCD. <http://multitext.ucc.ie/d/Dublin_1913Strike_and_Lockout>

Doherty, L. and Teague, P. (2011) 'Building Better Employment Relations: Conflict Management Systems in Subsidiaries of Non-Union Multinational Organisations Located in the Republic of Ireland'. Labour Relations Commission Symposium. Dublin, 23 February.

Donaghey, J., Cullinane, N., Dundon, T. and Wilkinson, A. (2011) 'Re-Conceptualising Employee Silence: Problems and Prognosis' *Work, Employment and Society*, 25(1), 51–67.

Donovan, Lord (1968) *Report on the Royal Commission on Trade Unions and Employers' Associations 1965–1968.* London: HMSO.

Drucker, P.F. (1950) *The New Society: The Anatomy of the Industrial Order*. New York: Harper & Bros.

Dubin, R., Kornhauser, A. and Ross, A.M. (eds.) (1954) *Industrial Conflict*. New York: McGraw-Hill.

Duffy, K. (1993) 'Industrial Relations Act 1990 – the Trade Union Experience', *Irish Industrial Relations Review*, January.

Duffy, K. (2010) 'The View of the Labour Court', in A. Kerr (ed.) *The Industrial Relations Act 1990: Twenty Years On*. Dublin: Round Hall.

Duffy, K. and Walsh, F. (2011) *Report of Independent Review of Employment Regulation Orders and Registered Employment Agreement Wage Setting Mechanisms*. Dublin: Department for Jobs, Enterprise and Innovation.

Duncan, R. (1979) 'What Is the Right Organisation Structure? Decision Tree Analysis Provides the Answer', *Organisational Dynamics*, Winter, 429–31.

Dundon, T. (2002) 'Employer Hostility and Union Avoidance in the UK', *Industrial Relations Journal*, 33(3), 234–45.

Dundon, T., Curran, D., Maloney, M. and Ryan, P. (2008) 'The Transposition of the European Employee Information and Consultation Directive Regulations in the Republic of Ireland'. Working Series Research Paper No. 26. Centre for Innovation and Structural Change, National University of Ireland, Galway.

Dunlop, J. (1958) *Industrial Relations Systems*. Carbondale, IL: Southern Illinois University Press.

Dunlop, J.T. (1993) *Industrial Relations Systems: Revised Edition*. Boston, MA: Harvard Business School Press.

Ebbinghaus, B. and Visser, J. (1999) 'When Institutions Matter: Union Growth and Decline in Western Europe, 1950–1995', *European Sociological Review*, 15(2), 135–58.

Edwards, P.K. (1977) 'A Critique of Kerr–Siegel Hypothesis of Strikes and the Isolated Mass: A Study of the Falsification of Sociological Knowledge', *The Sociological Review*, 25(3), 551–74.

Edwards, P.K. (1986) *Conflict at Work: A Materialist Analysis of Workplace Relations*. Oxford: Blackwell.

Edwards, P.K. (1992) 'Industrial Conflict: Themes and Issues in Recent Research', *British Journal of Industrial Relations*, 30(3), 361–404.

Edwards, P.K. (2003) 'The Employment Relationship and the Field of Industrial Relations', in P. Edwards (ed.) *Industrial Relations: Theory and Practice* (2nd edn.). Oxford: Blackwell.

Edwards, P.K. (2005) 'Discipline and Attendance: a Murky Aspect of People Management', in S. Bach (ed.) *Managing Human Resources: Personnel Management in Transition*. Oxford: Basil Blackwell.

Einarsen, S. and Skogstad, A. (1996) 'Bullying at Work: Epidemiological Findings in Public and Private Organizations', *European Journal of Work and Organizational Psychology*, 5, 185–202.

Employment Appeals Tribunal (EAT) (1985–2011) *Annual Reports* (various). Dublin: Employment Appeals Tribunal/Stationery Office.

Employment Status Group (2000) *Report of the Employment Status Group*. Dublin: Department of Enterprise, Trade and Employment.

Equality Authority (2002) *Code of Practice on Sexual Harassment and Harassment at Work*. Dublin: Equality Authority.

Equality Tribunal (2011) *Mediation Review 2010*. Dublin: Equality Tribunal.

Equality Tribunal (2000–2011) *Annual Reports* (various years). Dublin: Equality Tribunal.

European Industrial Relations Intelligence (EIRI) Associates (2004) 'Employee Involvement in a "European company"', *EIRI European Review*, March/April, 14–5.

Ewing, K.D. (2012) 'The Draft Monti II Regulation: An Inadequate Response to Viking and Laval', *The Institute of Employment Rights*, 1–16. <http://www.ier.org.uk/sites/ier.org.uk/files/The%20Draft%20Monti%2011%20Regulatioin%20by%20Keith%20Ewing%20March%202012.pdf>

Farnham, D. and Pimlott, J. (1990) *Understanding Industrial Relations*. London: Cassell.

Farrelly, R. (2010a) 'Dispute Over Compulsory Redundancies at Blarney Woollen Mills', *Industrial Relations News*, 2, 14 January, 16.

Farrelly, R. (2010b) 'Local Authority Waste Collection Outsourcing Issues Resolved', *Industrial Relations News*, 30, 26 August, 10–11.

Farrelly, R. (2011a) 'Campaign Against Student Nurse Cuts', *Industrial Relations News*, 5, 2 February, 16.

Farrelly, R. (2011b) 'Stud Farm Owners are Latest to Launch JLC Challenge', *Industrial Relations News*, 19, 12 May, 19.

Farrelly, R. (2011e) 'Davenport Hotel Told to Reinstate Workers on Contracted Pay Rates', *Industrial Relations News*, 10, 9 March, 9–10.

Fenley, A. (1998) 'Models, Styles and Metaphors: Understanding the Management of Discipline', *Employee Relations*, 20(4), 349–64.

Fennell, C. and Lynch, I. (1993) *Labour Law in Ireland*. Dublin: Gill & Macmillan.

Ferner, A. and Hyman, R. (1998) *Changing Industrial Relations in Europe* (2nd edn.). Oxford: Blackwell.

Fine, J. (2007) 'A Marriage Made in Heaven? Mismatches and Misunderstandings Between Worker Centres and Unions', *British Journal of Industrial Relations*, 45(2), 335–60.

Fisher, R. and Ury, W. (1986) *Getting to Yes*. London: Hutchinson.

Fisher, R., Ury, W. and Patton, B. (1997) *Getting to Yes: Negotiating Agreement without Giving In* (2nd edn.). London: Arrow Books.

Fitzgerald, K. (2006) 'Business Leaders Back Social Partnership, Few Plan to Relocate', *Industrial Relations News*, 12, January, 27.

Fitzpatrick, P.J. (2012) 'Reflections on the Croke Park Deal'. Lecture prepared for the Countess Markievicz Memorial Lecture Series. Irish Association for Industrial Relations: 29 November. <http://www2.ul.ie/pdf/742954018.pdf>

Flanders, A. (1956) 'Collective Bargaining', in A. Flanders and H.A. Clegg (eds.) *The System of Industrial Relations in Great Britain*. Oxford: Basil Blackwell.

Flanders, A. (1965) *Industrial Relations – What's Wrong with the System?* London: Faber & Faber.

Flanders, A. (1968) 'Collective Bargaining: A Theoretical Analysis', *British Journal of Industrial Relations*, 6(1), 1–26.

Flavin, P., Pacek, A. and Radcliff, B. (2010) 'Labor Unions and Life Satisfaction: Evidence from New Data', *Social Indicator Research*, 98(3), 435–49.

Flood, P.C. and Toner, B. (1997) 'How Do Large Non-Union Companies Avoid a Catch 22?', *British Journal of Industrial Relations*, 35(2), 257–77.

Fogarty, M.P., Egan, D. and Ryan, W.J.L. (1981) *Pay Policy for the 1980s*. Dublin: FUE.

Fombrun, C. (1986) 'Environmental Trends Create New Pressures on Human Resources', in S.L. Rynes and G.T. Milkovich (eds.) *Current Issues in Human Resource Management: Commentary and Readings*. Plano, TX: Business Publications Inc.

Forde, M. (1991) *Industrial Relations Law*. Dublin: Round Hall Press.

Forfás (2011) *Forfás Annual Employment Survey 2010*. Dublin: Forfás.

Fox, A. (1966) 'Industrial Sociology and Industrial Relations'. Research Paper No. 3 to the Royal Commission on Trade Unions and Employers' Associations. London: HMSO.

Fox, A. (1973) 'Industrial Relations: A Social Critique of Pluralist Ideology', in J. Child (ed.) *Man and Organisation*. London: Allen & Unwin.

Fox, A. (1974) *Beyond Contract: Work, Power and Trust Relations*. London: Faber & Faber.

Fox, A. (1975) 'Collective Bargaining, Flanders and the Webbs', *British Journal of Industrial Relations*, 13(2), 151–74.

Fox, A. (1977) 'The Myth of Pluralism and a Radical Alternative', in T. Clarke and L. Clements (eds.) *Trade Unions under Capitalism*. London: Faber & Faber.

Franzosi, R. (1989) 'Strike Data in Search of a Theory: The Italian Case in the Post-War Period', *Politics and Society*, 17, 453–87.

Frawley, M. (2002) 'Technology Teachers Latest Group to Switch to LRC, Labour Court', *Industrial Relations News*, 24, 14–5.

Freeman, R.B. (2007) 'What Do Unions Do? The 2004 M-Brane Stringtwister Edition', in J.T. Bennett and B.E. Kaufman (eds.) *What Do Unions Do? A Twenty-Year Perspective*. New Brunswick, NJ: Transaction.

Freeman, R. and Rogers, J. (1999) *What Workers Want*. Ithaca: Cornell University Press and the Russell Sage Foundation.

Fuerstenberg, F. (1987) 'The Federal Republic of Germany', in G.J. Bamber and R.D. Lansbury (eds.) *International and Comparative Industrial Relations: A Study of Developed Market Economies*. London: Allen & Unwin.

Gall, G. (1999) 'A Review of Strike Activity at the End of the Second Millennium', *Employee Relations*, 23(4), 357–77.

Garavan, T. (2002) *The Irish Health and Safety Handbook* (2nd edn.). Dublin: Oak Tree Press.

Gardner, M. and Palmer, G. (1992) *Employment Relations: Industrial Relations and Human Resource Management in Australia*. Sydney: Macmillan.

Geary, J. (1994) 'Task Participation: Employee's Participation – Enabled or Constrained', in K. Sisson (ed.) *Personnel Management: A Comprehensive Guide to Theory and Practice in Britain*. Oxford: Blackwell.

Geary, J. (1996) 'Working at Restructuring Work in Europe: The Case of Team-working', *Irish Business and Administrative Research*, 17, 44–57.

Geary, J. (1998) 'New Work Structures and the Diffusion of Team Working Arrangements in Ireland'. Paper presented at the 6th John Lovett Memorial Lecture Series. University of Limerick, 2 April.

Geary, J. (1999) 'The New Workplace: Change at Work in Ireland', *International Journal of Human Resource Management*, 10(5), 870–90.

Geary, J. (2008) 'Do Unions Benefit from Working in Partnership with Employers? Evidence from Ireland', *Industrial Relations: A Journal of Economy and Society*, 47(4), 530–68.

Geary, J. and Roche, W.K. (2001) 'Multinationals and Human Resource Practices in Ireland: A Rejection of the "New Conformance Thesis"', *International Journal of Human Resource Management*, 12(1), 109–27.

Geary, J. and Trif, A. (2011) 'Workplace Partnership and the Balance of Advantage: A Critical Case Analysis', *British Journal of Industrial Relations*, 49(1), 44–69.

Gennard, J. and Judge, G. (2010) *Managing Employment Relations*. London: Chartered Institute of Personnel and Development.

Geoghegan, B. (1996) 'IBEC Expert Defends PCW', *Sunday Business Post*, 30 August.

Gernigon, B., Odero, A. and Guido, H. (2000) 'Principles Concerning Collective Bargaining, *International Labour Review,* 139(1), 33–55.

Gilbraith, J. and Nathanson, D. (1978) *Strategy Implementation: The Role of Structure*. St Paul, MN: West Publishing.

Golden, M., Wallerstein, M. and Lange, P. (1999) 'Postwar Trade-Union Organisation and Industrial Relations in Twelve Countries', in H. Kitschelt, P. Lange, G. Marks and J. Stephens (eds.) *Continuity and Change in Contemporary Capitalism*. Cambridge: Cambridge University Press.

Goetschy, J. (2000) 'The European Union and National Social Pacts: Employment and Social Protection Put to the Test of Joint Regulation', in G. Fajertag and P. Pochet (eds.) *Social Pacts in Europe – New Dynamics*. Brussels: European Trade Union Institute.

Goldthorpe, J. (1974) 'Industrial Relations in Great Britain: A Critique of Reformism', *Politics and Society*, 4(4), 419–52.

Gouldner, A.W. (1954) *Wildcat Strike*. New York: Harper.

Green, F. (1990) 'Trade Union Availability and Trade Union Membership in Britain', *The Manchester School*, 58(4), 378–94.

Green, G. (1991) *Industrial Relations*. London: Pitman.

Griffin, J.I. (1939) *Strikes: A Study in Quantitative Economics*. New York: Colombia University Press.

Grint, K. (1991) *The Sociology of Work: An Introduction*. Oxford: Polity Press.

Grote, J., Lang, A. and Traxler, F. (2007) 'Germany', in F. Traxler and G. Huemer (eds.) *Handbook of Business Interest Associations, Firm Size and Governance*. London/New York: Routledge.

Guest, D. (1987) 'Human Resource Management and Industrial Relations', *Journal of Management Studies*, 24(5), 503–21.

Gunnigle, P. (1995a) 'Collectivism and the Management of Industrial Relations in Greenfield Sites', *Human Resource Management Journal*, 4, 24–40.

Gunnigle, P. (1995b) 'Management Styles in Employee Relations in Greenfield Sites: Challenging a Collectivist Tradition'. Unpublished PhD thesis, Cranfield School of Management.

Gunnigle, P. (1998a) 'Human Resource Management and the Personnel Function', in W.K. Roche, K. Monks and J. Walsh (eds.) *Human Resource Management Strategies: Policy and Practice in Ireland*. Dublin: Oak Tree Press.

Gunnigle, P. (1998b) 'More Rhetoric than Reality: Industrial Relations Partnerships in Ireland', *Economic and Social Review*, 28(4), 179–200.

Gunnigle, P. and Brady, T. (1984) 'The Management of Industrial Relations in the Small Firm', *Employee Relations*, 6(5), 21–4.

Gunnigle, P. and Flood, P. (1990) *Personnel Management in Ireland: Practice, Trends and Developments*. Dublin: Gill & Macmillan.

Gunnigle, P. and McGuire, D. (2001) 'Why Ireland? A Qualitative Review of the Factors Influencing the Location of US Multinationals in Ireland with Particular Reference to the Impact of Labour Issues', *The Economic and Social Review*, 32(1), 43–67.

Gunnigle, P. and Roche, W.K. (1995) *New Challenges to Irish Industrial Relations*. Dublin: Oak Tree Press.

Gunnigle, P., Foley, K. and Morley, M. (1994) 'A Review of Organisational Reward Practices', in P. Gunnigle, P. Flood, M. Morley and T. Turner (eds.) *Continuity and Change in Irish Employee Relations*. Dublin: Oak Tree Press.

Gunnigle, P., Heraty, N. and Morley, M. (2002) *Human Resource Management in Ireland*. Dublin: Gill & Macmillan.

Gunnigle, P., Heraty, N. and Morley, M. (2011) *Human Resource Management in Ireland* (4th edn.). Dublin: Gill & Macmillan.

Gunnigle, P., Lavelle, J. and McDonnell, A. (2009) 'Subtle but Deadly? Union Avoidance through "Double Breasting" among Multinational Companies', *Advances in Industrial and Labor Relations*, 16, 51–74.

Gunnigle, P., Lavelle, J. and Monaghan, S. (2013) 'weathering the Storm? Multinational Companies and Human Resource Management through the Global Financial Crisis', *International Journal of Manpower*, 34(3), forthcoming.

Gunnigle, P., MacCurtain, S. and Morley, M. (2001) 'Dismantling Pluralism: Industrial Relations in Irish Greenfield Sites', *Personnel Review*, 30(3), 263–79.

Gunnigle, P., Morley, M. and Turner, T. (1997) 'Challenging Collectivist Traditions: Individualism and the Management of Industrial Relations in Greenfield Sites', *Economic and Social Review*, (28)2, 105–34.

Gunnigle, P., O'Sullivan, M. and Kinsella, M. (2002) 'Organised Labour in the New Economy: Trade Unions and Public Policy in the Republic of Ireland', in D. D'Art and T. Turner (eds.) *Irish Employment Relations in the New Economy*. Dublin: Blackhall Publishing.

Guthrie, J., Flood, P.C., Liu, W. and MacCurtain, S. (2009) 'High Performance Work Systems in Ireland: Human Resource and Organisational Outcomes', *International Journal of Human Resource Management*, 20(1), 112–25.

Guthrie, J., Flood, P.C., Liu, W., MacCurtain, S. and Armstrong, C.A. (2011) 'Big Hat, No Cattle? High Performance Work Systems and Executives' Perceptions of HR Capability', *International Journal of Human Resource Management*, 22(8), 1,470–4,684.

Handy, L.J. (1968) 'Absenteeism and Attendance in the British Coal Mining Industry', *British Journal of Industrial Relations*, 6(1), 27–50.

Hann, D. and Teague, P. (2008) *The Role of the Rights Commissioners in the Irish Employment System: Solving Problems and Vindicating Rights*. Dublin: Labour Relations Commission.

Hardiman, N. (1988) *Pay, Politics and Economic Performance in Ireland 1970–1987*. Oxford: Clarendon.

Hardiman, N. (2000) 'Social Partnership, Wage Bargaining, and Growth', in B. Nolan, J. O'Connell and C. Whelan (eds.) *Bust to Boom? The Irish Experience of Growth and Inequality*. Dublin: Institute of Public Administration.

Hardiman, N. (2006) 'Political and Social Partnership: Flexible Network Governance', *Economic and Social Review*, 37(3), 343–74.

Hastings, T. (2003) *Politics, Management and Industrial Relations: Semi-State Companies and the Challenges of Marketization*. Dublin: Blackhall Publishing.

Haynes, P., Vowles, J. and Boxall, P. (2005) 'Explaining the Younger–Older Worker Union Density Gap: Evidence from New Zealand', *British Journal of Industrial Relations*, 43(1), 93–116.

Hawkins, K. (1979) *A Handbook of Industrial Relations Practice*. London: Kogan Page.

Hawkins, K. (1982) *Case Studies in Industrial Relations*. London: Kogan Page.

Hebdon, R.P. and Stern, R.N. (1998) 'Trade-Offs Among Expressions of Industrial Conflict: Public Sector Strike Bans and Arbitrations', *Industrial and Labour Relations Review*, 51(2), 204–21.

Heery, E. (2010) 'Debating Employment Law: Responses to Juridification', in P. Blyton, E. Heery and P. Turnbull (eds.) *Reassessing the Employment Relationship*. Basingstoke: Palgrave Macmillan.

Heery, E., Simms, M., Simpson, D., Delbridge, R. and Salmon, J. (2000) 'Organising Unionism Comes to the UK', *Employee Relations*, 22(1), 38–57.

Heery, E., Williams, S. and Abbott, B. (2012) 'Civil Society Organisations and Trade Unions: Co-operation, Conflict, Indifference', *Work, Employment & Society*, 26(1), 145–60.

Heffernan, M., Harney, B., Cafferkey, K. and Dundon, T. (2008) *People Management & Innovation in Ireland*. Working Series, Research Paper No. 27. Centre for Innovation and Structural Change, National University of Ireland, Galway.

Hepple, B. (2002) 'Introduction', in B. Hepple (ed.) *Social and Labour Rights in a Global Context: International and Comparative Perspectives*. Cambridge: Cambridge University Press.

Hepple, B. (2010) 'Rethinking Laws Against Strikes'. Lecture prepared for the 34th Countess Markievicz Lecture of the Irish Association for Industrial Relations. University College Dublin: 11 October.

Heraty, N., Morley, M. and Turner, T. (1994) 'Trends and Developments in the Organisation of the Employment Relationship', in P. Gunnigle *et al.* (eds.) *Continuity and Change in Irish Employee Relations*. Dublin: Oak Tree Press.

Herzberg, F. (1968) *Work and the Nature of Man*. London: Staples Press.

Higgins, C. (2000a) 'European Company Statute – Worker Participation Logjam Resolved', *Industrial Relations News,* 47, 13 December, 16.

Higgins, C. (2000b) 'Train Drivers' Group Not Entitled to Recognition, Says High Court', *Industrial Relations News*, 16, 20 April, 22–3.

Higgins, C. (2001) 'European Company Statute – Details on Worker Participation Agreed', *Industrial Relations News,* 3, 17 January, 13.

Higgins, C. (2009a) 'SIPTU's New Sectoral Structure to Take Shape in 2010', *Industrial Relations News*, 37, 15 October, 21–30.

Higgins, C. (2009b) 'Dell–Consultation Ruling Will Be Watched by Non-union Sector', *Industrial Relations News*, 42, 18 November, 17.

Higgins, C. (2010a) 'Electrical Contactors' REA Challenge Dismissed as "Out of Time"', *Industrial Relations News,* 26, 8 July, 29–30.

Higgins, C. (2010b) 'Electrical REA Review Goes Ahead Without AECI', *Industrial Relations News*, 44, 2 December, 9–10.

Higgins, C. (2010c) 'Employers Concerned over "Inability to Pay" for Individual Companies', *Industrial Relations News*, 8, 25 February, 3–4.

Higgins, C. (2010d) 'Construction Sector's Response to Proposed 7.5% Pay Cut Crucial', *Industrial Relations News*, 26, 7 July, 20–2.

Higgins, C. (2010e) 'Croke Park Deal "Over the Line" Unions Call for Swift Implementation', *Industrial Relations News*, 23, 16 June, 9.

Higgins, C. (2011a) 'Construction Employers Expected to Seek Further Pay Cut', *Industrial Relations News*, 46, 15 December, 5–6.

Higgins, C. (2011b) 'JLC Reforms Set for End September, as Five Legal Cases Loom', *Industrial Relations News*, 17, 4 May, 10–11.

Higgins, C. (2011c) 'US Chamber Warns on Collective Bargaining, Agency Working', *Industrial Relations News*, 26, 7 July, 8–9.

Higgins, C. (2012a) 'Construction Employers' Pay Cut Claim Heard in Labour Court', *Industrial Relations News*, 36, 4 October, 10–11.

Higgins, C. (2012b) 'Major Electrical Firms Agree 6–10% Pay Cut for REA', *Industrial Relations News*, 11, 15 March, 4–5.

Higgins, C. (2012c) 'Security REA Proposal Cuts Premium Payments, Rounds Up Pay Rate', *Industrial Relations News*, 32, 6 September, 4–6.

Higgins, C. (2012d) 'Supreme Court Priority Sought By Electrical Contractors for REA Appeal', *Industrial Relations News*, 3, 18 January, 9.

Hillery, B. (1994) 'The Institutions of Industrial Relations', in T.V. Murphy and W.K. Roche (eds.) *Irish Industrial Relations in Practice*. Dublin: Oak Tree Press.

Hiltrop, J.M. and Udall, S. (1995) *The Essence of Negotiation*. London: Prentice Hall.

Hoffer, E. (2002) *The True Believer: Thoughts on the Nature of Mass Movements*. US: Harper Perennial Modern Classics.

Horgan, J. (1989) 'The Future of Collective Bargaining', in Department of Industrial Relations, UCD (eds.) *Industrial Relations in Ireland: Contemporary Issues and Developments*. Dublin: University College Dublin.

Howell, C. (2005) *Trade Unions and the State*. Princeton, NJ: Princeton University Press.

Huczynski, A.A. and Buchanan, D.A. (1991) *Organizational Behaviour: An Introductory Text*. London: Prentice Hall.

Hug, A. and Tudor, O. (2012) 'Single Market, Equal Rights? UK Perspectives on EU Employment and Social Law'. UK: The Foreign Policy Centre. <http://fpc.org.uk/publications/singlemarketequalrights>

Huselid, M.A. (1995) 'The Impact of Human Resource Management Practices on Turnover, Productivity and Corporate Financial Performance', *Academy of Management Journal*, 38(3), 635–72.

Hutchinson, M., Jackson, D., Wilkes, L. and Vickers, M.H. (2008) 'A New Model of Bullying in the Nursing Workplace: Organizational Characteristics as Critical Antecedents', *Advances in Nursing Science*, 31(2), 60–71.

Hutchinson, S. and Purcell, J. (2003) *Bringing Policies to Life: The Vital Role of Line Managers in People Management*. London: Chartered Institute of Personnel and Development.

Hyman, R. (1975) *Industrial Relations: A Marxist Introduction*. London: Macmillan.

Hyman, R. (1989) *Strikes*. London: Macmillan.

Hyman, R. and Mason, B. (1995) *Managing Employee Involvement and Participation*. London: Sage.

ICTU (2010) 'Analysis of OP/Ed Coverage in the Irish Newspapers'. Dublin: ICTU (unpublished).

Incomes Data Service (IDS) (1992) *Pay and Benefits*. London: IPM.

Incomes Data Service (IDS)/Institute of Personnel and Development (IPD) (1996) *European Management Guides: Industrial Relations and Collective Bargaining*. London: Institute of Personnel and Development.

Industrial Relations News (2004) 'New Labour Court Chair Would Like Major Overhaul of Employment Law', *Industrial Relations News*, 5, 29 January, 21–3.

Industrial Relations News (2006) 'Irish Multinationals Have 14% European Works Council Compliance Rate', *Industrial Relations News*, 37, 4 October.

Industrial Relations News (2010) 'Partnership – How It Looks After the Fall', *Industrial Relations News*, 45, 9 December, 19–21.

Industrial Relations News (2012) 'Vita Cortex Update: Workers Vote to Endorse Resolution Proposals', 17, 3 May, online version of *IRN*.

International Labour Office (ILO) (1960) *Collective Bargaining: A Workers' Manual*. Geneva: ILO.

International Labour Office (ILO) (1973) *Collective Bargaining in Industrial Market Economies*. Geneva: ILO.

International Labour Office (ILO) (1975) *Collective Bargaining in Industrialised Market Economies*. Geneva: ILO.

International Labour Office (ILO) (2012) *Reports of the Committee on Freedom of Association: 363rd Report of the Committee on Freedom of Association*. Geneva: ILO.

Ireland (1990) *Dáil Éireann Parliamentary Debates Official Report*, 396. Dublin: Stationery Office.

Irish Small and Medium Enterprises Association (ISME) (2009) Address by ISME Chairperson Eilis Quinlan at the Association's Annual Conference: 13 November. <www.isme.ie>

Jackson, M.P. (1982) *Industrial Relations: A Textbook*. London: Kogan Page.

Jackson, M.P. (1987) *Strikes: Industrial Conflict in Britain, USA and Australia*. London: Wheatsheaf.

Jackson, M.P. (1991) *An Introduction to Industrial Relations*. London: Routledge.

Jacoby, S.M. (1997) *Modern Manors: Welfare Capitalism since the New Deal*. New Jersey: Princeton University Press.

Jones, P. and Saundry, R. (2011) 'The Practice of Discipline: Evaluating the Roles and Relationship between Managers and HR Professionals', *Human Resource Management Journal*, 22(3), 252–66.

Kahn-Freund, O. (1977) *Labour and the Law*. London: Stevens.

Kavanagh, R. (1987) *Labour from the Beginning – 75 Years*. Dublin: The Labour Party.

Kelleher, O. (2003) 'E-mails a Potential Source of Libels', *The Sunday Business Post*, 21 September.

Keller, B. (2002) 'The European Company Statute: Employee Involvement – and Beyond', *Industrial Relations Journal*, 33(5), 424–45.

Kelly, A. (1975) 'Changes in the Occupational Structure and Industrial Relations in Ireland', *Management*, 22(6/7), 33–7.

Kelly, A. (1989a) 'The Rights Commissioner: Conciliator, Mediator or Arbitrator', in Department of Industrial Relations, UCD (eds.) *Industrial Relations in Ireland: Contemporary Issues and Developments*. Dublin: University College Dublin.

Kelly, A. (1989b) 'The Worker Director in Irish Industrial Relations', in Department of Industrial Relations, UCD (eds.) *Industrial Relations in Ireland: Contemporary Issues and Developments*. Dublin: University College Dublin.

Kelly, A. and Brannick, T. (1983) 'The Pattern of Strike Activity in Ireland, 1960–1979', *Irish Business and Administrative Research*, 5(1), 65–77.

Kelly, A. and Brannick, T. (1988) 'Explaining the Strike Proneness of British Companies in Ireland', *British Journal of Industrial Relations*, 26(1), 37–57.

Kelly, A. and Brannick, T. (1989) 'Strikes in Ireland: Measurement, Indices and Trends', in Department of Industrial Relations, UCD (eds.) *Industrial Relations in Ireland: Contemporary Issues and Developments*. Dublin: University College Dublin.

Kelly, A. and Hourihan, F. (1997) 'Employee Participation', in T.V. Murphy and W.K. Roche (eds.) *Irish Industrial Relations in Practice: Revised and Expanded Edition*. Dublin: Oak Tree Press.

Kelly, A. and Roche, W.K. (1983) 'Institutional Reform in Irish Industrial Relations', *Studies: An Irish Quarterly Review*, 72(287), 221–30.

Kelly, D. (2006) 'Workplace Bullying – a Complex Issue Needing IR/HRM Research?', in B. Pocock, C. Provis and E. Willis (eds.) 'Twenty-first Century Work: Proceedings of the 20th Conference of the Association of Industrial Relations Academics of Australia and New Zealand'. University of South Australia: February.

Kelly, J. (1998) *Rethinking Industrial Relations: Mobilization, Collectivism and Long Waves*. London: Routledge.

Kelly, J. (2003) 'Labour Movement Revitalization? A Comparative Perspective'. Lecture prepared for the Countess Markievicz Memorial Lecture Series. Dublin: 7 April.

Kelly, J. and Hamann, K. (2010) 'General Strikes in Western Europe: 1980–2008'. Paper presented at the Political Studies Association Annual Conference. Manchester: 7–9 April.

Kennedy, G. (1998) *The New Negotiating Edge: A Behavioural Approach for Results and Relationships*. London: Nicholas Brearly.

Kerr, A. (1989) 'Trade Unions and the Law', in Department of Industrial Relations, UCD (eds.) *Industrial Relations in Ireland: Contemporary Issues and Developments*. Dublin: University College Dublin.

Kerr, A. (1991) *The Trade Union and Industrial Relations Acts of Ireland*. London: Sweet & Maxwell.

Kerr, A. (1992) 'Why Public Sector Workers Join Unions: An Attitude Survey of Workers in the Health Service and Local Government', *Employee Relations*, 14(2), 39–54.

Kerr, A. (2010) 'The Involvement of the Courts', in A. Kerr (ed.) *The Industrial Relations Act Twenty Years On*. Dublin: Round Hall.

Kerr, C. and Siegel, A. (1954) 'The Interindustry Propensity to Strike – an International Comparison', in A. Kornhauser, R. Dubin and A.M. Ross (eds.) *Industrial Conflict*. New York: McGraw-Hill.

Kerr, A. and Whyte, G. (1985) *Irish Trade Union Law*. Abingdon: Professional Books.

Kerr, C., Harbinson, F. and Myers, H. (1962) *Industrialism and Industrial Man*. London: Heineman.

Kidner, R. (1982) 'Lessons in Trade Union Reform: The Origins and Passage of the Trade Disputes Act 1906', *Legal Studies*, 2(1), 34–52.

Klein, J. (1989) 'The Human Cost of Manufacturing Reform', *Harvard Business Review*, March/April.

Kochan, T.A. and Osterman, P. (1994) *The Mutual Gains Enterprise*. Cambridge, MA: Harvard Business School Press.

Kochan, T.A. and Rubenstein, S. (2000) 'Towards a Stakeholder View of the Firm: The Saturn Partnership', *Organization Science*, 11(4), 367–86.

Kochan, T.A., Katz, H.C. and McKersie, R.B. (1986) *The Transformation of American Industrial Relations*. New York: Basic Books.

Korpi, W. (1983) *The Democratic Class Struggle*. London: Routledge & Kegan Paul.

Koukiadaki, A. and Kretsos, L. (2012) 'Opening Pandora's Box: The Sovereign Debt Crisis and Labour Market Regulation in Greece', *Industrial Law Journal,* 41(3), 276–304.

Labour Court (1948–2011) *Annual Reports* (various). Dublin: Stationery Office.

Labour Relations Commission (1992–2011) *Annual Reports* (various). Dublin: Stationery Office.

Labour Relations Commission (2006) *Procedures for Addressing Bullying in the Workplace: Code of Practice No.6.* Dublin: Labour Relations Commission.

Larkin, E. (1965) *James Larkin: 1876–1947 – Irish Labour Leader.* London: Routledge.

Larragy, J. (2010) 'Asymmetric Engagement: The Community and Voluntary Pillar in Irish Social Partnership: A Case Study'. Unpublished PhD thesis, University College Dublin Library.

Lavelle, J. (2008) 'Charting the Contours of Union Recognition in Foreign-Owned MNCs: Survey Evidence from the Republic of Ireland', *Irish Journal of Management,* 29(1), 45–64.

Lavelle, J., Gunnigle, P. and McDonnell, A. (2010) 'Patterning Employee Voice in Multinational Companies', *Human Relations,* 63(3), 395–418.

Lavelle, J., McDonnell, A. and Gunnigle, P. (2009a), 'Employee Representation and Consultation', in J. Lavelle, A. McDonnell and P. Gunnigle (eds.) *Human Resource Practices in Multinational Companies in Ireland: A Contemporary Analysis.* Dublin: Stationery Office.

Lavelle, J., McDonnell, A. and Gunnigle, P. (2009b) *Human Resource Practices in Multinational Companies in Ireland: A Contemporary Analysis.* Dublin: Government of Ireland.

Law Reform Commission (2010) *Report: Alternative Dispute Resolution: Mediation and Conciliation.* Dublin: Law Reform Commission.

Lawler, E. (1978) 'The New Plant Revolution', *Organizational Dynamics,* Winter, 3–12.

Lawler, E. (1982) 'Increasing Worker Involvement to Enhance Organisational Effectiveness', in P.S. Goodman (ed.) *Change in Organisations.* San Francisco: Jossey-Bass.

Lee, J. (1980) 'Worker and Society since 1945', in D. Nevin (ed.) *Trade Unions and Change in Irish Society.* Dublin: Mercier Press/RTÉ.

Lewicki, R.J., Barry, B. and Saunders, D.M. (2010) *Negotiation.* Boston: McGraw-Hill/Irwin.

Lewicki, R.J., Saunders, D.M. and Minton, J.W. (1999) *Negotiation* (3rd edn.). Boston: McGraw-Hill.

Lewicki, R.J., Saunders, D.M. and Minton, J.W. (2001) *Essentials of Negotiation*. Boston: McGraw-Hill.

Liu, W., Guthrie, J., Flood, P.C. and MacCurtain, S. (2009) 'Unions and High Performance Work Systems: Does Job Security Play a Role?', *Industrial and Labor Relations Review*, 69(1), 108–26.

Logan, J. (1999) *Teachers' Union: The TUI and Its Forerunners 1899–1994*. Dublin: A. & A. Farmar.

Macey, W.H. and Schneider, B. (2008) 'The Meaning of Employee Engagement', *Industrial and Organizational Psychology*, 1, 3–30.

MacMahon, J. (2002) 'Owner Managers and Employment Relations in Small Irish Firms'. Unpublished PhD thesis, University of Limerick.

MacMahon, J., MacCurtain, S. and O'Sullivan, M. (2009) 'Bullying in Health Care Organizations', in J. Braithwaite, P. Hyde and P. Pope (eds.) *Culture, Climate and Teams in Health Care Organizations*. UK: Palgrave Macmillan.

MacSharry, R. and White, P. (2000) *The Making of the Celtic Tiger: The Inside Story of Ireland's Boom Economy*. Cork: Mercier Press.

Madden, D. and Kerr, A. (1996) *Unfair Dismissal: Cases and Commentary* (2nd edn.). Dublin: Irish Business and Employers Confederation.

Marchington, M. (1982) *Managing Industrial Relations*. London: McGraw-Hill.

Marchington, M. and Parker, P. (1990) *Changing Patterns of Employee Relations*. Hemel Hempstead: Harvester Wheatsheaf.

Marchington, M. and Wilkinson, A. (2000) 'Direct Participation', in S. Bach and K. Sisson (eds.) *Personnel Management: A Comprehensive Guide to Theory and Practice* (3rd edn.). Oxford: Blackwell.

Marginson, P., Hall, M. and Hoffman, A. (2004) 'The Impact of European Works Councils on Management Decision-Making in the UK and US-based Multinationals', *British Journal of Industrial Relations*, 412(2), 209–33.

Marshall, R. (1992) 'Work Organisation, Unions and Economic Performance', in L. Mishel and P. Voos (eds.) *Unions and Economic Competitiveness*. New York: ME Sharpe Inc.

Maslow, A.H. (1954) *Motivation and Personality*. New York: Harper & Row.

Mayo, E. (1949) *The Social Problems of an Industrial Civilization*. London: Routledge & Kegan Paul.

McCarthy, C. (1973) *The Decade of Upheaval*. Dublin: Institute of Public Administration.

McCarthy, C. (1977) *Trade Unions in Ireland: 1894–1960*. Dublin: Institute of Public Administration.

McCarthy, C. (1982) 'Reform: A Strategy for Research', in H. Pollock (ed.) *Reform of Industrial Relations.* Dublin: O'Brien Press.

McCarthy, C. (1984) *Elements in a Theory of Industrial Relations.* Dublin: Trinity College Dublin.

McCarthy, C. and von Prondzynski, F. (1982) 'The Reform of Industrial Relations', *Administration*, 29(3), 220–59.

McCarthy, W.E.J., O'Brien, J.F. and O'Dowd, V.G. (1975) *Wage Inflation and Wage Leadership.* Paper No. 79. Dublin: Economic and Social Research Institute.

McCartney, J. and Teague, P. (2004) 'The Use of Workplace Innovations in Ireland: A Review of the Evidence', *Personnel Review*, (33)1, 81–109.

McDonough, T. and Dundon, T. (2010) 'Thatcherism Delayed? The Irish Crisis and the Paradox of Social Partnership', *Industrial Relations Journal,* 41(6), 544–62.

McDonough, T., Loughrey, J., Klemm, A., Dunne, F. and Pentony, S. (2009) *Hierarchy of Earnings, Attributes and Privilege, Analysis.* Dublin: TASC, 1–17.

McGinley, M. (1989a) 'Pay in the 1980s – the Issue of Control', *Industrial Relations News*, 30, 17–24.

McGinley, M. (1989b) 'Pay Increases Between 1981–1987', in *Institute of Public Administration: Personnel and Industrial Relations Directory.* Dublin: Institute of Public Administration.

McGinley, M. (1990) 'Trade Union Law – Look Back in Anguish', *Industrial Relations News*, 16, 19–23.

McGinley, M. (1997) 'Industrial Relations in the Public Sector', in T.V. Murphy and W.K. Roche (eds.) *Irish Industrial Relations in Practice.* Dublin: Oak Tree Press.

McGinty, B. (2010) 'The Employers' Perspective', in A. Kerr (ed.) *The Industrial Relations Act Twenty Years On.* Dublin: Round Hall.

McGovern, P. (1989) 'Union Recognition and Union Avoidance in the 1980s', in Department of Industrial Relations, UCD (eds.) *Industrial Relations in Ireland: Contemporary Issues and Developments.* Dublin: University College Dublin.

McGovern, P., Hill, S., Mills, C. and White, M. (2007) *Market, Class and Employment.* Oxford: Oxford University Press.

McKersie, R.B. (1996) 'Labour–Management Partnerships: US Evidence and Implications for Ireland', *Irish Business and Administrative Research*, 17(1), 1–16.

McKersie, R.B. (2002) 'Labour–Management Partnerships: US Evidence and the Implications for Ireland', in P. Gunnigle, M. Morley and M. McDonnell (eds.) *The Lovett Lectures: A Decade of Developments in Human Resource Management.* Dublin: Liffey Press.

McMahon, G. (1990) 'Multinationals: The Labour Relations Experience in Ireland', *Advances in Business Studies*, 2(2), 86–98.

McMahon, G. (1991) 'Statutory Minimum Wage Regulation and Low Pay in the Republic of Ireland'. Unpublished PhD thesis, Trinity College Dublin.

McMahon, G. (2001) *Recruitment and Selection: How to Get It Right*. Dublin: Oak Tree Press.

McMahon, G. (2009a) 'No Place to Hide for Workplace Bullies', *Village Magazine*. <www.villagemagazine.ie>

McMahon, G. (2009b) *Successful Performance Management*. Dublin: Liffey Press.

McMahon, G. (2011) 'Pay Cuts and Redundancies – Through the Legal Minefield', *Industrial Relations News*, 14, 6 May, 27–30.

McNamara, G., Williams, K. and West, D. (1988) *Understanding Trade Unions: Yesterday and Today*. Dublin: O'Brien Educational Press in association with the Irish Congress of Trade Unions.

McNamara, G., Williams, K. and West, D. (1994) *Understanding Trade Unions: Yesterday and Today*. Dublin: ELO Publications in association with the Irish Congress of Trade Unions.

McPartlin, B. (1997) 'The Development of Trade Union Organisation', in T.V. Murphy and W.K. Roche (eds.) *Irish Industrial Relations in Practice: Revised and Expanded Edition*. Dublin: Oak Tree Press.

Meager, N., Tyers, C., Perryman, S., Rick, J. and Willison, R. (2002) *Awareness, Knowledge and Experience of Individual Employment Rights*. London: DTI. <http://www.bis.gov.uk/files/file13207.pdf>

Meenan, F. (1999) *Working within the Law: A Practical Guide for Employers and Employees* (2nd edn.). Dublin: Oak Tree Press.

Michels, R. (1962) *Political Parties*. New York: Free Press.

Mills, D.Q. (1989) *Labor–Management Relations*. New York: McGraw-Hill.

Moene, K. and Wallerstein, M. (1999) 'Social Democratic Labour Market Institutions: A Retrospective Analysis', in H. Kitschelt, P. Lange, G. Marks and J. Stephens (eds.) *Continuity and Change in Contemporary Capitalism*. Cambridge: Cambridge University Press.

Moffatt, J. (ed.) (2006) *Employment Law*. Dublin/Oxford: Law Society of Ireland/ Oxford University Press.

Molloy, E. (2012) 'Breaking Down the Croke Park Monolith', *Sunday Business Post*, 25 November.

Morley, M., Moore, S., Heraty, N., Linehan, M. and MacCurtain, S. (2004) *Principles of Organisational Behaviour: An Irish Text*. Dublin: Gill & Macmillan.

Muller-Camen, M., Almond, P., Gunnigle, P., Quintanilla, J. and Tempel, A. (2001) 'Between Home and Host Country: Multinationals and Employment Relations in Europe', *Industrial Relations Journal*, 32(5), 435–48.

Murphy, C. and Turner, T. (2011) 'Determining the Meaning of Union Organising Success in Ireland'. Paper presented at the Industrial Relations in Europe Conference. Universitat Pompeu Fabra, Barcelona: 1 September.

Murphy, C. and Turner, T. (2012) 'Fear and Leadership: The Role of Workplace Activists in Union Organising Campaigns'. Paper presented at the International Labour Process Conference. Stockholm University: 28 March.

Murphy, T. (1989) 'The Impact of the Unfair Dismissals Act 1977 on Workplace Industrial Relations', in Department of Industrial Relations, UCD (eds.) *Industrial Relations in Ireland: Contemporary Issues and Developments*. Dublin: University College Dublin.

Murphy, T. and Walsh, D. (1980) *The Worker Director and His Influence on the Enterprise: Expectations, Experience and Effectiveness in Seven Irish Companies*. Dublin: Irish Productivity Centre.

National Centre for Partnership and Performance (2010a) *NCPP 2009 National Employee Workplace Survey*. Dublin: National Centre for Partnership and Performance.

National Centre for Partnership and Performance (2010b) *NCPP 2009 National Employer Workplace Survey*. Dublin: National Centre for Partnership and Performance.

National Economic and Social Council (NESC) (1986) *A Strategy for Development 1986–1990*. Dublin: NESC.

Nevin, D. (1994) *Trade Union Century*. Dublin: Irish Congress of Trade Unions and RTÉ.

Nierenberg, G.I. (1968) *The Art of Negotiating*. New York: Cornerstone.

Nolan, J. (2002) 'The Intensification of Everyday Life', in B. Burchell, D. Ladipo and F. Wilkinson (eds.) *Job Insecurity and Work Intensification*. London: Routledge.

O'Brien, J.F. (1989) 'Pay Determination in Ireland', in Department of Industrial Relations, UCD (eds.) *Industrial Relations in Ireland: Contemporary Issues and Developments*. Dublin: University College Dublin.

O'Connell, P., Calvert, E. and Watson, D. (2007) *Bullying in the Workplace, Survey Reports*. Dublin: Department of Enterprise, Trade and Employment.

O'Connell, P., Russell, H., Watson, D. and Byrne, D. (2010) 'The Changing Workplace: A Survey of Employees' Views and Experiences'. Research Series No.7. Dublin: National Centre for Partnership and Performance.

O'Connor, E. (1988) *Syndicalism in Ireland 1917–1923*. Cork: Cork University Press.

O'Donnell, R. and O'Reardon, C. (1996) 'Irish Experiment: Social Partnership Has Yielded Economic Growth and Social Progress'. Dublin: National Economic and Social Council/Economic and Social Research Institute.

O'Donnell, R. and O'Reardon, C. (2000) 'Social Partnership in Ireland's Economic Transformation', in G. Fajertag and P. Pochett (eds.) *Social Pacts in Europe – New Dynamics*. Brussels: ETUI.

O'Donnell, R. and Thomas, D. (2002) 'Ireland in the 1990s', in S. Berger and H. Compston (eds.) *Policy Concertation and Social Partnership in Western Europe: Lessons for the Twenty-first Century*. New York/Oxford: Berghann Books.

Oechslin, J.J. (1985) 'Employer Organisations', in R. Blanpain (ed.) *Labour Law and Industrial Relations*. The Hague: Kluwer.

Ó Gráda, C. (1994) *Ireland: A New Economic History 1780–1939*. Oxford: Clarendon Press.

Ó Gráda, C. (1997) *A Rocky Road: The Irish Economy since the 1920s*. Manchester: Manchester University Press.

O'Hagan, J.W. (1987) *The Economy of Ireland: Policy and Performance* (5th edn.). Dublin: Irish Management Institute.

O'Hara, B. (1981) *The Evolution of Irish Industrial Relations: Law and Practice*. Dublin: Folens.

Oireachtas Library and Research Service (2011) 'Trade Unions, Collective Bargaining and the Economic Crisis: Where Now?', Houses of the Oireachtas, Dublin, No. 4. <www.oireachtas.ie/housesoftheoireachtas/spotTradeunion04061>

O'Keeffe, S. (1998) 'Industrial Action Ballots in Ireland – *Nolan Transport* v. *Halligan and Others*', *Industrial Law Journal*, 28(4), 347–52.

O'Kelly, K. and Compton, P. (2003) 'Workers' Participation at Board Level – the Irish Approach'. Paper presented to the European Trade Union Institute and the Hans Boeckler Stiftung, Elewijt. Belgium: 27–28 June.

O'Leary, A. (2000) 'Rights Commissioners: What Methods of Third Party Intervention Do They Adopt?' Unpublished MBS thesis, University of Limerick.

O'Mahony, D. (1964) *Industrial Relations in Ireland*. Dublin: Economic and Social Research Institute.

O'Neill, T. and Higgins, C. (2010) 'IRN Review of Cuts in Basic Pay and Salaries, 2008–2010', *Industrial Relations News*, 39, 27 October, 15–17.

Osigweh, C.A.B. and Hutchison, W.R. (1989) 'Positive Discipline', *Human Resource Management*, 28(3), 367–83.

Osigweh, C.A.B. and Hutchison, W.R. (1990) 'To Punish or Not to Punish? Managing Human Resources through "Positive Discipline"', *Employment Relations*, 12(3), 27–32.

O'Sullivan, M. and Gunnigle, P. (2009) '"Bearing All the Hallmarks of Oppression": Union Avoidance in Europe's Largest Low-cost Airline', *Labour Studies Journal*, 34(2), 252–70.

O'Sullivan, M. and Hartigan, C. (2011) 'The Citizens' Information Service in Ireland: Protecting the Nonunionised Employee?', *Journal of Workplace Rights*, 15(1), 65–82.

O'Sullivan, M. and Royle, T. (forthcoming) 'Everything and Nothing Changes: Fast-Food Employers and the Threat to Minimum Wage Regulation in Ireland', *Economic and Industrial Democracy*.

O'Sullivan, M. and Wallace, J. (2011) 'Minimum Labour Standards in a Social Partnership System – the Persistence of the Irish Variant of Wages Councils', *Industrial Relations Journal*, 42(1), 18–35.

Paldam, M. and Pederson, P.J. (1982) 'The Macro-Economic Strike Model: A Study of Seventeen Countries 1948–1975', *Industrial and Labour Relations Review*, 35(4), 504–21.

Palmer, G. (1983) *British Industrial Relations*. London: Allen & Unwin.

Panitch, L. (1979) 'The Development of Corporatism in Liberal Democracies', in P.C. Schmitter and G. Lehmbruch (eds.) *Trends Towards Corporatist Intermediation*. London: Sage.

Parker, P.A.L., Hayes, W.R. and Lumb, A.L. (1971) *The Reform of Collective Bargaining at Plant and Company Level*. London: HMSO.

Pateman, C. (1970) *Participation and Democratic Theory*. Cambridge: Cambridge University Press.

Pedersini, R. (2010) *Trade Union Strategies to Recruit New Groups of Workers*. European Foundation for the Improvement of Living and Working Conditions. <www.eurofound.europa.eu>

Peetz, D. (1997) *Union Membership Trends: Statistics and Selected Analysis*. Melbourne: Australian Council of Trade Unions.

Pekkarinen, J., Pohjola, M. and Rowthorn, B. (1992) 'Social Corporatism and Economic Performance: Introduction and Conclusions', in J. Pekkarinen, M. Pohjola and B. Rowthorn (eds.) *Social Corporatism: A Superior Economic System*. Oxford: Clarendon Press.

Pelling, H. (1976) *A History of British Trade Unionism*. Middlesex: Penguin.

Piore, M. and Sabel, C. (1984) *The Second Industrial Divide*. New York: Basic Books.

Pochet, P. and Fajertag, G. (2000) 'A New Era for Social Pacts in Europe', in G. Fajertag and P. Pochet (eds.) *Social Pacts in Europe – New Dynamics*. Brussels: European Trade Union Institute.

Pollert, A. (2008) 'Injustice at Work: How Britain's Low-Paid Non-Unionised Employees Experience Workplace Problems', *Journal of Workplace Rights*, 13(3), 223–44.

Poole, M. (1986) *Industrial Relations: Origins and Patterns of National Diversity*. London: Routledge.

Porter, M. (1980) *Competitive Strategy: Techniques for Analysing Industries and Competitors*. New York: The Free Press.

Purcell, J. (1987) 'Mapping Management Styles in Employee Relations', *Journal of Management Studies*, 24(5), 533–48.

Purcell, J. (1992) 'The Impact of Corporate Strategy on Human Resource Management', in G. Salamon (ed.) *Human Resource Strategies*. London: Sage/Open University.

Purcell, J. and Sisson, K. (1983) 'Strategies and Practice in the Management of Industrial Relations', in G. Bain (ed.) *Industrial Relations in Britain*. Oxford: Blackwell.

Rabbitte, P. and Gilmore, E. (1990) *Bertie's Bill*. Dublin: The Workers' Party.

Reed, M. (1989) *The Sociology of Management: Themes, Perspectives and Prospects*. London: Harvester Wheatsheaf.

Registry of Friendly Societies (2011) *Annual Report 2010*. Dublin: Registry of Friendly Societies.

Resnick, S. and Wolff, R. (2010) 'The Economic Crisis: A Marxian Interpretation', *Rethinking Marxism*, 22(2), 170–86.

Reynaud, J.P. (1978) *Problems and Prospects for Collective Bargaining in the EEC Member States*. Brussels: Commission of the European Community Document No.V/394/78-EN.

Rhodes, M. (1998) 'Globalisation, Labour Markets and Welfare States: A Future of Competitive Corporatism', in M. Rhodes and Y. Meny (eds.) *The Future of European Welfare: A New Social Contract*. London: Macmillan.

Riccucci, N.M. (1988) 'Nonpunitive Discipline in the Public Sector', *International Journal of Public Administration*, 11(1), 117–34.

Ridgely, P. (1988) 'How Relevant Is the FUE?', *Irish Business*, February, 21–2.

Rigby, M. and Aledo, M.L.M. (2001) 'The Worst Record in Europe? A Comparative Analysis of Industrial Conflict in Spain', *European Journal of Industrial Relations*, 7(3), 287–305.

Roche, W.K. (1989) 'State Strategies and the Politics of Industrial Relations in Ireland', in Department of Industrial Relations, UCD (eds.) *Industrial Relations in Ireland: Contemporary Issues and Developments*. Dublin: University College Dublin.

Roche, W.K. (1990) 'Industrial Relations Research in Ireland and the Trade Union Interest'. Paper presented to the Irish Congress of Trades Unions Conference on Joint Research between Trade Unions, Universities, Third-Level Colleges and Research Institutes. Dublin.

Roche, W.K. (1995) 'The New Competitive Order and Employee Relations in Ireland'. Paper presented to the Irish Business and Employers IBEC conference on Human Resources in the Global Market. Dublin: November.

Roche, W.K. (1997) 'The Trend of Unionisation', in W.K. Roche and T.V. Murphy (eds.) *Irish Industrial Relations in Practice, Revised and Expanded Edition*. Dublin: Oak Tree Press.

Roche, W.K. (2007a) 'Developments in Industrial Relations and Human Resource Management in Ireland', *Quarterly Economic Commentary*, March, 62–77. Dublin: Economic and Social Research Institute.

Roche, W.K. (2007b) 'Social Partnership and Workplace Regimes in Ireland', *Industrial Relations Journal*, 38(3), 188–209.

Roche, W.K. (2008a) 'Social Partnership in Ireland and New Social Pacts', *Industrial Relations*, 46(3), 395–425.

Roche, W.K. (2008b) 'The Trend of Unionisation in Ireland since the mid-1990s', in T. Hastings (ed.) *The State of the Unions: Challenges Facing Organised Labour in Ireland*. Dublin: Liffey Press.

Roche, W.K. (2009) 'Social Partnership: From Lemass to Cowen', *Economic and Social Review*, 40(2), 183–205.

Roche, W.K. (2012a) 'Austerity without Solidarity: Industrial Relations, Employment and Welfare in the Irish Crisis'. Paper presented at Varieties of Capitalism and Responses to the European Employment Crisis research conference. Centre for the Study of Europe and the World, University of Denver, Colorado: 1–2 June.

Roche, W.K. (2012b) '"After the Ball Is Over": Accounts of the Functioning and Demise of Social Partnership', in B. Sheehan (ed.) *The Labour Relations Commission: Recalling 21 Years: 1999–2012*. Labour Relations Commission, 114–49.

Roche, W.K. (2012c) Contribution to Panel Session on the Croke Park Agreement: Performance to Date and Future. 'The Future of HR in the Public Sector', Public Affairs Ireland Annual Conference. Dublin: 27 September.

Roche, W.K. and Ashmore, J. (2001) 'Irish Unions in the 1990s: Testing the Limits of Social Partnership', in G. Griffin (ed.) *Changing Patterns of Trade Unionism: A Comparison of English Speaking Countries*. London: Mansell.

Roche, W.K. and Geary, J.F. (2002) 'Collaborative Production and the Irish Boom: Work Organisation, Partnership and Direct Involvement in Irish Workplaces', in D. D'Art and T. Turner (eds.) *Irish Employment Relations in the New Economy*. Dublin: Blackhall Publishing.

Roche, W.K. and Gunnigle, P. (1997) 'Competition and the New Industrial Relations Agenda', in W.K. Roche and T.V. Murphy (eds.) *Industrial Relations in Practice: New and Revised Edition*. Dublin: Oak Tree Press.

Roche, W.K. and Larragy, J. (1986) 'The Formation of the Irish Trade Union Movement and Organisational Developments since 1945'. Working paper. Department of Industrial Relations, University College Dublin.

Roche, W.K. and Larragy, J. (1989) *The Determinants of the Annual Rate of Trade Union Growth and Decline in the Irish Republic: Evidence from the DUES Membership Series*. Dublin: University College Dublin.

Roche, W.K. and Teague, P. (2011) 'Firms and Innovative Conflict Management Systems in Ireland', *British Journal of Industrial Relations*, 49(3), 436–59.

Roche, W.K. and Turner, T. (1998) 'Human Resource Management and Industrial Relations: Substitution, Dualism and Partnership', in W.K. Roche, K. Monks and J. Walsh (eds.) *Human Resource Management Strategies: Policy and Practice in Ireland*. Dublin: Oak Tree Press.

Roche, W.K., Teague, P., Coughlan, A. and Fahy, M. (2011) *Human Resources in the Recession: Managing and Representing People at Work in Ireland*. Dublin: Labour Relations Commission.

Rollinson, D. (1993) *Understanding Employee Relations: A Behavioural Approach*. Wokingham: Addison-Wesley.

Rose, E. (2001) *Employment Relations*. Essex: *Financial Times*/Prentice Hall.

Rose, M. (1977) *Industrial Behaviour: Theoretical Development since Taylor*. Middlesex: Penguin.

Ross, A.M. and Hartman, P. (1960) *Changing Patterns of Industrial Conflict*. New York: Wiley.

Roth, S. (1993) 'Lean Production in German Motor Manufacturing', *P+: European Participation Monitor*, 1(5), 35–9. Dublin: European Foundation for the Improvement of Living and Working Conditions.

Royle, T. and Towers, B. (2002) *Labour Relations in the Global Fast-Food Industry*. London: Routledge.

RTÉ (2012) 'Gilmore Warns Against "Season of Kite-Flying"', 12 September. <http://www.rte.ie/news/2012/0912/gilmore-says-croke-park-deal-will-be-honoured.html>

Salamon, M. (1998) *Industrial Relations: Theory and Practice* (3rd edn.). London: Prentice Hall.

Salamon, M. (2000) *Industrial Relations: Theory and Practice* (4th edn.). Essex: Financial Times/Prentice Hall.

Salin, D. (2003) 'Ways of Explaining Workplace Bullying: A Review of Enabling, Motivating and Precipitating Structures and Processes in the Work Environment', *Human Relations*, 56, 1,213–32.

Salin, D. (2008) 'The Prevention of Workplace Bullying as a Question of Human Resource Management: Measures Adopted and Underlying Organizational Factors', *Scandinavian Journal of Management*, 24(3), 221–31.

Saundry, R., Jones, C. and Antcliff, V. (2011) 'Discipline, Representation and Dispute Resolution – Exploring the Role of Trade Unions and Employee Companions in Workplace Discipline', *Industrial Relations Journal*, 42(2), 195–211.

Saville, J. (1967) 'Trade Unions and Free Labour: The Background to the Taff Vale Decision', in A. Briggs and J. Saville (eds.) *Essays in Labour History*. London: Macmillan.

Schmitt, J. and Mitukiewicz, A. (2011) *Politics Matter: Changes in Unionization Rates in Rich Countries, 1960–2010*. Washington: Center for Economic and Policy Research.

Schmitter, P.C. (1979) 'Introduction', in P.C. Schmitter and G. Lehmbruch (eds.) *Trends towards Corporatist Intermediation*. London: Sage.

Schmitter, P.C. and Lehmbruch, G. (eds.) (1979) *Trends towards Corporatist Intermediation*. London: Sage.

Schmitter, P. and Streeck, W. (1999) 'The Organization of Business Interests: Studying the Associative Action of Business in Advanced Industrial Societies'. Discussion Paper 99/1. Max-Planck Institut für Gesellschaftsforschung.

Schregle, J. (1974) 'Labour Relations in Western Europe: Some Topical Issues', *International Labour Review*, January–June.

Scott, J.F. and Homans, G.C. (1947) 'Reflections on the Wildcat Strikes', *American Sociological Review*, 12, 278–87.

Sebenius, J.K. (2001) 'Six Habits of Merely Effective Negotiators', *Harvard Business Review*, 79(4), 89–95.

Shalev, M. (1992) 'The Resurgence of Labour Quiescence', in M. Regini (ed.) *The Future of Labour Movements*. London: Sage.

Sheehan, B. (1997) 'ISME's Case for Inclusion in the Partnership Process', *Industrial Relations News*, 30, 31 July, 14.

Sheehan, B. (2001) 'Social Partnership and the State of Industrial Relations', *Industrial Relations News*, 28, 19 July, 23–7.

Sheehan, B. (2002) 'Irish Industrial Relations and HRM: An Overview of the Lovett Years', in P. Gunnigle, M. Morley and M. McDonnell (eds.) *The Lovett Lectures: A Decade of Developments in Human Resource Management*. Dublin: The Liffey Press.

Sheehan, B. (2004) 'Looking Forward – "Stage Two" of National Pay Deal in Prospect', *Industrial Relations News*, 1 and 2, 6 January, 16–7.

Sheehan, B. (2007) 'SIPTU Leader Says "Paradox in Social Partnership Must Be Tackled"', *Industrial Relations News*, 41, 14 November, 19–20.

Sheehan, B. (2008a) 'Employment Tribunal Holding Up Well in New Era of Individual Rights', *Industrial Relations News*, 25, 3 July, 22–6.

Sheehan, B. (2008b) 'New Deal Backed in Record Vote, but Big Challenge for Social Partners', *Industrial Relations News*, 42, 18 November, 2–3.

Sheehan, B. (2010a) 'US Chamber: Wage Levels "Unsustainable" but Policy Direction Correct', *Industrial Relations News*, 3, 21 January, 21–3.

Sheehan, B. (2010b) 'Employer Body Withdraws from National Pay Deal', Euronline, February. <http://www.eurofound.europa.eu/eiro/2010/01/articles/IE1001029I.htm>

Sheehan, B. (2010c) '"Croke Park" Has Potential to Deliver for This Government, or the Next One', *Industrial Relations News*, 23, 16 June, 20–2.

Sheehan, B. (2011a) 'Bruton's Plan to Change "Haphazard" Employment Rights System', *Industrial Relations News*, 30, 25 August, 26–6.

Sheehan, B. (2011b) 'Dáil Answers Reveal Fees Paid to IBEC by Some State Agencies', *Industrial Relations News*, 20, 26 May, 6–7.

Sheehan, B. (2011c) 'Government's Policy Continues Shift towards "Social Dialogue", Away from Partnership', *Industrial Relations News*, 14, 6 April, 1–3.

Sheehan, B. (2011d) 'IBEC's Warning on "Bias towards Collective Ethos" and "Legal Industry"', *Industrial Relations News*, 35, 29 September, 22–3.

Sheehan, B. (2011e) 'Social Partnership Gets Mixed Reviews from Consultants', *Industrial Relations News*, 9, 3 March, 17–18.

Sheehan, B. (2012a) 'Bruton Moves on Reform Plan, Rejects Criticism from "Interest Groups"', *Industrial Relations News*, 27, 12 July, 26.

Sheehan, B. (2012b) 'Bruton's Plan Will Limit Right to a "Fair Trial", Says EAT Committee', *Industrial Relations News*, 23, 14 June, 2–3.

Sheehan, B. (2012c) 'Collective Bargaining – ILO Findings May Move "Solution" a Step Closer', *Industrial Relations News*, 14, 4 April, 3–6.

Sheehan, B. (2012d) 'Expert Believes Government Will Try to Partially Reverse "Ryanair" Ruling', *Industrial Relations News*, 13, 28 March, 24.

Sheehan, B. (2012e) '"No Independent Enquiry" into Ryanair Case – Bruton', *Industrial Relations News*, 35, 27 September, 6–7.

Sheldon, P. and Thornthwaite, L. (2005) 'Members or Clients? Employer Associations, the Decentralization of Bargaining, and the Reorientation of Service Provision: Evidence from Europe and Australia', *Business and Economic History*, 3, 1–21.

Sherman, M. and Lucia, A. (1992) 'Option: Positive Discipline and Labor Arbitration', *Arbitration Journal,* June, 56–8.

Siggins, L. (2004) 'Abuse of Sportswear Workers Highlighted', *The Irish Times,* 27 March.

Silverman, J. (1970) *The Theory of Organisations.* London: Heinemann.

Silvia, S. and Schroeder, W. (2007) 'Why Are German Employer Associations Declining? Arguments and Evidence', *Comparative Political Studies*, 40(12), 1,433–59.

Sisson, K. (1994) 'Workplace Europe. Direct Participation in Organisational Change: Introducing the EPOC Project'. Paper presented to the International Industrial Relations Association 4th European Regional Congress on Transformation of European Industrial Relations: Consequences of Integration and Disintegration. Helsinki.

Skogstad, A., Einarsen, S., Torsheim, T., Aasland, M.S. and Hetland, H. (2007) 'The Destructiveness of Laissez-Faire Leadership Behavior', *Journal of Occupational Health Psychology*, 12(1), 80–92.

Smith, P. and Morton, G. (2006) 'Nine Years of New Labour: Neoliberalism and Workers' Rights', *British Journal of Industrial Relations*, 44(3), 401–20.

Smith, S. (2003) *Labour Economics* (2nd edn.). London: Routledge.

Social Justice Ireland (2009) *Income and Poverty.* Dublin: Social Justice Ireland.

Sparrow, P.R. and Hiltrop, J.M. (1994) *European Human Resource Management in Transition.* London: Prentice Hall.

Special Correspondent (2008) 'Building Competitive Organisations – the Role of HR', Chartered Institute of Personnel and Development Conference/*Industrial Relations News*, 20, 29 May, 19–23.

Stafford, P. (2011) 'The Rise and Fall of Social Partnership: Its Impact on Interest Group Lobbying in Ireland', *Journal of Public Affairs*, 11(2), 74–9.

Stokke, T.A. and Thörnqvist, C. (2001) 'Strikes and Collective Bargaining in the Nordic Countries', *European Journal of Industrial Relations*, 7(3), 245–67.

Storey, J. (1992) *Developments in the Management of Human Resources.* Oxford: Blackwell.

Strauss, G. and Sayles, L.R. (1980) *Personnel* (4th edn.). Englewood Cliffs, NJ: Prentice-Hall.

Sturdy, A., Knights, D. and Willmott, H. (1992) 'Introduction: Skill and Consent in the Labour Process', in A. Sturdy, D. Knights and H. Willmott (eds.) *Skill and Consent: Contemporary Studies in the Labour Process.* London: Routledge.

Sweeney, P. (1998) *The Celtic Tiger – Ireland's Economic Miracle Explained.* Dublin: Oak Tree Press.

Sweeney, P. and O'Brien, F. (2011) 'Is the State's Wage-Setting System Necessary?' *The Irish Times*, 18 June.

Teague, P. (2009) 'Path Dependency and Comparative Industrial Relations Conflict Management Systems in Sweden and the Republic of Ireland', *British Journal of Industrial Relations*, 47(3), 499–520.

Teague, P. and Doherty, L. (2009) 'Reforming our IR Institutions – A Snip in the Wrong Direction?', *Industrial Relations News*, 28, 24 July, 15–18.

Teague, P. and Doherty, L. (2012) 'Reforming Dispute Resolution: A Response to Minister Bruton's "Blueprint"', *Industrial Relations News*, 18, 10 May, 18–21.

Teague, P. and Donaghey, J. (2009) 'Why Has Irish Social Partnership Survived?', *British Journal of Industrial Relations*, 47(1), 55–78.

Teague, P. and Donaghey, J. (2012) 'The Death of Irish Social Partnership: Should We Care?' Working paper supplied by the authors.

Teague, P. and Thomas, D. (2008) *Employment Dispute Resolution and Standard Setting in the Republic of Ireland*. Dublin: Oak Tree Press.

Teague, P., Roche, W.K. and Hann, D. (2012) 'The Diffusion of Workplace ADR in Ireland', *Economic and Industrial Democracy*, 33(4), 581–604.

Thelen, K. and van Wijnbergen, C. (2003) 'The Paradox of Globalization: Labor Relations in Germany and Beyond', *Comparative Political Studies*, 36(8), 859–80.

Thomas, D., Brannick, T. and Kelly, A. (2003) 'Social Partnership and Industrial Conflict in Ireland: Securing the Peace Dividend?' Working paper. University College Dublin.

Thomason, G. (1984) *A Textbook of Industrial Relations Management*. London: Institute of Personnel Management.

Thompson, L. (2009) *The Mind and Heart of the Negotiator* (5th edn.). New Jersey: Prentice Hall.

Thornthwaite, L. and Sheldon, P. (1997) 'Employer Associations, Dual Membership and the Problem of Conflicting Policies', in T. Bramble *et al.* (eds.) *Current Research in Industrial Relations, Proceedings of the 11th AIRAANZ Conference*. Brisbane: January.

Todd, P. (2012) 'Employer and Employer Association Matters in 2011', *Journal of Industrial Relations*, 54(3), 344–60.

Tolich, P. and Harcourt, M. (1999) 'Why Do People Join Unions? A Case Study of the New Zealand Engineering, Printing and Manufacturing Union', *New Zealand Journal of Industrial Relations*, 24(1), 63–74.

Tolliday, S. and Zeitlin, J. (1991) 'Employers and Industrial Relations between Theory and History', in S. Tolliday and J. Zeitlin (eds.) *The Power to Manage? Employers and Industrial Relations in Comparative-Historical Perspective*. London: Routledge.

Torrington, D. and Hall, L. (1998) *Human Resource Management*. London: Prentice Hall.

Traxler, F. (2004) 'Employer Associations, Institutions and Economic Change: A Crossnational Comparison', *Industrielle Beziehungen,* 11(2), 42–60.

Turner, H. (1969) 'Is Britain Really Strike Prone? A Review of the Incidence, Character and Costs of Industrial Conflict'. Occasional Paper No. 20. Cambridge: Cambridge University Press.

Turner, T. (1993) 'Unionisation and Human Resource Management in Irish Companies', *Industrial Relations Journal,* 25(39), 39–51.

Turner, T. (2006) 'Industrial Relations Systems, Economic Efficiency and Social Equity in the 1990s', *Review of Social Economy,* 64(1), 93–108.

Turner, T. and D'Art, D. (2000) 'A Review of Centralised Wage Agreements in Ireland 1987–2000', *Croner's Employee Relations Review,* 12, 16–9.

Turner, T. and D'Art, D. (2012) 'Public Perceptions of Trade Unions in Countries of the European Union: A Causal Analysis', *Labor Studies Journal,* 37(1), 33–55.

Turner, T. and O'Sullivan, M. (2011) 'The Economic Crisis and the Restructuring of Wage Setting Mechanisms for Vulnerable Workers in Ireland'. Paper presented at the Foundation for European Progressive Studies/TASC Seminar on Incomes: Instruments for Recovery. Cork: 29 September.

Turner, T. and Wallace, J. (2000) 'The Irish Model of Social Partnership: Achievements and Limitations'. Paper presented to the European Congress of the International Industrial Relations Association. Oslo: 25–29 June.

Turner, T., D'Art, D. and O'Sullivan, M. (2008) 'Union Availability, Union Membership and Immigrant Workers: An Empirical Investigation of the Irish Case', *Employee Relations,* 30(5), 479–93.

Tyson, S. and Fell, A. (1986) *Evaluating the Personnel Function*. London: Hutchinson.

Undy, R. (2008) *Trade Union Merger Strategies*. Oxford: Oxford University Press.

Ury, W. (1992) *Getting Past NO: Negotiating with Difficult People*. London: Century Business.

Vahabi, M. (2011) 'The Economics of Destructive Power', in D.L. Braddon and K. Hartley (2011) *Handbook on the Economics of Conflict*. Cheltenham: Edward Elgar Publishing.

von Prondzynski, F. (1989) 'Collective Labour Law', in Department of Industrial Relations, UCD (eds.) *Industrial Relations in Ireland: Contemporary Issues and Developments*. Dublin: University College Dublin.

von Prondzynski, F. (1992) 'Ireland Between Centralism and the Market', in A. Ferner and R. Hyman (eds.) *Industrial Relations in the New Europe.* Oxford: Blackwell.

von Prondzynski, F. (1998) 'Ireland: Corporatism Revived', in A. Ferner and R. Hyman (eds.) *Changing Industrial Relations in Europe.* Oxford: Blackwell.

von Prondzynski, F. and McCarthy, C. (1984) *Employment Law.* London: Sweet & Maxwell.

Waddington, J. (2005) 'Trade Union Membership in Europe: The Extent of the Problem and the Range of Trade Union Responses'. Background Paper for the ETUC/ETUI-REHS Top-level Summer School. Florence: July.

Waddington, J. and Whitson, C. (1997) 'Why Do People Join Unions in a Period of Membership Decline?', *British Journal of Industrial Relations,* 35(4), 515–46.

Wajcman, J. (2000) 'Feminism Facing I.R. in Britain', *British Journal of Industrial Relations,* 38(2), 183–201.

Wall, M. (2011a) 'IBEC Accuses Government of Prejudicing Wage-Rules Review', *The Irish Times,* 15 March.

Wall, M. (2011b) 'Reilly Drops Plan to Axe Student Nurse Pay', *The Irish Times,* 29 October.

Wall, M. (2012a) 'Bruton Stands by His Dispute Reform Plans', *The Irish Times,* 6 July.

Wall, M. (2012b) 'Unions Say "New" Croke Park Will be Difficult', *The Irish Times,* 29 November.

Wallace, J. (1982) *Industrial Relations in Limerick City and Environs.* Employment Research Programme, Limerick: University of Limerick.

Wallace, J. (1989) 'Procedure Agreements and Their Place in Workplace Industrial Relations', in Department of Industrial Relations, UCD (eds.) *Industrial Relations in Ireland: Contemporary Issues and Developments.* Dublin: University College Dublin.

Wallace, J. (1991) 'The Industrial Relations Act 1990 and Other Developments in Labour Law'. Paper presented to the Mid-West Chapter of the Institute of Personnel Management, University of Limerick. Limerick: November 1991.

Wallace, J. (1999) 'Investigating Employment Pacts: Collective Agreements Dealing with the Relationship Between Employment and Competitiveness'. Report to the European Foundation for the Improvement of Working and Living Conditions.

Wallace, J. and Clifford, N. (1998) *Collective Bargaining and Flexibility in Ireland.* Geneva: International Labour Office.

Wallace, J. and Delany, B. (1997) 'Back to the Future? The Irish Industrial Relations Act 1990', in F. Meenan (ed.) *Legal Perspectives – The Juridification of the Employment Relationship.* Dublin: Oak Tree Press.

Wallace, J. and McDonnell, C. (2000) 'The Institutional Provisions of the Industrial Relations Act 1990 in Operation', *Irish Business and Administrative Research*, (21)1, 169–88.

Wallace, J. and O'Shea, F. (1987) *A Study of Unofficial Strikes in Ireland*. Dublin: Government Publications Office.

Wallace, J. and O'Sullivan, M. (2002) 'The Industrial Relations Act 1990: A Critical Review', in D. D'Art and T. Turner (eds.) *Irish Employment Relations in the New Economy*. Dublin: Blackhall Publishing.

Wallace, J. and O'Sullivan, M. (2006) 'Contemporary Strike Trends since 1980: Peering through the Wrong End of a Telescope', in M. Morley, P. Gunnigle and D.G. Collins (eds.) *Global Industrial Relations*. London: Routledge.

Wallace, J. and White, L. (2008) 'Collaborative Bargaining – Annualised Hours Agreements in Ireland'. Proceedings of the 25th International Labour Process Conference. Amsterdam: 2–4 April.

Wallace, J., McDonnell, C. and Kennedy, V. (2000) 'A Review of Trade Union Rationalisation in Ireland'. Paper presented to the Irish Academy of Management Conference, 7–8 September.

Wallace, J., Turner, T. and McCarthy, A. (1998) 'EMU and the Impact on Irish Industrial Relations', in T. Kauppinen (ed.) *The Impact of EMU on Industrial Relations in Europe*. Publication No. 9. Helsinki: Finnish Labour Relations Association.

Wallerstein, M. and Lange, P. (1999) 'Postwar Trade-Union Organisation and Industrial Relations in Twelve Countries', in H. Kitschelt, P. Lange, G. Marks and J. Stephens (eds.) *Continuity and Change in Contemporary Capitalism*. Cambridge: Cambridge University Press.

Walters, S. (2002) 'Female Part-time Workers' Attitudes to Trade Unions in Britain', *British Journal of Industrial Relations*, 40(1), 49–68.

Walton, R.E. and McKersie, R.B. (1965) *A Behavioral Theory of Labour Negotiations: An Analysis of a Social Interaction System*. New York: McGraw-Hill.

Watson, D., Galway J., O'Connell, P.J. and Russell, H. (2010) *The Changing Workplace: A Survey of Employers' Views and Experiences*. Economic and Social Research Institute/ National Economic and Social Development Office.

Webb, S. and Webb, B. (1897) *Industrial Democracy: Vol. I*. London: Longman.

Webb, S. and Webb, B. (1920) *The History of Trade Unionism*. London: Longman.

Wedderburn, W.K. (1965) *The Worker and the Law*. London: Penguin.

Wedderburn, W.K. (1986) *The Worker and the Law* (3rd edn.). London: Penguin.

Wheeler, H.N. (1976) 'Punishment Theory and Industrial Discipline', *Industrial Relations*, 15(2), 235–43.

Wheeler, H.N. and McClendon, J.A. (1991) 'The Individual Decision to Unionize', in G. Strauss, D.G. Gallagher and J. Fiorito (eds.) *The State of the Unions.* Madison, WI: Industrial Relations Research Association.

Whelan, C. (1982) *Worker Priorities, Trust in Management and Prospects for Worker Participation, Paper III.* Dublin: Economic and Social Research Institute.

Whyte, W.F. (1951) *Pattern for Industrial Peace.* New York: Harper.

Wichert, I. (2002) 'Stress Intervention', in B. Burchell, D. Ladipo and F. Wilkinson (eds.) *Job Insecurity and Work Intensification.* London: Routledge.

Wilkinson, A. (1998) 'Empowerment', in M. Poole and M. Warner (eds.) *International Encyclopaedia of Business and Management Handbook of Human Resource Management.* London: ITB Press.

Wilkinson, A. and Dundon, T. (2010) 'Direct Employee Participation', in A. Wilkinson, P.J. Gollan, M. Marchington and D. Lewin (eds.) *The Oxford Handbook of Participation in Organizations.* Oxford/New York: Oxford University Press.

Wilkinson, A., Gollan, P.J., Marchington, M. and Lewin, D. (2010) *The Oxford Handbook of Participation in Organizations.* Oxford/New York: Oxford University Press.

Williams, S., Abbott, B. and Heery, E. (2011) 'Non-Union Worker Representation through Civil Society Organisations: Evidence from the United Kingdom', *Industrial Relations Journal,* 42(1), 69–85.

Windmuller, J.P. (1984) 'Employer Associations in Comparative Perspective: Organisation, Structure and Administration', in J.P. Windmuller and A. Gladstone (eds.) *Employer Associations and Industrial Relations.* Oxford: Clarendon.

Womack, J.P., Jones, D.T. and Roos, D. (1990) *The Machine That Changed the World.* New York: Rawson Associates.

Wood, S. (1978) 'Ideology in Industrial Relations Theory', *Industrial Relations Journal,* 9(4).

Wood, S. and Peccei, R. (1990) 'Preparing for 1992? Business-Led Versus Strategic Human Resource Management', *Human Resource Management,* 1(1), 63–89.

Woodward, J. (1958) *Management and Technology.* London: HMSO.

Yeates, P. (1993) 'Personnel Managers Favour a New PESP', *The Irish Times*, 21 December.

Yeates, P. (2000) *Lockout: Dublin 1913.* Dublin: Gill & Macmillan.

Yeates, P. (2003) '1913 Lockout', *The Irish Times*, 25 August.

Zhang, L. (2012) 'China's Foxconn Workers: From Suicide Threats to a Trade Union?' *Guardian*, 16 January.

Index